Advisory Editor: M.M. Willcock

GREEK ORATORS IV

ANDOCIDES

edited and translated

by

Michael Edwards

Aris & Phillips Ltd – Warminster – England

For Nan and Mum

τῇ μητρὶ καὶ τῇ θυγατρί

British Library Cataloguing-in-Publication Data
A catalogue record for this book is available from the
British Library.

ISBNs   **0 85668 527 5** (cloth)
            0 85668 528 3 (limp)

Contents

Preface

Any commentary on the *De Mysteriis* cannot but be deeply influenced by Douglas MacDowell's edition of the speech, which remains one of the outstanding modern commentaries on any ancient text. I have attempted to provide an alternative view on some of the major issues, as well as incorporating material published since 1962, but my debt to Professor MacDowell is evident at every turn. I am pleased to acknowledge it. Anna Missiou's excellent analysis of Andocides' rhetorical strategies must also now be a starting-point, in particular for discussion of the *De Pace*.

The translation aims at accuracy rather than elegance (a quality, indeed, that is not always present in the original). This will hopefully enable students who have recently begun their study of the language to follow the Greek text without the need for explanatory notes.

These conventions may be noted. References to Andocides' speeches are in bold type: those to a speech within its introduction and commentary are given by section number only, while cross-references to the other speeches include the speech number. References to Plutarch's *Lives* are cited by the section numbers of the Loeb edition. References to Develin are to the entries in Index I (Persons) and those to Austin/Vidal-Naquet are to passage numbers, except where otherwise indicated; references to Goodwin are to section numbers. Dates are B.C. unless otherwise stated.

Finally, it is my pleasant duty to thank those who have helped me in the preparation of this volume for the *Greek Orators* series. The work has been long delayed, but Adrian Phillips and Janet Davis have been extremely patient and understanding. I am very fortunate in being able to draw upon the computing expertise of John Wilkins, who wrote a Greek conversion programme that saved me many hours of re-typing. John's friendship and support, and the encouragement of other colleagues old and new, have helped me through difficult times. Earlier drafts were read by Stephen Usher and Malcolm Willcock, and Professor Willcock also acted as proof-reader. Their many comments and suggestions have improved the final version beyond recognition, and any faults that remain are mine alone.

Abbreviations

(1) Ancient Authors

Aesch.	Aeschines
Ag. And.	ps.-Lysias 6
Life of And.	ps.-Plutarch's *Life of Andocides* in *Lives of the Ten Orators* (*Moralia* 834B-835B)
Ant.	Antiphon
Ar.	Aristophanes
Arist.	Aristotle
Ath. Pol.	ps.-Aristotle, *Athenaion Politeia*
Dem.	Demosthenes
Din.	Dinarchus
Diod.	Diodorus Siculus
Dion. Hal.	Dionysius of Halicarnassus
Eur.	Euripides
Hdt.	Herodotus
Hyp.	Hyperides
Is.	Isaeus
Isoc.	Isocrates
Lyc.	Lycurgus
Lys.	Lysias
Paus.	Pausanias
Pl.	Plato
Plut.	Plutarch
Quint.	Quintilian
Soph.	Sophocles
Thuc.	Thucydides
Xen.	Xenophon

(2) Modern Works

AJP	American Journal of Philology
ATL	B. D. Meritt, H. T. Wade-Gery and M. F. McGregor, *The Athenian Tribute Lists*, vol. 3 (Princeton, 1950)
AVN	M. M. Austin and P. Vidal-Naquet, *Economic and Social History of Ancient Greece: An Introduction* (London, 1977)
CP	Classical Philology
CQ	Classical Quarterly
CR	Classical Review
CW	M. H. Crawford and D. Whitehead, *Archaic and Classical Greece* (Cambridge, 1983)
GRBS	Greek, Roman and Byzantine Studies

HCT	A. W. Gomme, A. Andrewes and K. J. Dover, *A Historical Commentary on Thucydides*, 5 vols (Oxford, 1945-81)
JHS	Journal of Hellenic Studies
LSJ	H. G. Liddell and R. Scott, *A Greek-English Lexicon*, revised by H. Stuart Jones
ML	R. Meiggs and D. M. Lewis, *A Selection of Greek Historical Inscriptions to the End of the Fifth Century B.C.* (Oxford, 1969)
PCPS	Proceedings of the Cambridge Philological Society
SIFC	Studi Italiani di Filologia Classica
TAPA	Transactions and Proceedings of the American Philological Association

Bibliography

Works on Andocides

U. Albini, *Andocide. De Reditu* (Florence, 1961)

U. Albini, *Andocide. De Pace* (Florence, 1964)

F. Blass and C. Fuhr, *Andocidis orationes* (4th ed., Leipzig, 1913)

G. Dalmeyda, *Andocide: Discours* (Paris, 1930)

S. Feraboli, 'Lingua e stile della orazione "Contro Alcibiade" attribuita ad Andocide', *SIFC* 44 (1972) 5-37

L. L. Forman, *Index Andocideus, Lycurgeus, Dinarcheus* (Oxford, 1897)

W. J. Hickie, *Andocides de Mysteriis* (London, 1885)

S. S. Kingsbury, *A Rhetorical Study of the Style of Andocides* (Baltimore, 1899)

D. M. MacDowell, *Andokides. On the Mysteries* (Oxford, 1962)

K. J. Maidment, *Minor Attic Orators I* (Loeb, London and Cambridge, Mass., 1941)

A. D. J. Makkink, *Andokides' Eerste Rede* (Amsterdam, 1932)

E. C. Marchant, *Andocides, de Mysteriis and de Reditu* (London, 1889)

J. L. Marr, 'Andocides' part in the Mysteries and Hermae affairs 415 B.C.', *CQ* 21 (1971) 326-38

A. Missiou, *The Subversive Oratory of Andokides* (Cambridge, 1992)

A. N. W. Saunders, *Greek Political Oratory* (Penguin, Harmondsworth, 1970)

Other works

O. Aurenche, *Les groupes d'Alcibiade, de Leogoras et de Teucros. Remarques sur la vie politique athénienne en 415 avant J.-C.* (Paris, 1974)

R. A. Bauman, *Political Trials in Ancient Greece* (London and New York, 1990)

F. Blass, *Die attische Beredsamkeit*, vol. 1 (2nd ed., Leipzig, 1887)

C. Carey, *Lysias: Selected Speeches* (Cambridge, 1989)

C. Carey, *Greek Orators VI, Apollodorus Against Neaera [Demosthenes 59]* (Warminster, 1992)

P. A. Cartledge, *Agesilaos and the Crisis of Sparta* (London and Baltimore, 1987)

Crux = P. A. Cartledge and F. D. Harvey (eds), *CRUX. Essays in Greek History Presented to G. E. M. de Ste. Croix on his 75th Birthday* (Exeter and London, 1985)

J. K. Davies, *Athenian Propertied Families 600-300 B.C.* (Oxford, 1971)

J. D. Denniston, *The Greek Particles* (2nd ed., Oxford, 1954)

R. Develin, *Athenian Officials 684-321 B.C.* (Cambridge, 1989)

J. F. Dobson, *The Greek Orators* (London, 1919)

K. J. Dover, *Lysias and the Corpus Lysiacum* (Berkeley and Los Angeles, 1968)

K. J. Dover, *Greek Popular Morality in the Time of Plato and Aristotle* (Oxford, 1974)

M. Edwards and S. Usher, *Greek Orators I, Antiphon and Lysias* (Warminster, 1985)

W. M. Ellis, *Alcibiades* (London and New York, 1989)

C. W. Fornara, *Archaic Times to the End of the Peloponnesian War* (2nd. ed., Cambridge, 1983)

viii

W. W. Goodwin, *Syntax of the Moods and Tenses of the Greek Verb* (repr. London, 1966)

M. H. Hansen, *Eisangelia. The Sovereignty of the People's Court in Athens in the Fourth Century B.C. and the Impeachment of Generals and Politicians* (Odense, 1975)

M. H. Hansen, *Apagoge, Endeixis and Ephegesis against Kakourgoi, Atimoi and Pheugontes: A Study in the Athenian Administration of Justice in the Fourth Century B.C.* (Odense, 1976)

M. H. Hansen, *The Athenian Democracy in the Age of Demosthenes* (Oxford, 1991)

A. R. W. Harrison, *The Law of Athens*, 2 vols (Oxford, 1968-71)

J. Hatzfeld, *Alcibiade* (Paris, 1940)

R. J. Hopper, *Trade and Industry in Classical Greece* (London and New York, 1979)

S. Hornblower, *A Commentary on Thucydides Volume I: Books I-III* (Oxford, 1991)

R. C. Jebb, *The Attic Orators from Antiphon to Isaeus*, vol. 1 (2nd ed., London, 1893)

G. A. Kennedy, *The Art of Persuasion in Greece* (Princeton, 1963)

W. K. Lacey, *The Family in Classical Greece* (London, 1968)

D. M. MacDowell, *Athenian Homicide Law in the Age of the Orators* (Manchester, 1963)

D. M. MacDowell, *Aristophanes Wasps* (Oxford, 1971)

D. M. MacDowell, *The Law in Classical Athens* (London, 1978)

D. M. MacDowell, *Demosthenes Against Meidias (Oration 21)* (Oxford, 1990)

R. Meiggs, *The Athenian Empire* (Oxford, 1972)

P. C. Millett, *Lending and Borrowing in Ancient Athens* (Cambridge, 1991)

G. E. Mylonas, *Eleusis and the Eleusinian Mysteries* (Princeton, 1961)

Nomos = P. A. Cartledge, P. C. Millett and S. C. Todd (eds), *Nomos. Essays in Athenian Law, Politics and Society* (Cambridge, 1990)

M. Nouhaud, *L'utilisation de l'histoire par les orateurs attiques* (Paris, 1982)

M. Ostwald, *From Popular Sovereignty to the Sovereignty of Law: Law, Society and Politics in Fifth-Century Athens* (Berkeley, Los Angeles and London, 1986)

H. W. Parke, *Festivals of the Athenians* (Ithaca, 1977)

L. Pearson, 'Historical allusions in the Attic orators', *CP* 36 (1941) 209-29

P. J. Rhodes, *The Athenian Boule* (Oxford, 1972)

P. J. Rhodes, *A Commentary on the Aristotelian Athenaion Politeia* (Oxford, 1981)

T. J. Saunders, *Plato's Penal Code: Tradition, Controversy, and Reform in Greek Penology* (Oxford, 1991)

A. H. Sommerstein, *Aristophanes: Wasps* (Warminster, 1983)

A. H. Sommerstein, *Aristophanes: Birds* (Warminster, 1987)

R. Thomas, *Oral Tradition and Written Record in Classical Athens* (Cambridge, 1989)

M. N. Tod, *A Selection of Greek Historical Inscriptions to the End of the Fifth Century B.C.*, vol. 2 (Oxford, 1948)

S. C. Todd, *The Shape of Athenian Law* (Oxford, 1993)

S. Usher, *Greek Orators III, Isocrates* (Warminster, 1990)

General Introduction

(i) Andocides' family

Andocides, son of Leogoras of the deme Cydathenaeum, was born into an aristocratic family shortly before 440.[1] He boasts in 1.147 that his house was the oldest in Athens,[2] and the fifth century historian Hellanicus traced his family's descent from Hermes and Odysseus.[3] The family was very wealthy, and Andocides' earliest known relative was a treasurer of Athena in the mid-sixth century.[4] In the family tradition other ancestors had fought against the Peisistratids;[5] and his grandfather Andocides was prominent in the 440s as a supporter of Pericles, leading an expedition to the Megarid as general in 446/5, going on the embassy to Sparta which concluded the Thirty Years' Peace and serving again as general with Pericles at Samos in 441/0.[6] But Andocides' father, Leogoras, failed to emulate these achievements, even though he had connections with the king of Macedonia and led an embassy to him in 426. His luxurious lifestyle was repeatedly satirised in comedy, and Andocides never cites his father's public services in his own defence.[7]

(ii) The life and career of Andocides

Andocides' life begins for us in 415. By then he was a member of a group of associates (*hetaireia*) which was almost certainly a political club with oligarchic sympathies, and it was probably for this group that he wrote a piece of propaganda entitled *To his Comrades*.[8] These comrades were soon to become notorious. In April of this year the Athenian assembly voted to send the ill-fated expedition to Sicily on the prompting of Alcibiades.[9] While the preparations were being made, it was discovered that during one night in May or June nearly all the stone images in the city of Hermes, the god of travellers, had been mutilated.[10] A commission of inquiry was appointed, and rewards offered for information. The alarm caused by this bad

---

1   He was young in 415 (**2.7**) and over forty in 400 (*Ag. And.* 46), still with the prospect of having children (**1.148**). *Life of And.* 835A wrongly gives 468/7.

2   He may mean either his family or the house itself was ancient (see MacDowell *ad loc.*).

3   Plut. *Alc.* 21.1; *Life of And.* 834B; Suda s.v.

4   **1.144**; *IG* i² 393.4. See Davies 27; Develin 137. This office was only open to the wealthiest property class, the *pentakosiomedimnoi* (*Ath. Pol.* 8.1).

5   See notes on **1.106, 2.26**.

6   ML 51 (= Fornara 101); **3.6**; Aesch. 2.174; Androtion F38. See Davies 29-30; Develin 138.

7   **2.11**; ML 65.51 (= Fornara 128); Ar. *Wasps* 1269 (with Sommerstein). See Davies 30; Develin 1784.

8   See **1.49**n.; cf. Plut. *Them.* 32.3; schol. Ar. *Wasps* 1007; Suda s.v. σκάνδιξ.

9   Thuc. 6.8-26. For different versions of the dates of these events see MacDowell App. F; *HCT* 4.271-6. Hansen (1975) 80 n. 5 notes that Diocleides' journey to collect his slave's earnings (**1.38**) is more likely to have taken place at the end of a month than in the middle, i.e. the mutilations were carried out the night before the beginning of the month Thargelion.

10   Thuc. 6.27. On how they were mutilated see **Introd. 1.I.b.**

omen was intensified when a certain Pythonicus stated in the assembly that Alcibiades and others had recently parodied the secret ceremonies of the Eleusinian Mysteries in private houses and with non-initiates present.[11] Alcibiades' enemies seized the opportunity to implicate him in both crimes, claiming they were part of a plot to overthrow the democracy, and when Alcibiades denied the charges and demanded an immediate trial, they succeeded in having the trial postponed. After Alcibiades' departure for Sicily there were further denunciations: some of those implicated in one or both affairs were executed, while others fled into exile. Alcibiades was recalled to Athens for trial, but escaped to the Peloponnese and was condemned to death in his absence.[12]

One of the informers was Diocleides, and among the forty-two names on his list was that of Andocides. Thrown into prison and facing execution, Andocides turned informer, on the guarantee of immunity, and he revealed that his *hetaireia* had been responsible for the mutilation.[13] Andocides thereby saved his own life and those of his father and several members of his family, but he had made himself extremely unpopular; and it has been widely accepted by scholars that the decree of Isotimides, which debarred all who were guilty of impiety and had confessed to it from the temples and agora of Athens, was aimed directly at Andocides. With his immunity effectively revoked, Andocides was forced to withdraw into exile.

In the period of his exile Andocides travelled around the Mediterranean, spending time especially in Cyprus.[14] He then made two unsuccessful attempts to return to Athens: the first, in 411, unfortunately coincided with the rule of the Four Hundred and led to his imprisonment;[15] the second, not later than 405, saw the delivery of his earliest extant speech, *On his Return*. It was not until after the amnesty of 403 that Andocides was finally able to resume his citizenship, and he was soon prosecuting Archippus for mutilating a Hermes dedicated by his family, getting involved in politics and holding offices.[16] Then, in autumn 400, came his own prosecution for violating the decree of Isotimides, and Andocides delivered the *On the Mysteries* speech to secure his acquittal.

Andocides' final mark on the historical record comes in 392/1, when he was a member of the peace embassy to Sparta. In his *On the Peace with the Spartans* he recommends acceptance of the proposed terms, but the speech failed to convince the assembly and the envoys were prosecuted by Callistratus, nephew of one of

---

11   **1.11**; Thuc. 6.28.
12   Thuc. 6.29, 61.
13   **1.37-68, 2.22-3**.
14   **1.4**, cf. **132, 2.20-1**; *Ag. And.* 6; *Life of And.* 834E-F.
15   **2.13-16**. On his release, Andocides returned to Cyprus and landed in more trouble (cf. *Ag. And.* 28).
16   *Ag. And.* 11, 33; **1.132**. At some point (perhaps after his acquittal in 400) he was choregus, winning with a boys' chorus at the Dionysia (*IG* ii² 1138.21; *Life of And.* 835B), and a commissioner of inquiry (Harpoc. s.v. ζητητής).

Andocides' accusers in 400, Agyrrhius. Fleeing to avoid trial, Andocides and his colleagues were condemned to death in their absence.[17]

(iii) Andocides' works

Andocides was the second in the canon of ten Attic orators, which was established in the late first century B.C. or early first century A.D. by the Augustan literary critic Caecilius of Calcacte.[18] Four speeches attributed to our author survive today; in the manuscript order these are *On the Mysteries, On his Return, On the Peace with the Spartans* and *Against Alcibiades*. The fourth speech is widely regarded as being spurious,[19] but its presence in the manuscripts under the name of Andocides and, it seems, its acceptance as a genuine work of his by the author of the *Life of Andocides* (as well as by some modern scholars) justify its inclusion in this volume.[20] Additionally, we possess a small number of fragments, all of which may come from the early propaganda piece *To his Comrades*;[21] and it is likely that the three certainly genuine speeches and this pamphlet were the sum total of Andocides' literary output.[22]

Andocides' speeches are of utmost importance, both as works of literature and as historical documents. On the literary side, they are amongst the earliest works of the rhetorical genre, which was to play a central role in Graeco-Roman culture and education for centuries to come. Their merits and defects as literature are considered in section (iv). From an historical point of view, the speeches are primary source material, and provide evidence - often the only evidence - for events in a momentous period of Greek history, supplementing the narratives of Thucydides and Xenophon. Thus, the *Mysteries* speech gives a fascinating insight into life at Athens towards and after the end of the Peloponnesian War, and contains invaluable details about the greatest scandal in Athenian history. Again, the speech *On the Peace with the Spartans* preserves vital indications of Athenian attitudes to war, empire and past history in the late 390s. On the other hand, this evidence is frequently controversial, and we must always bear in mind that the speeches were delivered for a specific purpose, to persuade the assembly to adopt a certain course of action or, in the case of the *Mysteries* speech, to secure Andocides' acquittal in a law-court. Because of this they are biased and selective in the details they provide, and may simply be lying or deceitful.

---

17 This is MacDowell's inference from Dem. 19.276-80. The sources simply record his banishment (cf. Philochorus F149; *Life of And.* 835A).
18 See most recently on this view I. Worthington, 'The canon of the ten Attic orators', in I. Worthington (ed.), *Persuasion: Greek Rhetoric in Action* (London, 1994) 244-63.
19 See **Introd. 4.**
20 *Life of And.* 835A refers to a *Defence against Phaeax*, which is almost certainly a confused reference to the *Against Alcibiades*.
21 This work apparently was no longer extant at the time when the *Life of Andocides* was written, since it is not listed among Andocides' works at 835A.
22 *Life of And.* 835A refers to a speech *On the Indictment*, which was probably an alternative title of the *On the Mysteries*.

(iv) The oratory and style of Andocides

The paucity of Andocides' writings reflects the fact that, unlike the other members of the canon, he was neither a professional speech-writer (*logographos*) nor a regular political speaker (*rhetor*). This makes his inclusion in the canon all the more remarkable and serves to underline his excellent oratorical ability. Andocides suffered a poor reputation as an orator in antiquity,[23] but the ancient critics were primarily interested in the literary products of the orators' activities and based their opinions largely on subjective stylistic criteria. Dionysius of Halicarnassus, a contemporary of Caecilius, mentions Andocides only twice (*Lysias* 2, *Thucydides* 51), but gives a clue to the continuing value of his prose, when he passes the verdict that Lysias was the perfect model of the Attic dialect current in his day, as exemplified in the speeches of Andocides and others.[24] Lysias, a professional speech-writer, devoted his considerable talents to producing graceful and apparently artless prose, which he then published in order to advertise his skills. Andocides, on the other hand, who seems to have spoken in public only when he had to do so, relied on his innate fluency and a thorough command of the everyday (if upper-class) language of his time. We do not know how closely our texts correspond to what Andocides actually said on the occasions in question, but the stylistic infelicities they contain suggest that he was not overly concerned with retouching his speeches for a reading public. The speeches of Andocides, therefore, are an example of a pure Attic Greek of the late fifth and early fourth centuries, and should be valued as such.

Andocides spoke with a natural vigour, and the essence of his Greek is its simplicity. Above all, he concentrates on what he is trying to say rather than on how he is saying it,[25] and the *Mysteries* speech in particular contains some quite brilliant rhetorical effects. His narrative passages are almost Lysianic in their simplicity and clarity (**1.11ff.**), and can be exciting (**1.38ff.**), emotive (**1.48ff., 2.10ff.**), intriguing (**1.117ff.**) and scandalous (**1.124ff.**). Andocides holds the jurors' attention by the use of direct speech and dialogue (**1.101**), by directly addressing them (**1.23, 33, 37**) and asking rhetorical questions (**1.148** with hypophora, cf. **3.13-15**), and by the use of anecdotes, jokes and irony (**1.130-1; 100, 129; 133, our gentleman friend Agyrrhius**). When, on the other hand, he interrupts himself in **1.4** (ἐγώ has no verb and the sentence is interrupted by the direct speech; cf. **39**), this is an indication of how there is frequently a lack of elegance in his style,[26] and how he can, at times,

---

23 Only Dinarchus was ranked lower (cf. Hermogenes, *On Characteristics* 11, p. 416 Spengel; Philostratus, *Lives of the Sophists* 2.1.14, p. 564 Kayser; Quint. 12.10.21). He has fared little better with modern scholars, who classify him pejoratively as an amateur or 'gentleman' orator (see B. L. Gildersleeve, review of Hickie in *AJP* 6 [1885] 489) and censure his treatment of subject-matter and argumentation techniques (see, e.g., Jebb 98-101; Kennedy 146-8).

24 *Life of And.* 835B says 'he is simple and free from artifice in his speeches, plain and sparing in the use of figures of speech'.

25 See further MacDowell 20-3.

26 Andocides' frequent omission of connective particles between sentences (asyndeton) was taken as a sign of 'a certain naive awkwardness' by Denniston xlv, but his criticism

get carried away with himself (e.g. **1.144-5** consists of one sentence in the Greek). He repeats words and sometimes whole phrases (e.g. **1.6, to show more goodwill to me than to my accusers**), joins together synonyms (e.g. **1.105, flee and leave**) or uses the same word in different senses in the same sentence (e.g. **1.107**, γιγνώσκω, **realising...decided**). But these technical flaws only add to the vivacity of Andocides' writing, and, in the hubbub of the law-court and on trial for his life, he evidently considered keeping the jurors entertained far more important than stylistic elegance.

In spite of his seeming lack of training, Andocides could not fail to be influenced by the developments in rhetorical technique that were taking place towards the end of the fifth century. He was a teenager when the Sicilian rhetorician Gorgias came to Athens in 427 on an embassy from Leontini and made a profound impression on the Athenian assembly with his exuberant style of speaking.[27] Gorgianic figures such as balanced antithesis do not abound in Andocides, but examples may be found (e.g. **1.30, 57, 93, 107; 3.12**). Then, Andocides' young adulthood coincided with the activity of Antiphon, the first member of the canon, who shared with him an oligarchic political standpoint. There are traces of the so-called grand style of Antiphon (and Thucydides) in Andocides' speeches, including poetic words and expressions, which derive mainly from tragedy (**1.29**, φρικώδη ἀνωρθίαζον, **they shouted aloud these horrors**; **1.31**, ἀρασάμενοι τὰς μεγίστας ἀρὰς, **invoking the greatest curses**; **1.68**, ὁρῶσι τοῦ ἡλίου τὸ φῶς, **see the light of day**; **1.99**, ἐπίτριπτον κίναδος, **practised rogue**; **1.130**, κληδών, **rumour**; **1.146**, οἴχεται πᾶν πρόρριζον, **it is completely and utterly destroyed**; **2.16**, εὐθαρσεῖν, **to be of good courage**; **3.7**, ὑψηλὸν ἦρε, **raised high**); and old-fashioned features such as the use of the indirect reflexive dative oἱ (**1.15, 38, 40, 41, 42, 126**); single τε to mean 'and' (**1.21, 61, 107, 111; 2.15 twice, 19; 3.7 twice, 9, 30, 33, 39, 40**); antithesis formed by τοῦτο μέν...τοῦτο δέ... (**1.103; 2.16, 17; 3.40**); and numerous periphrastic expressions such as λόγους ποιεῖσθαι instead of simply λέγειν for 'to say' (**1.1**). On the whole, however, these older features are rare in Andocides,[28] and his style bears more resemblance to the newer and far less florid style of Lysias.[29]

The success of the *Mysteries* speech is indicative of the persuasive potential of Andocides' natural oratory.[30] Even as an amateur he displays an increasing awareness of rhetorical methods, as closer analysis of his works than has regularly been made will indicate. The somewhat arrogant young aristocrat of the *On his Return* learned from his failure, and the more mature Andocides of the *Mysteries* trial is careful for the most part to hide his political views, while winning over the jurors with his wit and enthusiasm, as well as by a clever arrangement of his defence.

---

was rightly countered by MacDowell, App. P. MacDowell shows that the link is usually provided by another word or feature of the sentence.

27 Cf. Thuc. 3.86.3; Pl. *Hippias Major* 282b.

28 The use of metaphor (cf. **1.9**, θηρεύειν, **hunt after**; **2.9**, ἰαθῆναι, **to be remedied**) and abstract subjects (e.g. **3.7**, εἰρήνη, **peace**) is also rare.

29 For a detailed analysis of Andocides' style see Kingsbury.

30 See further Jebb 93-4; Kingsbury 9-10; Dobson 60-1.

By the time he came to deliver his final speech, *On the Peace with the Spartans*, Andocides could employ the regular topics of deliberative oratory and bring considerable rhetorical prowess to bear in making out a convincing case for his peace proposal. His failure on this occasion was due not so much to flaws in his oratory as to the fact that on a matter of such importance this proud, dyed-in-the-wool aristocrat would only recommend to the assembly the opposite course of action to the one it wanted to hear.

The Manuscripts and Text

The text of Andocides derives from two manuscripts only: A, the Crippsianus (British Museum Burneianus 95) of the thirteenth century, which contains all four speeches; and Q, the inferior Ambrosianus D 42 sup. of the fourteenth century, which contains the *De Pace* and *In Alcibiadem*. The other surviving manuscripts (BLMPZ) were shown by a series of critical studies in the 1870s and 1880s, beginning with A. Hug's *Commentatio de arte critica in Antiphontis orationibus factitanda* (Zürich, 1872), to be ultimately dependent on A. The folios of A containing Andocides' speeches (which begin the manuscript) were corrected by their copyist, and by probably the same hand but in a slightly darker ink. A full description of A and Q, with the history of their transmission, may be found in the critical introduction to W. Wyse's edition of Isaeus (Cambridge, 1904).

The standard modern edition of Andocides is the Teubner of F. Blass and C. Fuhr, *Andocidis orationes* (4th ed., Leipzig, 1913), but, in my opinion, MacDowell's generally more conservative approach to textual editing makes his text of the *De Mysteriis* superior. I have therefore based my text of the *De Mysteriis* on MacDowell, and of the *De Reditu*, *De Pace* and *In Alcibiadem* on Blass/Fuhr, with the following differences (excluding some minor changes in spelling, punctuation and accentuation which do not affect the sense):

	This edition	*MacDowell*
	Andocides 1	

74. MacDowell transposes ὁπόσοι κλοπῆς...ἀτίμους εἶναι to the last sentence of **73** (after πεπρᾶσθαι), following U. E. Paoli, *Studi di diritto attico* (Florence, 1930) 304-7, and puts δ' αὖ after ὁπόσοι. The order of the MS. is defended by Hansen (1976) 86-9.

	This edition	*MacDowell*
78.	<οἷς>	<οἷς, ἢ>
120.	προτέρῳ μὲν Λεάγρῳ, <λέγων> ὅτι	πρότερον μὲν <λέγων> Λεάγρῳ ὅτι
121.	ἵνα μὴ...ταῖς δ'	ἵνα <δὲ>...ταῖς [δ']
132.	ταμίαν	ταμίας <ἦν>

	This edition	*Blass/Fuhr*
	Andocides 2	
6.	ὦ 'Αθηναῖοι	ὦ <ἄνδρες> 'Αθηναῖοι (**2-4** *passim*)
16.	ὑπ' ἐμοῦ <cὺ>	<cὺ> ὑπ' ἐμοῦ
19.	αἰτίαν <ἂν>	<ἂν> αἰτίαν

8

22.	ὠφεληθήσεσθε	ὠφελήσεσθε
23.	διδόντας τε	τε διδόντας
26.	πρόπαππος	πάππος
	αὐτῶν	αὐτοῦ

Andocides 3

30.	βουλοίμεθα	βουλόμεθα
39.	καὶ <τὰς> ναῦς	καὶ ναῦς
40.	οὐ πρακτέον	οὐκ ἀκτέον

[Andocides] 4

3.	οὔτε διαψηφισαμένων	[οὔτε] διαψηφισαμένων
7.	ἕκαστον	ἑκάστου
8.	οὐ ῥᾴδιον εἰδέναι	οὐ ῥᾴδιον ἦν εἰδέναι
9.	δημεύεσθαι	δημεύειν <ὑμᾶς>
	τοὺς δὲ νικήσαντας	τῶν δὲ νικησάντων
	χρῆσθαι	χρήσεσθαι
12.	ἐπιμελεῖται	<μόνον> ἐπιμελεῖται
15.	Blass/Fuhr keep the manuscript order, with ἀλλὰ μὴν...βοηθήσοντας following περὶ πλείονος.	
17.	τὴν οἰκίαν	οἴκαδε τὴν οἰκίαν
23.	τὴν πόλιν	ἧς τὴν πόλιν
26.	τὸν ἐπιτυχόντα	<οὐ> τὸν ἐπιτυχόντα
34.	ἐξωστρακίσθησαν	<δὶς> ἐξωστρακίσθησαν

Earlier editions of Andocides, following the *editio princeps* of Aldus Manutius in 1513, include:

H. Stephanus, *Oratorum veterum orationes* (Paris, 1575)
J. J. Reiske, *Oratores graeci* (Leipzig, 1771)
I. Bekker, *Oratores attici*, vol. 1 (Oxford, 1822)
W. S. Dobson, *Antiphontis et Andocidis quae exstant omnia* (London, 1828)
J. G. Baiter and H. Sauppe, *Oratores attici* (Zürich, 1839)
F. Blass, *Andocidis orationes* (Leipzig, 1880)
J. H. Lipsius, *Andocidis orationes* (Leipzig, 1888)

THE SPEECHES

INTRODUCTION 1: *ON THE MYSTERIES*

(i) The religious background to the trial

The first speech in the Crippsianus manuscript of Andocides, though the second in time, is his *On the Mysteries*. Andocides devotes a large part of the speech to the events of 415, which were outlined in the **General Introduction** and were the long-term causes of his prosecution in 400, namely the profanation of the Mysteries and the mutilation of the Hermae. Discussion of his trial must therefore begin with a brief description of the religious beliefs and practices that were outraged by these scandals.

(a) The Eleusinian Mysteries

The Greater Eleusinian Mysteries were held every Boedromion (September and the beginning of October) at the time of sowing, in honour of 'the two goddesses' Demeter (goddess of the earth and agriculture) and her daughter Core (Persephone, queen of Hades). By the late fifth century initiates, including men, women, children and slaves, came from all over the Greek world to take part in the secret rites at Eleusis, about fourteen miles west of Athens, in the belief that they would enjoy everlasting happiness when they reached the land of the dead. The main part of the ritual was the showing of the *hiera* ('sacred things'), which at the beginning of the festival were taken from Eleusis to the Eleusinium in Athens. Various preliminary ceremonies followed, including the cleansing of the participants in the sea, each carrying a small pig which was then sacrificed, and rites in honour of Asclepius, the god of healing, before the *hiera* were carried back along the Sacred Way to Eleusis in a great procession. After a day of fasting, the main sacrifice was made under the supervision of the archon basileus, his assistant (*paredros*) and four superintendents (*epimeletai*); and then the Mysteries were conducted by priests, led by the hierophant ('shower of the sacred things', a member of the Eumolpidae family), the dadouchos ('torch-bearer', a member of the Ceryces) and the herald (*keryx*). The second day at Eleusis culminated in the revelation of the *hiera*, and the third day was devoted to libations and rites for the dead. Finally (on the ninth day of the festival, Boedromion 23) the initiates dispersed, and the next day the basileus reported to the council at Athens, meeting in the Eleusinium, on the conduct of the celebration.[1]

How the Mysteries were profaned in 415 is uncertain. Citizens who were non-initiates were cleared from the assembly before the first of the informers made his statement, which contains no specific details of this kind.[2] But we do know that

---

1   See further Mylonas chap. ix; Parke 55-72.
2   **12.** The jury at Andocides' trial also consisted of initiates (**29, 31**).

the participants acted out the roles of the priests and the initiates, and Andocides was alleged to have imitated the showing of the *hiera* and spoken the sacred words.[3]

(b) The Hermae

Hermae were quadrangular stone pillars surmounted by a carved representation of the head of the god Hermes and often bearing an erect phallus. These pillars replaced the heaps of stones which were the customary markers of paths, boundaries, meeting-places and graves (Hermes was the god of travellers, private property and the agora, and the conductor of the souls of the dead to Hades); and they were set up in front of houses and at many different points in Athens' streets. The phallus indicates that their function was apotropaic (i.e. to ward off evil).

As with the profanation, the details of the mutilation are not entirely clear. Thucydides says their faces were disfigured, but presumably the erect *phalloi* were also broken off where these were present.[4]

(c) The purposes of the profanation and mutilation

The reports of the impieties caused panic in Athens. The late fifth century was a time when traditional religious beliefs were being questioned, but it is hardly surprising that particularly an offence against the god of travellers caused outrage, given the imminent departure of the fleet.[5] Nevertheless, was there more to these affairs than the affronting of religious sensibilities, as Thucydides hints?[6] A first point to be borne in mind is that, even though some men were accused of both impieties, there was probably no direct or causal relationship between them.[7] The profanations were performed repeatedly in private houses and were evidently not intended to be publicised. This implies that they had no political purpose,[8] nor did they pose any real threat to the established religion;[9] rather, they were a form of private entertainment, perhaps even mock initiation ceremonies for a club.[10] The mutilations, on the other hand, were of a different order (though again there were precedents[11]). They were carried out on a large scale, and in a planned and very public operation, which seems to rule out any idea that they were simply the high jinks of wild, drunk young men. According to Andocides,[12] the act was to serve as a

---

3   Plut. *Alc.* 19.1, 22.3; *Ag. And.* 51.
4   Thuc. 6.27.1 (with *HCT*); cf. Ar. *Lys.* 1094. See further R. G. Osborne, 'The erection and mutilation of the *Hermai*', *PCPS* 31 (1985) 47-73.
5   *Contra* MacDowell 9. But see Osborne, *art. cit.* 64-7.
6   Thuc. 6.27.3. See Osborne, *art.cit.*67; Todd (1993) 312-15.
7   See Ellis 59 with n. 40.
8   Alcibiades, e.g., was no oligarch in 415.
9   Religious ceremonies were frequently parodied in comedy, including the Eleusinian festival in Aristophanes' *Frogs*.
10   See MacDowell App. G; *HCT* 4.283.
11   Plut. *Alc.* 19.1.
12   **67.**

pledge, which would ensure the loyalty of the group's members. But it is most unlikely that such a crime would have served merely as a pledge, and what has been seen as the group's further motive was the preventing of the departure of the fleet for Sicily.[13] The oligarchic leanings of Andocides' *hetaireia* will have meant that its members preferred peace to war and feared the strengthening of the democracy by a successful expedition.[14] But it has also been argued[15] that the timing of the act, at least a fortnight before the departure of the expedition, goes against this theory; there was no reason to believe such action would cause the abandonment of the expedition, which was strongly supported; and there was indeed no discussion of cancellation after the discovery of the mutilations. Furthermore, the oligarchs themselves actually stood a better chance of gaining power when the fleet was away (as happened in 411), and both oligarchs and radical democrats like Androcles might benefit from Alcibiades' absence.[16] It does not follow, of course, that the mutilators' thoughts were quite so logical, but either way Alcibiades' enemies seized their opportunity to whip up religious fervour and to get rid of him, as they hoped, once and for all.

(ii) Andocides' quarrel with Callias

Moving on now to the immediate background to Andocides' trial after his return to Athens in 403, we come to his quarrel with Callias, son of Hipponicus. Callias' extremely wealthy family belonged to the clan of the Ceryces and provided the dadouchos at the Mysteries.[17] His grandfather Callias,[18] who was married to Cimon's sister Elpinice and was a cousin of Aristeides, negotiated the Peace of Callias with Persia (450/49), was a member with Andocides' grandfather of the embassy which made the Thirty Years' Peace with Sparta, and was an official Spartan representative (*proxenos*) at Athens. His father Hipponicus[19] was general in 426/5, but is better known to us for divorcing Callias' mother, who then married Pericles. Callias[20] was born about 450. General in 391/0 and three times an envoy to the Spartans (he too was their *proxenos*), he was renowned for his culture[21] and also

---

13 As MacDowell App. G.
14 This does not necessarily carry the further implication that they were attempting the overthrow of the democracy (cf. Thuc. 6.27.3). They may have been friends of Nicias, who was opposed to the expedition; there was also, not surprisingly, a tradition that the Corinthians were involved on behalf of their colonists and allies the Syracusans (cf. *Life of And.* 834D; Plut. *Alc.* 18.3). See MacDowell *ibid.*
15 By Marr 337-8. See further *HCT* 4.284-6.
16 See also Ellis 58-62. For Androcles cf. Plut. *Alc.* 19.
17 For Callias' family tree see App. B.
18 See Davies 258-62; Develin 1501.
19 See Davies 262-3; Develin 1426.
20 See Davies 263-9; Develin 1502.
21 Especially as a patron of the sophists (Pl. *Ap.* 20a). His house in Athens is the setting of Plato's *Protagoras*, that at Peiraeus of Xenophon's *Symposium*.

his luxurious lifestyle, which greatly diminished his vast fortune.[22] The brother-in-law of Alcibiades, Callias first married the daughter of Glaucon, but his alleged activities when married to the daughter of Ischomachus afforded Andocides the opportunity for a stinging personal attack in **124-9**.

We only have Andocides' version of the feud, which is related in **117-23**. He says it stemmed from the claims of himself and Callias to the daughter of Epilycus, though the bitterness that evidently existed between the two men suggests there may be more to the story than Andocides tells us. It is clear, however, that both men stubbornly refused to give way, for whatever reasons. According to Andocides, Callias then determined to stop Andocides pursuing his claim by threatening him with prosecution, counting on him once again withdrawing into exile instead of facing trial;[23] and he paid the sycophant[24] Cephisius 1,000 drachmas to lodge an *endeixis* against Andocides for infringing the decree of Isotimides by attending the Mysteries of 400. During the festival Cephisius pointed out Andocides to the basileus, who reported this to the council meeting held after the Mysteries.[25] When, however, Andocides stayed in Athens, Callias had an olive-branch placed on the altar of the Eleusinium, which was illegal during the Mysteries, and accused Andocides of putting it there (**110-16**). This ruse also failed, and apparently the relationship between the two had so deteriorated that Andocides preferred to face trial than accept a final offer to pay him compensation.

Andocides' account is, of course, biased, and we have no way of testing its veracity. It is possible, however, to analyse its rhetorical purpose (see below, section v).

(iii) The date of the trial

There are two main clues to the date of Andocides' trial: it was held soon after the Mysteries (**121**), and he had by then been back in Athens for three years (**132**). If, as seems likely, he returned immediately after the amnesty, the trial should be dated to the autumn of 400.[26] Blass 291 n. 6 argued that the offices held by Andocides after his return (**132**) are listed in chronological order, in which case he cannot have been treasurer before 400/399, and the trial will have taken place in the autumn of 399. But inscriptional evidence shows Andocides was not treasurer in 400/399 or 399/8, and 401/0 is more likely.[27]

---

22   Cf. Ar. *Birds* 284-6 (with Sommerstein). See also **130**n.
23   See **2**n.
24   See **86**n.
25   See **111**n.
26   Cf. Plut. *Mor.* 349F; *Life of And.* 835A.
27   Further on these and other even more tenuous pieces of evidence see MacDowell App. J.

(iv) The prosecution

Andocides was prosecuted by the procedure *endeixis* on two charges of impiety (*asebeia*): that he attended the Mysteries when debarred by the decree of Isotimides, because he had committed impiety and confessed; and that he had laid an olive-branch on the altar of the Eleusinium at the time of the Mysteries, which was illegal. The case was heard by a jury of initiates (29), under the presidency of the basileus (the archon in charge of religious affairs), and if condemned Andocides faced the death penalty (4, 32, 146, 149-50; *Ag. And.* 55).[28]

The prosecution was conducted by a team of four, led by Cephisius with Meletus, Epichares and Agyrrhius in supporting roles. Andocides treats them all as professional accusers (cf. 105), actually calling Cephisius and Epichares sycophants (93, 99) and stating that Cephisius was in the pay of Callias (121). But Agyrrhius, at least, had a personal motive for his attack (133-6). A large section of one of the supporting speeches (*deuterologiai*) survives in the Lysianic corpus:[29] poorly composed, it deals mainly with the religious side of the case.

(v) The defence

The complex nature of the charges against him and their history meant that Andocides was faced with the problem of making, in effect, three separate defences in one long speech. The origins of his alleged crime lay in events that took place some fifteen years previously; there was the question as to whether the decree of Isotimides was invalidated by the amnesty of 403; and finally there was the affair of the olive-branch just prior to the trial. Andocides deals with each of these in turn, and what might have been a very difficult speech for the jurors to follow is in fact well-ordered and for the most part clear. This very orderliness and clarity betrays the careful and thorough preparation of the oration,[30] and the following is a breakdown of the its main sections.

After a standard introduction, in which he asks the jury for a fair hearing (1-10), Andocides deals at some length with the main charge, employing two lines of argument: firstly, he did not commit impiety in 415 (11-70); and secondly, the decree of Isotimides was no longer valid (71-91). His treatment of the Mysteries and Hermae affairs does not follow the standard narrative/proofs sequence, but is divided logically into two sections (11-33, 34-70). These too display an inventive variety: in the former narrative is followed by proof, but in the latter these two

---

28   It is not clear from these passages whether the death penalty was fixed by law (i.e. the case was an ἀγὼν ἀτίμητος) or by the proposal of the prosecution (i.e. an ἀγὼν τιμητός). See Hansen (1976) 129 with n. 37; MacDowell (1978) 253-4 on τίμησις.

29   Ps.-Lys. 6, *Against Andocides*.

30   Following the regular view that the speech as we have it was essentially the one which was actually delivered, with perhaps a few extemporaneous remarks (inserted during the course of delivery in answer to points made by the prosecution) added before publication. See MacDowell 18.

elements are mixed. Andocides thereby adopts a method for which Isaeus was to become noted,[31] and the complexity of the second section may reflect its relative difficulty for Andocides' case.[32] The rest of the speech is branded by Jebb 125 as 'a mere string of topics, unconnected with each other, and but slightly connected with the case', but his damning judgment completely fails to appreciate Andocides' clever handling of the secondary charge against him. This part of the defence (110-16) is sandwiched between two sets of personal attacks, on Cephisius, Meletus and Epichares (92-100) and on Callias and Agyrrhius (117-36); and it is immediately preceded by the underlining of the implications of this loyal citizen's acquittal for the unity of the city as a whole, with examples from Athens' past history in which his own ancestors featured prominently (101-9).[33] In other words, Andocides impugns the low morals and base motives of his accusers Cephisius, Meletus and Epichares, juxtaposing them with the high importance of his own position; and then his rejection of the secondary charge is bolstered by further character assassination of his two private enemies, Callias and Agyrrhius. Andocides again claims the moral high ground in this second set of attacks. He contrasts his upright and impeccable behaviour with the degenerate and vindictive motives of Callias, the well-known Sybarite; and he sets his dutiful patriotic actions against the selfish greed of Agyrrhius and his cronies, ending with another statement of the benefits that the city will gain from his acquittal. The proofs section of the speech is rounded off, in response to one of the prosecution's arguments, by the contention that his innocence is confirmed by the favour of the gods (137-9); and the defence ends in a forceful epilogue with a final plea for acquittal (140-50).

His plea was accepted. It is perhaps idle to speculate that any single argument rather than the combined weight of Andocides' arguments won him the case, but one area in particular may have had a strong influence on the outcome.[34] The depiction of Callias as an 'evil spirit' (130-1) and the refutation of the prosecution's argument about divine revenge (137-9) may well imply that the jurors, all initiates in the Mysteries,[35] were very concerned to maintain religious beliefs and fears. This conservatism was consistent with the political climate after 404, in which the democracy was restored but subject to the direction of Sparta, and beliefs of this kind tended to reinforce passive political attitudes. In such a context Andocides' religious services since his return to Athens will have stood him in good stead.

---

31 Cf. Dion. Hal. *Isaeus* 14.
32 See below section vi.2.
33 Attacks on the opponents, the argument that acquittal was in the state's interests and examples from past history are all regular features of forensic oratory.
34 See for this view Missiou 53-4.
35 See above section i.a (n. 1).

(vi) Andocides' part in the Mysteries and Hermae affairs

Despite his acquittal, was Andocides in truth guilty of profaning the Mysteries and/or of mutilating the Hermae? In his speech Andocides seeks to prove that he did not himself mutilate a Hermes, although he was a member of the group that carried out the mutilations, and he flatly denies involvement in the Mysteries affair. But a very different version persisted in the ancient world, that he was guilty, at least as an informer, of involvement in the profanation as well - and of informing against his father.[36] How far can we believe Andocides?

The only other near-contemporary account we have of these events (apart from the one in the *Ag. And.*) is found in Thucydides, who emphasises the way in which the scandals were used to attack Alcibiades. In 6.27-9 Thucydides tells us that in one night nearly all the Hermae had their faces disfigured, but no one knew who had committed the deed. Large rewards for information were offered, and a decree was passed guaranteeing immunity to anyone, citizen, alien or slave, who offered information about any sacrilege of which he was cognisant. Some metics and servants did come forward, although they had nothing to say about the Hermae,[37] but told of other cases in which statues were mutilated and of mock celebrations of the Mysteries in private houses. One of those accused of the latter was Alcibiades, and this was seized on by his political enemies, who exaggerated the affair as being part of a plot to overthrow the democracy. But wary of Alcibiades' current popularity, his opponents managed to have the trial put off until he returned from Sicily. Then in 6.53 Thucydides relates how Alcibiades and others in Sicily were ordered to return to Athens in the light of investigations that took place after the departure of the fleet. The Athenians believed the evidence of informers, regardless of their character, because they were afraid of tyranny. Finally, in 6.60 Thucydides describes the situation in Athens:

> Deeply mindful of these events and recalling everything they had heard about them,[38] the people of Athens were now angry and suspicious towards those who had been accused in connection with the Mysteries, and the whole affair seemed to them to be part of a plot aiming at oligarchy or tyranny. With public opinion inflamed by these suspicions, there were already a number of worthy citizens in prison and there seemed to be no end in sight, but every day saw an increase in savagery and led to more arrests being made. At last one of the prisoners, who was thought to be deeply implicated, was persuaded

---

36   Cf. *Ag. And.* 23-4, 51; *Life of And.* 834C-E; Tzetzes, *Historia* 49.

37   If the metic Teucrus gave his information before the expedition left, this statement is false; if after, the mention of metics is merely misleading and due to rhetorical exaggeration. That the latter is the case is suggested by 6.53.2, where Thucydides emphasises that many good men were arrested on the testimony of bad. See *HCT* 4.273-4.

38   Viz. the conspiracy of Harmodius and Aristogeiton.

by a fellow-prisoner to give information which may have been true or false. Opinions are divided, and no one, either then or later, was able to say for certain who did the deed. The one, however, succeeded in persuading the other that even if he had not done it, he ought to make himself safe by obtaining immunity and to put an end to the prevailing state of suspicion in the city; for he would be in a safer position if he made a confession with immunity than if he denied the charges and stood trial. So the man in question gave information incriminating himself and others with regard to the Hermae. The Athenian people were delighted at discovering what they imagined to be the truth, after previously being in despair at the idea that the conspirators against the democracy might never be found out. They immediately released the informer and the others with him whom he had not denounced. Those he had accused were brought to trial, and all who were secured were executed; while the death sentence was passed on all who had escaped, and a reward was proclaimed to anyone who should kill them. In all this no one could say whether those who suffered were justly punished, but the beneficial effect on the rest of the city at the time was quite clear.

Thucydides' account is broadly consistent with that of Andocides: it connects his confession with the mutilation of the Hermae and supports his contention in 66 that his information was held to clear up the matter. On the other hand, the historian also indicates that there were people in Athens who were by no means convinced of the whole truth of Andocides' confession. We do not know why this was (it may, of course, have been connected with the identity of Thucydides' informants), or indeed why Thucydides does not mention Andocides by name. Thucydides' overall opinion clearly is that what mattered most to the Athenians in 415 was not the truth of the matter, which was never certainly discovered, but ending their state of panic. This, however, is of little help in resolving the question of Andocides' guilt, and we are therefore thrown back onto the versions given by Andocides himself and the author of the *Against Andocides*.

The most detailed modern analysis of the problem is that of MacDowell in Appendices A-E of his Commentary, although an opposing viewpoint was taken by Marr in *CQ* 21 (1971) 326-38. MacDowell quite properly examines statements made by Andocides in the speech with an extremely critical eye, and concludes that Andocides was guilty of profanation but probably never declared himself guilty of mutilation. Attributing considerable weight to *Ag. And.* 21-4 at the expense of the accounts given by Thucydides and Plutarch (*Alcibiades* 21-2), who like Thucydides connects Andocides' confession with the mutilation not the profanation, MacDowell offers the following reconstruction. Andocides gave information about the mutilation of the Hermae, as he describes in 60-6, but was kept in prison (because he failed to hand over a slave for questioning as promised) until he also confessed to involvement in the Mysteries affair. To secure immunity (*adeia*), he denounced his father Leogoras (among others) and then, repentant after his release, he helped him avoid prosecution by the counter-prosecution of Speusippus (17).

It is my belief that MacDowell's theory, brilliant though it may be, is not borne out by the evidence available to us. This does not mean that he is wrong, and my purpose here is not by any means to whitewash Andocides, who by his own admission was cognisant of the mutilation plot (61). In assessing the trustworthiness of Andocides' story we must constantly bear in mind that he was on trial for his life, and persuading the jurors was more important to him than necessarily telling the whole truth.[39] It is natural for him to claim that he is innocent and that he has proved his case (29), and he appeals in regular rhetorical fashion to the knowledge of the jurors (30, 37). But there are good grounds for accepting Andocides' denial of the charge of profanation, and he perhaps deserves a fairer hearing than he receives as a result of over-reliance on the ps.-Lysias passage, to which the same critical principle concerning persuasion should be applied. The main points at issue are as follows.

I. Firstly, the profanation of the Mysteries (11-33). Andocides attempts to prove (a) that he did not commit impiety himself; (b) that he did not denounce anybody else for so doing (especially Leogoras); and (c) that he never confessed his guilt (10).

(a) The strongest argument that Andocides did not profane the Mysteries is that his name almost certainly did not appear on any of the lists provided by the various informers. If it had appeared, the only way he could have avoided being prosecuted or forced into exile was by denouncing Leogoras and others under a grant of immunity. But in that case Leogoras could hardly have escaped prosecution himself, despite his successful counter-attack against Speusippus (17), and it must be doubted whether Andocides, after confessing, could have played any active part in the latter. The assembly, in its excited state in 415, would not have allowed both guilty men to escape prosecution by legal technicalities. MacDowell notes that Andocides quotes the names of those denounced by Andromachus (13), Teucrus (15) and Agariste (16, though here he produces no documentary evidence), but not the names on the list furnished by Lydus (17). Since, in his view, Andocides does not prove that his name was not on Lydus' list, MacDowell concludes that it probably was. But while Philippus and Alexippus (18), relatives of two of those denounced, may not have been able in 400 to remember all the names on Lydus' list, it is quite possible that they remembered whether Andocides' name was on it, and we do not know precisely what testimony they gave. Lydus' list may not have survived for Andocides to quote, perhaps because he had not received a public reward, and Andocides'

---

39   For this principle see MacDowell App. A. But equally, we should not reject Andocides' evidence unless we can show clearly how it is to his advantage to misrepresent or conceal facts. See *HCT* 4.273.

challenge in **23** suggests that no official list containing his name was still in existence at the time of his trial.

MacDowell finds a further indication of Andocides' guilt in Plutarch's *Life of Alcibiades* 22.3-4. Plutarch quotes a document in which Thessalus, son of Cimon, impeaches Alcibiades for profaning the Mysteries in his own house, the leading roles being taken by Alcibiades, Pulytion and Theodorus. These details cannot, in MacDowell's opinion, be reconciled with the information provided by the four informers in Andocides' account: Andromachus reports a profanation in Pulytion's house by Alcibiades, Nicides and Meletus; the list of names furnished by Teucrus does not contain any of those given by Thessalus (Theodorus appears on Teucrus' list of those involved in the mutilation of the Hermae, **35**); Agariste and Lydus name the houses of Charmides and Pherecles respectively. MacDowell therefore posits a fifth denunciation as the basis of Thessalus' charge, which Andocides suppressed because he was implicated in it. If, however, there really was a fifth denunciation, the question again arises as to why Andocides was not prosecuted. In addition, Marr[40] examines the identities of those behind Thessalus' charge against Alcibiades, which was made after the conclusion of the Hermae investigation as part of a renewed attempt by Alcibiades' enemies to implicate him in the Mysteries affair.[41] Marr sees these enemies as acting in retaliation for Dioclcides' story (**37-43**), which in turn had been prompted by friends of Alcibiades (cf. **65**).[42] Similarly, Agariste, the wife of Alcmaconides, may have given information against Alcibiades in retaliation for Diocleides' denunciation of Callias, son of Alcmacon (**47**). In other words, the Philaid family to which Thessalus belonged was behind the attack on Alcibiades, in alliance with the Alcmaconids (because Thessalus' father, Cimon, had married the Alcmaconid Isodice). Then, since Andocides' family had close connections with the Alcmaconids and several of his relatives were also denounced by Diocleides, it is unlikely that Thessalus' charge against Alcibiades would also have incriminated Andocides and Leogoras. But are the accounts of Andocides and Plutarch truly irreconcilable? Marr suggests that although the precise details in Andocides and Plutarch do not match up, the combination in Thessalus' charge may have resulted from the various investigations and examinations which were conducted, and was chosen as the one most damaging to Alcibiades. But, more specifically, Plutarch's account indicates that Thessalus' prosecution was based on information supplied by informants connected with Alcibiades' bitter enemy, the demagogue Androcles.[43] Now their information concerned previous mutilations of images as well as parodies of the Mysteries, and despite being amongst the first informers, they were not rewarded (**28**). This suggests that they only in fact gave

---

40   Compare the discussion of Diocleides' motives at *HCT* 4.286-8, noting its warning about the dangers of inferences drawn from political prosopography.

41   Thuc. 6.61.1-4.

42   Note that Alcibiades of Phegus (**65**) was the cousin of *the* Alcibiades.

43   *Alc.* 19.1; cf. Thuc. 6.28.1.

information about the previous impieties, which Andocides did not consider worth recording.[44] It could also be the case that this early information was embarrassing to Andocides because, according to the *Life of Andocides*, he had himself on a previous occasion been indicted for breaking a Hermes during a night-time revel.[45] Andocides, of course, had no reason to mention Thessalus' charge, and we do not need to imagine a fifth denunciation as its basis.

(b) Andocides argues in **20-2** that, if he had denounced his father, one of them would have been executed. MacDowell counters this by emphasising that Leogoras never was actually tried for impiety and therefore never was proved innocent. Consequently, Andocides was not shown to have provided false information, and he has therefore failed to prove that he did not secure immunity by informing against Leogoras. But the same argument applies once more that both father and son could not have escaped prosecution if Andocides had informed against Leogoras.[46]

(c) Andocides does not, indeed, produce evidence to show that he never confessed his guilt, but equally we do not know that his opponents produced evidence to show he did. The assertion in *Ag. And.* 51 that he confessed is unsupported by witnesses, as are all the other accusations made in the speech, though admittedly this was not the main prosecution speech, during which such witnesses may have been produced.[47] Further, Andocides' hints at his guilt in *On his Return* are more naturally taken to refer (*pace* MacDowell) to the mutilation of the Hermae (see below section 2).

(d) As has already been mentioned, MacDowell puts great emphasis on *Ag. And.* 21-4, a version of which therefore follows:

> **[21]** Consider also Andocides' own life since he committed impiety, and whether there is any other such as he. For when he had done wrong, he was brought before the court and deliberately imprisoned himself, having assessed prison as the penalty if he did not hand over his slave; **[22]** but he knew well that he would not be able to hand him over, since he had been put to death because of this man and his wrongs, so that he might not become an informer. Yet how was it not one of the gods that destroyed this man's reason, when he

---

44   As MacDowell himself admits (p. 183-4).
45   *Life of And.* 834D; cf. Thuc. *ibid.*
46   See further Hansen (1975) 78-9 n. 11, who rightly contends that if Andocides had denounced his father before the latter's prosecution of Speusippus, Leogoras would not have won his case, and if afterwards, he would certainly have been tried.
47   Marr 335 argues that there may be a deliberate ambiguity in the word order here, since this statement could refer either to both scandals or to the Hermae affair alone, but not solely to the Mysteries affair.

thought it easier to assess prison as the penalty than money when his expectation was the same either way? [23] Therefore, as a result of this assessment, he was in prison for nearly a year, and in prison he gave information against his own relatives and friends, with immunity granted him if he was deemed to be giving true information. What soul do you think he had, when he was doing the most extreme and shameful things in informing against his own friends, but his safety was uncertain? [24] After this, when he had caused the deaths of those whom he said he valued most highly, he was deemed to have given true information and released, and you voted besides that he was to be barred from the agora and the temples, so that even if wronged by his enemies he could not gain redress.

MacDowell ties Andocides' failure to hand over his slave (*Ag. And.* 22) to his own statement in **64** that he did in fact hand over his slave for questioning, which must be a lie. Andocides secured the release of his relatives from prison (**66**), but due to this failure remained there himself (though not for nearly a year) until he denounced his relatives and friends for profanation of the Mysteries. MacDowell then sees Andocides' denunciation as the basis of Thessalus' impeachment of Alcibiades. This would also help to explain how, in Plutarch, Timaeus (not Andocides' Charmides) became an intimate friend of Andocides and persuaded him to confess, confusing this denunciation over the Mysteries with his earlier one over the Hermae. MacDowell's ingenious reconstruction additionally explains Andocides' continuing reputation in antiquity for denouncing his father.[48] But again, his reliance on the *Ag. And.* passage may be regarded as excessive. Does it really contain as much detail as MacDowell maintains, and how much of this is reliable? Stripping away the rhetoric, the passage in fact offers very few details, none of which is supported by evidence and three of which are particularly problematic.

(e) Firstly, Andocides was brought before the court and was imprisoned as a result of his failure to comply with the terms of his assessment, i.e. the production of his slave. This, MacDowell suggests, indicates that Andocides was referred to the court by the council in the same way as Diocleides (**65-6**). But the phrase 'brought before the court' (εἰσαχθεὶς εἰς τὸ δικαστήριον), taken in its normal sense, would imply that he was being prosecuted,[49] when he should have been given immunity by the council in return for his information; and this contradicts Thucydides, who says the informer obtained immunity and was immediately released.[50] Also, the comparison

48 *Life of And.* 834E; Tzetzes, *Historia* 49. But this reputation could easily have arisen as a result of the conflation of various imprecise recollections of events in 415. See Marr 336-7.

49 See LSJ, s.v. εἰσάγω II.3.b.

50 Thuc. 6.60.3-4 (though Thucydides does not name Andocides); cf. *Ag. And.* 36, which again refers to Andocides' *adeia.*

with what happened to Diocleides is unsound, because Diocleides admitted to the council that he had been lying. Furthermore, what are we to make of the phrase 'having assessed prison as the penalty' (τιμησάμενος δεσμοῦ)? It should reflect the procedure in cases where the penalty on conviction was not fixed, but was decided by the court in the light of proposals made by both parties after the verdict had been announced.[51] But at that stage it would have been too late to promise the submission of a slave for corroborative testimony, and in any case the jurors would presumably not have accepted imprisonment when other offenders were being executed.[52] So what court and trial can the speaker be referring to here? The order of the passage is that Andocides was brought before the court and imprisoned as a result of his assessment (21, 23), then he gave information (23) and was ultimately released (24); and the clear implication of this is that there was a preliminary hearing in the period between Andocides' arrest (ordered by the council in 45) and his imprisonment (48).[53] In that case the whole basis of MacDowell's version is undermined. But more than that, the emergency measures taken by the council and the arrest orders might be seen to have removed the opportunity or necessity for such preliminary proceedings, and we may well begin to wonder if there is any truth in the *Ag. And.* story at all. MacDowell comments that it is an odd story to invent, but there are clearly elements of it which are themselves very odd, such as the apparently invented trial before an ordinary dicastic court and the 'assessment'.[54] Again, given that there was only one slave (in itself a highly questionable premise), are we to prefer the *Ag. And.* version that the slave was already dead[55] to Andocides' statement that he did hand over his slave, which may have been supported by the witnesses at the end of 69? Andocides' defence clearly is weakened if there was no such testimony, but equally we should beware of too readily accepting his opponent's dubious allegation that he deliberately imprisoned himself through an act of folly brought about by a hostile deity.[56] Moreover, in *Ag. And.* 21-32 the speaker's aim is to depict Andocides as a jail-bird (almost everywhere he goes he gets himself imprisoned), and this can indeed explain the invention of such an unlikely story.

---

51   See MacDowell (1978) 253-4.

52   Further, imprisonment was very rare as a punishment in Athenian law; see Todd (1993) 140.

53   See W. D. Furley, 'A Note on [Lysias] 6, *Against Andokides*', *CQ* 39 (1989) 550-3. Andocides had no reason to mention this first stage, especially if he did in fact fail to produce his slave as promised.

54   Furley, *art. cit.* 552 with n. 9 notes that the use of the verb 'assess' here is metaphorical, since Andocides has been imprisoned not for mutilating the Hermae but for failing to produce his slave. His accuser thereby heightens the sense of Andocides' guilt.

55   And how did the speaker know that Andocides knew this when he made his 'assessment'?

56   Note the prominence given to religious matters in the *Ag. And.*

(f) Secondly, Andocides was in prison for nearly a year. On no conceivable reconstruction is it likely that Andocides languished in custody for so long before spilling the beans: if he was the shameless reprobate he is portrayed as being in this speech, would he have waited for more than a few days? It may be that he was held pending the council's further investigations (as is implied in *Ag. And.* 24), but these would not have been protracted. This would also explain Andocides' silence in **66** as to when he was himself released, though, as Marr points out,[57] Andocides' main concern in **51-9** is to emphasise how his actions were in the best interests of the state, and this does not sit well with an admission that he secured his own release by these same actions. On the other hand, Thucydides says (6.60.4) that he was released immediately on giving his information, along with the others whom he had not accused. If we accept Thucydides' account taken literally, any idea that Andocides remained in prison after his denunciation must, of course, be rejected (but see [g] below). Once again, the rhetorical exaggeration here is part of the jail-bird motif, and it casts doubt on the truth of the accuser's other remarks.[58]

(g) Thirdly, while in prison Andocides informed against his relatives and friends, after being granted immunity. It is this statement in particular that might hint at a second denunciation concerning the Mysteries, since (on MacDowell's reconstruction) Andocides has already given his information about the Hermae affair, and this did not include the names of relatives. But it is possible that Andocides did in fact denounce more than the four men he names in **52** and **67**. These, he says (**68**), all fled, but Thucydides and Plutarch both talk in addition of men who were executed.[59] Andocides had obvious motives for hiding this, especially if some of his relatives were actually involved. Did he, perhaps, make a second set of denunciations over the Hermae (not the Mysteries) affair? This would help to resolve the conflict mentioned above between the theory of an investigation and Thucydides' account (which then is merely telescoped), and would also be consistent with the version in the *Ag. And.* As for Andocides' narrative, he either suppresses certain details or simply curtails his story before it reaches its damaging ending. He instead minimises the time he spent in jail, in order to highlight how the alarm caused by Dioclides' information was relieved by his prompt action.[60]

---

57 Cf. Furley, *art. cit.* 550 n. 3.
58 An alternative but less satisfactory solution is to emend the text. Furley proposes ἐγγυήσας ἑαυτόν ('having pledged his own person as security') for ἐγγὺς ἐνιαυτόν.
59 Including some of Andocides' slaves, according to Plutarch, though Marr 331 explains this as a mistake deriving from **64**, where Andocides says the prytaneis arrested some of his slaves for questioning.
60 MacDowell employs this argument on p. 184 in support of his order of events, here agreeing with Thucydides (6.61.2-3) that the night the Athenians spent under arms followed the resolution of the Hermae affair, *pace* Andocides' account in **45**.

(h) Two final problems connected with the Mysteries affair remain. Andocides says that he was persuaded to inform by his cousin Charmides (48-50), but his account conflicts with that of Plutarch,[61] who says it was one Timaeus who persuaded him. For MacDowell there were two separate occasions on which Andocides was prevailed upon to confess, but this coincidence is rightly rejected by Marr, who also dismisses the alleged contradiction between Plutarch and Andocides over the time Andocides spent in jail. In Plutarch (and Thucydides) Andocides is imprisoned for far longer than the one night implied (though never actually stated) in 48-61, and the reason for this will again be that Andocides' account is deliberately confused, in order to exaggerate his role in relieving the city's alarm. Andocides himself says that there were others who entreated him (51), and there is certainly no reason to think that Plutarch twice writes 'Timaeus' for 'Charmides' by mistake.

II. We come now to the mutilation of the Hermae. Both Thucydides and Plutarch associate the charge against Andocides with this affair, and he himself admits some involvement, whilst denying that he actually took part in it (61-4). As MacDowell argues, there can be little doubt that none of those who were guilty of the mutilation was actually called as a witness in 400. At least four of the conspirators were back in Athens at the time of the trial (53), but they can hardly have given evidence for Andocides (who had denounced them) or against him (this could not simply have been ignored by Andocides). This also applies to Euphiletus, probably the only person apart from Andocides who really knew whether Andocides had agreed to take part in the mutilation (cf. 62).[62] MacDowell concludes that Andocides promised Euphiletus he would mutilate the Hermes near the shrine of Phorbas, but in the event was ill and did not do so; and that Andocides never later admitted that he had taken part. So he tends to accept Andocides' denials of involvement, connects his hints that he was guilty of impiety in *On his Return* (2.6, 7, 8, 10, 15) with the Mysteries affair, and rejects the versions of Plutarch and Thucydides that Andocides confessed to involvement, since he would not have accused himself of a crime he did not commit.

MacDowell's general conclusion about Andocides' innocence of actual involvement is cogent, but his further arguments are unnecessary and are, of course, undermined if Andocides did not in fact give information about the Mysteries. His confession need only have been to involvement in the plot for him to be disgraced (i.e. intention, or *bouleusis*, to mutilate the Hermes).[63] It will have been this confession of *bouleusis* to which Thucydides and Plutarch refer, and it is this guilt to which he refers in *On his Return*.[64] Furthermore, not only was Andocides a member of the club that carried out the mutilations and had intended to take part himself, but

---

61   *Alc.* 21.2-4.
62   MacDowell assumes Euphiletus was dead by the time of the trial.
63   Cf. **94**; Hansen (1975) 81 n. 21.
64   As Marr 333. See **2.7n**.

also he kept quiet about the matter until forced to confess, despite the ensuing panic in Athens and fear of an oligarchic revolution.[65] He was therefore so deeply involved that he needed immunity before confessing, and it is not really necessary to adopt Marr's conjecture that to make sure of obtaining this immunity Andocides may even have confessed to an actual mutilation. Marr goes on, however, to argue plausibly that the reason Andocides never admits to receiving *adeia* is that the jurors would at once have thought him simply 'guilty'. All this, finally, does then explain why Andocides spends more time defending himself over the Hermae than the Mysteries affair: he was guilty of involvement in the one but not the other. The charge of mutilation was, after all, the weaker part of his case.

---

65   Cf. Thuc. 6.27.3.

ΑΝΔΟΚΙΔΟΥ

ΠΕΡΙ ΤΩΝ ΜΥΣΤΗΡΙΩΝ

[1] Τὴν μὲν παρασκευήν, ὦ ἄνδρες, καὶ τὴν προθυμίαν τῶν ἐχθρῶν τῶν ἐμῶν, ὥστ' ἐμὲ κακῶς ποιεῖν ἐκ παντὸς τρόπου καὶ δικαίως καὶ ἀδίκως, ἐξ ἀρχῆς ἐπειδὴ τάχιστα ἀφικόμην εἰς τὴν πόλιν ταυτηνί, σχεδόν τι πάντες ἐπίστασθε, καὶ οὐδὲν δεῖ περὶ τούτων πολλοὺς λόγους ποιεῖσθαι· ἐγὼ δέ, ὦ ἄνδρες, δεήσομαι ὑμῶν δίκαια καὶ ὑμῖν τε ῥᾴδια χαρίζεσθαι καὶ ἐμοὶ ἄξια πολλοῦ τυχεῖν παρ' ὑμῶν. [2] καὶ πρῶτον μὲν ἐνθυμηθῆναι ὅτι νῦν ἐγὼ ἥκω οὐδεμιᾶς μοι ἀνάγκης οὔσης παραμεῖναι, οὔτ' ἐγγυητὰς καταστήσας οὔθ' ὑπὸ δεσμῶν ἀναγκασθείς, πιστεύσας δὲ μάλιστα μὲν τῷ δικαίῳ, ἔπειτα δὲ καὶ ὑμῖν, γνώσεσθαι τὰ δίκαια καὶ μὴ περιόψεσθαί με ἀδίκως ὑπὸ τῶν ἐχθρῶν τῶν ἐμῶν διαφθαρέντα, ἀλλὰ πολὺ μᾶλλον σώσειν δικαίως κατά τε τοὺς νόμους τοὺς ὑμετέρους καὶ τοὺς ὅρκους οὓς ὑμεῖς ὀμόσαντες μέλλετε τὴν ψῆφον οἴσειν. [3] εἰκότως δ' ἄν, ὦ ἄνδρες, τὴν αὐτὴν γνώμην ἔχοιτε περὶ τῶν ἐθελόντων εἰς τοὺς κινδύνους καθισταμένων, ἥνπερ αὐτοὶ περὶ αὑτῶν ἔχουσιν. ὁπόσοι μὲν γὰρ μὴ ἠθέλησαν ὑπομεῖναι καταγνόντες αὑτῶν ἀδικίαν, εἰκότως τοι καὶ ὑμεῖς τοιαῦτα περὶ αὐτῶν γιγνώσκετε οἷά περ καὶ αὐτοὶ περὶ σφῶν αὑτῶν ἔγνωσαν· ὁπόσοι δὲ πιστεύσαντες μηδὲν ἀδικεῖν ὑπέμειναν, δίκαιοί ἐστε καὶ ὑμεῖς περὶ τούτων τοιαύτην ἔχειν τὴν γνώμην οἵαν περ καὶ αὐτοὶ περὶ αὑτῶν ἔσχον, καὶ μὴ προκαταγιγνώσκειν ἀδικεῖν. [4] αὐτίκα ἐγὼ πολλῶν μοι ἀπαγγελλόντων ὅτι λέγοιεν οἱ ἐχθροὶ ὡς ἄρα ἐγὼ οὔτ' ἂν ὑπομείναιμι οἰχήσομαί τε φεύγων - "Τί γὰρ ἂν καὶ βουλόμενος Ἀνδοκίδης ἀγῶνα τοσοῦτον ὑπομείνειεν, ᾧ ἔξεστι μὲν ἀπελθόντι ἐντεῦθεν ἔχειν πάντα τὰ ἐπιτήδεια, ἔστι δὲ πλεύσαντι εἰς Κύπρον, ὅθεν περ ἥκει, γῆ πολλὴ καὶ ἀγαθὴ διδομένη καὶ δωρεὰ ὑπάρχουσα; οὗτος ἄρα βουλήσεται περὶ τοῦ σώματος τοῦ ἑαυτοῦ κινδυνεῦσαι; εἰς τί ἀποβλέψας; οὐχ ὁρᾷ τὴν πόλιν ἡμῶν ὡς διάκειται;" ἐγὼ δέ, ὦ ἄνδρες, πολὺ τὴν ἐναντίαν τούτοις γνώμην ἔχω. [5] ἄλλοθί τε γὰρ ὢν πάντα τὰ ἀγαθὰ ἔχειν στερόμενος τῆς πατρίδος οὐκ ἂν δεξαίμην, τῆς πόλεως οὕτω διακειμένης ὥσπερ αὐτοὶ οἱ ἐχθροὶ λέγουσι, πολὺ δ' ἂν αὐτῆς μᾶλλον ἐγὼ πολίτης δεξαίμην εἶναι ἢ ἑτέρων πόλεων, αἳ ἴσως πάνυ μοι δοκοῦσιν ἐν τῷ παρόντι εὐτυχεῖν. ἅπερ γιγνώσκων ἐπέτρεψα διαγνῶναι ὑμῖν περὶ τοῦ σώματος τοῦ ἐμαυτοῦ.

ANDOCIDES

ON THE MYSTERIES

[1] The preparation, gentlemen, and the zeal of my enemies to do me injury in every possible way, by fair means or foul, right from the very moment that I arrived in this city, almost all of you know, and it is not necessary to say much about this. I shall instead ask of you, gentlemen, what is just, and what is both easy for you to grant and valuable for me to obtain from you. [2] Firstly, I shall ask you to bear in mind that I have not come into court today as a result of any compulsion on me to stay in Athens, having neither given sureties nor been kept in prison; rather, I trusted especially in justice and then also in you, that you will make the right decision and not allow me to be unjustly destroyed by my enemies, but will far sooner save me justly in accordance both with your laws and with the oaths you have sworn before the vote you are going to cast. [3] It would be reasonable, gentlemen, for you to hold the same opinion about those who voluntarily submit themselves to danger as they hold about themselves. For just as in the case of those who are unwilling to stay to face trial and so admit their guilt, it is reasonable for you too to pass the same judgment on them as they passed on themselves, so in the case of those who are confident that they are not guilty and have stayed to face trial, you too should hold the same opinion about these as they held about themselves and not prejudge them to be guilty. [4] For example, in my case many people have reported to me that my enemies were talking as if I would not stay to face trial but would certainly flee into exile. "What would be the point of Andocides staying to face so dangerous a trial? If he goes away from here, he can have everything he needs, and if he sails to Cyprus, where he has come from, there is plenty of good land being offered him and a gift which he already has. Do you think a man in his position will want to risk his life? What would he be looking for? Does he not see the state of our city?" I, on the other hand, gentlemen, hold completely the opposite view to them. [5] I would never accept living elsewhere with every comfort but being deprived of my country, even if the city is in as bad a state as my enemies say, I would far sooner accept being a citizen of hers than of other cities which may seem to me to be exceedingly prosperous at the present time. These being my thoughts, I left it to you to give judgment on my life.

[6] Αἰτοῦμαι οὖν ὑμᾶς, ὦ ἄνδρες, εὔνοιαν πλείω παρασχέσθαι ἐμοὶ τῷ ἀπολογουμένῳ ἢ τοῖς κατηγόροις, εἰδότας ὅτι κἂν ἐξ ἴσου ἀκροᾶσθε, ἀνάγκη τὸν ἀπολογούμενον ἔλαττον ἔχειν. οἱ μὲν γὰρ ἐκ πολλοῦ χρόνου ἐπιβουλεύσαντες καὶ συνθέντες, αὐτοὶ ἄνευ κινδύνων ὄντες, τὴν κατηγορίαν ἐποιήσαντο· ἐγὼ δὲ μετὰ δέους καὶ κινδύνου καὶ διαβολῆς τῆς μεγίστης τὴν ἀπολογίαν ποιοῦμαι. εἰκὸς οὖν ὑμᾶς ἐστιν εὔνοιαν πλείω παρασχέσθαι ἐμοὶ ἢ τοῖς κατηγόροις. [7] ἔτι δὲ καὶ τόδε ἐνθυμητέον, ὅτι πολλοὶ ἤδη πολλὰ καὶ δεινὰ κατηγορήσαντες παραχρῆμα ἐξηλέγχθησαν ψευδόμενοι οὕτω φανερῶς ὥστε ὑμᾶς πολὺ ἂν ἥδιον δίκην λαβεῖν παρὰ τῶν κατηγόρων ἢ παρὰ τῶν κατηγορουμένων· οἱ δὲ αὖ, μαρτυρήσαντες τὰ ψευδῆ ἀδίκως ἀνθρώπους ἀπολέσαντες, ἑάλωσαν παρ' ὑμῖν ψευδομαρτυρίων, ἡνίκ' οὐδὲν ἦν ἔτι πλέον τοῖς πεπονθόσιν. ὁπότ' οὖν ἤδη πολλὰ τοιαῦτα γεγένηται, εἰκὸς ὑμᾶς ἐστι μήπω τοὺς τῶν κατηγόρων λόγους πιστοὺς ἡγεῖσθαι. εἰ μὲν γὰρ δεινὰ κατηγόρηται ἢ μή, οἷόν τε γνῶναι ἐκ τῶν τοῦ κατηγόρου λόγων· εἰ δὲ ἀληθῆ ταῦτά ἐστιν ἢ ψευδῆ, οὐχ οἷόν τε ὑμᾶς πρότερον εἰδέναι πρὶν ἂν καὶ ἐμοῦ ἀκούσητε ἀπολογουμένου.

[8] Σκοπῶ μὲν οὖν ἔγωγε, ὦ ἄνδρες, πόθεν χρὴ ἄρξασθαι τῆς ἀπολογίας, πότερον ἐκ τῶν τελευταίων λόγων, ὡς παρανόμως με ἐνέδειξαν, ἢ περὶ τοῦ ψηφίσματος τοῦ Ἰσοτιμίδου, ὡς ἄκυρόν ἐστιν, ἢ περὶ τῶν νόμων καὶ τῶν ὅρκων τῶν γεγενημένων, εἴτε καὶ ἐξ ἀρχῆς ὑμᾶς διδάξω τὰ γεγενημένα. ὃ δέ με ποιεῖ μάλιστ' ἀπορεῖν, ἐγὼ ὑμῖν ἐρῶ, ὅτι οὐ πάντες ἴσως ἐπὶ πᾶσι τοῖς κατηγορουμένοις ὁμοίως ὀργίζεσθε, ἀλλ' ἕκαστός τι ὑμῶν ἔχει πρὸς ὃ βούλοιτο ἄν με πρῶτον ἀπολογεῖσθαι· ἅμα δὲ περὶ πάντων εἰπεῖν ἀδύνατον. κράτιστον οὖν μοι εἶναι δοκεῖ ἐξ ἀρχῆς ὑμᾶς διδάσκειν πάντα τὰ γενόμενα καὶ παραλιπεῖν μηδέν. ἂν γὰρ ὀρθῶς μάθητε τὰ πραχθέντα, ῥᾳδίως γνώσεσθ' ἅ μου κατεψεύσαντο οἱ κατήγοροι. [9] τὰ μὲν οὖν δίκαια γιγνώσκειν ὑμᾶς ἡγοῦμαι καὶ αὐτοὺς παρεσκευάσθαι, οἷσπερ ἐγὼ πιστεύσας ὑπέμεινα, ὁρῶν ὑμᾶς καὶ ἐν τοῖς ἰδίοις καὶ ἐν τοῖς δημοσίοις περὶ πλείστου τοῦτο ποιουμένους, ψηφίζεσθαι κατὰ τοὺς ὅρκους (ὅπερ καὶ συνέχει μόνον τὴν πόλιν, ἀκόντων τῶν οὐ βουλομένων ταῦτα οὕτως ἔχειν)· τάδε δὲ ὑμῶν δέομαι, μετ' εὐνοίας μου τὴν ἀκρόασιν τῆς ἀπολογίας ποιήσασθαι, καὶ μήτε μοι ἀντιδίκους καταστῆναι μήτε ὑπονοεῖν τὰ λεγόμενα μήτε ῥήματα θηρεύειν, ἀκροασαμένους δὲ διὰ τέλους τῆς ἀπολογίας τότε ἤδη ψηφίζεσθαι τοῦτο ὅ τι ἂν ὑμῖν αὐτοῖς ἄριστον καὶ εὐορκότατον νομίζητε εἶναι. [10] ὥσπερ δὲ καὶ προεῖπον ὑμῖν,

[6] So I ask you, gentlemen, to show more goodwill to me, the defendant, than to my accusers, since you know that even if you listen impartially, the defendant is necessarily at a disadvantage. For they have made their accusation after plotting and scheming at length, and being in no danger themselves; but I am making my defence in fear and danger and against the greatest prejudice. It is therefore reasonable for you to show more goodwill to me than to my accusers. [7] Besides, this should also be borne in mind, that many before have laid many serious accusations and have immediately been proved liars so manifestly that you would far rather have punished the accusers than the accused. Others again, after unjustly destroying men by giving false evidence, have been convicted before you of perjury when it was too late to be of advantage to their victims. When many things of this kind have happened before, it is reasonable for you for the time being not to consider the statements of my accusers as trustworthy. Whether the accusation is serious or not you can judge from the statements of my accuser, but whether it is true or false you cannot know until you have also heard my defence.

[8] I am therefore wondering, gentlemen, at what point I should begin my defence - with the end of the story, how they lodged a denunciation against me illegally, or with the decree of Isotimides, how it is invalid, or with the laws passed and oaths taken, or again should I tell you the story right from the beginning? I shall tell you what is especially making me hesitant, that you are not all perhaps growing equally angry at all the charges, but each of you has something to which he would like me to reply first; yet it is impossible to speak about everything at once. So I think the best thing is to tell you the whole story from the beginning and to omit nothing. For if you learn the facts correctly, you will easily see the falsehoods which my accusers have alleged against me. [9] I think that you are anyway prepared to make a just decision, and it was because I trusted in you that I stayed to face trial, seeing that in both private and public cases you reckon this the most important thing, that you vote according to your oaths (and indeed it is this alone which holds the city together, frustrating certain persons who wish it were to dissolve). I do, however, ask this of you, that you listen to the defence with goodwill towards me; and that you neither become opponents to me nor view what I say with suspicion nor hunt after my words, but hear my defence from beginning to end and only then vote as you think is best for you yourselves and most in accordance with your oaths. [10] As I have already told you, gentlemen, I shall make my defence from

ὦ ἄνδρες, ἐξ ἀρχῆς περὶ πάντων ποιήσομαι τὴν ἀπολογίαν, πρῶτον μὲν περὶ αὐτῆς τῆς αἰτίας ὅθεν περ ἡ ἔνδειξις ἐγένετο, διόπερ εἰς τὸν ἀγῶνα τόνδε κατέστην, περὶ τῶν μυστηρίων ὡς οὔτ' ἐμοὶ ἠσέβηται οὐδὲν οὔτε μεμήνυται οὔθ' ὡμολόγηται, οὔτ' οἶδα τοὺς μηνύσαντας ὑμῖν περὶ αὐτῶν οὔτ' εἰ ψευδῆ οὔτ' εἰ ἀληθῆ ἐμήνυσαν· ταῦθ' ὑμᾶς διδάξω.

[11] Ἦν μὲν γὰρ ἐκκλησία τοῖς στρατηγοῖς τοῖς εἰς Σικελίαν, Νικίᾳ καὶ Λαμάχῳ καὶ Ἀλκιβιάδῃ, καὶ τριήρης ἡ στρατηγὶς ἤδη ἐξώρμει ἡ Λαμάχου· ἀναστὰς δὲ Πυθόνικος ἐν τῷ δήμῳ εἶπεν· "Ὦ Ἀθηναῖοι, ὑμεῖς μὲν στρατιὰν ἐκπέμπετε καὶ παρασκευὴν τοσαύτην, καὶ κίνδυνον ἀρεῖσθαι μέλλετε· Ἀλκιβιάδην δὲ τὸν στρατηγὸν ἀποδείξω ὑμῖν τὰ μυστήρια ποιοῦντα ἐν οἰκίᾳ μεθ' ἑτέρων, καὶ ἐὰν ψηφίσησθε ἄδειαν <ᾧ> ἐγὼ κελεύω, θεράπων ὑμῖν ἑνὸς τῶν ἐνθάδε ἀνδρῶν ἀμύητος ὢν ἐρεῖ τὰ μυστήρια· εἰ δὲ μή, χρῆσθε ἐμοὶ ὅ τι ἂν ὑμῖν δοκῇ, ἐὰν μὴ τἀληθῆ λέγω." [12] ἀντιλέγοντος δὲ Ἀλκιβιάδου πολλὰ καὶ ἐξάρνου ὄντος, ἔδοξε τοῖς πρυτάνεσι τοὺς μὲν ἀμυήτους μεταστήσασθαι, αὐτοὺς δ' ἰέναι ἐπὶ τὸ μειράκιον ὃ ὁ Πυθόνικος ἐκέλευε. καὶ ᾤχοντο, καὶ ἤγαγον θεράποντα Ἀλκιβιάδου [πολέμαρχον]· Ἀνδρόμαχος αὐτῷ ὄνομα ἦν. ἐπεὶ δὲ ἐψηφίσαντο αὐτῷ τὴν ἄδειαν, ἔλεγεν ὅτι ἐν τῇ οἰκίᾳ τῇ Πουλυτίωνος γίγνοιτο μυστήρια· Ἀλκιβιάδην μὲν οὖν καὶ Νικίδην καὶ Μέλητον, τούτους μὲν αὐτοὺς εἶναι τοὺς ποιοῦντας, συμπαρεῖναι δὲ καὶ ὁρᾶν τὰ γιγνόμενα καὶ ἄλλους, παρεῖναι δὲ καὶ δούλους, ἑαυτόν τε καὶ τὸν ἀδελφὸν καὶ Ἱκέσιον τὸν αὐλητὴν καὶ τὸν Μελήτου δοῦλον. [13] πρῶτος μὲν οὗτος ταῦτα ἐμήνυσε, καὶ ἀπέγραψε τούτους· ὧν Πολύστρατος μὲν συνελήφθη καὶ ἀπέθανεν, οἱ δὲ ἄλλοι φεύγοντες ᾤχοντο, καὶ αὐτῶν ὑμεῖς θάνατον κατέγνωτε. καί μοι λαβὲ καὶ ἀνάγνωθι αὐτῶν τὰ ὀνόματα.

ΟΝΟΜΑΤΑ. Τούσδε Ἀνδρόμαχος ἐμήνυσεν· Ἀλκιβιάδην, Νικίδην, Μέλητον, Ἀρχεβιάδην, Ἄρχιππον, Διογένην, Πολύστρατον, Ἀριστομένη, Οἰωνίαν, Παναίτιον.

[14] Πρώτη μέν, ὦ ἄνδρες, μήνυσις ἐγένετο αὕτη ὑπὸ Ἀνδρομάχου κατὰ τούτων τῶν ἀνδρῶν. καί μοι κάλει Διόγνητον.

Ἦσθα ζητητής, ὦ Διόγνητε, ὅτε Πυθόνικος εἰσήγγειλεν ἐν τῷ δήμῳ περὶ Ἀλκιβιάδου;

Ἦν.

Οἶσθα οὖν μηνύσαντα Ἀνδρόμαχον τὰ ἐν τῇ οἰκίᾳ τῇ Πουλυτίωνος γιγνόμενα;

Οἶδα.

the beginning and include everything, dealing firstly with the actual accusation which gave rise to the lodging of the denunciation whereby I am submitting to this trial: that is, concerning the Mysteries, that I have committed no act of impiety, nor turned informer nor admitted any guilt; and that, as regards those who did turn informer about them to you, I do not know whether their information was true or false. These things I shall prove to you.

[11] A meeting of the assembly was held for the generals about to leave for Sicily, Nicias, Lamachus and Alcibiades, and indeed Lamachus' flagship was already at sea when Pythonicus stood up before the people and said: "Athenians, you are sending out an army and this great armament, and you are about to undertake danger; but I shall prove to you that your general Alcibiades has been performing the Mysteries in a house with others, and if you vote immunity to the one I name, a slave of one of the men here today, although a non-initiate he will recite the Mysteries to you. Otherwise you can do whatever you like to me, if I am not telling the truth." [12] Alcibiades replied at length and denied the charge, and the prytaneis decided to dismiss the uninitiated and go themselves to find the boy Pythonicus named. They went off and returned with a slave of Alcibiades, whose name was Andromachus. When they had voted him immunity, he said that Mysteries were celebrated in the house of Pulytion, and that Alcibiades, Nicides and Meletus were the actual performers, but others too were present and saw what happened; there were also slaves there, himself, his brother, Hicesius the flute-player and Meletus' slave. [13] Andromachus was the first to give this information, and he denounced the following persons, of whom Polystratus was arrested and executed, while the rest fled into exile and were condemned to death by you. Take the list, please, and read out their names.

NAMES. Andromachus informed against the following: Alcibiades, Nicides, Meletus, Archebiades, Archippus, Diogenes, Polystratus, Aristomenes, Oeonias, Panaetius.

[14] This was the first information, gentlemen, given by Andromachus against these men. Now call Diognetus, please.

Were you a commissioner of inquiry, Diognetus, when Pythonicus impeached Alcibiades before the assembly?

I was.

Do you recall that Andromachus gave information concerning the events in Pulytion's house?

I do.

Τὰ ὀνόματα οὖν τῶν ἀνδρῶν ἐστι ταῦτα, καθ' ὧν ἐκεῖνος ἐμήνυσεν;

Ἔστι ταῦτα.

[15] Δευτέρα τοίνυν μήνυσις ἐγένετο. Τεῦκρος ἦν ἐνθάδε μέτοικος, ὃς ᾤχετο Μέγαράδε ὑπεξελθών, ἐκεῖθεν δὲ ἐπαγγέλλεται τῇ βουλῇ, εἴ οἱ ἄδειαν δοῖεν, μηνύσειν περὶ τῶν μυστηρίων, συνεργὸς ὤν, καὶ τοὺς ἄλλους τοὺς ποιοῦντας μεθ' ἑαυτοῦ, καὶ περὶ τῶν Ἑρμῶν τῆς περικοπῆς ἃ ᾔδει. ψηφισαμένης δὲ τῆς βουλῆς (ἦν γὰρ αὐτοκράτωρ) ᾤχοντο ἐπ' αὐτὸν Μέγαράδε· καὶ κομισθείς, ἄδειαν εὑρόμενος, ἀπογράφει τοὺς μεθ' ἑαυτοῦ. καὶ οὗτοι κατὰ τὴν Τεύκρου μήνυσιν ᾤχοντο φεύγοντες. καί μοι λαβὲ καὶ ἀνάγνωθι τὰ ὀνόματα αὐτῶν.

ΟΝΟΜΑΤΑ. Τούσδε Τεῦκρος ἐμήνυσε· Φαῖδρον, Γνιφωνίδην, Ἰσόνομον, Ἡφαιστόδωρον, Κηφισόδωρον, ἑαυτόν, Διόγνητον, Σμινδυρίδην, Φιλοκράτην, Ἀντιφῶντα, Τείσαρχον, Παντακλέα.

Μέμνησθε δέ, ὦ ἄνδρες, ὅτι καὶ ταῦθ' ὑμῖν προσομολογεῖται ἅπαντα.

[16] Τρίτη μήνυσις ἐγένετο. ἡ γυνὴ Ἀλκμεωνίδου, γενομένη δὲ καὶ Δάμωνος (Ἀγαρίστη ὄνομα αὐτῇ), αὕτη ἐμήνυσεν ἐν τῇ οἰκίᾳ τῇ Χαρμίδου τῇ παρὰ τὸ Ὀλυμπιεῖον μυστήρια ποιεῖν Ἀλκιβιάδην καὶ Ἀξίοχον καὶ Ἀδείμαντον· καὶ ἔφυγον οὗτοι πάντες ἐπὶ ταύτῃ τῇ μηνύσει.

[17] Ἔτι μήνυσις ἐγένετο μία. Λυδὸς ὁ Φερεκλέους τοῦ Θημακέως ἐμήνυσε μυστήρια γίγνεσθαι ἐν τῇ οἰκίᾳ Φερεκλέους τοῦ δεσπότου τοῦ ἑαυτοῦ ἐν Θημακῷ· καὶ ἀπογράφει τούς τε ἄλλους, καὶ τὸν πατέρα ἔφη τὸν ἐμὸν παρεῖναι μέν, καθεύδειν δὲ ἐγκεκαλυμμένον. Σπεύσιππος δὲ βουλεύων παραδίδωσιν αὐτοὺς τῷ δικαστηρίῳ. κἄπειτα ὁ πατὴρ καταστήσας ἐγγυητὰς ἐγράψατο τὸν Σπεύσιππον παρανόμων, καὶ ἠγωνίσατο ἐν ἑξακισχιλίοις Ἀθηναίων, καὶ μετέλαβε δικαστῶν τοσούτων οὐδὲ διακοσίας ψήφους ὁ Σπεύσιππος. ὁ δὲ πείσας καὶ δεόμενος μεῖναι τὸν πατέρα ἐγὼ ἦν μάλιστα, εἶτα δὲ καὶ οἱ ἄλλοι συγγενεῖς. [18] καί μοι κάλει Καλλίαν καὶ Στέφανον. κάλει δὲ καὶ Φίλιππον καὶ Ἀλέξιππον· οὗτοι γάρ εἰσιν Ἀκουμενοῦ καὶ Αὐτοκράτορος συγγενεῖς, οἳ ἔφυγον ἐπὶ τῇ Λυδοῦ μηνύσει· τοῦ μὲν ἀδελφιδοῦς ἐστιν Αὐτοκράτωρ, τοῦ δὲ θεῖος Ἀκουμενός· οἷς προσήκει μισεῖν μὲν τὸν ἐξελάσαντα ἐκείνους, εἰδέναι δὲ μάλιστα δι' ὅντινα ἔφυγον. βλέπετε εἰς τούτους, καὶ μαρτυρεῖτε εἰ ἀληθῆ λέγω.

Are these, then, the names of the men against whom he gave the information?

> They are.

[15] Now, a second information followed. There was a man named Teucrus, a metic resident in Athens who had secretly departed to Megara. From there he notified the council that, if they were to grant him immunity, he would give information about the Mysteries, in which he had participated, naming the other performers besides himself, and also tell what he knew about the mutilation of the Hermae. The council (which had full power to act) voted immunity, and they went to Megara to fetch him. He was brought back, and having obtained immunity for himself, he denounced his associates. These fled into exile on Teucrus' information. Take the list, please, and read out their names.

> NAMES. Teucrus informed against the following: Phaedrus, Gniphonides, Isonomus, Hephaestodorus, Cephisodorus, himself, Diognetus, Smindyrides, Philocrates, Antiphon, Teisarchus, Pantacles.

Remember, gentlemen, that all this is also being admitted to you.

[16] A third information followed. The wife of Alcmaeonides, who had also been the wife of Damon (her name was Agariste), gave information that Alcibiades, Axiochus and Adeimantus performed Mysteries in Charmides' house near the Olympieum. These too all fled on this information.

[17] There was yet one more information. Lydus, the slave of Pherecles of Themacus, gave information that Mysteries were celebrated in the house of his master Pherecles at Themacus. He denounced others, and he said that my father was present but was asleep with his face covered. Speusippus, a member of the council, proposed handing them over to the court, but then my father gave sureties and prosecuted Speusippus for illegality. The case was tried before 6000 Athenians, and Speusippus failed to gain even two hundred votes from so many jurors. The man principally responsible for persuading and entreating my father to stay in Athens was I myself, and then also his other relatives. [18] Call Callias and Stephanus, please. Call as well Philippus and Alexippus, for they are relatives of Acumenus and Autocrator, who fled on the information of Lydus (Autocrator is a nephew of the one, Acumenus is an uncle of the other). They may properly hate the one who drove out their relatives, and they of all people should know who caused their exile. Face the jury and give evidence as to whether I am telling the truth.

ΜΑΡΤΥΡΕΣ

[19] Τὰ μὲν γενόμενα ἠκούσατε, ὦ ἄνδρες, καὶ ὑμῖν οἱ μάρτυρες μεμαρτυρήκασιν· ἃ δὲ οἱ κατήγοροι ἐτόλμησαν εἰπεῖν, ἀναμνήσθητε. οὕτω γὰρ καὶ δίκαιον ἀπολογεῖσθαι, ἀναμιμνήσκοντα τοὺς τῶν κατηγόρων λόγους ἐξελέγχειν. ἔλεξαν γὰρ ὡς ἐγὼ μηνύσαιμι περὶ τῶν μυστηρίων, ἀπογράψαιμί τε τὸν πατέρα τὸν ἐμαυτοῦ παρόντα, καὶ γενοίμην μηνυτὴς κατὰ τοῦ πατρὸς τοῦ ἐμαυτοῦ, λόγον οἶμαι πάντων δεινότατόν τε καὶ ἀνοσιώτατον λέγοντες. ὁ μὲν γὰρ ἀπογράψας αὐτὸν Λυδὸς ἦν ὁ Φερεκλέους, ὁ δὲ πείσας ὑπομεῖναι καὶ μὴ οἴχεσθαι φεύγοντα ἐγώ, πολλὰ ἱκετεύσας καὶ λαμβανόμενος τῶν γονάτων. [20] καίτοι τί ἐβουλόμην, εἰ ἐμήνυσα μὲν κατὰ τοῦ πατρός, ὡς οὗτοί φασιν, ἱκέτευον δὲ τὸν πατέρα μείναντά τι παθεῖν ὑπ' ἐμοῦ; καὶ ὁ πατὴρ ἐπείσθη ἀγῶνα τοιοῦτον ἀγωνίσασθαι, ἐν ᾧ δυοῖν τοῖν μεγίστοιν κακοῖν οὐκ ἦν αὐτῷ ἁμαρτεῖν; ἢ γὰρ ἐμοῦ δόξαντος τὰ ὄντα μηνῦσαι κατ' ἐκείνου ὑπ' ἐμοῦ ἀποθανεῖν, ἢ αὐτῷ σωθέντι ἐμὲ ἀποκτεῖναι. ὁ γὰρ νόμος οὕτως εἶχεν· εἰ μὲν τἀληθῆ μηνύσειέ τις, εἶναι τὴν ἄδειαν, εἰ δὲ τὰ ψευδῆ, τεθνάναι. καὶ μὲν δὴ τοῦτό γε ἐπίστασθε πάντες, ὅτι ἐσώθην καὶ ἐγὼ καὶ ὁ ἐμὸς πατήρ· οἷόν τε δ' οὐκ ἦν, εἴπερ ἐγὼ μηνυτὴς ἐγενόμην περὶ τοῦ πατρός, ἀλλ' ἢ ἐμὲ ἢ ἐκεῖνον ἔδει ἀποθανεῖν. [21] φέρε δὴ τοίνυν, εἰ καὶ ὁ πατὴρ ἐβούλετο ὑπομένειν, τοὺς φίλους ἂν οἴεσθε ἢ ἐπιτρέπειν αὐτῷ μένειν ἢ ἐγγυήσασθαι, ἀλλ' οὐκ ἂν παραιτεῖσθαι καὶ δεῖσθαι ἀπιέναι ὅπου ἂν ἔμελλεν αὐτὸς σωθήσεσθαι ἐμέ τε οὐκ ἀπολεῖν; [22] ἀλλὰ γὰρ καὶ ὅτε Σπεύσιππον ἐδίωκεν ὁ πατὴρ τῶν παρανόμων, αὐτὰ ταῦτα ἔλεγεν, ὡς οὐδεπώποτε ἔλθοι εἰς Θημακὸν ὡς Φερεκλέα· ἐκέλευε δὲ βασανίσαι τὰ ἀνδράποδα, καὶ μὴ τοὺς μὲν παραδιδόντας μὴ ἐθέλειν ἐλέγχειν, τοὺς δὲ μὴ θέλοντας ἀναγκάζειν. ταῦτα δὲ λέγοντος τοῦ πατρὸς τοῦ ἐμοῦ, ὡς ἅπαντες ἴστε, τί ὑπελείπετο τῷ Σπευσίππῳ λέγειν, εἰ ἀληθῆ οἶδε λέγουσιν, ἀλλ' ἢ " Ὦ Λεωγόρα, τί βούλει περὶ θεραπόντων λέγειν; οὐχ ὁ υἱὸς οὑτοσὶ μεμήνυκε κατὰ σοῦ, καί φησί σε παρεῖναι ἐν Θημακῷ; ἔλεγχε σὺ τὸν πατέρα, ἢ οὐκ ἔστι σοι ἄδεια." ταυτὶ ἔλεγεν ἂν ὁ Σπεύσιππος, ὦ ἄνδρες, ἢ οὔ; ἐγὼ μὲν οἶμαι. [23] εἰ τοίνυν ἀνέβην ἐπὶ δικαστήριον, ἢ λόγος τις περὶ ἐμοῦ ἐγένετο, ἢ μήνυσίς τις ἐμὴ ἔστιν ἢ ἀπογραφή, μὴ ὅτι ἐμὴ καθ' ἑτέρου, ἀλλ' εἰ καὶ ἄλλου τινὸς κατ' ἐμοῦ, ἐλεγχέτω με ὁ βουλόμενος ἐνταῦθα ἀναβάς. ἀλλὰ γὰρ λόγον ἀνοσιώτερον καὶ ἀπιστότερον οὐδένας πώποτ' ἐγὼ

WITNESSES

[19] You have heard what happened, gentlemen, and the witnesses have given their evidence; now recall what my accusers had the audacity to say. For it is indeed right to make a defence in this way, by recalling the words of one's accusers and refuting them. They said that I gave information about the Mysteries, and that I denounced my own father as having been present and became an informer against my own father, which I think is the most abominable and outrageous story imaginable. The one who denounced him was Lydus, the slave of Pherecles, the one who persuaded him to stay and not take off in flight was I myself, after numerous entreaties and by grasping his knees. [20] What, indeed, was my objective in informing against my father, as they say, and then entreating him to stay and be ill treated by me? Again, was my father persuaded to contest such a trial in which he could not avoid one of two extreme evils? For either I must cause his death, if my information against him were thought to be true, or he must cause mine, if he were acquitted, because the law ran that if an informer told the truth, he should be granted immunity, but if he told lies, he should be executed. Yet you all indeed know this, that both I and my father survived, which could not have happened if I had become an informer against my father - one of us would have had to die. [21] Well then, even if my father wanted to stay, do you think that his friends would have allowed him to remain or would have gone bail for him, instead of entreating and begging him to go away where he would be likely to survive himself and also not destroy me? [22] Further, even when my father was prosecuting Speusippus for illegality, he repeatedly insisted on this, that he never at any time went to Themacus to visit Pherecles. He urged Speusippus to torture his slaves and not to refuse to examine those who offered, while compelling those who refused. When my father said this, as you all know he did, what was there left for Speusippus to say, if these men are telling the truth, but: "Leogoras, why do you want to talk about slaves? Has not your own son here informed against you, and does he not say that you were at Themacus? Prove your father guilty, Andocides, or there is no immunity for you." Is this what Speusippus would have said, gentlemen, or not? I for one think it is. [23] If in fact I did go into court, or if there was some story about me, or if there is some information or denunciation containing my name, to say nothing of one of mine against another but even another's against me, let anyone who wishes stand up here and refute me. But nobody can, for I have never known anyone tell a more

εἰπόντας οἶδα, οἳ τοῦτο μόνον ἡγήσαντο δεῖν, τολμῆσαι κατηγορῆσαι· εἰ δ' ἐλεγχθήσονται ψευδόμενοι, οὐδὲν αὐτοῖς ἐμέλησεν. [24] ὥσπερ οὖν, εἰ ἀληθῆ ἦν ταῦτα ἅ μου κατηγόρησαν, ἐμοὶ ἂν ὠργίζεσθε καὶ ἠξιοῦτε δίκην τὴν μεγίστην ἐπιτιθέναι, οὕτως ἀξιῶ ὑμᾶς, γιγνώσκοντας ὅτι ψεύδονται, πονηρούς τε αὐτοὺς νομίζειν χρῆσθαί τε τεκμηρίῳ ὅτι εἰ τὰ δεινότατα τῶν κατηγορηθέντων περιφανῶς ἐλέγχονται ψευδόμενοι, ἦ που τά γε πολλῷ φαυλότερα ῥᾳδίως ὑμῖν ἀποδείξω ψευδομένους αὐτούς.

[25] Αἱ μὲν μηνύσεις ὧδε περὶ τῶν μυστηρίων αὗται ἐγένοντο τέτταρες· οἳ δὲ ἔφυγον καθ' ἑκάστην μήνυσιν, ἀνέγνων ὑμῖν τὰ ὀνόματα αὐτῶν, καὶ οἱ μάρτυρες μεμαρτυρήκασιν. ἔτι δὲ πρὸς τούτοις ἐγὼ πιστότητος ὑμῶν ἕνεκα, ὦ ἄνδρες, τάδε ποιήσω. τῶν γὰρ φυγόντων ἐπὶ τοῖς μυστηρίοις οἱ μέν τινες ἀπέθανον φεύγοντες, οἱ δ' ἥκουσιν καί εἰσιν ἐνθάδε καὶ πάρεισιν ὑπ' ἐμοῦ κεκλημένοι. [26] ἐγὼ οὖν ἐν τῷ ἐμῷ λόγῳ δίδωμι τῷ βουλομένῳ ἐμὲ ἐξελέγξαι ὅτι ἔφυγέ τις αὐτῶν δι' ἐμὲ ἢ ἐμήνυσα κατ' αὐτοῦ, ἢ οὐχ ἕκαστοι ἔφυγον κατὰ τὰς μηνύσεις ταύτας ἃς ἐγὼ ὑμῖν ἀπέδειξα. καὶ ἐάν τις ἐλέγξῃ με ὅτι ψεύδομαι, χρήσασθέ μοι ὅ τι βούλεσθε. καὶ σιωπῶ καὶ παραχωρῶ, εἴ τις ἀναβαίνειν βούλεται.

[27] Φέρε δή, ὦ ἄνδρες, μετὰ ταῦτα τί ἐγένετο; ἐπειδὴ αἱ μηνύσεις ἐγένοντο, περὶ τῶν μηνύτρων (ἦσαν γὰρ κατὰ τὸ Κλεωνύμου ψήφισμα χίλιαι δραχμαί, κατὰ δὲ τὸ Πεισάνδρου μύριαι) περὶ δὲ τούτων ἠμφισβήτουν οὗτοί τε οἱ μηνύσαντες καὶ Πυθόνικος, φάσκων πρῶτος εἰσαγγεῖλαι, καὶ Ἀνδροκλῆς ὑπὲρ τῆς βουλῆς. [28] ἔδοξεν οὖν τῷ δήμῳ ἐν τῷ τῶν θεσμοθετῶν δικαστηρίῳ τοὺς μεμυημένους, ἀκούσαντας τὰς μηνύσεις ἃς ἕκαστος ἐμήνυσε, διαδικάσαι. καὶ ἐψηφίσαντο πρώτῳ μὲν Ἀνδρομάχῳ, δευτέρῳ δὲ Τεύκρῳ, καὶ ἔλαβον Παναθηναίων τῷ ἀγῶνι Ἀνδρόμαχος μὲν μυρίας δραχμάς, Τεῦκρος δὲ χιλίας. καί μοι κάλει τούτων τοὺς μάρτυρας.

ΜΑΡΤΥΡΕΣ

[29] Περὶ μὲν τῶν μυστηρίων, ὦ ἄνδρες, ὧν εἵνεκα ἡ ἔνδειξις ἐγένετο καὶ περὶ ὧν ὑμεῖς οἱ μεμυημένοι εἰσεληλύθατε, ἀποδέδεικταί μοι ὡς οὔτε ἠσέβηκα οὔτε μεμήνυκα περὶ οὐδενὸς

outrageous and unbelievable story than these men, who thought they only had to have the nerve to bring a charge: they cared not one iota if they should be proved liars. [24] Therefore, just as you would have been angry with me, if these charges of theirs had been true, and would have thought it right to impose on me the severest penalty, so do I think it right that you, perceiving them to be liars, should both consider them to be scoundrels and infer that, if they are manifestly proved to have lied about their most serious charges, then *a fortiori* I shall all the more easily prove to you they are lying about the far more paltry ones.

[25] Such, then, were the informations laid concerning the Mysteries, four in number; I had the names of those who went into exile after each information read to you, and the witnesses have given their evidence. In addition to this I shall do one more thing to confirm your belief, gentlemen. Of those who went into exile over the affair of the Mysteries some died in exile, but others have returned and are in Athens and are present in court at my request. [26] So, in the time allotted for me to speak, I shall allow anyone who wishes to refute me by showing that any one of them went into exile because of me, or that I informed against him, or that each and every one of them did not go into exile as a result of these informations which I described to you. If someone proves me a liar, you may do with me whatever you wish. I shall now be silent and make way for anyone who wishes to stand up.

[27] Well now, gentlemen, what happened after this? When the informations had been given, there was a dispute over the rewards (they were fixed at 1000 drachmas by the decree of Cleonymus, 10,000 by that of Peisander), a dispute between these informers, Pythonicus, who claimed he was the first to bring an impeachment, and Androcles on behalf of the council. [28] It was therefore resolved by the people that those who had been initiated should hear the informations which each claimant gave and decide between them in the court of the thesmothetae. They voted the rewards first to Andromachus and second to Teucrus, and at the festival of the Panathenaea Andromachus received 10,000 drachmas, Teucrus 1000. Please call the witnesses to this.

WITNESSES

[29] Concerning the Mysteries, gentlemen, on account of which the denunciation was lodged and about which you who are initiates have come into court, I have shown that I have neither committed any act of impiety nor

οὔτε ὡμολόγηκα περὶ αὐτῶν, οὐδὲ ἔστι μοι ἁμάρτημα περὶ τὼ θεὼ οὔτε μεῖζον οὔτ' ἔλαττον οὐδέν. ὅπερ ἐμοὶ περὶ πλείστου ἐστὶν ὑμᾶς πεῖσαι. καὶ γὰρ οἱ λόγοι τῶν κατηγόρων ‑ ταῦτα τὰ δεινὰ καὶ φρικώδη ἀνωρθίαζον, καὶ λόγους εἶπον ὡς πρότερον ἑτέρων ἁμαρτόντων καὶ ἀσεβησάντων περὶ τὼ θεώ, οἷα ἕκαστος αὐτῶν ἔπαθε καὶ ἐτιμωρήθη ‑ [30] τούτων οὖν ἐμοὶ τῶν λόγων ἢ τῶν ἔργων τί προσήκει; ἐγὼ γὰρ πολὺ μᾶλλον ἐκείνων κατηγορῶ, καὶ δι' αὐτὸ τοῦτό φημι δεῖν ἐκείνους μὲν ἀπολέσθαι, ὅτι ἠσέβησαν, ἐμὲ δὲ σῴζεσθαι, ὅτι οὐδὲν ἡμάρτηκα. ἢ δεινόν γ' ἂν εἴη, εἰ ἐμοὶ ὀργίζοισθε ἐπὶ τοῖς ἑτέρων ἁμαρτήμασι, καὶ τὴν εἰς ἐμὲ διαβολὴν εἰδότες ὅτι ὑπὸ τῶν ἐχθρῶν τῶν ἐμῶν λέγεται, κρείττω τῆς ἀληθείας ἡγήσεσθε. δηλονότι γὰρ τοῖς μὲν ἡμαρτηκόσι τὰ τοιαῦτα ἁμαρτήματα οὐκ ἔστιν ἀπολογία ὡς οὐκ ἐποίησαν (ἡ γὰρ βάσανος δεινὴ παρὰ τοῖς εἰδόσιν), ἐμοὶ δὲ ὁ ἔλεγχος ἥδιστος, ἐν οἷς ὑμῶν οὐδέν με δεῖ δεόμενον οὐδὲ παραιτούμενον σωθῆναι ἐπὶ τοιαύτῃ αἰτίᾳ, ἀλλ' ἐλέγχοντα τοὺς τῶν κατηγόρων λόγους. [31] καὶ ὑμᾶς ἀναμιμνήσκω τὰ γεγενημένα, οἵτινες ὅρκους μεγάλους ὀμόσαντες οἴσετε τὴν ψῆφον περὶ ἐμοῦ, καὶ ἀρασάμενοι τὰς μεγίστας ἀρὰς ὑμῖν τε αὐτοῖς καὶ παισὶ τοῖς ὑμετέροις αὐτῶν, ἦ μὴν ψηφιεῖσθαι περὶ ἐμοῦ τὰ δίκαια, πρὸς δὲ τούτοις μεμύησθε καὶ ἑοράκατε τοῖν θεοῖν τὰ ἱερά, ἵνα τιμωρήσητε μὲν τοὺς ἀσεβοῦντας, σῴζητε δὲ τοὺς μηδὲν ἀδικοῦντας. [32] νομίσατε τοίνυν ἀσέβημα οὐδὲν ἔλαττον εἶναι τῶν μηδὲν ἠδικηκότων ἀσεβεῖν καταγνῶναι ἢ τοὺς ἠσεβηκότας μὴ τιμωρεῖσθαι. ὥστ' ἐγὼ ὑμῖν πολὺ μᾶλλον τῶν κατηγόρων πρὸς τοῖν θεοῖν ἐπισκήπτω, ὑπέρ τε τῶν ἱερῶν ἃ εἴδετε, καὶ ὑπὲρ τῶν Ἑλλήνων οἳ τῆς ἑορτῆς ἕνεκεν ἔρχονται δεῦρο· εἰ μέν τι ἠσέβηκα ἢ ὡμολόγηκα ἢ ἐμήνυσα κατά τινος ἀνθρώπων, ἢ ἄλλος τις περὶ ἐμοῦ, ἀποκτείνατέ με, οὐ παραιτοῦμαι· [33] εἰ δὲ οὐδὲν ἡμάρτηταί μοι, καὶ τοῦτο ὑμῖν ἀποδείκνυμι σαφῶς, δέομαι ὑμῶν αὐτὸ φανερὸν τοῖς Ἕλλησι πᾶσι ποιῆσαι, ὡς ἀδίκως εἰς τόνδε τὸν ἀγῶνα κατέστην. ἐὰν γὰρ μὴ μεταλάβῃ τὸ πέμπτον μέρος τῶν ψήφων καὶ ἀτιμωθῇ ὁ ἐνδείξας ἐμὲ Κηφίσιος οὑτοσί, οὐκ ἔξεστιν αὐτῷ εἰς τὸ ἱερὸν τοῖν θεοῖν εἰσιέναι, ἢ ἀποθανεῖται. εἰ οὖν ὑμῖν δοκῶ ἱκανῶς περὶ τούτων ἀπολελογῆσθαι, δηλώσατέ μοι, ἵνα προθυμότερον περὶ τῶν ἄλλων ἀπολογῶμαι.

turned informer against anyone nor admitted any guilt about them, and that I have done no wrong whatsoever, either large or small, against the two goddesses. It is of the greatest importance for me to convince you of this. For the words of my accusers - they shouted aloud these terrible horrors and told stories about how in the past others had done wrong and committed impious acts against the two goddesses, and how every one of them suffered and was punished - what do these words or deeds have to do with me? [30] In fact I may far more justly accuse them, and for this reason I claim that they should perish, because they have committed impiety, and I should be acquitted, because I have done nothing wrong. Otherwise it would really be terrible, if you were to be angry with me on account of the wrongs of others and are going to consider the false accusation against me weightier than the truth, when you know that it has been made by my enemies. Plainly for those who have committed such wrongs as this there is no defence that they did not do them (for trial before men who know the truth is a dreadful ordeal), but for me the investigation is very pleasant in a case in which I do not need to secure my acquittal on such a charge by entreating or appealing to you, but by disproving the words of my accusers. [31] I am reminding you of what happened, men who have sworn great oaths before casting your votes in my case and invoked the greatest curses on yourselves and your children, swearing that you would vote justly in my case, and men who, in addition, are initiates and have seen the sacred objects of the two goddesses, so that you may punish those guilty of impiety and acquit those who are not guilty. [32] Consider, then, that it is no less an impious act to convict of impiety those who have committed no offence than not to punish those who have committed impiety. So I call on you, far more earnestly than my accusers, in the name of the two goddesses, both for the sake of the sacred objects which you have seen and for the sake of the Greeks who come here for the festival, if I have committed any impiety or admitted guilt or informed against another human being, or if someone else has done so about me, then put me to death, I do not ask for mercy. [33] If, on the other hand, I have done nothing wrong and I clearly prove this to you, then I ask you to make it plain to all the Greeks that I have been brought to this trial wrongfully. If Cephisius here, who lodged the denunciation against me, does not gain one-fifth of the votes and is disfranchised, he is forbidden to enter the sanctuary of the two goddesses on pain of death. So if you consider my defence against these charges adequate, show this to me, so that I may make my defence against the other charges more readily.

[34] Περὶ δὲ τῶν ἀναθημάτων τῆς περικοπῆς καὶ τῆς μηνύσεως, ὥσπερ καὶ ὑπεσχόμην ὑμῖν, οὕτω καὶ ποιήσω· ἐξ ἀρχῆς γὰρ ὑμᾶς διδάξω ἅπαντα τὰ γεγενημένα. ἐπειδὴ Τεῦκρος ἦλθε Μεγαρόθεν ἄδειαν εὑρόμενος, μηνύει περί τε τῶν μυστηρίων ἃ ᾔδει καὶ τῶν περικοψάντων τὰ ἀναθήματα, καὶ ἀπογράφει δυοῖν δέοντας εἴκοσιν ἄνδρας. ἐπειδὴ δὲ οὗτοι ἀπεγράφησαν, οἱ μὲν αὐτῶν φεύγοντες ᾤχοντο, οἱ δὲ συλληφθέντες ἀπέθανον κατὰ τὴν Τεύκρου μήνυσιν. καί μοι ἀνάγνωθι αὐτῶν τὰ ὀνόματα.

[35] ΟΝΟΜΑΤΑ. Τεῦκρος ἐπὶ τοῖς Ἑρμαῖς ἐμήνυσεν Εὐκτήμονα, Γλαύκιππον, Εὐρύμαχον, Πολύευκτον, Πλάτωνα, Ἀντίδωρον, Χάριππον, Θεόδωρον, Ἀλκισθένην, Μενέστρατον, Ἐρυξίμαχον, Εὐφίλητον, Εὐρυδάμαντα, Φερεκλέα, Μέλητον, Τιμάνθην, Ἀρχίδαμον, Τελένικον.

Τούτων τοίνυν τῶν ἀνδρῶν οἱ μὲν ἥκουσι καί εἰσιν ἐνθάδε, τῶν δὲ ἀποθανόντων εἰσὶ πολλοὶ προσήκοντες· ὧν ὅστις βούλεται, ἐν τῷ ἐμῷ λόγῳ ἀναβάς με ἐλεγξάτω ἢ ὡς ἔφυγέ τις δι' ἐμὲ τούτων τῶν ἀνδρῶν ἢ ὡς ἀπέθανεν.

[36] Ἐπειδὴ δὲ ταῦτα ἐγένετο, Πείσανδρος καὶ Χαρικλῆς, ὄντες μὲν τῶν ζητητῶν, δοκοῦντες δ' ἐν ἐκείνῳ τῷ χρόνῳ εὐνούστατοι εἶναι τῷ δήμῳ, ἔλεγον ὡς εἴη τὰ ἔργα τὰ γεγενημένα οὐκ ὀλίγων ἀνδρῶν ἀλλ' ἐπὶ τῇ τοῦ δήμου καταλύσει, καὶ χρῆναι ἔτι ζητεῖν καὶ μὴ παύσασθαι. καὶ ἡ πόλις οὕτως διέκειτο, ὥστ' ἐπειδὴ τὴν βουλὴν εἰς τὸ βουλευτήριον ὁ κῆρυξ ἀνείποι ἰέναι καὶ τὸ σημεῖον καθέλοι, τῷ αὐτῷ σημείῳ ἡ μὲν βουλὴ εἰς τὸ βουλευτήριον ᾔει, οἱ δ' ἐκ τῆς ἀγορᾶς ἔφευγον, δεδιότες εἰς ἕκαστος μὴ συλληφθείη.

[37] Ἐπαρθεὶς οὖν τοῖς τῆς πόλεως κακοῖς, εἰσαγγέλλει Διοκλείδης εἰς τὴν βουλήν, φάσκων εἰδέναι τοὺς περικόψαντας τοὺς Ἑρμᾶς, καὶ εἶναι αὐτοὺς εἰς τριακοσίους· ὡς δ' ἴδοι καὶ περιτύχοι τῷ πράγματι, ἔλεγε. (καὶ τούτοις, ὦ ἄνδρες, δέομαι ὑμῶν προσέχοντας τὸν νοῦν ἀναμιμνήσκεσθαι, ἐὰν ἀληθῆ λέγω, καὶ διδάσκειν ἀλλήλους· ἐν ὑμῖν γὰρ ἦσαν οἱ λόγοι, καί μοι ὑμεῖς τούτων μάρτυρές ἐστε.) **[38]** ἔφη γὰρ εἶναι μὲν ἀνδράποδόν οἱ ἐπὶ Λαυρείῳ, δεῖν δὲ κομίσασθαι ἀποφοράν. ἀναστὰς δὲ πρῲ ψευσθεὶς τῆς ὥρας βαδίζειν· εἶναι δὲ πανσέληνον. ἐπεὶ δὲ παρὰ τὸ προπύλαιον τοῦ Διονύσου ἦν, ὁρᾶν ἀνθρώπους πολλοὺς ἀπὸ τοῦ Ὠιδείου καταβαίνοντας εἰς τὴν ὀρχήστραν· δείσας δὲ αὐτούς, εἰσελθὼν ὑπὸ τὴν σκιὰν καθέζεσθαι μεταξύ του κίονος καὶ τῆς

[34] Concerning the mutilation of the images and the information, I shall do as I promised and tell you from the beginning all that happened. When Teucrus returned from Megara and obtained immunity, he gave the information he knew about the Mysteries and the mutilators of the images, and denounced eighteen men. When these were denounced, some fled into exile, others were arrested and executed on Teucrus' information. Please read out their names.

[35] NAMES. In the matter of the Hermae Teucrus informed against Euctemon, Glaucippus, Eurymachus, Polyeuctus, Plato, Antidorus, Charippus, Theodorus, Alcisthenes, Menestratus, Eryximachus, Euphiletus, Eurydamas, Pherecles, Meletus, Timanthes, Archidamus, Telenicus.

Now, some of these men have returned to Athens and are present in court, as are a number of relatives of those who have died; any one of these who wishes is welcome to stand up in the time allotted me to speak and prove against me that I was responsible for either the exile or the death of any of these men.

[36] After this Peisander and Charicles, who were among the commissioners of inquiry and seemed at that time to be very well-disposed towards the democracy, declared that what had happened was not the work of a few men but was an attempt to overthrow the democracy, and that inquiries should still proceed and not cease. The city was in such a state that when the herald summoned the council to proceed to the council-chamber and took down the signal, as well as being the signal for the council to proceed to the chamber it was the signal for those in the agora to flee from it, each in fear of arrest.

[37] Encouraged by the city's ills, Diocleides brought an impeachment before the council, claiming that he knew who had mutilated the Hermae and that there were about three hundred of them; and he told how he saw the deed and how he happened on it. (I ask you, gentlemen, to turn your minds to these things, recall whether I am telling the truth and inform one another; for his speech was made before you, and you are my witnesses to these things.) [38] He said that he had a slave at Laurium and had to collect a fee. He got up early, mistaking the time, and began his walk; there was a full moon. When he was by the gateway to the theatre of Dionysus, he saw a large number of men going down from the Odeum into the orchestra. Afraid of them, he moved into the shadow and sat down

στήλης ἐφ' ᾗ ὁ στρατηγός ἐστιν ὁ χαλκοῦς. ὁρᾶν δὲ ἀνθρώπους τὸν <μὲν> ἀριθμὸν <μάλιστα> τριακοσίους, ἑστάναι δὲ κύκλῳ ἀνὰ πέντε καὶ δέκα ἄνδρας, τοὺς δὲ ἀνὰ εἴκοσιν· ὁρῶν δὲ αὐτῶν πρὸς τὴν σελήνην τὰ πρόσωπα τῶν πλείστων γιγνώσκειν. [39] (καὶ πρῶτον μέν, ὦ ἄνδρες, τοῦθ' ὑπέθετο - δεινότατον πρᾶγμα, οἶμαι - ὅπως ἐν ἐκείνῳ εἴη ὅντινα βούλοιτο Ἀθηναίων φάναι τῶν ἀνδρῶν τούτων εἶναι, ὅντινα δὲ μὴ βούλοιτο, λέγειν ὅτι οὐκ ἦν.) ἰδὼν δὲ ταῦτ' ἔφη ἐπὶ Λαύρειον ἰέναι, καὶ τῇ ὑστεραίᾳ ἀκούειν ὅτι οἱ Ἑρμαῖ εἶεν περικεκομμένοι· γνῶναι οὖν εὐθὺς ὅτι τούτων εἴη τῶν ἀνδρῶν τὸ ἔργον. [40] ἥκων δὲ εἰς ἄστυ ζητητάς τε ἤδη ᾑρημένους καταλαμβάνειν καὶ μήνυτρα κεκηρυγμένα ἑκατὸν μνᾶς. ἰδὼν δὲ Εὔφημον τὸν Καλλίου τοῦ Τηλοκλέους ἀδελφὸν ἐν τῷ χαλκείῳ καθήμενον, ἀναγαγὼν αὐτὸν εἰς τὸ Ἡφαιστεῖον λέγειν ἅπερ ὑμῖν ἐγὼ εἴρηκα, ὡς ἴδοι ἡμᾶς ἐν ἐκείνῃ τῇ νυκτί· οὔκουν δέοιτο παρὰ τῆς πόλεως χρήματα λαβεῖν μᾶλλον ἢ παρ' ἡμῶν, ὥσθ' ἡμᾶς ἔχειν φίλους. εἰπεῖν οὖν τὸν Εὔφημον ὅτι καλῶς ποιήσειεν εἰπών, καὶ νῦν ἥκειν κελεῦσαί οἱ εἰς τὴν Λεωγόρου οἰκίαν, "ἵνα ἐκεῖ συγγένῃ μετ' ἐμοῦ Ἀνδοκίδῃ καὶ ἑτέροις οἷς δεῖ". [41] ἥκειν ἔφη τῇ ὑστεραίᾳ καὶ δὴ κόπτειν τὴν θύραν· τὸν δὲ πατέρα τὸν ἐμὸν τυχεῖν ἐξιόντα, καὶ εἰπεῖν αὐτόν· " Ἆρά γε σὲ οἴδε περιμένουσι; χρὴ μέντοι μὴ ἀπωθεῖσθαι τοιούτους φίλους." εἰπόντα δὲ αὐτὸν ταῦτα οἴχεσθαι. (καὶ τούτῳ μὲν τῷ τρόπῳ τὸν πατέρα μου ἀπώλλυε, συνειδότα ἀποφαίνων.) εἰπεῖν δὲ ἡμᾶς ὅτι δεδογμένον ἡμῖν εἴη δύο μὲν τάλαντα ἀργυρίου διδόναι οἱ ἀντὶ τῶν ἑκατὸν μνῶν τῶν ἐκ τοῦ δημοσίου, ἐὰν δὲ κατάσχωμεν ἡμεῖς ἃ βουλόμεθα, ἕνα αὐτὸν ἡμῶν εἶναι, πίστιν δὲ τούτων δοῦναί τε καὶ δέξασθαι. [42] ἀποκρίνασθαι δὲ αὐτὸς πρὸς ταῦτα ὅτι βουλεύσοιτο· ἡμᾶς δὲ κελεύειν αὐτὸν ἥκειν εἰς Καλλίου τοῦ Τηλοκλέους ἵνα κἀκεῖνος παρείη. (τὸν δ' αὖ κηδεστήν μου οὕτως ἀπώλλυεν.) ἥκειν ἔφη εἰς Καλλίου, καὶ καθομολογήσας ἡμῖν πίστιν δοῦναι ἐν ἀκροπόλει, καὶ ἡμᾶς συνθεμένους οἱ τὸ ἀργύριον εἰς τὸν εἰσιόντα μῆνα δώσειν διαψεύδεσθαι καὶ οὐ διδόναι· ἥκειν οὖν μηνύσων τὰ γενόμενα.

[43] Ἡ μὲν εἰσαγγελία αὐτῷ, ὦ ἄνδρες, τοιαύτη· ἀπογράφει δὲ τὰ ὀνόματα τῶν ἀνδρῶν ὧν ἔφη γνῶναι, δύο καὶ τετταράκοντα, πρώτους μὲν Μαντίθεον καὶ Ἀψεφίωνα, βουλευτὰς ὄντας καὶ καθημένους ἔνδον, εἶτα δὲ καὶ τοὺς ἄλλους. ἀναστὰς δὲ Πείσανδρος ἔφη χρῆναι λύειν τὸ ἐπὶ Σκαμανδρίου ψήφισμα καὶ ἀναβιβάζειν ἐπὶ τὸν τροχὸν τοὺς ἀπογραφέντας, ὅπως μὴ πρότερον νὺξ ἔσται πρὶν πυθέσθαι τοὺς ἄνδρας ἅπαντας. ἀνέκραγεν ἡ βουλὴ

between the pillar and the pedestal on which the bronze statue of the general stands. He saw in total about three hundred men, but standing in groups of fifteen or twenty; he saw their faces in the moonlight and recognised most of them. [39] (The first point, gentlemen, is that he gave his story this beginning - a monstrous business, in my opinion - with the purpose of being in a position to say that any Athenian he chose was one of these men, and any he did not choose was not one of them.) After seeing this, he said he went to Laurium and next day heard that the Hermae had been mutilated; he therefore knew immediately that it was the work of these men. [40] Returning to the city, he found that commissioners of inquiry had already been elected and a reward of 100 minas proclaimed. So when he saw Euphemus, the brother of Callias, son of Telocles, sitting in his smithy, he took him up to the temple of Hephaestus and told him what I have told you, how he had seen us that night; now, he said, he would prefer to take money from us than from the city, so as to keep us friends. Euphemus said it was good of him to say this and bade him please come now to Leogoras' house, "so that you and I may meet Andocides there and the others involved". [41] He said he did come the next day, and he knocks on the door; my father happens to be going out, and he said, "Are you the one they are waiting for? You certainly must not turn away friends like them." With these words he went off. (In this way Diocleides tried to destroy my father, by showing he was in the know.) According to Diocleides we said that we had decided firstly to give him two talents of silver instead of the 100 minas from the treasury, secondly that, if we got what we wanted, he should be one of us, and thirdly that pledges to do these things should be exchanged. [42] He said his reply to this was that he would think it over, and we told him to come to the house of Callias, son of Telocles, so that he too might be present. (In this way, again, Diocleides tried to destroy my brother-in-law.) Diocleides said he then went to Callias' house, and on reaching agreement made a pledge to us on the Acropolis, while we agreed to give him the money in the incoming month, but deceived him and did not do so. He therefore had come to give information about what happened.

[43] Such was his impeachment, gentlemen. He denounced the names of the men he said he knew, forty-two of them, beginning with Mantitheus and Apsephion, who were members of the council and sitting in the meeting, and then the rest. Peisander now stood up, and moved that the decree passed in the archonship of Scamandrius should be repealed and the men denounced should be sent to the wheel, to make sure that everyone involved should be discovered before nightfall. The council shouted out its

ὡς εὖ λέγει. [44] ἀκούσαντες δὲ ταῦτα Μαντίθεος καὶ Ἀψεφίων ἐπὶ τὴν ἑστίαν ἐκαθέζοντο, ἱκετεύοντες μὴ στρεβλωθῆναι ἀλλ' ἐξεγγυηθέντες κριθῆναι. μόλις δὲ τούτων τυχόντες, ἐπειδὴ τοὺς ἐγγυητὰς κατέστησαν, ἐπὶ τοὺς ἵππους ἀναβάντες ᾤχοντο εἰς τοὺς πολεμίους αὐτομολήσαντες, καταλιπόντες τοὺς ἐγγυητάς, οὓς ἔδει <ἐν> τοῖς αὐτοῖς ἐνέχεσθαι ἐν οἷσπερ οὓς ἠγγυήσαντο. [45] ἡ δὲ βουλὴ ἐξελθοῦσα ἐν ἀπορρήτῳ συνέλαβεν ἡμᾶς καὶ ἔδησεν ἐν τοῖς ξύλοις. ἀνακαλέσαντες δὲ τοὺς στρατηγοὺς ἀνειπεῖν ἐκέλευσαν Ἀθηναίων τοὺς μὲν ἐν ἄστει οἰκοῦντας ἰέναι εἰς τὴν ἀγορὰν τὰ ὅπλα λαβόντας, τοὺς δ' ἐν μακρῷ τείχει εἰς τὸ Θησεῖον, τοὺς δ' ἐν Πειραιεῖ εἰς τὴν Ἱπποδαμείαν ἀγοράν, τοὺς δὲ ἱππέας ἔτι νυκτὸς σημῆναι τῇ σάλπιγγι ἥκειν εἰς τὸ Ἀνάκειον, τὴν δὲ βουλὴν εἰς ἀκρόπολιν ἰέναι κἀκεῖ καθεύδειν, τοὺς δὲ πρυτάνεις ἐν τῇ θόλῳ. Βοιωτοὶ δὲ πεπυσμένοι τὰ πράγματα ἐπὶ τοῖς ὁρίοις ἦσαν ἐξεστρατευμένοι. τὸν δὲ τῶν κακῶν τούτων αἴτιον Διοκλείδην ὡς σωτῆρα ὄντα τῆς πόλεως ἐπὶ ζεύγους ἦγον εἰς τὸ πρυτανεῖον στεφανώσαντες, καὶ ἐδείπνει ἐκεῖ.

[46] Πρῶτον μὲν οὖν ταῦτα, ὦ ἄνδρες, ὁπόσοι ὑμῶν παρῆσαν ἀναμιμνήσκεσθε καὶ τοὺς ἄλλους διδάσκετε· εἶτα δέ μοι τοὺς πρυτάνεις κάλει τοὺς τότε πρυτανεύσαντας, Φιλοκράτη καὶ τοὺς ἄλλους. διδάσκετε.

ΜΑΡΤΥΡΕΣ

[47] Φέρε δή, καὶ τὰ ὀνόματα ὑμῖν ἀναγνώσομαι τῶν ἀνδρῶν ὧν ἀπέγραψεν, ἵν' εἰδῆτε ὅσους μοι τῶν συγγενῶν ἀπώλλυεν, πρῶτον μὲν τὸν πατέρα, εἶτα δὲ τὸν κηδεστήν, τὸν μὲν συνειδότα ἀποδεικνύς, τοῦ δ' ἐν τῇ οἰκίᾳ φάσκων τὴν σύνοδον γενέσθαι· τῶν δ' ἄλλων ἀκούσεσθε τὰ ὀνόματα. καὶ αὐτοῖς ἀναγίγνωσκε.

Χαρμίδης Ἀριστοτέλους.
Οὗτος ἀνεψιὸς ἐμός· ἡ μήτηρ ἐκείνου καὶ ὁ πατὴρ ὁ ἐμὸς ἀδελφοί.
Ταυρέας.
Οὑτοσὶ ἀνεψιὸς τοῦ πατρός.
Νισαῖος.
Υἱὸς Ταυρέου.
Καλλίας ὁ Ἀλκμέωνος.
Ἀνεψιὸς τοῦ πατρός.
Εὔφημος.

approval. [44] On hearing this, Mantitheus and Apsephion went to sit at the altar, begging not to be tortured but to be allowed bail and to stand trial. They barely managed to secure this, and as soon as they had given sureties, they mounted their horses and took off to desert to the enemy, leaving behind their sureties to be liable to the same penalties as those for whom they had gone bail. [45] When the council left the chamber, its secret decision to arrest us was carried out, and we were put in the stocks. They then summoned the generals and ordered them to proclaim that those citizens resident in Athens were to go to the agora under arms, those resident in the area between the Long Walls were to go to the Theseum and those in Peiraeus to the agora of Hippodamus, a trumpet-signal was to be given before daybreak for the knights to come to the Anaceum, the council was to go to the Acropolis and sleep there, the prytaneis in the Tholos. The Boeotians had heard about the events, had taken the field and were on the frontier. Meanwhile the cause of these troubles, Diocleides, hailed as the saviour of the city, was crowned and driven on a chariot to the Prytaneum, where he dined.

[46] Firstly, then, those of you who were present at these events, gentlemen, recall them and inform the others; next, please call the prytaneis who were then in office, Philocrates and the rest. Go on, tell them.

WITNESSES

[47] Well now, I am also going to have read to you the names of the men he denounced, so that you may see how many of my relatives he tried to destroy, firstly my father, then my brother-in-law: the one he named as being in the know, the other's house he claimed was where the meeting took place. You will hear the names of the rest. Read them out to the court.

Charmides, son of Aristoteles.

This is a cousin of mine; his mother and my father were brother and sister.

Taureas.

This is a cousin of my father's.

Nisaeus.

Son of Taureas.

Callias, son of Alcmaeon.

A cousin of my father's.

Euphemus.

48

Καλλίου τοῦ Τηλοκλέους ἀδελφός.
Φρύνιχος ὁ ὀρχησάμενος.
᾿Ανεψιός.
Εὐκράτης.
῾Ο Νικίου ἀδελφός· κηδεστὴς οὗτος Καλλίου.
Κριτίας.
᾿Ανεψιὸς καὶ οὗτος τοῦ πατρός· αἱ μητέρες ἀδελφαί.
Τούτους πάντας ἐν τοῖς τετταράκοντα ἀνδράσιν ἀπέγραψεν.
[48] Ἐπειδὴ δὲ ἐδεδέμεθα πάντες ἐν τῷ αὐτῷ, καὶ νύξ τε
ἦν καὶ τὸ δεσμωτήριον συνεκέκλητο, ἧκον δὲ τῷ μὲν μήτηρ, τῷ δὲ
ἀδελφή, τῷ δὲ γυνὴ καὶ παῖδες, ἦν δὲ βοὴ καὶ οἶκτος κλαιόντων
καὶ ὀδυρομένων τὰ παρόντα κακά, λέγει πρός με Χαρμίδης, ὢν μὲν
ἀνεψιός, ἡλικιώτης δὲ καὶ συνεκτραφεὶς ἐν τῇ οἰκίᾳ τῇ ἡμετέρᾳ
ἐκ παιδός, [49] ὅτι "᾿Ανδοκίδη, τῶν μὲν παρόντων κακῶν ὁρᾷς τὸ
μέγεθος, ἐγὼ δ᾽ ἐν μὲν τῷ παρελθόντι χρόνῳ οὐδὲν ἐδεόμην λέγειν
οὐδέ σε λυπεῖν, νῦν δὲ ἀναγκάζομαι διὰ τὴν παροῦσαν ἡμῖν
συμφοράν. οἷς γὰρ ἐχρῶ καὶ οἷς συνῆσθα ἄνευ ἡμῶν τῶν συγγενῶν,
οὗτοι ἐπὶ ταῖς αἰτίαις δι᾽ ἃς ἡμεῖς ἀπολλύμεθα οἱ μὲν αὐτῶν
τεθνᾶσιν, οἱ δὲ οἴχονται φεύγοντες, σφῶν αὐτῶν καταγνόντες
ἀδικεῖν..........[50] εἰ ἤκουσάς τι τούτου τοῦ πράγματος τοῦ
γενομένου, εἰπέ, καὶ πρῶτον μὲν σεαυτὸν σῶσον, εἶτα δὲ τὸν
πατέρα, ὃν εἰκός ἐστί σε μάλιστα φιλεῖν, εἶτα δὲ τὸν κηδεστήν,
ὃς ἔχει σου τὴν ἀδελφὴν ἥπερ σοι μόνη ἐστίν, ἔπειτα δὲ τοὺς
ἄλλους συγγενεῖς καὶ ἀναγκαίους τοσούτους ὄντας, ἔτι δὲ ἐμέ, ὃς
ἐν ἅπαντι τῷ βίῳ ἠνίασα μέν σε οὐδὲν πώποτε, προθυμότατος δὲ
εἰς σὲ καὶ τὰ σὰ πράγματά εἰμι, ὅ τι ἂν δέῃ ποιεῖν."
[51] Λέγοντος δέ, ὦ ἄνδρες, Χαρμίδου ταῦτα, ἀντιβολούντων
δὲ τῶν ἄλλων καὶ ἱκετεύοντος ἑνὸς ἑκάστου, ἐνεθυμήθην πρὸς
ἐμαυτόν· "῏Ω πάντων ἐγὼ δεινοτάτῃ συμφορᾷ περιπεσών, πότερα
περιίδω τοὺς ἐμαυτοῦ συγγενεῖς ἀπολλυμένους ἀδίκως, καὶ αὐτούς
τε ἀποθανόντας καὶ τὰ χρήματα αὐτῶν δημευθέντα, πρὸς δὲ
τούτοις ἀναγραφέντας ἐν στήλαις ὡς ὄντας ἀλιτηρίους τῶν θεῶν
τοὺς οὐδενὸς αἰτίους τῶν γεγενημένων, ἔτι δὲ τριακοσίους
᾿Αθηναίων μέλλοντας ἀδίκως ἀπολέσθαι, τὴν δὲ πόλιν ἐν κακοῖς
οὖσαν τοῖς μεγίστοις καὶ ὑποψίαν εἰς ἀλλήλους ἔχοντας, ἢ εἴπω
᾿Αθηναίοις ἅπερ ἤκουσα Εὐφιλήτου αὐτοῦ τοῦ ποιήσαντος;" [52] ἔτι
δὲ ἐπὶ τούτοις καὶ τόδε ἐνεθυμήθην, ὦ ἄνδρες, καὶ ἐλογιζόμην
πρὸς ἐμαυτὸν τοὺς ἐξημαρτηκότας καὶ τὸ ἔργον εἰργασμένους, ὅτι
οἱ μὲν αὐτῶν ἤδη ἐτεθνήκεσαν ὑπὸ Τεύκρου μηνυθέντες, οἱ δὲ

Brother of Callias, son of Telocles.

Phrynichus the former dancer.

A cousin.

Eucrates.

The brother of Nicias; this is Callias' brother-in-law.

Critias.

This is also a cousin of my father's; their mothers were sisters.

All these were among the forty he denounced.

[48] When we had all been thrown into the same prison, and it was night and the prison had been closed, and one person's mother had arrived, another's sister, another's wife and children, and there was the pitiful noise of people crying and bewailing their present troubles, Charmides, my cousin of the same age who had been brought up with me in our house from childhood, said to me, [49] "Andocides, you see the enormity of our present troubles, and while I have never needed in the past to say anything to vex you, I am now compelled to do so by our present plight. Your friends and associates outside our family, these are the ones who either have been executed on the charges through which we are perishing, or who have fled into exile and so pronounced themselves guilty. [50] If you have heard anything of this affair that has taken place, say so and save first of all yourself, then your father, whom you must love most of all, then your brother-in-law, who is the husband of your only sister, next all your other relations and kinsmen, and finally me, who in all my life have never done you any harm but am always devoted to you and your interests, whatever needs to be done."

[51] When Charmides said this, gentlemen, and the others entreated me, and each and every one beseeched me, I thought to myself, "I, of all men, have met with a most terrible misfortune! Am I to look on while my own relatives are perishing unjustly and are executed and are having their goods confiscated, and moreover are having their names inscribed on stelae as being sinners against the gods, when they are not to blame for any of what has happened, and three hundred Athenians are about to perish unjustly, and the city is suffering extreme troubles and mutual suspicion? Or am I to tell the Athenians what I heard from Euphiletus, the real culprit?" [52] Then I thought something else besides this, gentlemen, and I reckoned to myself that, of those who were guilty and had done the deed, some had already been executed on information given by Teucrus, while others had fled into exile

φεύγοντες ᾤχοντο καὶ αὐτῶν θάνατος κατέγνωστο, τέτταρες δὲ ἦσαν ὑπόλοιποι οἳ οὐκ ἐμηνύθησαν ὑπὸ Τεύκρου τῶν πεποιηκότων, Παναίτιος, Χαιρέδημος, Διάκριτος, Λυσίστρατος· [53] οὓς εἰκὸς ἦν ἁπάντων μάλιστα δοκεῖν εἶναι τούτων τῶν ἀνδρῶν οὓς ἐμήνυσε Διοκλείδης, φίλους ὄντας τῶν ἀπολωλότων ἤδη. καὶ τοῖς μὲν οὐδέπω βέβαιος ἦν ἡ σωτηρία, τοῖς δὲ ἐμοῖς οἰκείοις φανερὸς <ὁ> ὄλεθρος, εἰ μή τις ἐρεῖ Ἀθηναίοις τὰ γενόμενα. ἐδόκει οὖν μοι κρεῖττον εἶναι τέτταρας ἄνδρας ἀποστερῆσαι τῆς πατρίδος δικαίως, οἳ νῦν ζῶσι καὶ κατεληλύθασι καὶ ἔχουσι τὰ σφέτερα αὐτῶν, ἢ ἐκείνους ἀποθανόντας ἀδίκως περιιδεῖν.

[54] Εἰ οὖν τινι ὑμῶν, ὦ ἄνδρες, τῶν ἄλλων πολιτῶν γνώμη τοιαύτη παρειστήκει πρότερον περὶ ἐμοῦ, ὡς ἄρα ἐγὼ ἐμήνυσα κατὰ τῶν ἑταίρων τῶν ἐμαυτοῦ, ὅπως ἐκεῖνοι μὲν ἀπόλοιντο, ἐγὼ δὲ σωθείην (ἃ ἐλογοποίουν οἱ ἐχθροὶ περὶ ἐμοῦ βουλόμενοι διαβάλλειν με), σκοπεῖσθε ἐξ αὐτῶν τῶν γεγενημένων. [55] νῦν γὰρ ἐμὲ μὲν λόγον δεῖ δοῦναι τῶν ἐμοὶ πεπραγμένων μετὰ τῆς ἀληθείας, αὐτῶν παρόντων οἵπερ ἥμαρτον καὶ ἔφυγον ταῦτα ποιήσαντες, ἴσασι δὲ ἄριστα εἴτε ψεύδομαι εἴτε ἀληθῆ λέγω (ἔξεστι δὲ αὐτοῖς ἐλέγχειν με ἐν τῷ ἐμῷ λόγῳ, ἐγὼ γὰρ ἐφίημι)· [56] ὑμᾶς δὲ δεῖ μαθεῖν τὰ γενόμενα (ἐμοὶ γάρ, ὦ ἄνδρες, τοῦδε τοῦ ἀγῶνος τοῦτ᾽ ἔστι μέγιστον, σωθέντι μὴ δοκεῖν κακῷ εἶναι), εἶτα δὲ καὶ τοὺς ἄλλους ἅπαντας μαθεῖν ὅτι οὔτε μετὰ κακίας οὔτε μετ᾽ ἀνανδρίας οὐδεμιᾶς τῶν γεγενημένων πέπρακται ὑπ᾽ ἐμοῦ οὐδέν, ἀλλὰ διὰ συμφορὰν γεγενημένην μάλιστα μὲν τῇ πόλει, εἶτα <δὲ> καὶ ἡμῖν, εἶπον δὲ ἃ ἤκουσα Εὐφιλήτου προνοίᾳ μὲν τῶν συγγενῶν καὶ τῶν φίλων, προνοίᾳ δὲ τῆς πόλεως ἁπάσης, μετ᾽ ἀρετῆς ἀλλ᾽ οὐ μετὰ κακίας, ὡς ἐγὼ νομίζω. εἰ οὖν οὕτως ἔχει ταῦτα, σῴζεσθαί τε ἀξιῶ καὶ δοκεῖν ὑμῖν εἶναι μὴ κακός.

[57] Φέρε δή (χρὴ γάρ, ὦ ἄνδρες, ἀνθρωπίνως περὶ τῶν πραγμάτων ἐκλογίζεσθαι, ὥσπερ ἂν αὐτὸν ὄντα ἐν τῇ συμφορᾷ), τί ἂν ὑμῶν ἕκαστος ἐποίησεν; εἰ μὲν γὰρ ἦν †δυσὶ† τὸ ἕτερον ἑλέσθαι, ἢ καλῶς ἀπολέσθαι ἢ αἰσχρῶς σωθῆναι, ἔχοι ἄν τις εἰπεῖν κακίαν εἶναι τὰ γενόμενα (καίτοι πολλοὶ ἂν καὶ τοῦτο εἵλοντο, τὸ ζῆν περὶ πλείονος ποιησάμενοι τοῦ καλῶς ἀποθανεῖν). [58] ὅπου δὲ τούτων τὸ ἐναντιώτατον ἦν, σιωπήσαντι μὲν αὐτῷ τε αἴσχιστα ἀπολέσθαι μηδὲν ἀσεβήσαντι, ἔτι δὲ τὸν πατέρα περιιδεῖν ἀπολόμενον καὶ τὸν κηδεστὴν καὶ τοὺς συγγενεῖς καὶ ἀνεψιοὺς τοσούτους, οὓς οὐδεὶς ἄλλος ἀπώλλυεν ἢ ἐγὼ μὴ εἰπὼν ὡς ἕτεροι ἥμαρτον (Διοκλείδης μὲν γὰρ ψευσάμενος ἔδησεν αὐτούς, σωτηρία

and been condemned to death, but four were left who had not been informed against by Teucrus as being among the culprits, Panaetius, Chaeredemus, Diacritus and Lysistratus. [53] It was reasonable to think that they in particular were among these men against whom Diocleides gave information, since they were friends of the ones who had already been put to death. Their safety, then, was not yet assured, but the death of my relatives was certain, unless somebody told the Athenians what happened. I therefore thought it better to deprive four men of their country justly, men who are alive today and have been restored and are in possession of their property, than to look on while those others died unjustly.

[54] So, gentlemen, if any of you other citizens had previously got the idea about me that I informed against my own friends with the purpose of destroying them and saving myself (a story which my enemies invented about me in their desire to discredit me), consider the matter according to what actually happened. [55] For today not only must I give a truthful account of my actions, when there are present the very men who committed the crime and went into exile because they did it, and who know best of all whether I am lying or telling the truth (they may refute me in the time allotted for me to speak; I give my permission); [56] but also you must learn what happened (since for me, gentlemen, the most important thing in this trial is this, that on my acquittal my reputation should be clear), and then everyone else must know that none of what has happened has been done by me through any baseness or cowardice, but through disaster having afflicted most of all the city and then also us, and that I revealed what I heard from Euphiletus out of care for my relatives and friends, and out of care for the whole city, and in my opinion through virtue not baseness. If this is the case, I think it right both that I should be acquitted and that my reputation among you should be clear.

[57] Well now (for, gentlemen, you should consider the case by human standards, as one would if oneself were in this trouble), what would each of you have done? If it had been possible to choose one of these alternatives, either to die honourably or survive disgracefully, one would be able to call what I did baseness (although many men would have chosen this very option, valuing life more highly than an honourable death). [58] When, however, my alternatives were exactly the opposite to these, either by saying nothing to die in the utmost disgrace, although I had committed no impiety, and also to look on while my father died and my brother-in-law and so many relatives and cousins, whose death nobody else was going to cause except I, by not saying that others were guilty (Diocleides by his lying caused them to

δὲ αὐτῶν ἄλλη οὐδεμία ἦν ἢ πυθέσθαι Ἀθηναίους πάντα τὰ πραχθέντα· φονεὺς οὖν αὐτῶν ἐγιγνόμην ἐγὼ μὴ εἰπὼν ὑμῖν ἃ ἤκουσα) - ἔτι δὲ τριακοσίους Ἀθηναίων ἀπώλλυον, καὶ ἡ πόλις ἐν κακοῖς τοῖς μεγίστοις ἐγίγνετο· [59] ταῦτα μὲν οὖν ἦν ἐμοῦ μὴ εἰπόντος. εἰπὼν δὲ τὰ ὄντα αὐτός τε ἐσῳζόμην καὶ τὸν πατέρα ἔσῳζον καὶ τοὺς ἄλλους συγγενεῖς, καὶ τὴν πόλιν ἐκ φόβου καὶ κακῶν τῶν μεγίστων ἀπήλλαττον· φυγάδες δὲ δι' ἐμὲ τέτταρες ἄνδρες ἐγίγνοντο, οἵπερ καὶ ἥμαρτον· τῶν δ' ἄλλων, οἳ πρότερον ὑπὸ Τεύκρου ἐμηνύθησαν, οὔτε δήπου οἱ τεθνεῶτες δι' ἐμὲ μᾶλλον ἐτέθνασαν οὔτε οἱ φεύγοντες μᾶλλον ἔφευγον. [60] ταῦτα δὲ πάντα σκοπῶν εὕρισκον, ὦ ἄνδρες, τῶν παρόντων κακῶν ταῦτα ἐλάχιστα εἶναι, εἰπεῖν τὰ γενόμενα ὡς τάχιστα, καὶ ἐλέγξαι Διοκλείδην ψευσάμενον, καὶ τιμωρήσασθαι ἐκεῖνον, ὃς ἡμᾶς μὲν ἀπώλλυεν ἀδίκως, τὴν δὲ πόλιν ἐξηπάτα, ταῦτα δὲ ποιῶν μέγιστος εὐεργέτης ἐδόκει εἶναι καὶ χρήματα ἐλάμβανε.

[61] Διὰ ταῦτα εἶπον τῇ βουλῇ ὅτι εἰδείην τοὺς ποιήσαντας, καὶ ἐξέδειξα τὰ γενόμενα, ὅτι εἰσηγήσατο μὲν πινόντων ἡμῶν ταύτην τὴν βουλὴν [γενέσθαι] Εὐφίλητος, ἀντεῖπον δὲ ἐγώ, καὶ τότε μὲν οὐ γένοιτο δι' ἐμέ. ὕστερον δ' ἐγὼ μὲν ἐν Κυνοσάργει ἐπὶ πωλίον ὅ μοι ἦν ἀναβὰς ἔπεσον καὶ τὴν κλεῖν συνετρίβην καὶ τὴν κεφαλὴν κατεάγην, φερόμενός τε ἐπὶ κλίνης ἀπεκομίσθην οἴκαδε. [62] αἰσθόμενος δ' Εὐφίλητος ὡς ἔχοιμι, λέγει πρὸς αὐτοὺς ὅτι πέπεισμαι ταῦτα συμποιεῖν καὶ ὡμολόγηκα αὐτῷ μεθέξειν τοῦ ἔργου καὶ περικόψειν τὸν Ἑρμῆν τὸν παρὰ τὸ Φορβαντεῖον. ταῦτα δ' ἔλεγεν ἐξαπατῶν ἐκείνους· καὶ διὰ ταῦτα ὁ Ἑρμῆς ὃν ὁρᾶτε πάντες, ὁ παρὰ τὴν πατρῴαν οἰκίαν τὴν ἡμετέραν, ὃν ἡ Αἰγηὶς ἀνέθηκεν, οὐ περιεκόπη μόνος τῶν Ἑρμῶν τῶν Ἀθήνησιν, ὡς ἐμοῦ τοῦτο ποιήσοντος, ὡς ἔφη πρὸς αὐτοὺς Εὐφίλητος. [63] οἱ δ' αἰσθόμενοι δεινὰ ἐποίουν, ὅτι εἰδείην μὲν τὸ πρᾶγμα, πεποιηκὼς δὲ οὐκ εἴην. προσελθόντες δέ μοι τῇ ὑστεραίᾳ Μέλητος καὶ Εὐφίλητος ἔλεγον ὅτι "Γεγένηται, ὦ Ἀνδοκίδη, καὶ πέπρακται ἡμῖν ταῦτα. σὺ μέντοι εἰ μὲν ἀξιοῖς ἡσυχίαν ἔχειν καὶ σιωπᾶν, ἕξεις ἡμᾶς ἐπιτηδείους ὥσπερ καὶ πρότερον· εἰ δὲ μή, χαλεπώτεροί σοι ἡμεῖς ἐχθροὶ ἐσόμεθα ἢ ἄλλοι τινὲς δι' ἡμᾶς φίλοι." [64] εἶπον αὐτοῖς ὅτι νομίζοιμι μὲν διὰ τὸ πρᾶγμα Εὐφίλητον πονηρὸν εἶναι, ἐκείνοις δὲ οὐκ ἐμὲ δεινὸν εἶναι ὅτι οἶδα, ἀλλὰ μᾶλλον αὐτὸ τὸ ἔργον πολλῷ ὅτι πεποίηται.

Ὡς οὖν ἦν ταῦτ' ἀληθῆ, τόν τε παῖδα τὸν ἐμὸν παρέδωκα βασανίσαι, ὅτι ἔκαμνον καὶ οὐδ' ἀνιστάμην ἐκ τῆς κλίνης, καὶ τὰς

be imprisoned, and their safety depended entirely on the Athenians learning all the facts; so I was going to become their murderer by not telling you what I heard) - and again, I was going to destroy three hundred Athenians, and the city was going to fall into extreme troubles; [59] this would have been the result if I had not spoken. By telling the truth, however, I was going to save myself, and I was going to save my father and my other relatives, and I was going to free the city from fear and extreme troubles. Four men were going to become exiles because of me, who were in fact guilty; and of the others against whom Teucrus had previously informed neither, of course, did those who had died die the more because of me, nor were those in exile in exile the more because of me. [60] Considering all this, I found, gentlemen, that the least of my present troubles was to say what had happened as quickly as possible, prove Diocleides had lied and secure the punishment of the man who was destroying us unjustly and was thoroughly deceiving the city, but in so doing appeared to be its greatest benefactor and was going to receive money.

[61] As a result I told the council that I knew who were guilty, and I revealed what had happened, that Euphiletus had put forward this idea at one of our drinking-parties, but I opposed it and was responsible for its rejection at that time. Later in Cynosarges I mounted a pony of mine but fell off, broke my collar-bone and cut my head open; I was carried off home, borne on a stretcher. [62] When Euphiletus saw how I was, he told the others I had been persuaded to join in the scheme and had agreed with him to take part in the deed and mutilate the Hermes near the shrine of Phorbas. In saying this he deceived them, and for this reason the Hermes which you all see, the one near our family house which the Aegeis tribe dedicated, was the only one in Athens not to be mutilated, since I was to do this, as Euphiletus told them. [63] When they learned this, they expressed their anger that I knew about the affair but had not taken part in it. The next day Meletus and Euphiletus visited me and said, "It has happened, Andocides, and we have done it. As for you, if you see fit to keep quiet and say nothing, you will find us friends just like before; but if you do not, we will be more bitter enemies to you than any others will be friends through your betraying us." [64] I told them that I thought Euphiletus was wicked through the affair, but it was not I who was dangerous to them because I knew, but much rather the deed itself because it had been done.

To show that this account was true, I handed over my slave for torture, to prove that I had been ill and had not even been getting up, and the

54

θεραπαίνας ἔλαβον οἱ πρυτάνεις, ὅθεν ὁρμώμενοι ταῦτ' ἐποίουν ἐκεῖνοι. [65] ἐξελέγχοντες δὲ τὸ πρᾶγμα ἥ τε βουλὴ καὶ οἱ ζητηταί, ἐπειδὴ ἦν ᾗ ἐγὼ ἔλεγον καὶ ὡμολογεῖτο πανταχόθεν, τότε δὴ καλοῦσι τὸν Διοκλείδην· καὶ οὐ πολλῶν λόγων ἐδέησεν, ἀλλ' εὐθὺς ὡμολόγει ψεύδεσθαι καὶ ἐδεῖτο σώζεσθαι φράσας τοὺς πείσαντας αὐτὸν λέγειν ταῦτα· εἶναι δὲ Ἀλκιβιάδην τὸν Φηγούσιον καὶ Ἀμίαντον τὸν ἐξ Αἰγίνης. [66] καὶ οὗτοι μὲν δείσαντες ᾤχοντο φεύγοντες· ὑμεῖς δὲ ἀκούσαντες ταῦτα Διοκλείδην μὲν τῷ δικαστηρίῳ παραδόντες ἀπεκτείνατε, τοὺς δὲ δεδεμένους καὶ μέλλοντας ἀπολεῖσθαι ἐλύσατε, τοὺς ἐμοὺς συγγενεῖς, δι' ἐμέ, καὶ τοὺς φεύγοντας κατεδέξασθε, αὐτοὶ δὲ λαβόντες τὰ ὅπλα ἀπῆτε πολλῶν κακῶν καὶ κινδύνων ἀπαλλαγέντες. [67] ἐν οἷς ἐγώ, ὦ ἄνδρες, τῆς μὲν τύχης ᾗ ἐχρησάμην δικαίως ἂν ὑπὸ πάντων ἐλεηθείην, τῶν δὲ γενομένων ἕνεκεν εἰκότως <ἂν> ἀνὴρ ἄριστος δοκοίην εἶναι, ὅστις εἰσηγησαμένῳ μὲν Εὐφιλήτῳ πίστιν τῶν ἐν ἀνθρώποις ἀπιστοτάτην ἠναντιώθην καὶ ἀντεῖπον καὶ ἐλοιδόρησα ἐκεῖνον ὧν ἦν ἄξιος, ἁμαρτόντων δ' ἐκείνων τὴν ἁμαρτίαν αὐτοῖς συνέκρυψα, καὶ μηνύσαντος κατ' αὐτῶν Τεύκρου οἱ μὲν αὐτῶν ἀπέθανον, οἱ δὲ ἔφυγον, πρὶν ἡμᾶς ὑπὸ Διοκλείδου δεθῆναι καὶ μέλλειν ἀπολεῖσθαι. τότε δὲ ἀπέγραψα τέτταρας ἄνδρας, Παναίτιον, Διάκριτον, Λυσίστρατον, Χαιρέδημον· [68] οὗτοι μὲν ἔφυγον δι' ἐμέ, ὁμολογῶ· ἐσώθη δέ γε ὁ πατήρ, ὁ κηδεστής, ἀνεψιοὶ τρεῖς, τῶν ἄλλων συγγενῶν ἑπτά, μέλλοντες ἀποθανεῖσθαι ἀδίκως, οἳ νῦν ὁρῶσι τοῦ ἡλίου τὸ φῶς δι' ἐμέ, καὶ αὐτοὶ ὁμολογοῦσιν· ὁ δὲ τὴν πόλιν ὅλην συνταράξας καὶ εἰς τοὺς ἐσχάτους κινδύνους καταστήσας ἐξηλέγχθη· ὑμεῖς δὲ ἀπηλλάγητε μεγάλων φόβων καὶ τῶν εἰς ἀλλήλους ὑποψιῶν.

[69] Καὶ ταῦτ' εἰ ἀληθῆ λέγω, ὦ ἄνδρες, ἀναμιμνήσκεσθε, καὶ οἱ ἰδόντες διδάσκετε τοὺς ἄλλους. σὺ δέ μοι αὐτοὺς κάλει τοὺς λυθέντας δι' ἐμέ· ἄριστα γὰρ ἂν εἰδότες τὰ γενόμενα λέγοιεν εἰς τούτους. οὑτωσὶ δὲ ἔχει, ὦ ἄνδρες· μέχρι τούτου ἀναβήσονται καὶ λέξουσιν ὑμῖν, ἕως ἂν ἀκροᾶσθαι βούλησθε, ἔπειτα δ' ἐγὼ περὶ τῶν ἄλλων ἀπολογήσομαι.

<ΜΑΡΤΥΡΕΣ>

[70] Περὶ μὲν οὖν τῶν τότε γενομένων ἀκηκόατε πάντα καὶ ἀπολελόγηταί μοι ἱκανῶς (ὥς γ' ἐμαυτὸν πείθω· εἰ δέ τίς τι ὑμῶν ποθεῖ ἢ νομίζει τι μὴ ἱκανῶς εἰρῆσθαι ἢ παραλέλοιπά τι, ἀναστὰς

prytaneis arrested the maidservants of the house from where the culprits set out to commit the crime. [65] Both the council and the commissioners of inquiry investigated the affair, and when they established it was as I said and my story was corroborated by all concerned, they then summoned Diocleides. He did not need much questioning, rather he confessed at once that he had lied and begged for mercy if he named the men who had induced him to tell this story: they were Alcibiades of Phegus and Amiantus from Aegina. [66] These were terrified and fled into exile; while you, on hearing this, handed Diocleides over to the court and put him to death, and because of me freed those in prison and about to perish, my relatives, and recalled the exiles. You yourselves then picked up your weapons and dispersed, freed from numerous troubles and dangers. [67] In all this I, gentlemen, rightly deserve everybody's sympathy for the ill fortune I suffered, and for what I did I should reasonably be thought of as a man of utmost integrity. For when Euphiletus proposed one of the most treacherous pledges men could make, I opposed him and spoke against him and heaped on him the abuse he deserved, but when his friends had committed their crime, I joined with them in concealing it; and it was only when Teucrus informed against them that some of them died and others fled, before we were imprisoned by Diocleides and were about to perish. It was then that I denounced four men, Panaetius, Diacritus, Lysistratus and Chaeredemus. [68] These fled because of me, I confess, but my father was saved, my brother-in-law, three cousins and seven other relatives, who were about to be put to death unjustly but who still see the light of day because of me, as they themselves admit. Further, the one who threw the entire city into chaos and brought it into extreme dangers was convicted, and you were freed from great fears and mutual suspicions.

[69] Now, gentlemen, recall if I am telling the truth about this, and those of you who saw the events inform the others. Now, clerk, please call the ones who were released because of me, for those who know what happened can best tell it to the jurors. So it stands, gentlemen; they will go up on the platform and address you for just so long as you wish to listen, then I shall proceed to the rest of my defence.

<WITNESSES>

[70] Concerning what happened at that time, then, you have heard everything, and I have made a sufficient defence (at least I so persuade myself; if any of you requires something more or thinks something has not

ὑπομνησάτω, καὶ ἀπολογήσομαι καὶ πρὸς τοῦτο)· περὶ δὲ τῶν νόμων ἤδη ὑμᾶς διδάξω.

[71] Κηφίσιος γὰρ οὑτοσὶ ἐνέδειξε μέν με κατὰ τὸν νόμον τὸν κείμενον, τὴν δὲ κατηγορίαν ποιεῖται κατὰ ψήφισμα πρότερον γενόμενον ὃ εἶπεν Ἰσοτιμίδης, οὗ ἐμοὶ προσήκει οὐδέν. ὁ μὲν γὰρ εἶπεν εἴργεσθαι τῶν ἱερῶν τοὺς ἀσεβήσαντας καὶ ὁμολογήσαντας, ἐμοὶ δὲ τούτων οὐδέτερα πεποίηται· οὔτε ἠσέβηται οὔτε ὡμολόγηται. [72] ὡς δὲ καὶ τοῦτο τὸ ψήφισμα λέλυται καὶ ἄκυρόν ἐστιν, ἐγὼ ὑμᾶς διδάξω. καίτοιγε τοιαύτην ἀπολογίαν περὶ αὐτοῦ ποιήσομαι, ὅπου μὴ πείθων μὲν ὑμᾶς αὐτὸς ζημιώσομαι, πείσας δὲ ὑπὲρ τῶν ἐχθρῶν ἀπολελογημένος ἔσομαι. ἀλλὰ γὰρ τἀληθῆ εἰρήσεται.

[73] Ἐπεὶ γὰρ αἱ νῆες διεφθάρησαν καὶ ἡ πολιορκία ἐγένετο, ἐβουλεύσασθε περὶ ὁμονοίας, καὶ ἔδοξεν ὑμῖν τοὺς ἀτίμους ἐπιτίμους ποιῆσαι, καὶ εἶπε τὴν γνώμην Πατροκλείδης. οἱ δὲ ἄτιμοι τίνες ἦσαν καὶ τίνα τρόπον ἕκαστοι; ἐγὼ ὑμᾶς διδάξω. οἱ μὲν ἀργύριον ὀφείλοντες τῷ δημοσίῳ, ὁπόσοι εὐθύνας ὦφλον ἄρξαντες ἀρχάς, ἢ ἐξούλας ἢ γραφὰς ἢ ἐπιβολὰς ὦφλον, ἢ ὠνὰς πριάμενοι ἐκ τοῦ δημοσίου μὴ κατέβαλον τὰ χρήματα, ἢ ἐγγύας ἠγγυήσαντο πρὸς τὸ δημόσιον (τούτοις ἡ μὲν ἔκτισις ἦν ἐπὶ τῆς ἐνάτης πρυτανείας· εἰ δὲ μή, διπλάσιον ὀφείλειν καὶ τὰ κτήματα αὐτῶν πεπρᾶσθαι). [74] εἷς μὲν τρόπος οὗτος ἀτιμίας ἦν· ἕτερος δὲ ὢν τὰ μὲν σώματα ἄτιμα ἦν, τὴν δ' οὐσίαν εἶχον καὶ ἐκέκτηντο. οὗτοι δ' αὖ ἦσαν ὁπόσοι κλοπῆς ἢ δώρων ὄφλοιεν (τούτους ἔδει καὶ αὐτοὺς καὶ τοὺς ἐκ τούτων ἀτίμους εἶναι), καὶ ὁπόσοι λίποιεν τὴν τάξιν ἢ ἀστρατείας ἢ δειλίας ἢ ἀναυμαχίου ὄφλοιεν ἢ τὴν ἀσπίδα ἀποβάλοιεν, ἢ τρὶς ψευδομαρτυρίων ἢ τρὶς ψευδοκλητείας ὄφλοιεν, ἢ τοὺς γονέας κακῶς ποιοῖεν· οὗτοι πάντες ἄτιμοι ἦσαν τὰ σώματα, τὰ δὲ χρήματα εἶχον. [75] ἄλλοι αὖ κατὰ προστάξεις, οἵτινες οὐ παντάπασιν ἄτιμοι ἦσαν ἀλλὰ μέρος τι αὐτῶν, οἷον οἱ στρατιῶται, οἷς, ὅτι ἐπέμειναν ἐπὶ τῶν τυράννων ἐν τῇ πόλει, τὰ μὲν ἄλλα ἦν ἅπερ τοῖς ἄλλοις πολίταις, εἰπεῖν δ' ἐν τῷ δήμῳ οὐκ ἐξῆν αὐτοῖς οὐδὲ βουλεῦσαι. τούτων ἦσαν οὗτοι ἄτιμοι· αὕτη γὰρ ἦν τούτοις πρόσταξις. [76] ἑτέροις οὐκ ἦν γράψασθαι, τοῖς δὲ ἐνδεῖξαι· τοῖς δὲ μὴ ἀναπλεῦσαι εἰς Ἑλλήσποντον, ἄλλοις δ' εἰς Ἰωνίαν, τοῖς δ' εἰς τὴν ἀγορὰν μὴ εἰσιέναι πρόσταξις ἦν. ταῦτ'

been sufficiently covered, or if I have omitted something, let him stand up and mention it, and I shall make a defence against this as well). I shall now tell you about the laws.

[71] Cephisius here lodged the denunciation against me according to the established law, but he is basing his accusation on a previously enacted decree moved by Isotimides which has nothing at all to do with me. Isotimides moved that those who had committed impiety and confessed be excluded from the temples, but I have done neither of these: I have neither committed impiety nor confessed. [72] Furthermore, I shall prove to you that this decree has been repealed and is invalid. Yet I shall be making such a defence about it in a situation in which if I do not convince you, I shall be punished myself, but if I do convince you, I shall have made a defence for my opponents. Nevertheless, the truth will be told.

[73] When the fleet was destroyed and the siege began, you deliberated about unity and decided to re-enfranchise the disfranchised, and Patrocleides moved the resolution. Who were the disfranchised and what rights had each group lost? I will tell you. First, people owing money to the treasury: those who held public offices but failed the examinations of their conduct, those who lost ejectment cases or public cases or owed fines, those who bought privileges of tax-collection from the treasury but did not pay the money due, or those who gave security to the treasury (all these had to make their payment in the ninth prytany; otherwise they were to pay double and their possessions were to be sold). [74] This was one kind of disfranchisement; another concerned those who lost their personal rights but retained and held their property. These were persons who were convicted of theft or bribery (both they and their descendants were to be disfranchised), those who deserted their posts or were guilty of avoiding military service or of cowardice or of failing to bring a ship into battle or who threw away their shields, or those who were guilty of giving false evidence three times or falsely acting as summons-witnesses three times, or those who maltreated their parents; all these were deprived of their personal rights but retained their property. [75] Others again lost their rights according to limitations, that is they were not completely disfranchised but only lost a part of their rights, such as the soldiers who, because they remained in the city in the time of the tyrants, enjoyed all the rights of other citizens but were not allowed to speak in the assembly or be members of the council. These were deprived of these rights, this was the limitation imposed on them. [76] Others were not allowed to bring a public case or to lodge a denunciation; the limitation for some was not to sail to the Hellespont, for others to Ionia and others still not

οὖν ἐψηφίσασθε ἐξαλεῖψαι πάντα τὰ ψηφίσματα, καὶ αὐτὰ καὶ εἴ
πού τι ἀντίγραφον ἦν, καὶ πίστιν ἀλλήλοις περὶ ὁμονοίας δοῦναι
ἐν ἀκροπόλει. καί μοι ἀνάγνωθι τὸ ψήφισμα τὸ Πατροκλείδου καθ᾽
ὃ ταῦτα ἐγένετο.

[77] ΨΗΦΙΣΜΑ. Πατροκλείδης εἶπεν· ἐπειδὴ ἐψηφίσαντο
᾽Αθηναῖοι τὴν ἄδειαν περὶ <τῶν ἀτίμων καὶ> τῶν
ὀφειλόντων ὥστε λέγειν ἐξεῖναι καὶ ἐπιψηφίζειν,
ψηφίσασθαι τὸν δῆμον ταὐτὰ ἅπερ ὅτε ἦν τὰ
Μηδικά, καὶ συνήνεγκεν ᾽Αθηναίοις ἐπὶ τὸ ἄμεινον.
περὶ δὲ τῶν ἐπιγεγραμμένων εἰς τοὺς πράκτορας ἢ
τοὺς ταμίας τῆς θεοῦ καὶ τῶν ἄλλων θεῶν ἢ τὸν
βασιλέα, ἢ εἴ τις μὴ ἐξεγράφη, μέχρι τῆς
ἐξελθούσης βουλῆς ἐφ᾽ ἧς Καλλίας ἦρχεν, [78] ὅσοι
ἄτιμοι ἦσαν ἢ ὀφείλοντες, καὶ ὅσων εὔθυναί τινές
εἰσι κατεγνωσμέναι ἐν τοῖς λογιστηρίοις ὑπὸ τῶν
εὐθύνων καὶ τῶν παρέδρων, ἢ μήπω εἰσηγμέναι εἰς
τὸ δικαστήριον γραφαί τινές εἰσι περὶ τῶν εὐθυνῶν,
ἢ προστάξεις ἢ ἐγγύαι τινές εἰσι κατεγνωσμέναι,
εἰς τὸν αὐτὸν τοῦτον χρόνον, καὶ ὅσα ὀνόματα τῶν
τετρακοσίων τινὸς ἐγγέγραπται, ἢ ἄλλο τι περὶ τῶν
ἐν τῇ ὀλιγαρχίᾳ πραχθέντων ἐστί που γεγραμμένον -
πλὴν ὁπόσα ἐν στήλαις γέγραπται τῶν μὴ ἐνθάδε
μεινάντων ἢ <οἷς,> ἐξ ᾽Αρείου πάγου ἢ τῶν ἐφετῶν
ἢ ἐκ πρυτανείου ἢ Δελφινίου δικασθεῖσιν ὑπὸ τῶν
βασιλέων, ἢ ἐπὶ φόνῳ τίς ἐστι φυγὴ ἢ θάνατος
κατεγνώσθη ἢ σφαγεῦσιν ἢ τυράννοις - [79] τὰ δὲ
ἄλλα πάντα ἐξαλεῖψαι τοὺς πράκτορας καὶ τὴν
βουλήν, καὶ τὰ εἰρημένα πανταχόθεν, ὅπου τι ἔστιν
ἐν τῷ δημοσίῳ, καὶ εἰ ἀντίγραφόν που ἔστι,
παρέχειν τοὺς θεσμοθέτας καὶ τὰς ἄλλας ἀρχάς.
ποιεῖν δὲ ταῦτα τριῶν ἡμερῶν, ἐπειδὰν δόξῃ τῷ
δήμῳ. ἃ δ᾽ εἴρηται ἐξαλεῖψαι, μὴ κεκτῆσθαι ἰδίᾳ
μηδενὶ ἐξεῖναι μηδὲ μνησικακῆσαι μηδέποτε· εἰ δὲ
μή, ἔνοχον εἶναι τὸν παραβαίνοντα ταῦτα ἐν τοῖς
αὐτοῖς ἐν οἷσπερ οἱ ἐξ ᾽Αρείου πάγου φεύγοντες,

to enter the agora. You, then, voted to obliterate all these decrees, both the decrees themselves and any copies that might exist, and to exchange a pledge of unity on the Acropolis. Please read the decree of Patrocleides according to which these things happened.

[77] DECREE. Patrocleides moved: since the Athenians voted immunity concerning the disfranchised and state debtors, so that it is permissible to make proposals and put them to the vote, the people shall vote the same decree as the one passed during the Persian Wars, when it was beneficial to the Athenians. Concerning those registered with the revenue-collectors or the treasurers of the Goddess and the other gods or with the basileus, or anyone else whose name was not deleted, up to the expiry of the term of office of the council in the archonship of Callias, [78] all who were disfranchised or state debtors, and all who have been condemned for misconduct in office by the examiners and their assessors in the auditors' offices, or whose prosecutions concerning the examination of their conduct in office have not yet come into court, or who have been condemned to suffer limitations or fulfil guarantees, up to this same time, and all the names of any of the Four Hundred that are registered, or anything else written down about things done during the oligarchy - except for names inscribed on stelae of those who did not remain in Athens or who, after trial by either the Areopagus or the ephetae or at the Prytaneum or the Delphinium under the presidency of the basileis, either are in some kind of exile for homicide or were condemned to death either as murderers or as tyrants - [79] all the other names the revenue-collectors and the council are to obliterate, and they are to obliterate the said names from every place where any of them is recorded in public, and any copy that exists anywhere is to be produced by the thesmothetae and the other magistrates. They are to do this within three days after the resolution of the people. It is not to be permitted for anyone to keep privately the names which it has been decided to obliterate, nor ever to recall grievances; otherwise the transgressor of this rule is to be liable to the same penalties as those exiled by the

ὅπως ἂν ὡς πιστότατα ἔχῃ 'Αθηναίοις καὶ νῦν καὶ
εἰς τὸν λοιπὸν χρόνον.

[80] Κατὰ μὲν τὸ ψήφισμα τουτὶ τοὺς ἀτίμους ἐπιτίμους
ἐποιήσατε· τοὺς δὲ φεύγοντας οὔτε Πατροκλείδης εἶπε κατιέναι
οὔθ' ὑμεῖς ἐψηφίσασθε. ἐπεὶ δ' αἱ σπονδαὶ πρὸς Λακεδαιμονίους
ἐγένοντο, καὶ τὰ τείχη καθείλετε, καὶ τοὺς φεύγοντας
κατεδέξασθε, καὶ κατέστησαν οἱ τριάκοντα, καὶ μετὰ ταῦτα Φυλή
τε κατελήφθη Μουνυχίαν τε κατέλαβον, ἐγένετο ὑμῖν ὧν ἐγὼ οὐδὲν
δέομαι μεμνῆσθαι οὐδ' ἀναμιμνήσκειν ὑμᾶς τῶν γεγενημένων
κακῶν. [81] ἐπειδὴ δ' ἐπανήλθετε ἐκ Πειραιέως, γενόμενον ἐφ' ὑμῖν
τιμωρεῖσθαι, ἔγνωτε ἐᾶν τὰ γεγενημένα, καὶ περὶ πλείονος
ἐποιήσασθε σῴζειν τὴν πόλιν ἢ τὰς ἰδίας τιμωρίας, καὶ ἔδοξε μὴ
μνησικακεῖν ἀλλήλοις τῶν γεγενημένων. δόξαντα δὲ ὑμῖν ταῦτα,
εἵλεσθε ἄνδρας εἴκοσι· τούτους δὲ ἐπιμελεῖσθαι τῆς πόλεως, ἕως
ἄλλοι νόμοι τεθεῖεν· τέως δὲ χρῆσθαι τοῖς Σόλωνος νόμοις καὶ
τοῖς Δράκοντος θεσμοῖς. [82] ἐπειδὴ δὲ βουλήν τε ἀπεκληρώσατε
νομοθέτας τε εἵλεσθε, εὕρισκον τῶν νόμων τῶν τε Σόλωνος καὶ
τῶν Δράκοντος πολλοὺς ὄντας οἷς πολλοὶ τῶν πολιτῶν ἔνοχοι ἦσαν
τῶν πρότερον ἕνεκα γενομένων. ἐκκλησίαν ποιήσαντες ἐβουλεύσασθε
περὶ αὐτῶν, καὶ ἐψηφίσασθε, δοκιμάσαντες πάντας τοὺς νόμους,
εἶτ' ἀναγράψαι ἐν τῇ στοᾷ τούτους τῶν νόμων οἳ ἂν δοκιμασθῶσι.
καί μοι ἀνάγνωθι τὸ ψήφισμα.

[83] <ΨΗΦΙΣΜΑ.> Ἔδοξε τῷ δήμῳ, Τεισαμενὸς εἶπε·
πολιτεύεσθαι 'Αθηναίους κατὰ τὰ πάτρια, νόμοις δὲ
χρῆσθαι τοῖς Σόλωνος καὶ μέτροις καὶ σταθμοῖς,
χρῆσθαι δὲ καὶ τοῖς Δράκοντος θεσμοῖς, οἷσπερ
ἐχρώμεθα ἐν τῷ πρόσθεν χρόνῳ. ὁπόσων δ' ἂν
προσδέῃ, †οἷδε† ᾑρημένοι νομοθέται ὑπὸ τῆς βουλῆς
ἀναγραφέντας ἐν σανίσιν ἐκτιθέντων πρὸς τοὺς
ἐπωνύμους σκοπεῖν τῷ βουλομένῳ, καὶ παραδιδόντων
ταῖς ἀρχαῖς ἐν τῷδε τῷ μηνί. [84] τοὺς δὲ
παραδιδομένους νόμους δοκιμασάτω πρότερον ἡ βουλὴ
καὶ οἱ νομοθέται οἱ πεντακόσιοι, οὓς οἱ δημόται
εἵλοντο, ἐπειδὰν ὀμωμόκωσιν· ἐξεῖναι δὲ καὶ ἰδιώτῃ
τῷ βουλομένῳ εἰσιόντι εἰς τὴν βουλὴν συμβουλεύειν
ὅ τι ἂν ἀγαθὸν ἔχῃ περὶ τῶν νόμων. ἐπειδὰν δὲ
τεθῶσιν οἱ νόμοι, ἐπιμελείσθω ἡ βουλὴ ἡ ἐξ 'Αρείου
πάγου τῶν νόμων, ὅπως ἂν αἱ ἀρχαὶ τοῖς κειμένοις
νόμοις χρῶνται. τοὺς δὲ κυρουμένους τῶν νόμων

Areopagus, so that there may be the greatest possible trust among the Athenians both now and in the future.

[80] By this decree you re-enfranchised the disfranchised, but neither did Patrocleides move nor did you vote that the exiles return. When the peace was made with the Spartans, and you demolished the walls and recalled the exiles, and the Thirty were established, and afterwards Phyle was seized and they seized Munychia, you had things happen to you none of which I need recall, nor need I remind you of the troubles that occurred. [81] When you returned from Peiraeus, and it came into your power to seek vengeance, you decided to let bygones be bygones and placed more value on saving the city than private retributions; and you resolved not to recall grievances with one another over what had happened. After you had made this decision, you elected twenty men: these were to take charge of the city until other laws were passed, and until then the laws of Solon and the ordinances of Draco were to be employed. [82] When, however, you had chosen a council by lot and elected nomothetae, they found that there were a large number of the laws of Solon and Draco to which a large number of citizens were liable due to previous events. You called an assembly and deliberated about them, and you voted to examine all the laws and inscribe in the stoa those laws which were approved. Please read the decree.

[83] <DECREE.> The people resolved, Teisamenus moved: the Athenians are to conduct their affairs in the traditional manner, they are to employ the laws of Solon and his weights and measures, they are also to enforce the ordinances of Draco, which we employed in former time. Whatever additions may be needed are to be inscribed on boards by the nomothetae elected by the council, and are to be exhibited publicly in front of the tribal heroes for anyone who wishes to inspect and handed over to the magistrates during this month. [84] The laws being handed over are to be examined first by the council and the five hundred nomothetae elected by the demesmen, after they have taken the oath; also any individual who wishes is to be permitted to come before the council and give any good advice he can about the laws. When the laws have been passed, the council of the Areopagus is to take care of the laws, so that the magistrates may employ the established laws. Those laws which are being ratified are to be inscribed on the wall,

ἀναγράφειν εἰς τὸν τοῖχον, ἵνα περ πρότερον ἀνεγράφησαν, σκοπεῖν τῷ βουλομένῳ.

[85] Ἐδοκιμάσθησαν μὲν οὖν οἱ νόμοι, ὦ ἄνδρες, κατὰ τὸ ψήφισμα τουτί, τοὺς δὲ κυρωθέντας ἀνέγραψαν εἰς τὴν στοάν. ἐπειδὴ ἀνεγράφησαν, ἐθέμεθα νόμον, ᾧ πάντες χρῆσθε. καί μοι ἀνάγνωθι τὸν νόμον.

ΝΟΜΟΣ. Ἀγράφῳ δὲ νόμῳ τὰς ἀρχὰς μὴ χρῆσθαι μηδὲ περὶ ἑνός.

[86] Ἆρά γε ἔστιν οὕτως ὅ τι περιελείπετο περὶ ὅτου οἷόν τε ἢ ἀρχὴν εἰσάγειν ἢ ὑμῶν πρᾶξαί τινι, ἀλλ' ἢ κατὰ τοὺς ἀναγεγραμμένους νόμους; ὅπου οὖν δὴ ἀγράφῳ νόμῳ οὐκ ἔξεστι χρήσασθαι, ἢ που ἀγράφῳ γε ψηφίσματι παντάπασιν οὐ δεῖ γε χρήσασθαι. ἐπειδὴ τοίνυν ἑωρῶμεν ὅτι πολλοῖς τῶν πολιτῶν εἶεν συμφοραί, τοῖς μὲν κατὰ νόμους, τοῖς δὲ κατὰ ψηφίσματα τὰ πρότερον γενόμενα, τουτουσὶ τοὺς νόμους ἐθέμεθα, αὐτῶν εἵνεκα τῶν νυνὶ ποιουμένων, ἵνα τούτων μηδὲν γίγνηται μηδὲ ἐξῇ συκοφαντεῖν μηδενί. καί μοι ἀνάγνωθι τοὺς νόμους.

[87] ΝΟΜΟΙ. Ἀγράφῳ δὲ νόμῳ τὰς ἀρχὰς μὴ χρῆσθαι μηδὲ περὶ ἑνός. ψήφισμα δὲ μηδὲν μήτε βουλῆς μήτε δήμου νόμου κυριώτερον εἶναι. μηδὲ ἐπ' ἀνδρὶ νόμον ἐξεῖναι θεῖναι, ἐὰν μὴ τὸν αὐτὸν ἐπὶ πᾶσιν Ἀθηναίοις, ἐὰν μὴ ἑξακισχιλίοις δόξῃ κρύβδην ψηφιζομένοις.

Τί οὖν ἦν ἐπίλοιπον; οὑτοσὶ ὁ νόμος. καί μοι ἀνάγνωθι τοῦτον.

<ΝΟΜΟΣ.> Τὰς δὲ δίκας καὶ τὰς διαίτας κυρίας εἶναι, ὁπόσαι ἐν δημοκρατουμένῃ τῇ πόλει ἐγένοντο· τοῖς δὲ νόμοις χρῆσθαι ἀπ' Εὐκλείδου ἄρχοντος.

[88] Τὰς μὲν δίκας, ὦ ἄνδρες, καὶ τὰς διαίτας ἐποιήσατε κυρίας εἶναι, ὁπόσαι ἐν δημοκρατουμένῃ <τῇ> πόλει ἐγένοντο, ὅπως μήτε χρεῶν ἀποκοπαὶ εἶεν μήτε δίκαι ἀνάδικοι γίγνοιντο, ἀλλὰ τῶν ἰδίων συμβολαίων αἱ πράξεις εἶεν· τῶν δὲ δημοσίων, <ἐφ'> ὁπόσοις ἢ γραφαί εἰσιν ἢ φάσεις ἢ ἐνδείξεις ἢ ἀπαγωγαί, τούτων ἕνεκα τοῖς νόμοις ἐψηφίσασθε χρῆσθαι ἀπ' Εὐκλείδου ἄρχοντος. [89] ὁπότ' οὖν ἔδοξεν ὑμῖν δοκιμάσαι μὲν τοὺς νόμους, δοκιμάσαντας δὲ ἀναγράψαι, ἀγράφῳ δὲ νόμῳ τὰς ἀρχὰς μὴ χρῆσθαι μηδὲ περὶ ἑνός, ψήφισμα δὲ <μηδὲν> μήτε βουλῆς μήτε δήμου <νόμου> κυριώτερον εἶναι, μηδ' ἐπ' ἀνδρὶ νόμον τιθέναι, ἐὰν

where they were previously inscribed, for anyone who wishes to inspect.

[85] The laws were therefore examined, gentlemen, in accordance with this decree, and the ones ratified were inscribed in the stoa. When they had been inscribed, we passed a law which you all employ. Please read the law.

LAW. Magistrates are not under any circumstances to employ an unwritten law.

[86] This being so, is there anything which was left over about which it is possible either for a magistrate to bring a case into court or for any of you to take action, except in accordance with the inscribed laws? When, therefore, it is not permitted to employ an unwritten law, then *a fortiori* it is certainly not right at all to employ an unwritten decree. Since, then, we saw that a large number of citizens were suffering misfortunes, some on account of laws and others on account of decrees enacted previously, we passed the following laws to guard against the very things now being done, so that nothing of this kind should happen and nobody should be able to make false accusations. Please read the laws.

[87] LAWS. Magistrates are not under any circumstances to employ an unwritten law. No decree either of the council or of the people is to override a law. It is not to be permitted that any law be passed with reference to an individual, if the same law does not apply to all Athenians, unless it is passed by a secret vote of six thousand.

What, then, was remaining? This law. Please read it.

<LAW.> All judgments and arbitrations are to be valid which were given in the city under the democracy; but the laws are to be employed from the archonship of Eucleides.

[88] You enacted, gentlemen, that all the judgments and arbitrations which were given in the city under the democracy were valid, so that there might be neither cancellations of debts nor the retrying of suits, but that agreements between individuals might be carried out; but for all public offences, which are dealt with by public prosecutions, indictments, denunciations or summary arrests, for these you voted that the laws be employed from the archonship of Eucleides. [89] When you decided to examine the laws, and having examined them to inscribe them, and that magistrates are not under any circumstances to employ an unwritten law, that no decree either of the council or of the people is to override a law, that no law is to be passed with reference to an individual, if the same law does not

μὴ τὸν αὐτὸν ἐπὶ πᾶσιν Ἀθηναίοις, τοῖς δὲ νόμοις τοῖς κειμένοις χρῆσθαι ἀπ' Εὐκλείδου ἄρχοντος, ἐνταυθοῖ ἔστιν ὅ τι ὑπολείπεται ἢ μεῖζον ἢ ἔλαττον τῶν γενομένων πρότερον ψηφισμάτων πρὶν Εὐκλείδην ἄρξαι, ὅπως κύριον ἔσται; οὐκ οἶμαι ἔγωγε, ἄνδρες. σκοπεῖτε δὲ καὶ αὐτοί.

[90] Φέρε δὴ τοίνυν, οἱ ὅρκοι ὑμῖν πῶς ἔχουσιν; ὁ μὲν κοινὸς τῇ πόλει ἁπάσῃ, ὃν ὀμωμόκατε πάντες μετὰ τὰς διαλλαγάς· "Καὶ οὐ μνησικακήσω τῶν πολιτῶν οὐδενὶ πλὴν τῶν τριάκοντα καὶ τῶν ἕνδεκα, οὐδὲ τούτων ὃς ἂν ἐθέλῃ εὐθύνας διδόναι τῆς ἀρχῆς ἧς ἦρξεν." ὅπου τοίνυν αὐτοῖς τοῖς τριάκοντα ὤμνυτε μὴ μνησικακήσειν, τοῖς μεγίστων κακῶν αἰτίοις, εἰ διδοῖεν εὐθύνας, ἦ που σχολῇ τῶν γε ἄλλων πολιτῶν τινι ἠξιοῦτε μνησικακεῖν. [91] ἡ δὲ βουλὴ αὖ ἡ ἀεὶ βουλεύουσα τί ὄμνυσι; "Καὶ οὐ δέξομαι ἔνδειξιν οὐδὲ ἀπαγωγὴν ἕνεκα τῶν πρότερον γεγενημένων, πλὴν τῶν φυγόντων." ὑμεῖς δ' αὖ, ὦ Ἀθηναῖοι, τί ὀμόσαντες δικάζετε; "Καὶ οὐ μνησικακήσω οὐδὲ ἄλλῳ πείσομαι, ψηφιοῦμαι δὲ κατὰ τοὺς κειμένους νόμους." ἃ χρὴ σκοπεῖν, εἰ δοκῶ ὀρθῶς ὑμῖν λέγειν ὡς ὑπὲρ ὑμῶν λέγω καὶ τῶν νόμων.

[92] Σκέψασθε τοίνυν, ὦ ἄνδρες, καὶ τοὺς νόμους καὶ τοὺς κατηγόρους, τί αὐτοῖς ὑπάρχον ἑτέρων κατηγοροῦσι. Κηφίσιος μὲν οὑτοσὶ πριάμενος ὠνὴν ἐκ τοῦ δημοσίου, τὰς ἐκ ταύτης ἐπικαρπίας τῶν ἐν τῇ γῇ γεωργούντων ἐνενήκοντα μνᾶς ἐκλέξας, οὐ κατέβαλε τῇ πόλει, καὶ ἔφυγεν· εἰ γὰρ ἦλθεν, ἐδέδετ' ἂν ἐν τῷ ξύλῳ. [93] ὁ γὰρ νόμος οὕτως εἶχε· κυρίαν εἶναι τὴν βουλήν, ὃς ἂν πριάμενος τέλος μὴ καταβάλῃ, δεῖν εἰς τὸ ξύλον. οὗτος τοίνυν, ὅτι τοῖς νόμοις ἐψηφίσασθε ἀπ' Εὐκλείδου ἄρχοντος χρῆσθαι, ἀξιοῖ ἃ ἔχει ὑμῶν ἐκλέξας μὴ ἀποδοῦναι· καὶ νῦν γεγένηται ἀντὶ μὲν φυγάδος πολίτης, ἀντὶ δὲ ἀτίμου συκοφάντης, ὅτι τοῖς νόμοις τοῖς νῦν κειμένοις χρῆσθε.

[94] Μέλητος δ' αὖ οὑτοσὶ ἀπήγαγεν ἐπὶ τῶν τριάκοντα Λέοντα, ὡς ὑμεῖς ἅπαντες ἴστε, καὶ ἀπέθανεν ἐκεῖνος ἄκριτος. καὶ οὗτος ὁ νόμος καὶ πρότερον ἦν <καὶ> ὡς καλῶς ἔχων καὶ νῦν ἔστι καὶ χρῆσθε αὐτῷ· τὸν βουλεύσαντα ἐν τῷ αὐτῷ ἐνέχεσθαι καὶ τὸν τῇ χειρὶ ἐργασάμενον. Μέλητον τοίνυν τοῖς παισὶ τοῖς τοῦ Λέοντος οὐκ ἔστι φόνου διώκειν, ὅτι τοῖς νόμοις δεῖ χρῆσθαι ἀπ'

apply to all Athenians, and to employ the established laws from the archonship of Eucleides, is there anything there left remaining either greater or lesser than the decrees enacted previous to Eucleides' archonship that can be valid? I for one do not think so, gentlemen. But consider it also for yourselves.

[90] Well then, your oaths, how do they go? The one which is common to the whole city, which you all swore after the reconciliations: "And I shall not recall grievances against any citizens except the Thirty and the Eleven, and not even against any of these who is willing to render account of the office he conducted." When, then, you swore not to recall grievances even against the Thirty, the ones responsible for extreme evils, if they rendered account of their office, surely you could scarcely have thought it right to recall grievances against any of the other citizens. [91] Again, what is the oath of the council that holds office at any given time? "And I will not allow any denunciation or summary arrest arising out of past events, except in the case of those who fled." Again, what is your oath, Athenians, before you give judgment? "And I will not recall grievances nor will I do so at another's bidding, but I will vote according to the established laws." You must consider these oaths, to see whether you think I am right when I tell you that I am speaking on behalf of you and the laws.

[92] Moreover, gentlemen, consider my accusers in relation to the laws, what their own position is when they accuse others. Cephisius here bought a tax-collection privilege from the treasury, but after collecting the revenues from this of ninety minas from the farmers of the land concerned, he did not pay the money due to the city and fled. If he had come to Athens, he would have been put in the stocks. [93] For the law was this: the council is to have the power to put in the stocks anyone who has bought a tax and defaulted on payment. This man, then, because you voted that the laws be employed from the archonship of Eucleides, thinks himself entitled not to pay the money he has which he collected from you. He has now become a citizen instead of an exile, a false accuser instead of a man disfranchised, because you are enforcing the laws now established.

[94] Again, Meletus here arrested Leon under the Thirty, as you all know, and Leon was put to death without trial. Yet the following law not only was in force previously because it is a good one, but also is in force today and you employ it: the person planning a deed is to be liable to the same punishment as the one actually carrying it out. So Meletus cannot be prosecuted for murder by Leon's sons simply because the laws must be

Εὐκλείδου ἄρχοντος, ἐπεὶ ὥς γε οὐκ ἀπήγαγεν οὐδ' αὐτὸς ἀντιλέγει.

[95] Ἐπιχάρης δ' οὑτοσί, ὁ πάντων πονηρότατος καὶ βουλόμενος εἶναι τοιοῦτος, ὁ μνησικακῶν αὐτὸς αὑτῷ - οὗτος γὰρ ἐβούλευεν ἐπὶ τῶν τριάκοντα· ὁ δὲ νόμος τί κελεύει, ὃς ἐν τῇ στήλῃ ἔμπροσθέν ἐστι τοῦ βουλευτηρίου; ὃς ἂν ἄρξῃ ἐν τῇ πόλει ⸱τῆς δημοκρατίας καταλυθείσης, νηποινεὶ τεθνάναι, καὶ τὸν ἀποκτείναντα ὅσιον εἶναι καὶ τὰ χρήματα ἔχειν τοῦ ἀποθανόντος. ἄλλο τι οὖν, ὦ Ἐπίχαρες, ἢ νῦν ὁ ἀποκτείνας σε καθαρὸς τὰς χεῖρας ἔσται κατά γε τὸν Σόλωνος νόμον; [96] καί μοι ἀνάγνωθι τὸν νόμον τὸν ἐκ τῆς στήλης.

ΝΟΜΟΣ. Ἔδcξε τῇ βουλῇ καὶ τῷ δήμῳ· Αἰαντὶς ἐπρυτάνευε, Κλειγένης ἐγραμμάτευε, Βοηθὸς ἐπεστάτει. τάδε Δημόφαντος συνέγραψεν. ἄρχει χρόνος τοῦδε τοῦ ψηφίσματος ἡ βουλὴ οἱ πεντακόσιοι λαχόντες τῷ κυάμῳ, οἷς Κλειγένης πρῶτος ἐγραμμάτευεν.

Ἐάν τις δημοκρατίαν καταλύῃ τὴν Ἀθήνησιν, ἢ ἀρχήν τινα ἄρχῃ καταλελυμένης τῆς δημοκρατίας, πολέμιος ἔστω Ἀθηναίων καὶ νηποινεὶ τεθνάτω, καὶ τὰ χρήματα αὐτοῦ δημόσια ἔστω, καὶ τῆς θεοῦ τὸ ἐπιδέκατον· ὁ δὲ ἀποκτείνας τὸν ταῦτα ποιήσαντα καὶ ὁ συμβουλεύσας ὅσιος ἔστω καὶ εὐαγής. [97] ὀμόσαι δ' Ἀθηναίους ἅπαντας καθ' ἱερῶν τελείων κατὰ φυλὰς καὶ κατὰ δήμους, ἀποκτενεῖν τὸν ταῦτα ποιήσαντα. ὁ δὲ ὅρκος ἔστω ὅδε· "Κτενῶ <καὶ λόγῳ καὶ ἔργῳ καὶ ψήφῳ καὶ> τῇ ἐμαυτοῦ χειρί, ἂν δυνατὸς ὦ, ὃς ἂν καταλύσῃ τὴν δημοκρατίαν τὴν Ἀθήνησι, καὶ ἐάν τις ἄρξῃ τιν' ἀρχὴν καταλελυμένης τῆς δημοκρατίας τὸ λοιπόν, καὶ ἐάν τις τυραννεῖν ἐπαναστῇ ἢ τὸν τύραννον συγκαταστήσῃ. καὶ ἐάν τις ἄλλος ἀποκτείνῃ, ὅσιον αὐτὸν νομιῶ εἶναι καὶ πρὸς θεῶν καὶ δαιμόνων, ὡς πολέμιον κτείναντα τὸν Ἀθηναίων, καὶ τὰ κτήματα τοῦ ἀποθανόντος πάντα ἀποδόμενος ἀποδώσω τὰ ἡμίσεα τῷ ἀποκτείναντι [καὶ λόγῳ καὶ ἔργῳ καὶ ψήφῳ], καὶ οὐκ ἀποστερήσω οὐδέν. [98] ἐὰν δέ τις κτείνων τινὰ τούτων ἀποθάνῃ ἢ ἐπιχειρῶν, εὖ ποιήσω αὐτόν τε καὶ τοὺς παῖδας τοὺς ἐκείνου, καθάπερ Ἀρμόδιόν τε καὶ Ἀριστογείτονα καὶ τοὺς

employed from the archonship of Eucleides, when not even Meletus himself denies that he in fact made the arrest.

[95] Then Epichares here, the lowest of the low and proud of it, a man who even recalls grievances of his own making - for this man was a member of the council under the Thirty, but what does the law which is on the stele in front of the council-chamber prescribe? Anyone who holds office in the city after the overthrow of the democracy is to be killed with impunity, and his killer is to be free from guilt and is to keep the property of the dead man. So is it not the case, Epichares, that he who kills you today will have untainted hands, at least according to Solon's law? [96] Please read the law from the stele.

> LAW. The council and the people resolved; the Aeantis tribe were presidents, Cleigenes was secretary, Boethus was chairman. Demophantus drew up the following enactment. The commencement date of this decree is the council of five hundred appointed by lot for whom Cleigenes was the first secretary.

> If anyone overthrows the democracy at Athens or holds any office after the democracy has been overthrown, he shall be an enemy of the Athenians and shall be killed with impunity, and his property shall be confiscated and a tenth part of it given to the Goddess; and he who kills the man who has done this or helps plan the killing shall be pure and free from guilt. [97] All Athenians are to swear over unblemished sacrifices by tribes and by demes to kill the man who has done this. The oath shall be as follows: "I shall kill, by word and deed and vote and my own hand, if I can, anyone who overthrows the democracy at Athens and anyone who holds any office in the future, after the democracy has been overthrown, and anyone who sets himself up to be tyrant or helps to set up the tyrant. And if anyone else kills the man, I shall consider him to be pure in the eyes of both gods and spirits, because he has killed an enemy of the Athenians, and I shall sell all the property of the dead man and give half to the killer, and I shall not hold any back. [98] And if anyone dies in killing or attempting to kill any such man, I shall care for both him and his children, just as for Harmodius and Aristogeiton and their

ἀπογόνους αὐτῶν. ὁπόσοι δὲ ὅρκοι ὀμώμονται
'Αθήνησιν ἢ ἐν τῷ στρατοπέδῳ ἢ ἄλλοθί που
ἐναντίοι τῷ δήμῳ τῷ 'Αθηναίων, λύω καὶ ἀφίημι."
ταῦτα δὲ ὀμοσάντων 'Αθηναῖοι πάντες καθ' ἱερῶν
τελείων, τὸν νόμιμον ὅρκον, πρὸ Διονυσίων· καὶ
ἐπεύχεσθαι εὐορκοῦντι μὲν εἶναι πολλὰ καὶ ἀγαθά,
ἐπιορκοῦντι δ' ἐξώλη αὐτὸν εἶναι καὶ γένος.

[99] Πότερον, ὦ συκοφάντα καὶ ἐπίτριπτον κίναδος, κύριος ὁ
νόμος ὅδε ἐστὶν ἢ οὐ κύριος; διὰ τοῦτο δ' οἶμαι γεγένηται ἄκυρος,
ὅτι τοῖς νόμοις δεῖ χρῆσθαι ἀπ' Εὐκλείδου ἄρχοντος. καὶ σὺ ζῇς
καὶ περιέρχῃ τὴν πόλιν ταύτην, οὐκ ἄξιος ὤν· ὃς ἐν δημοκρατίᾳ
μὲν συκοφαντῶν ἔζης, ἐν ὀλιγαρχίᾳ δέ, ὡς μὴ ἀναγκασθείης τὰ
χρήματα ἀποδοῦναι ὅσα συκοφαντῶν ἔλαβες, ἐδούλευες τοῖς
τριάκοντα. [100] εἶτα σὺ περὶ ἑταιρείας ἐμοὶ μνείαν ποιῇ καὶ
κακῶς τινας λέγεις; ὃς ἑνὶ μὲν οὐχ ἡταίρησας (καλῶς γὰρ ἄν σοι
εἶχε), πραττόμενος δ' οὐ πολὺ ἀργύριον τὸν βουλόμενον ἀνθρώπων,
ὡς οὗτοι ἴσασιν, ἐπὶ τοῖς αἰσχίστοις ἔργοις ἔζης, καὶ ταῦτα
οὕτως μοχθηρὸς ὢν τὴν ἰδέαν. ἀλλ' ὅμως οὗτος ἑτέρων ἐτόλμα
κατηγορεῖν, ᾧ κατὰ τοὺς νόμους τοὺς ὑμετέρους οὐδ' αὐτῷ ὑπὲρ
αὑτοῦ ἔστιν ἀπολογεῖσθαι.

[101] 'Αλλὰ γάρ, ὦ ἄνδρες, καθήμενος ἡνίκα μου κατηγόρει,
βλέπων εἰς αὐτόν, οὐδὲν ἄλλο ἢ ὑπὸ τῶν τριάκοντα συνειλημμένος
ἔδοξα κρίνεσθαι. εἰ γὰρ τότε ἠγωνιζόμην, τίς ἄν μου κατηγόρει;
οὐχ οὗτος ὑπῆρχεν, εἰ μὴ ἐδίδουν ἀργύριον; καὶ γὰρ νῦν. ἀνέκρινε
δ' ἄν με τίς ἄλλος ἢ Χαρικλῆς, ἐρωτῶν, "Εἰπέ μοι, ὦ 'Ανδοκίδη,
ἦλθες εἰς Δεκέλειαν, καὶ ἐπετείχισας τῇ πατρίδι τῇ σεαυτοῦ;"
"Οὐκ ἔγωγε." "Τί δέ; ἔτεμες τὴν χώραν, καὶ ἐλῄσω ἢ κατὰ γῆν ἢ
κατὰ θάλατταν τοὺς πολίτας τοὺς σεαυτοῦ;" "Οὐ δῆτα." "Οὐδ'
ἐναυμάχησας ἐναντία τῇ πόλει, οὐδὲ συγκατέσκαψας τὰ τείχη,
οὐδὲ συγκατέλυσας τὸν δῆμον, οὐδὲ βίᾳ κατῆλθες εἰς τὴν πόλιν;"
"Οὐδὲν τούτων πεποίηκα." "Οὐδέν; δοκεῖς οὖν χαιρήσειν ἢ οὐκ
ἀποθανεῖσθαι, ὡς ἕτεροι πολλοί;" [102] ἆρ' <ἂν> οἴεσθε, ὦ ἄνδρες,
ἄλλων τινῶν τυχεῖν με δι' ὑμᾶς, εἰ ἐλήφθην ὑπ' αὐτῶν; οὐκ οὖν
δεινόν, εἰ ὑπὸ μὲν τούτων διὰ τοῦτ' ἂν ἀπωλόμην, ὅτι εἰς τὴν
πόλιν οὐδὲν ἥμαρτον, ὥσπερ καὶ ἑτέρους ἀπέκτειναν, ἐν ὑμῖν δὲ
κρινόμενος, οὓς οὐδὲν κακὸν πεποίηκα, οὐ σωθήσομαι; πάντως
δήπου· ἢ σχολῇ γέ τις ἄλλος ἀνθρώπων.

descendants. And all oaths that have been sworn at Athens or in the camp or anywhere else against the people of Athens I declare null and void." All Athenians shall swear this oath over unblemished sacrifices, in the customary manner, before the Dionysia, and they are to pray that he who keeps his oath may have many blessings, but he who breaks it may suffer destruction, himself and his family.

[99] Now, you false accuser and practised rogue, is this law valid or not? I think it has become invalid for this reason, that the laws must be employed from the archonship of Eucleides. You are alive and walking around this city, though you do not deserve to do so; you, who under the democracy lived by making false accusations and under the oligarchy, to avoid having to give up the money you made from making false accusations, were a slave to the Thirty. [100] And you mention association to me and speak badly of people? You, who did not associate with one man alone (that would be all right) but charged any man who wanted to very little, as the court knows, and lived on the foulest vice, and this despite your ugly appearance. But nevertheless this man still dared to accuse others, when according to your laws he does not even have the right to defend himself.

[101] Further, gentlemen, as I sat while he made his prosecution speech against me and as I looked at him, I felt as if I had been arrested and put on trial by none other than the Thirty. If I had been contesting a case at that time, who would have prosecuted me? Would not this man have been there, ready to do it had I not offered him money? Yes, as he is today too. Who but Charicles would have examined me before the trial, asking, "Tell me, Andocides, did you go to Decelea and fortify it against your own country?" "I did not." "Well, did you ravage Athens' territory and plunder your fellow-Athenians by land or by sea?" "Not at all." "You did not fight at sea against the city or help to demolish its walls or help to overthrow the democracy or return forcibly to the city?" "I have done none of these things." "None? Then do you expect to get away with it, or not suffer the fate of many others?" [102] Do you think, gentlemen, that I would have suffered any other treatment because of my loyalty to you if I had been captured by them? Is it not then a terrible thing if I would have been put to death by these people, as they indeed killed others, for doing nothing harmful to the city, but when on trial before you, to whom I have done nothing wrong, I should not be acquitted? Of course I should be, otherwise scarcely could any other man be.

[103] Ἀλλὰ γάρ, ὦ ἄνδρες, τὴν μὲν ἔνδειξιν ἐποιήσαντό μου κατὰ νόμον κείμενον, τὴν δὲ κατηγορίαν κατὰ τὸ ψήφισμα τὸ πρότερον γεγενημένον περὶ ἑτέρων. εἰ οὖν ἐμοῦ καταψηφιεῖσθε, ὁρᾶτε μὴ οὐκ ἐμοὶ μάλιστα τῶν πολιτῶν προσήκει λόγον δοῦναι τῶν γεγενημένων, ἀλλὰ πολλοῖς ἑτέροις μᾶλλον, τοῦτο μὲν οἷς ὑμεῖς ἐναντία μαχεσάμενοι διηλλάγητε καὶ ὅρκους ὠμόσατε, τοῦτο δὲ οὓς φεύγοντας κατηγάγετε, τοῦτο δὲ οὓς ἀτίμους ὄντας ἐπιτίμους ἐποιήσατε· ὧν εἵνεκα καὶ στήλας ἀνείλετε καὶ νόμους ἀκύρους ἐποιήσατε καὶ ψηφίσματα ἐξηλείψατε· οἳ νυνὶ μένουσιν ἐν τῇ πόλει πιστεύοντες ὑμῖν, ὦ ἄνδρες. [104] εἰ οὖν γνώσονται ὑμᾶς ἀποδεχομένους τὰς κατηγορίας τῶν πρότερον γεγενημένων, τίνα αὐτοὺς οἴεσθε γνώμην ἕξειν περὶ σφῶν αὐτῶν; ἢ τίνα αὐτῶν ἐθελήσειν εἰς ἀγῶνα καθίστασθαι ἕνεκα τῶν πρότερον γεγενημένων; φανήσονται γὰρ πολλοὶ μὲν ἐχθροὶ πολλοὶ δὲ συκοφάνται, οἳ καταστήσουσιν αὐτῶν ἕκαστον εἰς ἀγῶνα. [105] ἥκουσι δὲ νυνὶ ἀκροασόμενοι ἀμφότεροι, οὐ τὴν αὐτὴν γνώμην ἔχοντες ἀλλήλοις, ἀλλ᾿ οἱ μὲν εἰσόμενοι εἰ χρὴ πιστεύειν τοῖς νόμοις τοῖς κειμένοις καὶ τοῖς ὅρκοις οὓς ὠμόσατε ἀλλήλοις, οἱ δὲ ἀποπειρώμενοι τῆς ὑμετέρας γνώμης, εἰ αὐτοῖς ἐξέσται ἀδεῶς συκοφαντεῖν καὶ γράφεσθαι, τοὺς δὲ ἐνδεικνύναι, τοὺς δὲ ἀπάγειν. οὕτως οὖν ἔχει, ὦ ἄνδρες· ὁ μὲν ἀγὼν ἐν τῷ σώματι τῷ ἐμῷ καθέστηκεν, ἡ δὲ ψῆφος ἡ ὑμετέρα δημοσίᾳ κρινεῖ πότερον χρὴ τοῖς νόμοις τοῖς ὑμετέροις πιστεύειν, ἢ τοὺς συκοφάντας παρασκευάζεσθαι, ἢ φεύγειν αὐτοὺς ἐκ τῆς πόλεως καὶ ἀπιέναι ὡς τάχιστα.

[106] Ἵνα δὲ εἰδῆτε, ὦ ἄνδρες, ὅτι τὰ πεποιημένα ὑμῖν εἰς ὁμόνοιαν οὐ κακῶς ἔχει, ἀλλὰ τὰ προσήκοντα καὶ τὰ συμφέροντα ὑμῖν αὐτοῖς ἐποιήσατε, βραχέα βούλομαι καὶ περὶ τούτων εἰπεῖν. οἱ γὰρ πατέρες οἱ ὑμέτεροι γενομένων τῇ πόλει κακῶν μεγάλων, ὅτε οἱ τύραννοι μὲν εἶχον τὴν πόλιν, ὁ δὲ δῆμος ἔφευγε, νικήσαντες μαχόμενοι τοὺς τυράννους ἐπὶ Παλληνίῳ, στρατηγοῦντος Λεωγόρου τοῦ προπάππου τοῦ ἐμοῦ καὶ Χαρίου, οὗ ἐκεῖνος τὴν θυγατέρα εἶχεν, ἐξ ἧς ὁ ἡμέτερος ἦν πάππος, κατελθόντες εἰς τὴν πατρίδα τοὺς μὲν ἀπέκτειναν, τῶν δὲ φυγὴν κατέγνωσαν, τοὺς δὲ μένειν ἐν τῇ πόλει ἐάσαντες ἠτίμωσαν. [107] ὕστερον δὲ ἡνίκα βασιλεὺς ἐπεστράτευσεν ἐπὶ τὴν Ἑλλάδα, γνόντες τῶν συμφορῶν τῶν ἐπιουσῶν τὸ μέγεθος καὶ τὴν παρασκευὴν τὴν βασιλέως, ἔγνωσαν τούς τε φεύγοντας καταδέξασθαι καὶ τοὺς ἀτίμους ἐπιτίμους ποιῆσαι καὶ κοινὴν τήν τε σωτηρίαν καὶ τοὺς κινδύνους ποιήσασθαι. πράξαντες δὲ ταῦτα, καὶ δόντες ἀλλήλοις πίστεις καὶ

[103] Further, gentlemen, they made the denunciation against me according to the established law but the charge according to the decree previously enacted about others. So if you vote to condemn me, consider that it may be fitting not for me in particular to give an account of past events but rather for many other citizens, firstly the ones whom you fought against and with whom you were reconciled and swore oaths, secondly those in exile whom you restored and finally those whom you re-enfranchised when disfranchised. It was for their sakes that you removed stelae and made laws invalid and obliterated decrees; and they remain in the city today because they trust you, gentlemen. [104] So if they learn that you are allowing prosecutions for what has happened in the past, what do you think will be their inclination concerning themselves? Will any of them want to stand trial for what has happened in the past? For many enemies and many false accusers will appear, who will bring every one of them to trial. [105] Both sides have come today to listen, but not with the same inclination as one another: some in order to know whether they should trust the existing laws and the oaths which you swore to one another, others in order to make trial of your inclination, to see if they will be able without fear to accuse falsely and make public prosecutions, to lodge denunciations and make summary arrests. This is the case, gentlemen; the trial is concerned with my life, but your vote will decide for the public as a whole whether they should trust your laws or suborn the false accusers or flee from them and leave the city as quickly as possible.

[106] So that you may know, gentlemen, that the actions you took for unity have not been a failure, but you acted in a way both appropriate and advantageous to yourselves, I wish to say a few things also about these matters. After great troubles had befallen the city, when the tyrants were ruling the city and the democrats were in exile, your forefathers defeated the tyrants in battle near the temple at Pallenium, under the generalship of Leogoras my great-grandfather and Charias, whose daughter he married from whom was born my grandfather; then returning to their own country, they killed some, condemned others to exile and allowed others still to remain in the city, but disfranchised them. [107] Later, when the King of Persia invaded Greece, realising the size of the impending disasters and the King's armament, they decided to recall exiles, re-enfranchise the disfranchised, and make safety and dangers common to all. When they had

ὅρκους μεγάλους, ἠξίουν σφᾶς αὐτοὺς προτάξαντες πρὸ τῶν Ἑλλήνων ἁπάντων ἀπαντῆσαι τοῖς βαρβάροις Μαραθῶνάδε, νομίσαντες τὴν σφετέραν αὐτῶν ἀρετὴν ἱκανὴν εἶναι τῷ πλήθει τῷ ἐκείνων ἀντιτάξασθαι· μαχεσάμενοί τε ἐνίκων, καὶ τήν τε Ἑλλάδα ἠλευθέρωσαν καὶ τὴν πατρίδα ἔσωσαν. [108] ἔργον δὲ τοιοῦτον ἐργασάμενοι οὐκ ἠξίωσάν τινι τῶν πρότερον γενομένων μνησικακῆσαι. τοιγάρτοι διὰ ταῦτα, τὴν πόλιν ἀνάστατον παραλαβόντες ἱερά τε κατακεκαυμένα τείχη τε καὶ οἰκίας καταπεπτωκυίας, ἀφορμήν τε οὐδεμίαν ἔχοντες, διὰ τὸ ἀλλήλοις ὁμονοεῖν τὴν ἀρχὴν τῶν Ἑλλήνων κατηργάσαντο καὶ τὴν πόλιν ὑμῖν τοιαύτην καὶ τοσαύτην παρέδοσαν. [109] ὑμεῖς οὖν καὶ αὐτοὶ ὕστερον, κακῶν οὐκ ἐλαττόνων ἢ ἐκείνοις γεγενημένων, ἀγαθοὶ ἐξ ἀγαθῶν ὄντες ἀπέδοτε τὴν ὑπάρχουσαν ἀρετήν· ἠξιώσατε γὰρ τούς τε φεύγοντας καταδέξασθαι καὶ τοὺς ἀτίμους ἐπιτίμους ποιῆσαι. τί οὖν ὑμῖν ὑπόλοιπόν ἐστι τῆς ἐκείνων ἀρετῆς; μὴ μνησικακῆσαι, εἰδότας, ὦ ἄνδρες, ὅτι ἡ πόλις ἐκ πολὺ ἐλάττονος ἀφορμῆς ἐν τῷ ἔμπροσθεν χρόνῳ μεγάλη καὶ εὐδαίμων ἐγένετο· ἃ νῦν αὐτῇ ὑπάρχει, εἰ ἐθέλοιμεν οἱ πολῖται σωφρονεῖν τε καὶ ὁμονοεῖν ἀλλήλοις.

[110] Κατηγόρησαν δέ μου καὶ περὶ τῆς ἱκετηρίας, ὡς καταθείην ἐγὼ ἐν τῷ Ἐλευσινίῳ, νόμος δ' εἴη πάτριος, ὃς ἂν θῇ ἱκετηρίαν μυστηρίοις, τεθνάναι. καὶ οὕτως εἰσὶ τολμηροί, ὥσθ' ἃ αὐτοὶ κατεσκεύασαν, οὐκ ἀρκεῖ αὐτοῖς ὅτι οὐ κατέσχον ἃ ἐπεβούλευσαν, ἀλλὰ καὶ κατηγορίαν ἐμοῦ ποιοῦνται ὡς ἀδικοῦντος. [111] ἐπειδὴ γὰρ ἤλθομεν Ἐλευσινόθεν καὶ ἡ ἔνδειξις ἐγεγένητο, προσῄει ὁ βασιλεὺς περὶ τῶν γεγενημένων Ἐλευσῖνι κατὰ τὴν τελετήν, ὥσπερ ἔθος ἐστίν· οἱ δὲ πρυτάνεις προσάξειν ἔφασαν αὐτὸν πρὸς τὴν βουλήν, ἐπαγγεῖλαί τ' ἐκέλευον ἐμοί τε καὶ Κηφισίῳ παρεῖναι εἰς τὸ Ἐλευσίνιον. (ἡ γὰρ βουλὴ ἐκεῖ καθεδεῖσθαι ἔμελλε κατὰ τὸν Σόλωνος νόμον, ὃς κελεύει τῇ ὑστεραίᾳ τῶν μυστηρίων ἕδραν ποιεῖν ἐν τῷ Ἐλευσινίῳ.) [112] καὶ παρῆμεν κατὰ τὰ προειρημένα. καὶ ἡ βουλὴ ἐπειδὴ ἦν πλήρης, ἀναστὰς Καλλίας ὁ Ἱππονίκου τὴν σκευὴν ἔχων λέγει ὅτι ἱκετηρία κεῖται ἐπὶ τοῦ βωμοῦ, καὶ ἔδειξεν αὐτοῖς. κᾆθ' ὁ κῆρυξ ἐκήρυττε τίς τὴν ἱκετηρίαν καταθείη, καὶ οὐδεὶς ὑπήκουε. ἡμεῖς δὲ παρέσταμεν, καὶ οὗτος ἡμᾶς ἑώρα. ἐπειδὴ δὲ οὐδεὶς ὑπήκουεν, καὶ ᾤχετο εἰσιὼν ἐπεξελθὼν Εὐκλῆς οὑτοσί · καί μοι κάλει αὐτόν. πρῶτα μὲν οὖν ταῦτα εἰ ἀληθῆ λέγω μαρτύρησον, Εὔκλεις.

done this, and exchanged pledges and solemn oaths, they resolved to put themselves as a defence in front of all the Greeks and meet the barbarians at Marathon, considering that their own valour was sufficient to set against the large numbers of the enemy. They fought and conquered, and they freed Greece and saved their own country. [108] After doing such a deed they did not think it right to recall grievances over any past events. It was for this very reason that, receiving the city back devastated, its temples burnt down and its walls and houses fallen down, and with no resources whatsoever, through this living together in unity they acquired sovereignty over the Greeks and handed down to you this great and glorious city. [109] You yourselves later, when troubles no less than those had befallen you, as fine sons of fine fathers showed your own virtue, by deciding to recall exiles and re-enfranchise the disfranchised. What, then, is there remaining for you before you match their virtue? Not to recall grievances, remembering, gentlemen, that in earlier time the city became great and prosperous from far fewer resources. This is possible for it today, if we, its citizens, were willing to show self-control and live together in unity.

[110] They also accused me in connection with the olive-branch, that it was I who placed it in the Eleusinium, but there is an ancestral law that whoever lays an olive-branch at the time of the Mysteries is to be put to death. They are so bold that with a crime which they themselves contrived, it is not enough for them that they did not accomplish what they were plotting, but they even accuse me of being guilty of it. [111] When we returned from Eleusis and the denunciation had been lodged, the basileus came to report about the performance of the ritual at Eleusis, as is customary. The prytaneis said that they would bring him before the council, and ordered him to notify me and Cephisius to attend at the Eleusinium. (The council was to sit there in accordance with Solon's law, which prescribes that it hold a sitting in the Eleusinium on the day after the Mysteries.) [112] We appeared according to instructions. When the council was full, Callias, son of Hipponicus, stood up wearing his official dress and said that an olive-branch had been laid on the altar, and he showed it to them. The herald then called for the person who placed the olive-branch, and nobody responded. Yet we were standing close by, and Callias could see us. When nobody responded, and Eucles here went off inside again after making the enquiry - please call him. Give evidence as to whether I am telling the truth in this first of all, Eucles.

<MAPTYPIA>

[113] Ὡς μὲν ἀληθῆ λέγω μεμαρτύρηται· πολὺ δέ μοι δοκεῖ τὸ ἐναντίον εἶναι ἢ <ὃ> οἱ κατήγοροι εἶπον. ἔλεξαν γάρ, εἰ μέμνησθε, ὅτι αὐτώ με τὼ θεὼ περιαγάγοιεν ὥστε θεῖναι τὴν ἱκετηρίαν μὴ εἰδότα τὸν νόμον, ἵνα δῶ δίκην. ἐγὼ δέ, ὦ ἄνδρες, εἰ ὡς μάλιστα ἀληθῆ λέγουσιν οἱ κατήγοροι, ὑπ᾽ αὐτοῖν μέν φημι τοῖν θεοῖν σεσῶσθαι· [114] εἰ γὰρ ἔθηκα μὲν τὴν ἱκετηρίαν, ὑπήκουσα δὲ μή, ἄλλο τι ἢ αὐτὸς μὲν αὐτὸν ἀπώλλυον τιθεὶς τὴν ἱκετηρίαν, ἐσῳζόμην δὲ τῇ τύχῃ διὰ τὸ μὴ ὑπακοῦσαι, δηλονότι διὰ τὼ θεώ; εἰ γὰρ ἐβουλέσθην με ἀπολλύναι τὼ θεώ, ἐχρῆν δήπου καὶ μὴ θέντα με τὴν ἱκετηρίαν ὁμολογῆσαι. ἀλλ᾽ οὔτε ὑπήκουσα οὔτ᾽ ἔθηκα.

[115] Ἐπειδὴ δ᾽ ἔλεγε τῇ βουλῇ Εὐκλῆς ὅτι οὐδεὶς ὑπακούοι, πάλιν ὁ Καλλίας ἀναστὰς ἔλεγεν ὅτι εἴη νόμος πάτριος, εἴ τις ἱκετηρίαν θείη ἐν τῷ Ἐλευσινίῳ, ἄκριτον ἀποθανεῖν, καὶ ὁ πατήρ ποτ᾽ αὐτοῦ Ἱππόνικος ἐξηγήσατο ταῦτα Ἀθηναίοις, ἀκούσειε δὲ ὅτι ἐγὼ θείην τὴν ἱκετηρίαν. ἐντεῦθεν ἀναπηδᾷ Κέφαλος οὑτοσὶ καὶ λέγει· [116] "Ὦ Καλλία, πάντων ἀνθρώπων ἀνοσιώτατε, πρῶτον μὲν ἐξηγῇ Κηρύκων ὤν, οὐχ ὅσιον <ὂν> σοι ἐξηγεῖσθαι· ἔπειτα δὲ νόμον πάτριον λέγεις, ἡ δὲ στήλη παρ᾽ ᾗ ἕστηκας χιλίας δραχμὰς κελεύει ὀφείλειν, ἐάν τις ἱκετηρίαν θῇ ἐν τῷ Ἐλευσινίῳ. ἔπειτα δὲ τίνος ἤκουσας ὅτι Ἀνδοκίδης θείη τὴν ἱκετηρίαν; κάλεσον αὐτὸν τῇ βουλῇ, ἵνα καὶ ἡμεῖς ἀκούσωμεν." ἐπειδὴ δὲ ἀνεγνώσθη ἡ στήλη κἀκεῖνος οὐκ εἶχεν εἰπεῖν ὅτου ἤκουσεν, καταφανὴς ἦν τῇ βουλῇ αὐτὸς θεὶς τὴν ἱκετηρίαν.

[117] Φέρε δὴ τοίνυν, ὦ ἄνδρες, (τάχα γὰρ ἂν αὐτὸ βούλοισθε πυθέσθαι) ὁ δὲ Καλλίας τί βουλόμενος ἐτίθει τὴν ἱκετηρίαν; ἐγὼ δὲ ὑμῖν διηγήσομαι ὧν ὑπ᾽ αὐτοῦ εἵνεκα ἐπεβουλεύθην. Ἐπίλυκος ἦν ὁ Τεισάνδρου θεῖός μοι, ἀδελφὸς τῆς μητρὸς τῆς ἐμῆς· ἀπέθανε δὲ ἐν Σικελίᾳ ἄπαις ἀρρένων παίδων, θυγατέρας δὲ δύο καταλιπών, αἳ ἐγίγνοντο εἴς τε ἐμὲ καὶ Λέαγρον. [118] τὰ δὲ πράγματα τὰ οἴκοι πονήρως εἶχε· τὴν μὲν γὰρ φανερὰν οὐσίαν οὐδὲ δυοῖν ταλάντοιν κατέλιπε, τὰ δὲ ὀφειλόμενα πλέον ἦν ἢ πέντε τάλαντα. ὅμως δ᾽ ἐγὼ καλέσας Λέαγρον ἐναντίον τῶν φίλων ἔλεγον ὅτι ταῦτ᾽ εἴη ἀνδρῶν ἀγαθῶν, ἐν τοῖς τοιούτοις δεικνύναι τὰς οἰκειότητας ἀλλήλοις. [119] "Ἡμᾶς γὰρ οὐ δίκαιόν ἐστιν οὔτε χρήματα ἕτερα οὔτ᾽ εὐτυχίαν ἀνδρὸς

<EVIDENCE>

[113] Evidence has been given that I am telling the truth; and it seems to me that the truth is completely the opposite to what my accusers said. They said, if you remember, that the two goddesses themselves confused me into laying the olive-branch in ignorance of the law, so that I be punished. I, gentlemen, contend on the contrary that, even if my accusers are telling the absolute truth, I was saved by the two goddesses themselves. [114] Suppose I did lay the olive-branch but did not respond, was it not I myself who was destroying myself by laying the olive-branch, and was I not saved by the chance of my not responding, which was clearly due to the two goddesses? If the two goddesses had wanted to destroy me, I ought, of course, to have confessed, even if I had not laid the olive-branch. Yet neither did I respond nor did I lay it.

[115] When Eucles told the council that nobody had responded, Callias stood up again and said that there is an ancestral law that whoever lays an olive-branch in the Eleusinium is to be put to death without trial; also that his father Hipponicus had once given this interpretation to the Athenians, and he had heard that it was I who had laid the olive-branch. Thereupon Cephalus here leapt up and said, [116] "Callias, most impious of all men, first you are giving interpretations as one of the Ceryces, when it is not permitted for you to give interpretations; and then you talk of an ancestral law when the stele by which you are standing prescribes a fine of a thousand drachmas for anyone who lays an olive-branch in the Eleusinium. Finally, from whom did you hear that Andocides laid the olive-branch? Call him for the council, so that we too may hear." When the stele was read and Callias could not say where he heard it, it was clear to the council that he had laid the olive-branch himself.

[117] Well then, gentlemen, (perhaps you would like to know this) what was Callias' motive in laying the olive-branch? I shall describe to you in full the reasons why he plotted against me. Epilycus, son of Teisander, was my uncle, my mother's brother. He died in Sicily without male children but leaving two daughters, who were due to come into the charge of myself and Leagrus. [118] His financial affairs were in a bad state: he left visible property worth less than two talents, but his debts were more than five talents. Nevertheless, I summoned Leagrus and said in front of the members of the family that it was the duty of decent men in such circumstances to display friendly relations to each other. [119] "It is not right for us to prefer another estate or a successful man, and so look down on Epilycus' daughters.

ἑλέσθαι, ὥστε καταφρονῆσαι τῶν Ἐπιλύκου θυγατέρων. καὶ γὰρ εἰ ἔζη Ἐπίλυκος ἢ τεθνεὼς πολλὰ κατέλιπε χρήματα, ἠξιοῦμεν ἂν γένει ὄντες ἐγγυτάτω ἔχειν τὰς παῖδας. τοιγάρτοι ἐκεῖνα μὲν δι᾽ Ἐπίλυκον ἂν ἦν ἢ διὰ τὰ χρήματα· νῦν δὲ διὰ τὴν ἡμετέραν ἀρετὴν τάδε ἔσται. τῆς μὲν οὖν σὺ ἐπιδικάζου, τῆς δὲ ἐγώ." [120] ὡμολόγησέ μοι, ὦ ἄνδρες. ἐπεδικασάμεθα ἄμφω κατὰ τὴν πρὸς ἡμᾶς ὁμολογίαν. καὶ ἧς μὲν ἐγὼ ἐπεδικασάμην, ἡ παῖς τύχῃ χρησαμένη καμοῦσα ἀπέθανεν· ἡ δ᾽ ἑτέρα ἔστιν ἔτι. ταύτην Καλλίας ἔπειθε Λέαγρον χρήματα ὑπισχνούμενος ἐὰν αὐτὸν λαβεῖν. αἰσθόμενος δ᾽ ἐγὼ εὐθὺς ἔθηκα παράστασιν καὶ ἔλαχον προτέρῳ μὲν Λεάγρῳ, <λέγων> ὅτι "Εἰ μὲν σὺ βούλει ἐπιδικάζεσθαι, ἔχε τύχῃ ἀγαθῇ· εἰ δὲ μή, ἐγὼ ἐπιδικάσομαι." [121] γνοὺς ταῦτα Καλλίας λαγχάνει τῷ υἱεῖ τῷ ἑαυτοῦ τῆς ἐπικλήρου τῇ δεκάτῃ ἱσταμένου, ἵνα μὴ ἐπιδικάσωμαι ἐγώ. ταῖς δ᾽ εἰκάσι, μυστηρίοις τούτοις, δοὺς Κηφισίῳ χιλίας δραχμὰς ἐνδείκνυσί με καὶ εἰς τὸν ἀγῶνα τοῦτον καθίστησιν. ἐπειδὴ δ᾽ ἑώρα με ὑπομένοντα, τίθησι τὴν ἱκετηρίαν, ὡς ἐμὲ μὲν ἀποκτενῶν ἄκριτον ἢ ἐξελῶν, αὐτὸς δὲ πείσας Λέαγρον χρήμασι συνοικήσων τῇ Ἐπιλύκου θυγατρί. [122] ἐπειδὴ δ᾽ <οὐδ᾽> οὕτως ἄνευ ἀγῶνος ἑώρα ἐσόμενα τὰ πράγματα, τότε δὴ προσιὼν Λυσίστρατον, Ἡγήμονα, Ἐπιχάρην, ὁρῶν φίλους ὄντας ἐμοὶ καὶ χρωμένους, εἰς τοῦτο βδελυρίας ἦλθε καὶ παρανομίας, ὥστ᾽ ἔλεγε πρὸς τούτους ὡς εἰ ἔτι καὶ νῦν βουλοίμην ἀποστῆναι τῆς Ἐπιλύκου θυγατρός, ἕτοιμος εἴη παύσασθαί με κακῶς ποιῶν, ἀπαλλάξαι δὲ Κηφίσιον, δίκην δ᾽ ἐν τοῖς φίλοις δοῦναί μοι τῶν πεποιημένων. [123] εἶπον αὐτῷ καὶ κατηγορεῖν καὶ παρασκευάζειν ἄλλους· "Εἰ δ᾽ ἐγὼ αὐτὸν ἀποφεύξομαι καὶ γνώσονται Ἀθηναῖοι περὶ ἐμοῦ τὰ δίκαια, ἐγὼ αὐτὸν οἶμαι περὶ τοῦ σώματος τοῦ ἑαυτοῦ ἐν τῷ μέρει κινδυνεύσειν." ἅπερ αὐτὸν οὐ ψεύσομαι, ἐὰν ὑμῖν, ὦ ἄνδρες, δοκῇ. ὡς δ᾽ ἀληθῆ λέγω, κάλει μοι τοὺς μάρτυρας.

ΜΑΡΤΥΡΕΣ

[124] Ἀλλὰ γὰρ τὸν υἱὸν αὐτοῦ τοῦτον, ᾧ λαχεῖν ἠξίωσε τῆς Ἐπιλύκου θυγατρός, σκέψασθε πῶς γέγονε καὶ πῶς ἐποιήσατ᾽ αὐτόν· ταῦτα γὰρ καὶ ἄξιον ἀκοῦσαι, ὦ ἄνδρες. γαμεῖ μὲν Ἰσχομάχου θυγατέρα· ταύτῃ δὲ συνοικήσας οὐδ᾽ ἐνιαυτὸν τὴν μητέρα αὐτῆς ἔλαβε, καὶ συνῴκει ὁ πάντων σχετλιώτατος ἀνθρώπων τῇ μητρὶ καὶ τῇ θυγατρί, ἱερεὺς ὢν τῆς Μητρὸς καὶ τῆς

For after all, if Epilycus were alive or when he died had left a large estate, we would be expecting to claim the girls as their next of kin. In that case, then, we would have claimed them because of Epilycus or his estate, and now we shall claim them because of our virtue. So you enter a claim for the one, and I for the other." [120] He agreed, gentlemen. We did both enter claims according to our agreement. Now, the girl I claimed happened to fall ill and died, but the other is still alive. Callias tried to persuade Leagrus to let him take this one by promising money. When I heard of this, however, I immediately deposited a fee and firstly obtained leave to bring a case against Leagrus, saying "If you wish to continue the claim, keep her and good luck; if not, I shall enter a claim myself." [121] Learning this, Callias obtained leave to claim the heiress for his own son on the tenth of the month, in order to prevent me from obtaining her; and soon after the twentieth, during these last Mysteries, he gave Cephisius a thousand drachmas, had a denunciation lodged against me and brought me to this trial. When he saw that I was staying to face trial, he laid the olive-branch, in order to secure my death without trial or my banishment and to live with Epilycus' daughter himself after bribing Leagrus. [122] When he saw that he would not achieve his objective even in this way without a fight, he approached Lysistratus, Hegemon and Epichares, who he saw were my friends and associates, and sank to such a level of contempt for decency and the law as to say to them that if I was finally willing even now to give up Epilycus' daughter, he was ready to stop molesting me, to call off Cephisius and to give me compensation for what had been done in accordance with the decision of my friends. [123] I told him to go ahead both with his prosecution and with procuring others. "If I escape him and the Athenians return a just verdict in my case, I think that he will be in danger of his own life in his turn." With your permission, gentlemen, I shall not disappoint him in this. Please call the witnesses that I am telling the truth.

WITNESSES

[124] Further, consider this son of his, for whom he resolved to obtain leave to claim Epilycus' daughter, how he was born and how he acknowledged him: for this is also worth hearing, gentlemen. Callias married a daughter of Ischomachus, but he had not even lived with her for a year before he took up with her mother; and he, the most wicked of all men, lived with the mother and the daughter, when a priest of the Mother and the

78

θυγατρός, καὶ εἶχεν ἐν τῇ οἰκίᾳ ἀμφοτέρας. [125] καὶ οὗτος μὲν οὐκ ᾐσχύνθη οὐδ' ἔδεισε τὼ θεώ· ἡ δὲ τοῦ Ἰσχομάχου θυγάτηρ τεθνάναι νομίσασα λυσιτελεῖν ἢ ζῆν ὁρῶσα τὰ γιγνόμενα, ἀπαγχομένη μεταξὺ κατεκλίθη, καὶ ἐπειδὴ ἀνεβίω ἀποδρᾶσα ἐκ τῆς οἰκίας ᾤχετο, καὶ ἐξήλασεν ἡ μήτηρ τὴν θυγατέρα. ταύτης δ' αὖ διαπεπλησμένος ἐξέβαλε καὶ ταύτην. ἡ δ' ἔφη κυεῖν ἐξ αὐτοῦ· καὶ ἐπειδὴ ἔτεκεν υἱόν, ἔξαρνος ἦν μὴ εἶναι ἐξ αὐτοῦ τὸ παιδίον. [126] λαβόντες δὲ οἱ προσήκοντες τῇ γυναικὶ τὸ παιδίον ἧκον ἐπὶ τὸν βωμὸν Ἀπατουρίοις ἔχοντες ἱερεῖον, καὶ ἐκέλευον κατάρξασθαι τὸν Καλλίαν. ὁ δ' ἠρώτα τίνος εἴη τὸ παιδίον· ἔλεγον "Καλλίου τοῦ Ἱππονίκου." "Ἐγώ εἰμι οὗτος." "Καὶ ἔστι γε σὸν τὸ παιδίον." λαβόμενος τοῦ βωμοῦ ὤμοσεν ἦ μὴν μὴ εἶναί <οἱ> υἱὸν ἄλλον μηδὲ γενέσθαι πώποτε, εἰ μὴ Ἱππόνικον ἐκ τῆς Γλαύκωνος θυγατρός, ἢ ἐξώλη εἶναι καὶ αὐτὸν καὶ τὴν οἰκίαν - ὥσπερ ἔσται. [127] μετὰ ταῦτα τοίνυν, ὦ ἄνδρες, ὑστέρῳ πάλιν χρόνῳ τῆς γραὸς τολμηροτάτης γυναικὸς ἀνηράσθη, καὶ κομίζεται αὐτὴν εἰς τὴν οἰκίαν καὶ τὸν παῖδα ἤδη μέγαν ὄντα εἰσάγει εἰς Κήρυκας, φάσκων εἶναι υἱὸν αὐτοῦ. ἀντεῖπε μὲν Καλλικλῆς μὴ εἰσδέξασθαι, ἐψηφίσαντο δὲ οἱ Κήρυκες κατὰ τὸν νόμον ὅς ἐστιν αὐτοῖς, τὸν πατέρα ὀμόσαντα εἰσάγειν ἦ μὴν υἱὸν ὄντα ἑαυτοῦ εἰσάγειν. λαβόμενος τοῦ βωμοῦ ὤμοσεν ἦ μὴν τὸν παῖδα ἑαυτοῦ εἶναι γνήσιον, ἐκ Χρυσίλλης γεγονότα· ὃν <πρότερον> ἀπώμοσε. καί μοι τούτων ἁπάντων τοὺς μάρτυρας κάλει.

<ΜΑΡΤΥΡΕΣ>

[128] Φέρε δὴ τοίνυν, ὦ ἄνδρες, σκεψώμεθα εἰ πώποτε ἐν τοῖς Ἕλλησι πρᾶγμα τοιοῦτον ἐγένετο, ὅπου γυναῖκά τις γήμας ἐπέγημε τῇ θυγατρὶ τὴν μητέρα καὶ ἐξήλασεν ἡ μήτηρ τὴν θυγατέρα· ταύτῃ δὲ συνοικῶν βούλεται τὴν Ἐπιλύκου θυγατέρα λαβεῖν, ἵν' ἐξελάσῃ τὴν τήθην ἡ θυγατριδῆ. ἀλλὰ γὰρ τῷ παιδὶ αὐτοῦ τί χρὴ τοὔνομα θέσθαι; [129] οἶμαι γὰρ ἔγωγε οὐδένα οὕτως ἀγαθὸν εἶναι λογίζεσθαι, ὅστις ἐξευρήσει τοὔνομα αὐτοῦ. τριῶν γὰρ οὐσῶν γυναικῶν αἷς συνῳκηκὼς ἔσται ὁ πατὴρ αὐτοῦ, τῆς μὲν υἱός ἐστιν, ὥς φησι, τῆς δὲ ἀδελφός, τῆς δὲ θεῖος. τίς ἂν εἴη οὗτος; Οἰδίπους, ἢ Αἴγισθος; ἢ τί χρὴ αὐτὸν ὀνομάσαι;

[130] Ἀλλὰ γάρ, ὦ ἄνδρες, βραχύ τι ὑμᾶς ἀναμνῆσαι περὶ Καλλίου βούλομαι. εἰ γὰρ μέμνησθε, ὅτε ἡ πόλις ἦρχε τῶν Ἑλλήνων καὶ εὐδαιμόνει μάλιστα, Ἱππόνικος δὲ ἦν πλουσιώτατος

Daughter, and kept them both in his house. [125] He felt no shame, nor did he fear the two goddesses, but Ischomachus' daughter thought it better to be dead than alive and seeing what was happening, and tried to hang herself, but before she succeeded was taken down and put to bed. When she recovered, she ran away from the house, and the mother drove out the daughter. When he in turn had had enough of the mother, he threw her out too. She then said she was pregnant by him, but when she gave birth to a son, he denied that the child was his. [126] The woman's relatives took the child and came to the altar at the Apaturia with a sacrificial victim, then ordered Callias to begin the ceremony. He asked whose child it was, they said, "Of Callias, son of Hipponicus." "I am he." "Yes, and it is your child." Grasping the altar, he swore that he truly did not have, nor had ever had any son other than Hipponicus, whose mother was Glaucon's daughter, or let utter destruction fall both on himself and his family - as it will. [127] Now, some time after this, gentlemen, he fell in love again with the old battleaxe, and he both received her back into his house and introduced the boy, by now a grown lad, to the Ceryces, declaring he was his son. Callicles spoke against his admission, but the Ceryces voted according to the law by which they abide, that the father who swears he is introducing a son who is truly his own may introduce him. Grasping the altar, he swore that the boy truly was lawfully begotten of himself, born of Chrysilla - the one he previously disowned on oath. Please call the witnesses to all this.

<WITNESSES>

[128] Well then, gentlemen, let us consider whether such a thing has ever happened before among the Greeks, that a man married a woman, then married the mother in addition to the daughter, and the mother drove out the daughter; then, while living with the mother, he wants to take the daughter of Epilycus, so that the granddaughter can drive out the grandmother. Further, what on earth should we call his son? [129] I myself do not think there is anybody so good at reasoning as to work out his name. For there are three women with whom his father will have lived, and he is the son of one, so it is said, brother of another and uncle of the third. Who would he be himself? Oedipus or Aegisthus, or what should we call him?

[130] Further, gentlemen, I wish to remind you of a small matter concerning Callias. If you remember, when our city ruled the Greeks and was at the peak of its prosperity, and Hipponicus was the wealthiest of the

τῶν Ἑλλήνων, τότε μέντοι πάντες ἴστε ὅτι παρὰ τοῖς παιδαρίοις τοῖς μικροτάτοις καὶ τοῖς γυναίοις κληδὼν ἐν ἁπάσῃ τῇ πόλει κατεῖχεν, ὅτι Ἱππόνικος ἐν τῇ οἰκίᾳ ἀλιτήριον τρέφει ὃς αὐτοῦ τὴν τράπεζαν ἀνατρέπει. [131] μέμνησθε ταῦτα, ὦ ἄνδρες. πῶς οὖν ἡ φήμη ἡ τότε οὖσα δοκεῖ ὑμῖν ἀποβῆναι; οἰόμενος γὰρ Ἱππόνικος υἱὸν τρέφειν ἀλιτήριον αὑτῷ ἔτρεφεν, ὃς ἀνατέτροφεν ἐκείνου τὸν πλοῦτον, τὴν σωφροσύνην, τὸν ἄλλον βίον ἅπαντα. οὕτως οὖν χρὴ περὶ τούτου γιγνώσκειν, ὡς ὄντος Ἱππονίκου ἀλιτηρίου.

[132] Ἀλλὰ γάρ, ὦ ἄνδρες, διὰ τί ποτε τοῖς ἐμοὶ νυνὶ ἐπιτιθεμένοις μετὰ Καλλίου καὶ συμπαρασκευάσασι τὸν ἀγῶνα καὶ χρήματα εἰσενεγκοῦσιν ἐπ' ἐμοὶ τρία μὲν ἔτη ἐπιδημῶν καὶ ἥκων ἐκ Κύπρου οὐκ ἀσεβεῖν ἐδόκουν αὐτοῖς, μυῶν μὲν Ἀ<...> Δελφόν, ἔτι δὲ ἄλλους ξένους ἐμαυτοῦ, καὶ εἰσιὼν εἰς τὸ Ἐλευσίνιον καὶ θύων, ὥσπερ ἐμαυτὸν ἄξιον νομίζω εἶναι; ἀλλὰ τοὐναντίον λῃτουργεῖν οὗτοι προὐβάλλοντο, πρῶτον μὲν γυμνασίαρχον Ἡφαιστίοις, ἔπειτα ἀρχιθέωρον εἰς Ἰσθμὸν καὶ Ὀλυμπίαζε, εἶτα δὲ ταμίαν ἐν πόλει τῶν ἱερῶν χρημάτων· νῦν δὲ ἀσεβῶ καὶ ἀδικῶ εἰσιὼν εἰς τὰ ἱερά;

[133] Ἐγὼ ὑμῖν ἐρῶ διότι οὗτοι ταῦτα νῦν γιγνώσκουσιν. Ἀγύρριος γὰρ οὑτοσὶ ὁ καλὸς κἀγαθὸς ἀρχώνης ἐγένετο τῆς πεντηκοστῆς τρίτον ἔτος, καὶ ἐπρίατο τριάκοντα ταλάντων, μετέσχον δ' αὐτῷ οὗτοι πάντες οἱ παρασυλλεγέντες ὑπὸ τὴν λεύκην, οὓς ὑμεῖς ἴστε οἷοί εἰσιν· οἳ διὰ τοῦτο ἔμοιγε δοκοῦσι συλλεγῆναι ἐκεῖσε, ἵν' αὐτοῖς ἀμφότερα ᾖ, καὶ μὴ ὑπερβάλλουσι λαβεῖν ἀργύριον καὶ ὀλίγου πραθείσης μετασχεῖν. [134] κερδάναντες δὲ τρία τάλαντα, γνόντες τὸ πρᾶγμα οἷον εἴη, ὡς πολλοῦ ἄξιον, συνέστησαν πάντες, καὶ μεταδόντες τοῖς ἄλλοις ἐωνοῦντο πάλιν τριάκοντα ταλάντων. ἐπεὶ δ' οὐκ ἀντωνεῖτο οὐδείς, παρελθὼν ἐγὼ εἰς τὴν βουλὴν ὑπερέβαλλον, ἕως ἐπριάμην ἓξ καὶ τριάκοντα ταλάντων. ἀπελάσας δὲ τούτους καὶ καταστήσας ὑμῖν ἐγγυητὰς ἐξέλεξα τὰ χρήματα καὶ κατέβαλον τῇ πόλει, καὶ αὐτὸς οὐκ ἐζημιώθην, ἀλλὰ καὶ βραχέα ἀπεκερδαίνομεν οἱ μετασχόντες· τούτους δ' ἐποίησα τῶν ὑμετέρων μὴ διανείμασθαι ἓξ τάλαντα ἀργυρίου. [135] ἃ οὗτοι γνόντες ἔδοσαν σφίσιν αὐτοῖς λόγον, ὅτι "Ἄνθρωπος οὑτοσὶ οὔτε αὐτὸς λήψεται τῶν κοινῶν χρημάτων οὔθ' ἡμᾶς ἐάσει, φυλάξει δὲ καὶ ἐμποδὼν ἔσται διανείμασθαι τὰ κοινά· πρὸς δὲ τούτοις ὃν ἂν ἡμῶν ἀδικοῦντα λάβῃ εἰσάξει εἰς τὸ πλῆθος τὸ Ἀθηναίων καὶ ἀπολεῖ. δεῖ οὖν τοῦτον ἐκποδὼν ἡμῖν εἶναι καὶ

Greeks, well, at that time you all know that there was a rumour prevalent throughout the city among the tiniest young children and weak women, that Hipponicus was rearing an evil spirit in his house which was upsetting his balance. [131] You remember this, gentlemen. How, then, do you think the saying current at that time turned out? Hipponicus thought he was rearing a son, but he was actually rearing for himself an evil spirit, which has upset his wealth, his self-control, his whole way of life. This, therefore, is how we should think of this man, as being Hipponicus' evil spirit.

[132] Further, gentlemen, why was it that those who are now attacking me along with Callias, who have joined with him in preparing the trial and have contributed money to deal with me, that they never thought I was guilty of impiety during the three years I have been home since returning from Cyprus, even though I initiated A... from Delphi and other friends of mine from abroad, and even though I entered the Eleusinium and offered sacrifices, as I consider myself entitled to do? On the contrary, these men kept proposing me for public services, first as gymnasiarch at the festival of Hephaestus, then as architheorus at the Isthmian and Olympic games, and also as treasurer of the sacred monies on the Acropolis, but today I am guilty of impiety and am a wrongdoer for entering the temples?

[133] I shall tell you why these men now hold this opinion. Our gentleman friend Agyrrhius here became chief contractor of the two per cent tax two years ago and bought it for thirty talents. All these men, who assembled with him under the poplar tree, were his shareholders, and you know what kind of men they are. I think they met there for this double purpose, to be paid for not outbidding Agyrrhius and to get shares in the privilege sold at a low price. [134] They made a profit of three talents, and realising what the business was like, how profitable it was, they all banded together and, giving shares to the other bidders, tried to buy it again, for thirty talents. Since there was nobody bidding against them, I went myself before the council and kept outbidding them, until I bought it for thirty-six talents. After ousting them and giving you sureties, I collected the money and paid it over to the city; and I myself did not lose by it, but my shareholders and I even managed to make a small profit, and I prevented these people from dividing among themselves six talents of your money. [135] They realised this and deliberated among themselves: "This man will neither take any of the public money himself nor let us do so, but he will stand on guard and prevent us from dividing the state funds among ourselves. In addition, if he catches one of us committing an offence, he will bring him before the Athenian people and destroy him. So he must be got out

δικαίως καὶ ἀδίκως." **[136]** ταῦτα μὲν οὖν, ὦ ἄνδρες δικασταί, τούτοις ποιητέα ἦν, ὑμῖν δέ γε <τὸ> ἐναντίον τούτων. ὡς γὰρ πλείστους εἶναι ὑμῖν ἤθελον ἂν τοιούσδε οἷόσπερ ἐγώ, τούτους δὲ μάλιστα <μὲν> ἀπολωλέναι, εἰ δὲ μή, εἶναι τοὺς μὴ ἐπιτρέψοντας αὐτοῖς· οἷς καὶ προσήκει ἀνδράσιν εἶναι καὶ ἀγαθοῖς καὶ δικαίοις περὶ τὸ πλῆθος τὸ ὑμέτερον, καὶ βουλόμενοι δυνήσονται εὖ ποιεῖν ὑμᾶς. ἐγὼ οὖν ὑμῖν ὑπισχνοῦμαι ἢ παύσειν τούτους ταῦτα ποιοῦντας καὶ βελτίους παρέξειν, ἢ εἰς ὑμᾶς εἰσαγαγὼν κολάσειν τοὺς ἀδικοῦντας αὐτῶν.

[137] Κατηγόρησαν δέ μου καὶ περὶ τῶν ναυκληριῶν καὶ περὶ τῆς ἐμπορίας, ὡς ἄρα οἱ θεοὶ διὰ τοῦτό με ἐκ τῶν κινδύνων σώσαιεν, ἵνα ἐλθὼν δεῦρο, ὡς ἔοικεν, ὑπὸ Κηφισίου ἀπολοίμην. ἐγὼ δέ, ὦ Ἀθηναῖοι, οὐκ ἀξιῶ τοὺς θεοὺς τοιαύτην γνώμην ἔχειν, ὥστ', εἰ ἐνόμιζον ὑπ' ἐμοῦ ἀδικεῖσθαι, λαμβάνοντάς με ἐν τοῖς μεγίστοις κινδύνοις μὴ τιμωρεῖσθαι. τίς γὰρ κίνδυνος μείζων ἀνθρώποις ἢ χειμῶνος ὥρᾳ πλεῖν τὴν θάλατταν; ἐν οἷς ἔχοντες μὲν τὸ σῶμα τοὐμόν, κρατοῦντες δὲ τοῦ βίου καὶ τῆς οὐσίας τῆς ἐμῆς, εἶτα ἔσῳζον; **[138]** οὐκ ἐξῆν αὐτοῖς ποιῆσαι μηδὲ ταφῆς τὸ σῶμα ἀξιωθῆναι; ἔτι δὲ πολέμου γενομένου καὶ τριήρων ἀεὶ κατὰ θάλατταν οὐσῶν καὶ λῃστῶν, ὑφ' ὧν πολλοὶ ληφθέντες, ἀπολέσαντες τὰ ὄντα, δουλεύοντες τὸν βίον διετέλεσαν, οὔσης δὲ χώρας βαρβάρου, εἰς ἣν πολλοὶ ἤδη ἐκπεσόντες αἰκίαις ταῖς μεγίσταις περιέπεσον καὶ τὰ σφέτερα αὐτῶν σώματα αἰκισθέντες ἀπέθανον, **[139]** εἶτα οἱ μὲν θεοὶ ἐκ τοσούτων κινδύνων ἔσῳζόν με, σφῶν δὲ αὐτῶν προὐστήσαντο τιμωρὸν γενέσθαι Κηφίσιον τὸν πονηρότατον Ἀθηναίων, ὃν οὗτός φησι πολίτης εἶναι οὐκ ὤν, ᾧ οὐδ' ὑμῶν τῶν καθημένων οὐδεὶς ἂν ἐπιτρέψειεν οὐδὲν τῶν ἰδίων, εἰδὼς τοῦτον οἷός ἐστιν; ἐγὼ μὲν οὖν, ὦ ἄνδρες, ἡγοῦμαι χρῆναι νομίζειν τοὺς τοιούτους κινδύνους ἀνθρωπίνους, τοὺς δὲ κατὰ θάλατταν θείους. εἴπερ οὖν δεῖ τὰ τῶν θεῶν ὑπονοεῖν, πάνυ ἂν αὐτοὺς οἶμαι ἐγὼ ὀργίζεσθαι καὶ ἀγανακτεῖν εἰ τοὺς ὑφ' ἑαυτῶν σῳζομένους ὑπ' ἄλλων ἀπολλυμένους ὁρῷεν.

[140] Καὶ μὲν δὴ καὶ τάδε ὑμῖν ἄξιον, ὦ ἄνδρες, ἐνθυμηθῆναι, ὅτι νυνὶ πᾶσι τοῖς Ἕλλησιν ἄνδρες ἄριστοι καὶ εὐβουλότατοι δοκεῖτε γεγενῆσθαι, οὐκ ἐπὶ τιμωρίαν τραπόμενοι τῶν γεγενημένων, ἀλλ' ἐπὶ σωτηρίαν τῆς πόλεως καὶ ὁμόνοιαν τῶν πολιτῶν. συμφοραὶ μὲν γὰρ ἤδη καὶ ἄλλοις πολλοῖς ἐγένοντο οὐκ ἐλάττους ἢ καὶ ἡμῖν· τὸ δὲ τὰς γενομένας διαφορὰς πρὸς ἀλλήλους θέσθαι καλῶς, τοῦτ' εἰκότως ἤδη δοκεῖ ἀνδρῶν ἀγαθῶν

of our way by fair means or foul." [136] This then, gentlemen of the jury, was what they had to do, but you, indeed, must do the opposite to this. For I could wish that you have as many men like me as possible, and that these men are preferably destroyed or at least that there be men who will not commit themselves to them. They should also be men who are good and fair in matters concerning your people, and if they wish will be able to serve you well. I myself promise you either to stop these men doing these things and make them better citizens, or to bring before you and punish those of them who are wrongdoers.

[137] They also accused me in connection with my ship-owning and trade, as if the gods saved me from dangers for this reason, that I might come here and, apparently, be destroyed by Cephisius. I myself, Athenians, do not believe that the gods have such an inclination that if they thought they were being wronged by me, when they had me in the greatest dangers, they would not punish me. For what greater danger is there for men than to sail the sea in winter time? When they had my person in such a situation, and my life and property were in their hands, did they save me in spite of that? [138] Was it not possible for them to bring it about that my body should not even be given burial? Besides, war had broken out, there were triremes and pirates constantly at sea, and many men were captured by them and robbed of their possessions, and lived the rest of their lives in slavery. There was also foreign territory, on which many, already having suffered shipwreck, then suffered the most terrible maltreatment, and their very persons were maltreated before they died. [139] Yet in spite of that did the gods save me from such dangers and choose as their avenger Cephisius, the lowest man in Athens, of which he claims to be a citizen when he is not, and to whom not even any of you the judges would entrust any of your affairs, knowing what kind of man he is? No, gentlemen, I myself think that we should consider such legal dangers as human and those at sea as divine. So if we must conjecture about the affairs of the gods, I think myself that they would be exceedingly angry and annoyed if they saw those saved by themselves being destroyed by others.

[140] This is also, indeed, something else worth your bearing in mind, gentlemen, that at present you appear to all the Greeks to be excellent and highly prudent men for not turning to revenge for what has happened, but to the preservation of the city and the unity of its citizens. Misfortunes no less than ours have also befallen many others before now, but the happy reconciliation of existing differences may reasonably be considered still now

καὶ σωφρόνων ἔργον εἶναι. ἐπειδὴ τοίνυν παρὰ πάντων ὁμολογουμένως ταῦθ᾽ ὑμῖν ὑπάρχει, καὶ εἴ τις φίλος ὢν τυγχάνει καὶ εἴ τις ἐχθρός, μὴ μεταγνῶτε, μηδὲ βούλεσθε τὴν πόλιν ἀποστερῆσαι ταύτης τῆς δόξης, μηδὲ αὐτοὶ δοκεῖν τύχῃ ταῦτα μᾶλλον ἢ γνώμῃ ψηφίσασθαι.

[141] Δέομαι οὖν ἁπάντων <ὑμῶν> περὶ ἐμοῦ τὴν αὐτὴν γνώμην ἔχειν, ἥπερ καὶ περὶ τῶν ἐμῶν προγόνων, ἵνα κἀμοὶ ἐγγένηται ἐκείνους μιμήσασθαι, ἀναμνησθέντας αὐτῶν ὅτι ὅμοιοι τοῖς πλείστων καὶ μεγίστων ἀγαθῶν αἰτίοις τῇ πόλει γεγένηνται, πολλῶν ἕνεκεν σφᾶς αὐτοὺς παρέχοντες τοιούτους, μάλιστα δὲ τῆς εἰς ὑμᾶς εὐνοίας, καὶ ὅπως, εἴ ποτέ τις αὐτοῖς ἢ τῶν ἐξ ἐκείνων τινὶ κίνδυνος γένοιτο ἢ συμφορά, σῴζοιντο συγγνώμης παρ᾽ ὑμῶν τυγχάνοντες. [142] εἰκότως δ᾽ ἂν αὐτῶν μεμνῆσθε· καὶ γὰρ τῇ πόλει ἁπάσῃ αἱ τῶν ὑμετέρων προγόνων ἀρεταὶ πλείστου ἄξιαι ἐγένοντο. ἐπειδὴ γάρ, ὦ ἄνδρες, αἱ νῆες διεφθάρησαν, πολλῶν βουλομένων τὴν πόλιν ἀνηκέστοις συμφοραῖς περιβαλεῖν, Λακεδαιμόνιοι ἔγνωσαν ὅμως τότε ἐχθροὶ ὄντες σῴζειν τὴν πόλιν διὰ τὰς ἐκείνων τῶν ἀνδρῶν ἀρετάς, οἳ ὑπῆρξαν τῆς ἐλευθερίας ἁπάσῃ τῇ Ἑλλάδι. [143] ἐπειδὴ τοίνυν καὶ ἡ πόλις ἐσώθη δημοσίᾳ διὰ τὰς τῶν προγόνων τῶν ὑμετέρων ἀρετάς, ἀξιῶ κἀμοὶ διὰ τὰς τῶν προγόνων τῶν ἐμῶν ἀρετὰς σωτηρίαν γενέσθαι. καὶ γὰρ αὐτῶν τῶν ἔργων δι᾽ ἅπερ ἡ πόλις ἐσώθη οὐκ ἐλάχιστον μέρος οἱ ἐμοὶ πρόγονοι συνεβάλοντο· ὧν ἕνεκα καὶ ἐμοὶ δίκαιον ὑμᾶς μεταδοῦναι τῆς σωτηρίας, ἧσπερ καὶ αὐτοὶ παρὰ τῶν Ἑλλήνων ἐτύχετε.

[144] Σκέψασθε τοίνυν καὶ τάδε, ἄν με σώσητε, οἷον ἕξετε πολίτην· ὃς πρῶτον μὲν ἐκ πολλοῦ πλούτου, ὅσον ὑμεῖς ἴστε, οὐ δι᾽ ἐμαυτὸν ἀλλὰ διὰ τὰς τῆς πόλεως συμφορὰς εἰς πενίαν πολλὴν καὶ ἀπορίαν κατέστην, ἔπειτα δὲ καινὸν βίον ἠργασάμην ἐκ τοῦ δικαίου τῇ γνώμῃ καὶ τοῖν χεροῖν τοῖν ἐμαυτοῦ· ἔτι δὲ εἰδότα μὲν οἷόν ἐστι πόλεως τοιαύτης πολίτην εἶναι, εἰδότα δὲ οἷόν ἐστι ξένον εἶναι καὶ μέτοικον ἐν τῇ τῶν πλησίον, [145] ἐπιστάμενον δὲ οἷον τὸ σωφρονεῖν καὶ ὀρθῶς βουλεύεσθαι, ἐπιστάμενον δ᾽ οἷον τὸ ἁμαρτόντα πρᾶξαι κακῶς· <...> πολλοῖς συγγενόμενος καὶ πλείστων πειραθείς, ἀφ᾽ ὧν ἐμοὶ ξενίαι καὶ φιλότητες πρὸς πολλοὺς καὶ βασιλέας καὶ πόλεις καὶ ἄλλους ἰδίᾳ ξένους γεγένηνται, ὧν ἐμὲ σώσαντες μεθέξετε, καὶ ἔστιν ὑμῖν χρῆσθαι τούτοις, ὅπου ἂν ἐν καιρῷ τι ὑμῖν γίγνηται.

the action of good and moderate men. Since, then, it is agreed by everyone that you possess these qualities, both by those who happen to be friends and by those who happen to be enemies, do not change your minds, and do not be willing to deprive the city of this reputation or to appear yourselves to have voted for this by chance rather than by design.

[141] I therefore ask you all to hold the same opinion about me as you hold about my ancestors, so that it may be possible for me to imitate them, and remember that they have equalled those responsible for the most numerous and greatest benefactions to the city. They provided these themselves for many reasons, but especially out of goodwill towards you and in order that, if ever some danger or disaster befell them or any of their descendants, they might be saved by obtaining forgiveness from you. [142] It would indeed be reasonable for you to remember them, just as the valiant exploits of your ancestors came to be of the highest value to the whole city. For when, gentlemen, the fleet was destroyed and many wanted to involve the city in irreparable misfortunes, the Spartans, even though they were enemies at that time, nevertheless decided to spare the city because of the valiant exploits of those men who initiated freedom for the whole of Greece. [143] Since, then, the city as a whole was saved by the valiant exploits of your ancestors, I expect there to be safety for me too because of the valiant exploits of my ancestors. For not the least part of those very deeds by which the city was saved was contributed by my ancestors, and therefore it is right that you give me too a share of the safety which you yourselves obtained from the Greeks.

[144] Now, consider this as well, what kind of citizen you will have, if you acquit me. Firstly, from a position of great wealth, as you know, through no fault of my own but through the misfortunes of the city I was reduced to great poverty and penury, but then I made myself a new livelihood by honest means, with my own wits and with my own two hands. Further, I know what it is to be a citizen of such a city as this, and I know what it is to be a foreigner resident in the lands of neighbouring peoples; [145] and I understand what it is to show self-control and to deliberate soundly, and I understand what it is to suffer for one's mistakes. After meeting with many people and making the acquaintance of even more, from these experiences I have formed ties of hospitality and friendships with many kings and cities and other private individuals, in which you will share, if you acquit me, and it is possible for you to make use of these whenever you have an opportunity.

[146] Ἔχει δὲ καὶ ὑμῖν, ὦ ἄνδρες, οὕτως· ἐάν με νυνὶ διαφθείρητε, οὐκ ἔστιν ὑμῖν ἔτι λοιπὸς τοῦ γένους τοῦ ἡμετέρου οὐδείς, ἀλλ' οἴχεται πᾶν πρόρριζον. καίτοι οὐκ ὄνειδος ὑμῖν ἐστιν ἡ Ἀνδοκίδου καὶ Λεωγόρου οἰκία οὖσα, ἀλλὰ πολὺ μᾶλλον τότ' ἦν ὄνειδος, ὅτ' ἐμοῦ φεύγοντος Κλεοφῶν αὐτὴν ὁ λυροποιὸς ᾤκει. οὐ γὰρ ἔστιν ὅστις πώποτε ὑμῶν παριὼν τὴν οἰκίαν τὴν ἡμετέραν ἀνεμνήσθη ἢ ἰδίᾳ τι ἢ δημοσίᾳ κακὸν παθὼν ὑπ' ἐκείνων, [147] οἳ πλείστας μὲν στρατηγήσαντες στρατηγίας πολλὰ τρόπαια τῶν πολεμίων καὶ κατὰ γῆν καὶ κατὰ θάλατταν ὑμῖν ἀπέδειξαν, πλείστας δὲ ἄλλας ἀρχὰς ἄρξαντες καὶ χρήματα διαχειρίσαντες τὰ ὑμέτερα οὐδὲν πώποτε ὦφλον· οὐδ' ἡμάρτηται οὐδὲν οὔτε ἡμῖν εἰς ὑμᾶς οὔτε ὑμῖν εἰς ἡμᾶς, οἰκία δὲ πασῶν ἀρχαιοτάτη καὶ κοινοτάτη ἀεὶ τῷ δεομένῳ. οὐδ' ἔστιν ὅπου ἐκείνων τις τῶν ἀνδρῶν καταστὰς εἰς ἀγῶνα ἀπήτησεν ὑμᾶς χάριν τούτων τῶν ἔργων. [148] μὴ τοίνυν, εἰ αὐτοὶ τεθνᾶσι, καὶ περὶ τῶν πεπραγμένων αὐτοῖς ἐπιλάθησθε, ἀλλ' ἀναμνησθέντες τῶν ἔργων νομίσατε τὰ σώματα αὐτῶν ὁρᾶν αἰτουμένων ἐμὲ παρ' ὑμῶν σῶσαι. τίνα γὰρ καὶ ἀναβιβάσομαι δεησόμενον ὑπὲρ ἐμαυτοῦ; τὸν πατέρα; ἀλλὰ τέθνηκεν. ἀλλὰ τοὺς ἀδελφούς; ἀλλ' οὐκ εἰσί. ἀλλὰ τοὺς παῖδας; ἀλλ' οὔπω γεγένηνται. [149] ὑμεῖς τοίνυν καὶ ἀντὶ πατρὸς ἐμοὶ καὶ ἀντὶ ἀδελφῶν καὶ ἀντὶ παίδων γένεσθε· εἰς ὑμᾶς καταφεύγω καὶ ἀντιβολῶ καὶ ἱκετεύω· ὑμεῖς με παρ' ὑμῶν αὐτῶν αἰτησάμενοι σώσατε. καὶ μὴ βούλεσθε Θετταλοὺς καὶ Ἀνδρίους πολίτας ποιεῖσθαι δι' ἀπορίαν ἀνδρῶν, τοὺς δὲ ὄντας πολίτας ὁμολογουμένως, οἷς προσήκει ἀνδράσιν ἀγαθοῖς εἶναι καὶ βουλόμενοι δυνήσονται, τούτους δὲ ἀπόλλυτε. μὴ δῆτα. ἔπειτα καὶ ταῦθ' ὑμῶν δέομαι, εὖ ποιῶν ὑμᾶς ὑφ' ὑμῶν τιμᾶσθαι. ὥστ' ἐμοὶ μὲν πειθόμενοι οὐκ ἀποστερεῖσθε εἴ τι ἐγὼ δυνήσομαι ὑμᾶς εὖ ποιεῖν· ἐὰν δὲ τοῖς ἐχθροῖς τοῖς ἐμοῖς πεισθῆτε, οὐδ' ἂν ὑστέρῳ χρόνῳ ὑμῖν μεταμελήσῃ, οὐδὲν ἔτι πλέον ποιήσετε. [150] μὴ τοίνυν μήθ' ὑμᾶς αὐτοὺς τῶν ἀπ' ἐμοῦ ἐλπίδων ἀποστερήσητε μήτ' ἐμὲ τῶν εἰς ὑμᾶς.

Ἀξιῶ δ' ἔγωγε τούτους, οἵτινες ὑμῖν ἀρετῆς ἤδη τῆς μεγίστης εἰς τὸ πλῆθος τὸ ὑμέτερον ἔλεγχον ἔδοσαν, ἀναβάντας ἐνταυθοῖ συμβουλεύειν ὑμῖν ἃ γιγνώσκουσι περὶ ἐμοῦ. δεῦρο, Ἄνυτε, Κέφαλε, ἔτι δὲ καὶ οἱ φυλέται οἱ ᾑρημένοι μοι συνδικεῖν, Θράσυλλος καὶ οἱ ἄλλοι.

[146] Your position, gentlemen, is in fact as follows. If you cause me to perish today, there is not a single member of my family still left to you, but it is completely and utterly destroyed. Yet there is no disgrace to you in the existence of the house of Andocides and Leogoras, far more was there disgrace at the time when I was in exile and Cleophon the lyre-maker lived in it. There is not one of you who ever, on passing by our house, was reminded of any injury he suffered either privately or publicly at the hands of my family, [147] who have held innumerable commands and produced for you many trophies of victory over your enemies both on land and on sea, and who have held innumerable other offices and administered your finances, and never once failed the examination of their term. No wrong has been committed at all, either by us against you or by you against us, but our house is the oldest of all and always very open to anyone in need. There has been no occasion on which any of the family has appeared on trial and demanded any favour of you for these actions. [148] Do not, then, just because they are dead, forget about what they did, but remember their actions and imagine that you see their persons begging you for me, to acquit me. For whom can I bring before you to plead on my behalf? My father? He is dead. My brothers? I have none. My children? They have not yet been born. [149] You, then, act as my father and brothers and children. To you I flee for refuge and make my entreaties and make my supplications; you beg for my life from yourselves and save me. Do not be ready to enfranchise Thessalians and Andrians because of a shortage of manpower and at the same time destroy acknowledged citizens, who should be good men and if they wish will be able to be. Do not do this. Then I also ask this of you, that having served you well, I be held in honour by you. If you are so persuaded by me, you are not depriving yourselves of any good services I shall be able to do you; but if you are persuaded by my enemies, even if you regret this later, you will no longer be able to do anything more than that. [150] So do not deprive yourselves of what you hope to receive from me or me of my hopes in you.

I now ask that these men, who have already given you proof of their outstanding service to your people, come up here and advise you of what they think of me. Come up, Anytus, Cephalus and also you fellow-tribesmen who have been chosen to be my advocates, Thrasyllus and the others.

INTRODUCTION 2: *ON HIS RETURN*

(i) The background and date of the speech

The second speech in the MS. of Andocides is in fact the earliest of the four. Its date, however, cannot be determined with any precision, and indeed every year from 410 to 406 has been suggested. As we have seen, during the investigations into the Mysteries and Hermae affairs Andocides turned informer on the grant of immunity, but the decree of Isotimides made life in Athens so unbearable for him that he withdrew into exile. That this exile was voluntary, not dictated by the terms of the decree, is evidenced by his remarks in **10**, and after an appropriate length of time abroad Andocides began his efforts to return home. The timing of his first attempt was unfortunate, since his bitter enemy Peisander had recently led the oligarchic revolution of the Four Hundred, and Andocides was imprisoned. He was presumably released after the fall of the Four Hundred, and a further period of exile ensued before he made a second attempt to return, the occasion on which this speech was delivered. It must therefore be dated after the collapse of the oligarchic regime in September 411 (cf. **10-16**) and the restoration of the democracy (cf. **26-8**; *Ag. And.* 29), and a considerable time after the battle referred to in **12**, but before the battle of Aegospotami led to the closure of Peiraeus in 405 (cf. **21**). Another clue is that Andocides had secured a consignment of corn for Athens (**19-23**), which suggests that he was trying to secure the repeal of the decree of Isotimides in return for providing corn at a time of shortage.[66] The democracy was not restored until after the battle of Cyzicus (April 410),[67] and if this is the engagement to which Andocides refers, the speech may fall within the period between early 409, when the Spartans' attempt to secure the Bosporus threatened Athens' Black Sea corn route, and the autumn of 408, when control of it was restored by the capture of Byzantium.[68]

(ii) Analysis of the speech

Andocides delivered the *On his Return* before the assembly while making his second attempt to return to Athens. The speech is therefore a *demegoria* and falls under the first of Aristotle's three types of oratory,[69] but being on a private matter it is not strictly a deliberative speech.[70] At first sight the speech seems to be poorly ordered, and to consist of a series of short topics delivered in almost staccato fashion, but closer inspection reveals the following divisions.

---

66 *Contra* MacDowell 4 n. 9.

67 See Rhodes (1981) 415.

68 See in greater detail Maidment 454-8, who suggests late 409 or the first half of 408. MacDowell *ibid.* prefers a time after the return of Alcibiades in 408 or 407. The end of summer 406 was suggested by V. G. Ramírez, 'Sobre la fecha del discurso II de Andócides', *Nova Tellus* 6 (1988) 107-23

69 *Rhet.* 1.3.3 (the categories are deliberative, forensic and epideictic).

70 See Jebb 108-9.

Andocides' opening remarks are extensive (1-9), which is a feature of the oratory we possess from this period.[71] There follows (unusually for deliberative oratory) a section of pure and dramatic narrative, in which Andocides relates his services to Athens' armed forces during his exile and what happened on his first return to the city (10-16). In the proofs section (17-23) Andocides argues that he deserves to be rewarded for his personal expenditure on behalf of the state and his services to it, both past and taking place at that very moment. Finally, the epilogue (24-8) contains an appeal to the Athenians to lay aside their resentment of Andocides in the light of his repentance (his present actions are more befitting his family's record of service to Athens) and lack of ill-will towards them.

It will be apparent from the preceding summary of the speech that Andocides bases his appeal on the services performed by himself and his family on Athens' behalf. This was a commonplace argument in Attic oratory, but it is given a clever twist here. Andocides relates in detail the service he rendered at the time of his first attempt to return (10-12) and gives as an example of his family's service the actions taken on behalf of the democracy by his ancestor Leogoras (26). But when he talks about his present service (16-22) and proudly announces the imminent arrival of ships carrying corn, Andocides mysteriously alludes to another, secret service whose details are only known to members of the council. Having thereby raised the expectations of his audience, Andocides immediately moves on to his request that the assembly grant him in return a small favour (22-3).

Allusiveness and the juxtaposing of greater with lesser (in the above instance benefit for the Athenians with a small favour for Andocides) are a tactic which Andocides also uses to some effect in attempting to assuage his guilt concerning the events of 415. A striking feature of the speech is, indeed, Andocides' readiness to admit his guilt, or rather his past 'mistake'. In the *Mysteries* speech he has to admit to involvement in the mutilation plot because he had subsequently turned informer, but he flatly denies that he has committed impiety (1.58) and only once admits to having done anything wrong (1.145). He is a confident speaker, and his style is dramatic, lively and diffuse. In the *Return* speech, on the other hand, when the events of 415 were fresher in the minds of his audience, Andocides' tone is more humble and remorseful. He speaks plaintively, attempting to arouse pity for the situation in which he finds himself, and his style is correspondingly duller and far more compact, at times even rather abrupt. Nevertheless, Andocides is by no means abject in his remorse, and there are some traces of an aristocratic insolence in his manner of speaking (see below). Furthermore, the allusiveness of the references to his past tempers his admission. He does not in fact mention the Mysteries and Hermae affairs themselves, and this is clearly part of a rhetorical strategy by which Andocides attempts to lessen the importance of his own specific, but vaguely described wrongdoing by placing it within the wider context of human error. Thus, in the proem he talks in general terms of men making a mistake (5-6), then more specifically of himself deserving pity for what has happened (6), and of his youthful folly and act of madness (7). In the narrative he again refers to my own madness (10) and to my disgrace in the eyes of the gods (15), in each case

---

71   See 1.1-10n.

following his admission with how he has paid the penalty, through exile and imprisonment respectively. In the epilogue there is another general reference to **the mistakes which [men] make in their opinions (24)**, followed by the more specific **my mistake then (25)** and **if indeed I happen now at last to have regained my senses (26)**. All this builds to a climax in 27-8, once more with the sequence of general/greater followed by specific/lesser error: the Athenians were persuaded to inflict on themselves **the greatest of wrongs**, for which they were severely punished by the substitution of **domination for democracy**, just as they were persuaded to do Andocides a wrong. His case then seems insignificant in comparison with the overthrow of the democracy.[72]

Andocides, in sum, has produced a carefully constructed piece of rhetoric with the *Return* speech, employing in it a good number of the standard rhetorical devices. But we know that his appeal was unsuccessful. He must have been faced with an uphill struggle to persuade the Athenians at this stage to forgive and forget, and his task will not have been made easier by the insolent tone that has been detected at the beginning of the speech and in 9 and 12.[73] But two other, more telling reasons have been suggested by Missiou 28-49: the aristocratic Andocides failed to convince his audience either that his benefactions were performed out of allegiance to the democracy rather than simply for his personal advantage, or that his ideology was now democratic rather than oligarchic.

---

72   When it comes to performing a service, on the other hand, the private (i.e. specific) one is naturally greater than the public (**17-18**).

73   See Maidment 459; Missiou 26-8.

ΠΕΡΙ ΤΗΣ ΕΑΥΤΟΥ ΚΑΘΟΔΟΥ

[1] Εἰ μέν, ὦ ἄνδρες, ἐν ἑτέρῳ τῳ πράγματι οἱ παριόντες μὴ τὴν αὐτὴν γνώμην ἔχοντες πάντες ἐφαίνοντο, οὐδὲν ἂν θαυμαστὸν ἐνόμιζον· ὅπου μέντοι δεῖ τὴν πόλιν ἐμέ τι ποιῆσαι ἀγαθόν, ἢ εἴ τις ἕτερος βούλοιτο ἐμοῦ κακίων, δεινότατον ἁπάντων χρημάτων ἡγοῦμαι, εἰ τῷ μὲν δοκεῖ ταῦτα τῷ δὲ μή, ἀλλὰ μὴ πᾶσιν ὁμοίως. εἴπερ γὰρ ἡ πόλις ἁπάντων τῶν πολιτευομένων κοινή ἐστι, καὶ τὰ γιγνόμενα δήπου ἀγαθὰ τῇ πόλει κοινά ἐστι. [2] τουτὶ τοίνυν τὸ μέγα καὶ δεινὸν πάρεστιν ὑμῖν ὁρᾶν τοὺς μὲν ἤδη πράττοντας, τοὺς δὲ τάχα μέλλοντας· καί μοι μέγιστον θαῦμα παρέστηκε, τί ποτε οὗτοι οἱ ἄνδρες δεινῶς οὕτως περικαίονται, εἴ τι ὑμᾶς χρὴ ἀγαθὸν ἐμοῦ ἐπαυρέσθαι. δεῖ γὰρ αὐτοὺς ἤτοι ἀμαθεστάτους εἶναι πάντων ἀνθρώπων ἢ τῇ πόλει ταύτῃ δυσμενεστάτους. εἰ μέν γε νομίζουσι τῆς πόλεως εὖ πραττούσης καὶ τὰ ἴδια σφῶν αὐτῶν ἄμεινον ἂν φέρεσθαι, ἀμαθέστατοί εἰσι τὰ ἐναντία νῦν τῇ ἑαυτῶν ὠφελείᾳ σπεύδοντες· [3] εἰ δὲ μὴ ταὐτὰ ἡγοῦνται σφίσι τε αὐτοῖς συμφέρειν καὶ τῷ ὑμετέρῳ κοινῷ, δυσμενεῖς ἂν τῇ πόλει εἶεν· οἵτινες εἰσαγγείλαντός μου ἀπόρρητα εἰς τὴν βουλὴν περὶ τῶν πραγμάτων, ὧν ἀποτελεσθέντων οὐκ εἰσὶ τῇ πόλει ταύτῃ μείζονες ὠφέλειαι, καὶ τούτων ἀποδεικνύντος μου τοῖς βουλευταῖς σαφεῖς τε καὶ βεβαίους τὰς ἀποδείξεις, ἐκεῖ μὲν οὔτε τούτων τῶν ἀνδρῶν οἱ παραγενόμενοι ἐλέγχοντες οἷοί τ' ἦσαν ἀποδεῖξαι εἴ τι μὴ ὀρθῶς ἐλέγετο οὔτ' ἄλλος οὐδείς, ἐνθάδε δὲ νῦν πειρῶνται διαβάλλειν. [4] σημεῖον οὖν τοῦτο ὅτι οὗτοι οὐκ ἀφ' αὑτῶν ταῦτα πράττουσιν (εὐθὺς γὰρ ἂν τότε ἠναντιοῦντο) ἀλλ' ἀπὸ ἀνδρῶν ἑτέρων, οἷοί εἰσιν ἐν τῇ πόλει ταύτῃ, οὐδενὸς ἂν χρήματος δεξάμενοι ὑμᾶς τι ἀγαθὸν ἐξ ἐμοῦ πρᾶξαι. καὶ αὐτοὶ μὲν οὗτοι οἱ ἄνδρες οὐ τολμῶσι σφᾶς αὐτοὺς εἰς τὸ μέσον καταστήσαντες διισχυρίζεσθαι περὶ τούτων, φοβούμενοι ἔλεγχον διδόναι εἴ τι εἰς ὑμᾶς τυγχάνουσι μὴ εὖ φρονοῦντες· ἑτέρους δὲ εἰσπέμπουσι, τοιούτους ἀνθρώπους οἷς εἰθισμένοις ἤδη ἀναισχυντεῖν οὐδὲν διαφέρει εἰπεῖν τε καὶ ἀκοῦσαι τὰ μέγιστα τῶν κακῶν. [5] τὸ δ' ἰσχυρὸν τοῦτο μόνον εὕροι τις ἂν αὐτῶν ἐν τοῖς λόγοις, τὰς ἐμὰς συμφορὰς ἐπὶ παντὶ ὀνειδίζειν, καὶ ταῦτα ἐν εἰδόσι δήπου κάλλιον ὑμῖν, ὥστε μηδὲν ἂν τούτων δικαίως τιμὴν αὐτοῖς τινα φέρειν.

Ἐμοὶ δέ, ὦ ἄνδρες, καὶ τῷ πρώτῳ τοῦτο εἰπόντι ὀρθῶς δοκεῖ εἰρῆσθαι, ὅτι πάντες ἄνθρωποι γίγνονται ἐπὶ τῷ εὖ καὶ κακῶς πράττειν, μεγάλη δὲ δήπου καὶ τὸ ἐξαμαρτεῖν δυσπραξία

ON HIS RETURN

[1] If, gentlemen, on some other matter the speakers had not all clearly held the same opinion, I should not have thought it at all surprising. When, however, it is a question of whether I, or anyone else more lowly than I who wanted to do so, should perform the city some service, I think it the most terrible of all things if one person approves it but another does not, and there is no universal agreement. For if the city is common to all those who enjoy citizen rights, then, of course, the benefits accruing to the city are also common. [2] Now, this serious and terrible thing you can see some are already doing, while others are soon about to do it, and the greatest astonishment has come upon me why ever these men are so terribly excited if you should enjoy some benefit from me. They must be either the most stupid of all men or the most hostile towards this city. If, indeed, they think that with the city faring well their own private affairs too would turn out better, they are very stupid in pressing today for the opposite to their own benefit; [3] while if they do not think that their own private interests are the same as yours as a community, they would be hostile towards the city. When, indeed, I secretly made a report to the council concerning measures whose accomplishment would bring the greatest benefits to this city, and when I produced clear and certain proofs of these to the members of the council, there neither were any of these men who were present able to prove by questioning that anything I said was not right, nor was anybody else, but here they are now trying to discredit what I said. [4] This is proof, then, that these men are not doing these things on their own prompting (for they would immediately have opposed me then) but on that of other men, such as there are in this city, who would not allow you to receive any benefit from me for all the money in the world. These men do not dare themselves to come out into the open and make assertions about these things, being afraid to offer the opportunity of testing whether they have not always been well-disposed towards you. Rather, they suborn others, such men as are already accustomed to being shameless and to whom it makes no difference at all to speak or hear the greatest of evils. [5] But this is the only strong point anyone would find in their words, that they reproach me at every turn with my misfortunes, and this before you, who of course know better, so that none of these words would justly bring them any credit.

To me, gentlemen, it seems that the man who was the first to say this spoke correctly, that all men are born to meet with good and bad luck, and

ἐστί, [6] καὶ εἰσὶν εὐτυχέστατοι μὲν οἱ ἐλάχιστα ἐξαμαρτάνοντες, σωφρονέστατοι δὲ οἳ ἂν τάχιστα μεταγιγνώσκωσι. καὶ ταῦτα οὐ διακέκριται τοῖς μὲν γίγνεσθαι τοῖς δὲ μή, ἀλλ' ἔστιν ἐν τῷ κοινῷ πᾶσιν ἀνθρώποις καὶ ἐξαμαρτεῖν τι καὶ κακῶς πρᾶξαι. ὧν ἕνεκα, ὦ Ἀθηναῖοι, εἰ ἀνθρωπίνως περὶ ἐμοῦ γιγνώσκοιτε, εἴητε ἂν ἄνδρες εὐγνωμονέστεροι. οὐ γὰρ φθόνου μᾶλλον ἢ οἴκτου ἄξιά μοί ἐστι τὰ γεγενημένα· [7] ὃς εἰς τοσοῦτον ἦλθον τῆς ἐμαυτοῦ δυσδαιμονίας (εἴτε χρὴ εἰπεῖν νεότητί τε καὶ ἀνοίᾳ, εἴτε καὶ δυνάμει τῶν πεισάντων με ἐλθεῖν εἰς τοιαύτην συμφορὰν τῶν φρενῶν), ὥστ' ἀνάγκην μοι γενέσθαι δυοῖν κακοῖν τοῖν μεγίστοιν θάτερον ἑλέσθαι, ἢ μὴ βουληθέντι κατειπεῖν τοὺς ταῦτα ποιήσαντας οὐ περὶ ἐμοῦ μόνου ὀρρωδεῖν, εἴ τι ἔδει παθεῖν, ἀλλὰ καὶ τὸν πατέρα οὐδὲν ἀδικοῦντα σὺν ἐμαυτῷ ἀποκτεῖναι (ὅπερ ἀνάγκη παθεῖν ἦν αὐτῷ, εἰ ἐγὼ μὴ ἐβουλόμην ταῦτα ποιῆσαι), ἢ κατειπόντι τὰ γεγενημένα αὐτὸν μὲν ἀφεθέντα μὴ τεθνάναι, τοῦ δὲ ἐμαυτοῦ πατρὸς μὴ φονέα γενέσθαι (τί δ' ἂν οὐ πρό γε τούτου τολμήσειεν ἄνθρωπος ποιῆσαι;). [8] ἐγὼ τοίνυν ἐκ τῶν παρόντων εἱλόμην ταῦτα, ἃ ἐμοὶ μὲν λύπας ἐπὶ χρόνον πλεῖστον οἴσειν ἔμελλεν, ὑμῖν δὲ ταχίστην τοῦ παρόντος τότε κακοῦ μετάστασιν. ἀναμνήσθητε δὲ ἐν οἵῳ κινδύνῳ τε καὶ ἀμηχανίᾳ καθέστατε, καὶ ὅτι οὕτως σφόδρα σφᾶς αὐτοὺς ἐπεφόβησθε, ὥστ' οὐδ' εἰς τὴν ἀγορὰν ἔτι ἐξῇτε, ἕκαστος ὑμῶν οἰόμενος συλληφθήσεσθαι. ταῦτα τοίνυν ὥστε μὲν γενέσθαι τοιαῦτα, πολλοστὸν δή τι ἐγὼ μέρος τῆς αἰτίας εὑρέθην ἔχων, ὥστε μέντοι παυθῆναι, ἐγὼ εἰς ὢν μόνος αἴτιος. [9] καὶ ὅμως τό γε δυστυχέστατος εἶναι ἀνθρώπων οὐδαμῇ ἐκφεύγω, ὅτε δὴ προαγομένης μὲν τῆς πόλεως ἐπὶ ταύτας τὰς συμφορὰς οὐδεὶς ἐμοῦ ἤρχετο γίγνεσθαι δυσδαιμονέστερος, μεθισταμένης δὲ πάλιν εἰς τὸ ἀσφαλὲς ἁπάντων ἐγὼ ἀθλιώτατος. ὄντων γὰρ κακῶν τοσούτων τῇ πόλει ἀδύνατον ἦν ταῦτα ἰαθῆναι ἄλλως ἢ τῷ ἐμῷ αἰσχρῷ, ὥστ' ἐν αὐτῷ ᾧ ἐγὼ κακῶς ἔπραττον, ἐν τούτῳ ὑμᾶς σῴζεσθαι. χάριν οὖν εἰκός με, οὐ μῖσος τῷ δυστυχήματι τούτῳ φέρεσθαι παρ' ὑμῶν.

[10] Καίτοι ἐγὼ τότ' αὐτὸς γνοὺς τὰς ἐμαυτοῦ συμφοράς, ᾧ τινι κακῶν τε καὶ αἰσχρῶν οὐκ οἶδ' εἴ τι ἀπεγένετο, τὰ μὲν παρανοίᾳ τῇ ἐμαυτοῦ, τὰ δ' ἀνάγκῃ τῶν παρόντων πραγμάτων, ἔγνων ἥδιστον εἶναι πράττειν τε τοιαῦτα καὶ διαιτᾶσθαι ἐκεῖ, ὅπου ἥκιστα μέλλοιμι ὀφθήσεσθαι ὑφ' ὑμῶν. ἐπειδὴ δὲ χρόνῳ ὕστερον εἰσῆλθέ μοι, ὥσπερ εἰκός, ἐπιθυμία τῆς τε μεθ' ὑμῶν πολιτείας ἐκείνης καὶ διαίτης, ἐξ ἧς δευρὶ μετέστην, ἔγνων

that making a mistake is, of course, great ill luck, [6] and that they are luckiest who make the fewest mistakes but most sensible who repent the quickest. Nor is this predestined to happen to some and not others, but it is the common lot of all men both to make some mistake and to meet with bad luck. Wherefore, Athenians, if you were to pass judgment on me with fellow-feeling, you would be more reasonable men. For I deserve not so much ill-will as pity for what has happened; [7] I who reached such a depth of misery (whether, should I say, through my youthful folly or through the influence of those who persuaded me to enter into such an act of madness) that it became necessary for me to choose one of the two greatest evils, either by refusing to reveal the names of those who did these things not only to fear for myself alone, if I should have to suffer in some way, but also to kill my father, who had done nothing wrong, along with me (he would inevitably have suffered this fate, if I refused to do this), or by revealing what had happened to be released myself and not to die, and not to become my own father's murderer (and what would a man not dare to do in order to avoid this?). [8] So of the alternatives I chose the one which was likely to bring to me grief for a very long time but to you very fast relief from the evil existing at the time. Remember the danger and helplessness you were in, and that you were so exceedingly afraid of one another that you no longer went out even into the agora, every one of you thinking he would be arrested. Now, that such a state of affairs came into existence was only found to be in small part due to me, that it ceased, however, was due to me alone. [9] Yet I can in no way escape from being the unluckiest of men, since when the city was being led on into these disasters, no one was nearly becoming more ill-fated than I, and when it was moving again towards safety, of all men I was the most wretched. For when such great troubles were afflicting the city, it was impossible for them to be remedied other than by my disgrace, so that in my ruin lay your safety. It is therefore reasonable for me to receive gratitude, not hatred, from you for this ill-luck.

[10] Yet at the time I was myself aware of my misfortunes, for whom I think no troubles or disgrace were lacking, some through my own madness, others through force of circumstances, and I knew you would be best pleased were I to adopt that style of life and live in a place where I would be furthest from your sight. But when some time later there entered into me, as was reasonable, a longing for that public and private life with you

λυσιτελεῖν μοι ἢ τοῦ βίου ἀπηλλάχθαι, ἢ τὴν πόλιν ταύτην ἀγαθόν τι τοσοῦτον ἐργάσασθαι, ὥστε ὑμῶν ἑκόντων εἶναί ποτέ μοι πολιτεύσασθαι μεθ' ὑμῶν. [11] ἐκ δὲ τούτου οὐ πώποτε οὔτε τοῦ σώματος οὔτε τῶν ὄντων ἐμοὶ ἐφεισάμην, ὅπου ἔδει παρακινδυνεύειν· ἀλλ' αὐτίκα μὲν τότε εἰσήγαγον εἰς στρατιὰν ὑμῶν οὖσαν ἐν Σάμῳ κωπέας, τῶν τετρακοσίων ἤδη τὰ πράγματα ἐνθάδε κατειληφότων, ὄντος μοι Ἀρχελάου ξένου πατρικοῦ καὶ διδόντος τέμνεσθαί τε καὶ ἐξάγεσθαι ὁπόσους ἐβουλόμην. τούτους τε εἰσήγαγον τοὺς κωπέας, καὶ παρόν μοι πέντε δραχμῶν τὴν τιμὴν αὐτῶν δέξασθαι οὐκ ἠθέλησα πράξασθαι πλέον ἢ ὅσου ἐμοὶ κατέστησαν· εἰσήγαγον δὲ σῖτόν τε καὶ χαλκόν. [12] καὶ οἱ ἄνδρες ἐκεῖνοι ἐκ τούτων παρεσκευασμένοι ἐνίκησαν μετὰ ταῦτα Πελοποννησίους ναυμαχοῦντες, καὶ τὴν πόλιν ταύτην μόνοι ἀνθρώπων ἔσωσαν ἐν τῷ τότε χρόνῳ. εἰ τοίνυν μεγάλων ἀγαθῶν αἴτια ὑμᾶς ἠργάσαντο ἐκεῖνοι, μέρος ἐγὼ οὐκ ἂν ἐλάχιστον δικαίως ταύτης τῆς αἰτίας ἔχοιμι. εἰ γὰρ τοῖς ἀνδράσιν ἐκείνοις τότε τὰ ἐπιτήδεια μὴ εἰσήχθη, οὐ περὶ τοῦ σῶσαι τὰς Ἀθήνας ὁ κίνδυνος ἦν αὐτοῖς μᾶλλον ἢ περὶ τοῦ μηδ' αὐτοὺς σωθῆναι.

[13] Τούτων τοίνυν οὕτως ἐχόντων οὐκ ὀλίγῳ μοι παρὰ γνώμην εὑρέθη τὰ ἐνταῦθα πράγματα ἔχοντα. κατέπλευσα μὲν γὰρ ὡς ἐπαινεθησόμενος ὑπὸ τῶν ἐνθάδε προθυμίας τε εἵνεκα καὶ ἐπιμελείας τῶν ὑμετέρων πραγμάτων· πυθόμενοι δέ τινές με ἥκοντα τῶν τετρακοσίων ἐζήτουν τε παραχρῆμα, καὶ λαβόντες ἤγαγον εἰς τὴν βουλήν. [14] εὐθὺς δὲ παραστάς μοι Πείσανδρος "Ἄνδρες" ἔφη "βουλευταί, ἐγὼ τὸν ἄνδρα τοῦτον ἐνδεικνύω ὑμῖν σῖτόν τε εἰς τοὺς πολεμίους εἰσαγαγόντα καὶ κωπέας." καὶ τὸ πρᾶγμα ἤδη πᾶν διηγεῖτο ὡς ἐπέπρακτο. ἐν δὲ τῷ τότε τὰ ἐναντία φρονοῦντες δῆλοι ἦσαν ἤδη οἱ ἐπὶ στρατιᾶς ὄντες τοῖς τετρακοσίοις. [15] κἀγώ (θόρυβος γὰρ δὴ τοιοῦτος ἐγίγνετο τῶν βουλευτῶν) ἐπειδὴ ἐγίγνωσκον ἀπολούμενος, εὐθὺς προσπηδῶ πρὸς τὴν ἑστίαν καὶ λαμβάνομαι τῶν ἱερῶν. ὅπερ μοι καὶ πλείστου ἄξιον ἐγένετο ἐν τῷ τότε· εἰς γὰρ τοὺς θεοὺς ἔχοντα ὀνείδη οὗτοί με μᾶλλον τῶν ἀνθρώπων ἐοίκασι κατελεῆσαι, βουληθέντων τε αὐτῶν ἀποκτεῖναί με οὗτοι ἦσαν οἱ διασώσαντες. δεσμά τε ὕστερον καὶ κακὰ ὅσα τε καὶ οἷα τῷ σώματι ἠνεσχόμην, μακρὸν ἂν εἴη μοι λέγειν. [16] οὗ δὴ καὶ μάλιστ' ἐμαυτὸν ἀπωλοφυράμην· ὅστις τοῦτο μὲν ἐν ᾧ ἐδόκει ὁ δῆμος κακοῦσθαι, ἐγὼ ἀντὶ τούτου κακὰ εἶχον, τοῦτο δὲ ἐπειδὴ ἐφαίνετο ὑπ' ἐμοῦ <εὖ> πεπονθώς, πάλιν αὖ καὶ διὰ τοῦτ' ἐγὼ ἀπωλλύμην. ὥστε ὁδόν τε καὶ πόρον

which I had exchanged for this exile, I knew it was better for me either to die or to do this city such a service as to be able, with your assent, at some time to enjoy citizen rights with you. [11] From that moment I never spared either my life or my possessions when I had to risk some danger; but I at once supplied your army in Samos with oar-spars at the time when the Four Hundred had already seized power here, since Archelaus was an hereditary guest-friend of mine and allowed me to cut and export as many as I wished. I both supplied these spars and, although I could have got the price for them of five drachmas apiece, I did not care to charge more than they cost me; I also supplied corn and bronze. [12] So equipped, those men after this defeated the Peloponnesians at sea, and they alone saved this city at that time. Now, if those men rendered you great service by their actions, I might justly claim not the least part of this service. For if the supplies had not been brought in for those men at that time, the danger facing them was not so much to do with saving Athens as with not even being saved themselves.

[13] These being the circumstances, then, the situation here was found to be not a little different from my expectation. For I put in expecting to be commended by those here for my zeal and attention to your affairs, but instead certain of the Four Hundred, on learning of my arrival, immediately searched for me, then arrested and brought me before the council. [14] Peisander at once stood beside me and said, "Gentlemen of the council, I denounce this man to you for having supplied corn and oar-spars to the enemy." He went on to describe the whole business as it had happened. By then it was clear that opposite viewpoints were now held by the men on service and the Four Hundred. [15] As for me (for indeed such a great murmur was arising among the councillors), since I knew I was lost, I immediately leaped on the altar and grasped the sacred objects. This more than anything saved me at that moment, for despite my disgrace in the eyes of the gods they seem to have had more compassion on me than men, and when men wanted to kill me, the gods were the ones who saved me. My subsequent imprisonment and the number and nature of the physical sufferings I endured would take me a long time to tell. [16] It was there, indeed, that I most loudly bewailed my fate, who on the one hand, when the people seemed to be in ill plight, was the one suffering instead of it, and who on the other hand, when it had clearly been benefited by me, once again was being destroyed because of this. So I no longer had any way or means to be

μηδαμῇ ἔτι εἶναί μοι εὐθαρσεῖν· ὅποι γὰρ τραποίμην, πάντοθεν κακόν τί μοι ἐφαίνετο ἑτοιμαζόμενον. ἀλλ' ὅμως καὶ ἐκ τούτων τοιούτων ὄντων ἀπαλλαγεὶς οὐκ ἔστιν ὅ τι ἕτερον ἔργον περὶ πλείονος ἐποιούμην ἢ τὴν πόλιν ταύτην ἀγαθόν τι ἐργάσασθαι. [17] Ὁρᾶν δὲ χρή, ὦ Ἀθηναῖοι, ὅσῳ τὰ τοιαῦτα τῶν ὑπουργημάτων διαφέρει. τοῦτο μὲν γὰρ ὅσοι τῶν πολιτῶν τὰ ὑμέτερα πράγματα διαχειρίζοντες ἀργύριον ὑμῖν ἐκπορίζουσιν, ἄλλο τι ἢ τὰ ὑμέτερα ὑμῖν διδόασι; τοῦτο δὲ ὅσοι στρατηγοὶ γενόμενοι καλόν τι τὴν πόλιν κατεργάζονται, τί ἄλλο ἢ μετὰ τῆς τῶν ὑμετέρων σωμάτων ταλαιπωρίας τε καὶ κινδύνων, καὶ ἔτι τῶν κοινῶν χρημάτων δαπάνης, ποιοῦσιν ὑμᾶς εἴ τι τυγχάνουσιν ἀγαθόν; ἐν ᾧ καὶ ἄν τι ἐξαμάρτωσιν, οὐκ αὐτοὶ τῆς σφετέρας αὐτῶν ἁμαρτίας δίκην διδόασιν, ἀλλ' ὑμεῖς ὑπὲρ τῶν ἐκείνοις ἡμαρτημένων. [18] ἀλλ' ὅμως οὗτοι στεφανοῦνταί γε ὑφ' ὑμῶν καὶ ἀνακηρύττονται ὡς ὄντες ἄνδρες ἀγαθοί. καὶ οὐκ ἐρῶ ὡς οὐ δικαίως· μεγάλη γάρ ἐστιν ἀρετή, ὅστις τὴν ἑαυτοῦ πόλιν ὁτῳοῦν δύναται τρόπῳ ἀγαθόν τι ἐργάζεσθαι. ἀλλ' οὖν γιγνώσκειν γε χρὴ ὅτι ἐκεῖνος ἂν εἴη πολὺ πλείστου ἄξιος ἀνήρ, ὅστις τοῖς ἑαυτοῦ παρακινδυνεύων χρήμασί τε καὶ σώματι τολμῴη ἀγαθόν τι ποιεῖν τοὺς ἑαυτοῦ πολίτας.

[19] Ἐμοὶ τοίνυν τὰ μὲν ἤδη εἰς ὑμᾶς πεπραγμένα σχεδόν τι ἅπαντες ἂν εἰδεῖτε, τὰ δὲ μέλλοντά τε καὶ ἤδη πραττόμενα ἄνδρες ὑμῶν πεντακόσιοι ἐν ἀπορρήτῳ ἴσασιν· οὓς πολλῷ δήπου εἰκὸς· ἧττον ἄν τι ἐξαμαρτεῖν ἢ εἰ ὑμᾶς δέοι ἀκούσαντάς τι ἐν τῷ παραχρῆμα νῦν διαβουλεύσασθαι. οἱ μέν γε σχολῇ περὶ τῶν εἰσαγγελλομένων σκοποῦνται, ὑπάρχει τε αὐτοῖς, ἐάν τι ἐξαμαρτάνωσιν, αἰτίαν ἔχειν καὶ λόγον αἰσχρὸν ἐκ τῶν ἄλλων πολιτῶν· ὑμῖν δὲ οὐκ εἰσὶν ἕτεροι ὑφ' ὧν αἰτίαν <ἂν> ἔχοιτε· τὰ γὰρ ὑμέτερα αὐτῶν ἐφ' ὑμῖν δικαίως ἐστὶ καὶ εὖ καὶ κακῶς, ἐὰν βούλησθε, διαθέσθαι. [20] ἅ γε μέντοι ἔξω τῶν ἀπορρήτων οἷόν τέ μοί ἐστιν εἰπεῖν εἰς ὑμᾶς ἤδη πεπραγμένα, ἀκούσεσθε. ἐπίστασθε γάρ που ὡς ἠγγέλθη ὑμῖν ὅτι οὐ μέλλει ἐκ Κύπρου σῖτος ἥξειν ἐνταῦθα· ἐγὼ τοίνυν τοιοῦτός τε καὶ τοσοῦτος ἐγενόμην, ὥστε τοὺς ἄνδρας τοὺς ταῦτα βουλεύσαντας ἐφ' ὑμῖν καὶ πράξαντας ψευσθῆναι τῆς αὐτῶν γνώμης. [21] καὶ ὡς μὲν ταῦτα διεπράχθη, οὐδὲν προὔργου ἀκοῦσαι ὑμῖν· τάδε <δὲ> νυνὶ βούλομαι ὑμᾶς εἰδέναι, ὅτι αἱ μέλλουσαι νῆες ἤδη σιταγωγοὶ καταπλεῖν εἰς τὸν Πειραιᾶ εἰσιν ὑμῖν τέτταρες καὶ δέκα, αἱ δὲ λοιπαὶ τῶν ἐκ Κύπρου ἀναχθεισῶν ἥξουσιν ἀθρόαι οὐ πολὺ ὕστερον. ἐδεξάμην δ' <ἂν>

of good courage, for wherever I turned, from every side some trouble was clearly being prepared for me. But nevertheless, as soon as I was freed from all these woes, there was no deed I valued more than doing this city some service.

[17] You must see, Athenians, how far such actions differ from ordinary services. For on the one hand, when those citizens who administer your affairs furnish you with money, do they give you anything other than what is yours? On the other hand, when those who have become generals do something fine for the city, what do they do for you if they render some service other than with distress and dangers for your own persons and besides by the expenditure of public money? Even if they make some mistake, it is not they themselves who are punished for their own mistake, but you for the mistake made by them. [18] But nevertheless they are crowned by you and proclaimed as heroes. I will not say this is unjust; for it is a great virtue to be able to do some service for one's own city in any way whatsoever. But you must understand that that man is by far the worthiest who dares to venture his own money and person in performing some service for his fellow citizens.

[19] Now, the things I have already done for you almost all of you would know, but the things I am about to do and am already doing five hundred of you know in secret. It is, of course, far less likely that they would make some mistake than if you had to listen and immediately now debate the matter thoroughly. They are considering the report at leisure, and it is possible for them, if they make some mistake, to be accused and censured by the rest of the citizens; but you have no others by whom you might be accused, for it is rightly in your hands to manage your affairs well or badly as you wish. [20] However, the services that are not secret and I am able to tell you about since they have already been performed, you shall hear. You know, I think, how it was announced to you that no corn was to come here from Cyprus. Now, I acted so ably and with such effect that the men who planned this against you and put it into operation were disappointed in their intention. [21] It is no good for you to hear how this was accomplished, but I do now want you to know this, that the ships conveying corn which are already about to put in to Peiraeus for you are fourteen in number, and the rest of those that sailed from Cyprus will arrive together not long afterwards. I would have given all the money in the world to be in a safe position to tell

ἀντὶ πάντων χρημάτων εἶναι ἐν ἀσφαλεῖ φράσαι πρὸς ὑμᾶς ἃ καὶ τῇ βουλῇ ἐν ἀπορρήτῳ εἰσήγγειλα, ὅπως αὐτόθεν προῄδετε. [22] νῦν δὲ ἐκεῖνα μὲν τότε ὅταν ἀποτελεσθῇ γνώσεσθε ἅμα καὶ ὠφεληθήσεσθε· νῦν δέ, ὦ Ἀθηναῖοι, εἴ μοι βουληθεῖτε δοῦναι χάριν μικράν τε καὶ ἄπονον ὑμῖν καὶ ἅμα δικαίαν, πάνυ ἄν μοι τοῦτο ἐν μεγάλῃ ἡδονῇ γένοιτο. ὡς δὲ καὶ δικαία ἐστίν, εἴσεσθε. ἃ γάρ μοι αὐτοὶ γνόντες τε καὶ ὑποσχόμενοι ἔδοτε, ὕστερον δὲ ἑτέροις πειθόμενοι ἀφείλεσθε, ταῦθ' ὑμᾶς, εἰ μὲν βούλεσθε, αἰτῶ, εἰ δὲ μὴ βούλεσθε, ἀπαιτῶ. [23] ὁρῶ δὲ ὑμᾶς πολλάκις καὶ δούλοις ἀνθρώποις καὶ ξένοις παντοδαποῖς πολιτείαν διδόντας τε καὶ εἰς χρήματα μεγάλας δωρειάς, οἳ ἂν ὑμᾶς φαίνωνται ποιοῦντές τι ἀγαθόν. καὶ ταῦτα μέντοι ὀρθῶς ὑμεῖς φρονοῦντες δίδοτε· οὕτω γὰρ ἂν ὑπὸ πλείστων ἀνθρώπων εὖ πάσχοιτε. ἐγὼ τοίνυν τοσοῦτον ὑμῶν μόνον δέομαι· τὸ ψήφισμα ὃ Μενίππου εἰπόντος ἐψηφίσασθε, εἶναί μοι ἄδειαν, πάλιν ἀπόδοτε. ἀναγνώσεται δὲ ὑμῖν αὐτό· ἔτι γὰρ καὶ νῦν ἐγγέγραπται ἐν τῷ βουλευτηρίῳ.

ΨΗΦΙΣΜΑ

[24] Τουτὶ τὸ ψήφισμα ὃ ἠκούσατε ψηφισάμενοί μοι, ὦ Ἀθηναῖοι, ὕστερον ἀφείλεσθε χάριν ἑτέρῳ φέροντες. πείθεσθε οὖν μοι, καὶ ἤδη παύσασθε εἴ τῳ ὑμῶν διάβολόν τι ἐν τῇ γνώμῃ περὶ ἐμοῦ παρέστηκεν. εἰ γὰρ ὅσα οἱ ἄνθρωποι γνώμῃ ἁμαρτάνουσι, τὸ σῶμα αὐτῶν μὴ αἴτιόν ἐστιν, ἐμοῦ τὸ μὲν σῶμα τυγχάνει ταὐτὸν ἔτι ὄν, ὅπερ τῆς αἰτίας ἀπήλλακται, ἡ δὲ γνώμη ἀντὶ τῆς προτέρας ἑτέρα νυνὶ παρέστηκεν. οὐδὲν οὖν ἔτι ὑπολείπεται ὅτῳ ἄν μοι δικαίως διαβεβλῆσθε. [25] ὥσπερ δὲ τῆς τότε ἁμαρτίας τὰ ἀπὸ τῶν ἔργων σημεῖα ἔφατε χρῆναι πιστότατα ποιούμενοι κακόν με ἄνδρα ἡγεῖσθαι, οὕτω καὶ ἐπὶ τῇ νῦν εὐνοίᾳ μὴ ζητεῖτε ἑτέραν βάσανον ἢ τὰ ἀπὸ τῶν νυνὶ ἔργων σημεῖα ὑμῖν γιγνόμενα. [26] πολὺ δέ μοι προσήκει ταῦτα μᾶλλον ἐκείνων καὶ τῷ γένει συνηθέστερά ἐστι. τάδε γὰρ οὐ ψευσαμένῳ μοι λαθεῖν οἷόν τ' ἐστι τούς γε πρεσβυτέρους ὑμῶν, ὅτι ὁ τοῦ ἐμοῦ πατρὸς πρόπαππος Λεωγόρας στασιάσας πρὸς τοὺς τυράννους ὑπὲρ τοῦ δήμου, ἐξὸν αὐτῷ διαλλαχθέντι τῆς ἔχθρας καὶ γενομένῳ κηδεστῇ ἄρξαι μετ' ἐκείνων τῶν ἀνδρῶν τῆς πόλεως, εἵλετο μᾶλλον ἐκπεσεῖν μετὰ τοῦ δήμου καὶ φεύγων κακοπαθεῖν μᾶλλον ἢ προδότης αὐτῶν καταστῆναι. ὥστ' ἔμοιγε καὶ διὰ τὰ τῶν προγόνων ἔργα εἰκότως ὑπάρχει δημοτικῷ εἶναι, εἴπερ τι ἄλλα νῦν γε φρονῶν τυγχάνω. ὧν

you what I also reported in secret to the council, so that you might know it at once. [22] But as it is you will only know that at the same time as you have derived benefit from it, at the moment when it has been accomplished. But now, Athenians, if you would be willing to grant me a small favour, and one costing you no trouble and at the same time just, this would especially be a great pleasure for me. That it is indeed just, you will know. For it is what you yourselves decided, promised and gave, but afterwards were persuaded by others to rescind that I am asking of you if you are willing and demanding if you are not. [23] I often see you giving citizenship and large gifts of money to both slaves and foreigners of every country, if they are seen to be performing you some service. Of course, you are thinking correctly in giving these things, for in so doing you would receive benefits from most men. Now, I ask only this of you: restore again the decree which you voted on the motion of Menippus, that I be granted immunity. The herald will read it to you, for it is still registered even now in the council-chamber.

DECREE

[24] You voted me this decree to which you have been listening, Athenians, but afterwards rescinded it to do a favour to another. Believe me, then, and stop now if some prejudice has come upon any of you in your opinion about me. For if men's persons are not to blame for the mistakes which they make in their opinions, my person still happens to be the same and is free from blame, but my opinion has become different now from what it was before. So there is nothing still left remaining through which you might justly be filled with resentment against me. [25] Just as with my mistake then, considering me a criminal, you said you had to place the greatest trust in the signs provided by actions, so too with my present goodwill do not search for another test than the signs coming to you provided by my present actions. [26] These are far more befitting me than those and are more customary of my family. It is not possible for me to deceive the older ones among you in lying about this, that my father's great-grandfather Leogoras formed a faction against the tyrants on behalf of the democrats, and although it was possible for him to reconcile his enmity and become their relative by marriage, and so rule the city with those men, he chose instead to be banished with the democrats and suffer hardships in exile rather than become a traitor to them. So in my case too through the actions of my ancestors it is reasonable for me to be on the democratic side, if indeed I happen now at last to have regained my senses. Also because of this it is

καὶ ἕνεκα εἰκὸς ὑμᾶς, ἐὰν χρηστὸς ὢν ἀνὴρ εἰς ὑμᾶς φαίνωμαι, προθυμότερόν μου ἀποδέχεσθαι τὰ πραττόμενα. [27] τὸ δὲ δόντας ἐμοὶ τὴν ἄδειαν ἀφελέσθαι ὑμᾶς, εὖ ἴστε ὅτι οὐδεπώποτε ἠγανάκτησα· ὅπου γὰρ ὑπὸ τῶν ἀνδρῶν τούτων αὐτοὶ εἰς ὑμᾶς αὐτοὺς ἐπείσθητε τὰ μέγιστα ἐξαμαρτεῖν, ὥστε ἀντὶ τῆς ἀρχῆς δουλείαν ἀλλάξασθαι, ἐκ δημοκρατίας δυναστείαν καταστήσαντες, τί ἄν τις ὑμῶν θαυμάζοι καὶ εἰς ἐμὲ εἴ τι ἐπείσθητε ἐξαμαρτεῖν; [28] βουλοίμην μέντ' ἄν, ὥσπερ ἐν τοῖς ὑμετέροις αὐτῶν πράγμασιν, ἐπειδὴ ἐξουσίαν ἐλάβετε, τὰς τῶν ἐξαπατησάντων ὑμᾶς ἀκύρους ἔθετε βουλάς, οὕτω καὶ ἐν ᾧ περὶ ἐμοῦ ἐπείσθητε γνῶναί τι ἀνεπιτήδειον, ἀτελῆ τὴν γνώμην αὐτῶν ποιῆσαι, καὶ μήτε ἐν τούτῳ μήτε ἐν ἑτέρῳ τῳ τοῖς ὑμῶν αὐτῶν ἐχθίστοις ὁμόψηφοί ποτε γένησθε.

reasonable for you, if I am clearly a man who is devoted to you, to accept more readily from me the things I am doing. [27] As for the fact that you rescinded the immunity you gave me, be assured that I have never felt annoyed; when you were persuaded by these men to do to you yourselves the greatest of wrongs, with the result that you exchanged sovereignty for slavery and substituted domination for democracy, why should any of you wonder that you were persuaded to do some wrong to me too? [28] I could wish, however, that just as in your own affairs, when you had the power to do so, you invalidated the decisions of those who deceived you, so too in a matter in which you were persuaded to take some prejudicial decision about me you would make their judgment ineffectual, and do not ever become on this or any other matter voters in concert with those who are your worst enemies.

INTRODUCTION 3: *ON THE PEACE WITH THE SPARTANS*

(i) Deliberative oratory

The development of democracy at Athens during the fifth century B.C. provided the ideal conditions under which oratory was able to flourish.[74] Aristotle's later distinction[75] between political or deliberative oratory and judicial or forensic oratory hardly applies in this period, and the deliberative oratory which survives from the fifth and early fourth centuries indicates that similar techniques were employed in the assembly and law-courts, which were, after all, manned by the same citizens. These few speeches, found mainly in Herodotus and Thucydides, with a small number of other examples, have proems and epilogues like those in forensic speeches; while their proofs, as well as employing the regular deliberative themes of expediency, justice, possibility and necessity, also contain argument from probability and historical examples.[76] However, certain differences between deliberative and forensic oratory are already observable in the fifth century.

The first of these is in the matter of instruction. As techniques of public speaking were refined, the need for tuition grew among up-and-coming politicians. Professional speech-writers (*logographoi*) began to appear, but their main area of activity was forensic oratory. This was also the subject of the early rhetorical handbooks, and the politician's need was met instead by the sophists, who claimed expertise in a range of subjects, especially politics. These sophists, among whose number were Protagoras of Abdera, Prodicus of Ceos, Thrasymachus of Chalcedon and Gorgias of Leontini, would provide specimen speeches and examples of commonplace topics which could be adapted to suit the occasion.[77] But the audience in the assembly expected those who addressed it to speak without a text, and therein lies a second difference from forensic oratory. A litigant, indeed, would regularly memorise the speech he had purchased from a logographer, but for a politician the ability to speak extemporaneously was essential. Further, while he would employ the standard deliberative themes, he had to develop them in his own personal way if he was to be successful.

Another difference was that politicians in the fifth century did not publish their speeches. Deliberative oratory was not yet regarded as a separate literary form in its own right, and Plato says[78] that politicians were afraid of being themselves regarded as sophists if they did publish them. It has been suggested[79] that publication of political speeches was begun by non-citizens, who wished to influence public policy but were unable to address the assembly in person. Thus Thrasymachus wrote a speech *On Behalf of the Larissans*,[80] and a fragment of one

---

74 See further on this Edwards and Usher 7-10.
75 See **Introd.** 2 n. 69.
76 The separate narrative section was regularly dispensed with in deliberative oratory.
77 E.g. the proems of Critias (cf. Hermogenes, *On Characteristics* 2.11, p. 416 Spengel).
78 *Phaedrus* 257d.
79 By Kennedy 204.
80 Clement, *Miscellanies* 6.16.

of his demegoric speeches is quoted by Dionysius of Halicarnassus.[81] Similarly, Lysias 34, *Against the Subversion of the Ancestral Constitution of Athens*, was written by Lysias (a metic) for another to deliver.[82] On the other hand, we should note that although Antiphon, who was regarded in antiquity as the first logographer, remained aloof from politics,[83] he did nevertheless write speeches for the Lindians and Samothracians and was an Athenian citizen. Isocrates later adopted a similar practice, publishing but not actually delivering deliberative speeches. But whatever the origins of published political oratory, and while others may have done both, no examples survive of an Athenian politician delivering and publishing a deliberative speech before Demosthenes - with one exception. For despite the doubts that have been raised about its authenticity[84] and the lack of evidence to show when the speech was published or by whom, our earliest extant example of such a speech does appear to be Andocides' *On the Peace with the Spartans*.

(ii) Historical background

Sparta's victory in the Peloponnesian War, far from ending hostilities, was only the beginning of further troubles both on the Greek mainland and in Asia Minor. The Persian king, Artaxerxes, had supported Sparta in return for the promised surrender of the Asiatic Greek states, but the Spartans claimed to be champions of Greek freedom. They resolved their dilemma by declaring war on the Persians in 400, and there followed a decade of ultimately futile warfare. Meanwhile, on the mainland Sparta's self-interested policies quickly led to discontent among her allies, and in 395 the Corinthian War broke out against a confederacy led by Thebes, Corinth, Argos and Athens. Sparta won a technical victory under the leadership of Agesilaus at Coronea (394), but the war on land reached a stalemate. Then in 393 the Athenian Conon sailed into Peiraeus with large quantities of Persian money. He, alongside the Persian satrap Pharnabazus, had destroyed Spartan sea-power at the battle of Cnidus the year before, and now oversaw the rebuilding of Athens' fortifications and the Long Walls, which had been destroyed by Lysander in 404.

So by the summer of 392 Sparta had failed to secure leadership of mainland Greece and had lost her maritime hegemony. She had even seen part of her own territory (the island of Cythera) garrisoned, and worse still in 392 came the formation of the so-called Union of Corinth and Argos. Not surprisingly Sparta began to make peace overtures, firstly to Persia. Antalcidas was sent to Sardis, but his agreement with Tiribazus, which guaranteed the autonomy of the mainland Greek states and islands but once again involved the abandoning of the Asiatic Greeks, was ultimately rejected by Artaxerxes. A congress was also held at Sparta in the winter of 392/1, at which the Spartans modified these terms (but not the abandonment of the Asiatic Greeks) in order to achieve a 'common peace'. The

---

81   *Demosthenes* 3.
82   Dion. Hal. *Lysias* 32-3. On the publishing of speeches for propaganda purposes at the time of the Thirty see S. Usher, 'Xenophon, Critias and Theramenes', *JHS* 88 (1968) 128-35.
83   Cf. Thuc. 8.68.
84   See section (iii) below.

Athenian delegates, among them Andocides, secured the concession that Athens should control three islands vital to her corn-supply, Lemnos, Imbros and Scyros, and referred the terms of the treaty to the Athenian assembly. Andocides delivered his *On the Peace with the Spartans* (which is often referred to by its Latin title, *De Pace*), but the Athenians, along with the Corinthians and Argives, rejected the proposals. Andocides and his fellow-ambassadors were condemned *in absentia*, and the war continued until 387/6, when the King's Peace (also called the Peace of Antalcidas) was concluded on more or less the same terms as those on offer in 392/1.[85]

(iii) The authenticity of the *De Pace*

According to a *Hypothesis* added to the start of the speech in the Burneianus MS., Dionysius pronounced the *De Pace* spurious, and the lexicographer Harpocration also doubted its authenticity. Some scholars of the nineteenth century followed this line, and it has been suggested, for example, that the speech is in fact a political pamphlet published after the exile of the ambassadors to vindicate their actions. We do not know the grounds on which Dionysius made his judgment, and most commentators now accept the speech as genuine, but the following points may be noted.

Firstly, concerning the historical setting, the main source for the peace negotiations apart from Andocides is Xenophon, *Hellenica* 4.8.12-15. But just as Andocides does not mention Antalcidas' mission to Persia, so is Xenophon silent on the congress at Sparta. Doubts about the latter were removed by the discovery in 1901 of the papyrus fragments of the commentary on Demosthenes' *Philippics* by Didymus. He quotes a passage of Philochorus referring to both sets of negotiations and the subsequent banishment of the Athenian ambassadors in the archonship of Philocles (392/1).[86] Philochorus does not specifically mention Andocides' report to the assembly, but the passage makes it highly likely that the circumstances behind his speech are historical. Of more concern, therefore, is Andocides' omission of the negotiations in Sardis. Philochorus says the Athenians refused to accept the first Peace of Antalcidas because it sanctioned the abandonment of the Asiatic Greeks to Persia, but Xenophon's version is perhaps the more likely one, that they were in fact concerned with losing Lemnos, Imbros and Scyros. This was the very concession then made at the congress in Sparta, and an obvious inference from this is that the betrayal of the Asiatic Greeks was still on the agenda, hence the Spartans were attempting to buy off allied objections.[87] If so, Andocides' silence on the Asiatic

---

85   See in greater detail Cartledge, esp. chapters 17-18. The charges against the envoys were breach of instructions, making an incorrect report to the council, giving false evidence concerning the allies and taking bribes (Dem. 19.277-9). See Hansen (1975) 87-8. Bauman 87-9 overlooks the Demosthenes passage in suggesting impiety (ἀσέβεια).

86   Philochorus F149.

87   See Maidment 492-4, who argues that the congress may have taken place before news arrived that Artaxerxes had rejected the proposals brought from Sardis in person by Tiribazus. Albini (1964) 12-13 puts the congress *before* the embassy to Sparta.

Greeks is understandable: he concentrates on the benefits Athens will derive from the proposed peace terms, in a vain attempt to gloss over what will have been a very unpopular policy. A similar explanation applies to the guarantee of freedom for the remaining Greeks, which forestalled any ideas of imperialist expansion. But with such plans in mind, and still perhaps with some reluctance to abandon the Ionians whose mother-city Athens claimed to be, the assembly categorically rejected Andocides' proposal.

Secondly, scholars have noted the dreadful inaccuracy of the historical examples adduced in the speech. But that Andocides was capable of such gross errors is evidenced in his first two speeches and explicable in terms of his family's oral traditions, and so the historical errors have no bearing on the question of authenticity. Indeed, the fact that 3-12 are repeated almost verbatim at Aeschines 2.172-6 points to Aeschines copying Andocides, rather than a later 'pseudo-Andocides' copying Aeschines.[88]

Neither of these points, of course, proves that the *De Pace* is not a political pamphlet, and the problem of how close the surviving speech is to what was actually delivered is an insoluble one. But no adequate reason is apparent today for rejecting the attribution of the speech as a work of Andocides.

(iv) Analysis of the speech

There has been a wide divergence of opinion among scholars as to the organisation, or lack of it, of the *De Pace*. Thus, while Blass criticised the speech for its total lack of order or plan, Albini praised its precise and intelligent schema.[89] The truth perhaps lies somewhere in the middle. For while the speech has no simple proem/proofs/epilogue structure, a basic tripartite division may nevertheless be discerned.

It is essential, firstly, to recognise that Andocides' speech responds to a series of objections which he alleges were being made by his opponents. This is shown by his repeated use of the common verbs meaning 'to say' ($\lambda\acute{e}\gamma\omega$ and $\phi\eta\mu\acute{\iota}$): **for they say (1); I have already heard some people saying...those who say this (10-11); some say (13); some are saying (26); for they even say (33); there are already some people saying (36); some say (40).** These objections correspond to the passages where Andocides begins new arguments. Furthermore, the use of this technique reflects the fact that most of Andocides' arguments in the speech are refutative, his one confirmative argument in **17-23** being introduced by 'consider' ($\sigma\kappa\acute{e}\psi\alpha\sigma\theta\epsilon$). Significantly, this section stands almost in the middle of the speech, and we therefore arrive at the following division.

---

88   See Jebb 130. For example, there was no need for another writer to mention Andocides' grandfather (whom Aeschines makes the leader of the embassy) in connection with the Thirty Years' Peace.

        Dionysius may have adduced stylistic reasons for his rejection of the speech. There is no space here for an in-depth analysis, but in general terms there are insufficient stylistic differences between the *De Pace* and the earlier speeches to warrant such a rejection.

89   Blass 330 (cf. Kennedy 147); *contra* Albini (1964) 25.

Dispensing with a formal proem, Andocides goes straight into his first topic, employing historical examples to show that making peace with Sparta will not endanger the democracy (1-12). This section of the speech is subdivided into two parts, the peace agreements that were made during the Pentecontaetia (1-9) and the truce made at the end of the Peloponnesian War (10-12). He continues with a four-part discussion of the advantages of peace over continuing the war, beginning with a refutation of the claim that continuation was a necessity (13-16). Andocides now inserts his confirmative proof, demonstrating the advantages that peace will bring, in turn, to Sparta, Boeotia and finally (at about the mid-point of the speech) Athens (17-23). He then returns to refutation by immediately juxtaposing to these advantages the disadvantages of siding with Corinth and Argos (24-7), supporting this with a second set of historical examples which illustrate Athens' old fault of abandoning powerful friends for weak ones (28-32). The third topic of the speech is the ambassadors' referral of the decision to the assembly (33-41). Andocides justifies this action firstly against those who want peace to be concluded immediately (33-4), then against those who want war, the latter in two parts (35-6, 40-1) separated by a third use of historical example (37-9). This final topic is brought to an emphatic climax with the remark thanks to us (δι' ἡμᾶς); and the speech ends with a very brief epilogue (41).

(v) Evaluation of the speech
The attention of scholars has been mainly focused on the problems discussed in sections (iii) and (iv) above. These, and the ultimate failure of the plea, have detracted from the rhetorical merits that the *De Pace* contains. Andocides deals with the standard deliberative themes of necessity (13), practicability (15), expediency (17-23) and justice (26). Additionally, the speech has a number of effective rhetorical features, including the series of questions (hypophora) in 13-16; the debate with imaginary interlocutors (prosopopoeia) at 26; the ironical comment on the behaviour of the Argives (27); notable remarks such as the claim that joined with Boeotia Athens could face **the whole world (25), they call the precaution taken by us in making the reference fear (33)** and **the walls cannot feed them (36)**; other various frank statements at **19, 21, 28, 35**; and the sincerity of the plea at **32**. Finally, there is the employment of emotional appeal, discussed in section (vi). Andocides' failure, then, does not lie in rhetorical inadequacy.

(vi) Andocides the subversive orator
At the core of Missiou's thought-provoking thesis that Andocides' speeches were subversive to the Athenian democracy is her analysis of the *De Pace* (chapters 3-7).[90] This is lengthy and detailed, and cannot be fully discussed here, but the main arguments and conclusions merit recapitulation.

Andocides opens the *De Pace* with the contention that making peace with Sparta would not cause the fall of the democracy, adducing three historical

---

90 Subversive rhetoric is defined as occurring when a communicator attempts to weaken or destroy an ideology. See W. Fisher, 'A motive view of communication', *Quarterly Journal of Speech* 56 (1970) 131-9.

examples drawn from the Pentecontaetia period. In the first two of these (3-5, 6-7) the pattern is narrative/rhetorical question(s)/detailed description of the resulting benefits; in the third (8-9) the questions are omitted. A notable feature here is the very abundance of the historical references: Andocides' listeners are led to the inference from all these past benefits that similar benefits will accrue in the future from the proposed peace.[91] He then moves on to more recent history (10-12) and addresses the specific argument of his opponents that the peace made with Sparta in 404 led to the rule of the Thirty. Andocides avoids the emotional connotations these events must have had for the assembly and the role of Sparta in the establishment of the Thirty, and replies cleverly to this very real problem for his case that the settlement in 404 was a forced truce (σπονδαί) rather than, as before, a true peace (εἰρήνη). This raises the question as to whether Athens was now negotiating on equal terms with Sparta, which Andocides does not directly answer, though he later talks of Spartan victories and allied defeats (18-19). His emphasis lies rather on the causal relationship between peace with Sparta and Athenian prosperity (4-5, 7), and, since this was the opposite view to the popular one that Athens' prosperity was the direct result of her empire and willingness to take action,[92] on the sufferings of war (6, 8). Andocides was clearly adopting a very risky standpoint, which Missiou interprets as a subversive attempt to discredit the past empire and so hinder the revival of Athenian imperialism.

We should, in addition, note the absence of the regular term for 'empire' (ἀρχή) in 1-12,[93] which does however appear, along with other words recalling the empire (such as Hellenotamiae, walls and ships) when Andocides again refers to the past in 37-40. Andocides' argument in this part of the speech has three main elements, beginning in 35 with criticism of the Athenians' character - they do not know what they want. This is connected with his emphasis on the value of the walls and fleet. Although the importance of Athens' walls for her security was well known, it appears from 36 that there was some disagreement in Athens as to whether walls and ships were sufficient ends in themselves. Andocides attempts to exploit this - the walls and ships had acquired a symbolic significance, and the agreement over their retention reflected Sparta's acceptance that Athens was not in the same position now as she had been in 404. His opponents, on the other hand, were arguing that mere retention of the walls and ships did not go far enough - Athens should continue fighting, in order to recover the Chersonese and overseas settlements and thereby secure her vital food supply from the Black Sea. The slogans **they are not regaining their own private property from abroad** and **the walls cannot feed them** (36) therefore reflect the social demands of Athens' lower classes, who hoped for a revival of the empire as a solution to their post-war poverty; whereas the wealthier citizens supported the concept of self-sufficiency

---

91 This aim is in fact stated in **2**.
92 This view is reflected in numerous passages of Thucydides (e.g. 1.70.8-9, 2.64.3) and in funeral speeches (e.g. Lys. 2.43, 55; cf. Thuc. 2.36.2, 36.4, 41.4).
93 Though 'power' (δύναμις) is used in **5, 7, 12**.

(αὐτάρκεια).[94] Finally, Andocides' account of the empire is less than flattering. Power was acquired by stealth and bribery as well as by persuasion and force (37-8); defeat in the Peloponnesian War and its consequences are emphasised (39); he denies the Athenians credit for their empire by ascribing Athens' rise to others' lack of attention; and he makes no mention of Themistocles' role in the building of the walls. These are, once more, the marks of an oligarchic sympathiser.

Aware of the gulf in ideology between himself and the assembly, in 19-23 Andocides builds a strong ethical argument on the basis of the gratitude Athens owed Sparta. The highly moral Sparta is the polar opposite to the ungrateful Athens; and the rhetorical questions at the start of 21 indicate that he is reacting to a negative response from his audience, shielding himself behind his responsibility to state the facts. These include a sensational reference to the recent past in 21-2 (the negotiations leading to the treaty of 404) - the vivid presentation underlines Sparta's magnanimous behaviour then, in contrast with the behaviour of the Athenians' current allies, who were their direst enemies at the time. Since the Spartans had inverted the traditional Greek principle of helping friends and harming enemies, Athens should have returned the favour, but instead detached the Boeotians and Corinthians from them and, along with Argos, went to war. Similarly, Athens turned the Persian king against Sparta and enabled Conon to deprive her of her naval hegemony. Despite this Sparta continued to treat Athens like an ally, and Athens should now recognise that the peace is a goodwill gesture and advantageous only to Athens (23). Other sources which refer to the negotiations of 404 show that there was also a hostile tradition in which Sparta, far from being benevolent, actually played a destructive role in Athens' affairs.[95] Since Andocides in 21 (cf. Xen. *Hell.* 2.2.19-20) clearly prefers the Spartan code of international politics, the moral gratitude he says Athens owes Sparta is associated with the pursuit of Sparta's advantage (i.e. the conclusion of peace). Finally, Missiou raises the possibility that Andocides' version of events in 404 was fabricated and looks for their historical kernel,[96] to discover when the story developed (before 1.142) and how it was modified to meet changing demands - which were firstly of the Spartans, to rehabilitate their reputation as the patrons of the Thirty after the restoration of the democracy; and secondly of the Athenian oligarchs, to involve the Thebans and Corinthians because they had become Athens' allies against Sparta in the Corinthian War. If, therefore, Andocides was adopting a line which he anticipated would provoke a hostile reaction, it will have been his oligarchic ideology that was his motivation.

In 28-32 Andocides criticises Athenian foreign policy and adduces three historical examples to show that its main principle was to help the weak and the wronged, and to reject the strong. Missiou's examination of Greek interstate

---

94   Cf. Pl. *Menex.* 237e-238a. But see the reservation of S. C. Todd in his review of Missiou, *CR* 43 (1993) 21, that it is unsafe to assume the rich farmers were consistently anti-war.

95   Cf. Lys. 14.18-19; Isoc. 5.43-4; Dem. 19.65-6; Pl. *Menex.* 244c; Diod. 15.63; Plut. *Lysander* 15.

96   I.e. that Athens was not destroyed, although this was perhaps proposed at some point.

relations demonstrates that Andocides is attacking a characteristic feature of Athenian diplomacy under the democracy. Whereas the Greeks in general followed a pattern of diplomacy which was based on the demand for the return of a favour (χάρις), the Athenians tended to follow a second pattern, in which expectation of reciprocity was absent and emphasis was laid instead on the moral obligation to help the weak and the wronged. This policy distinguished democratic Athens from the other Greek states, and the Athenians' commitment to it is described positively in numerous texts, including the six extant funeral speeches and speeches in Thucydides.[97] But the negative view is also expressed, as by Andocides at **28** and Plato at *Menex.* 244c, and the close similarity between these two passages suggests oligarchic circles, in which Athens' coalition with anti-Spartan governments was caricatured as support for the inferior. In addition, Andocides is silent on Athens' obligation to stay loyal to existing allies, which was being stressed by his opponents: since the alliance with Argos was designed to safeguard the democracy, his criticism of Athenian foreign policy in **28-32** and advocation of alliance with Sparta reflects his ideological commitment to oligarchy.

Emotional appeal plays a crucial role in the *De Pace*. Andocides' opponents seem to have concentrated on the need to alter the current state of affairs, and in particular to abolish Spartan hegemony (**15**), and so their arguments will have been hortatory and oriented towards the future. Andocides, on the other hand, was attempting to preserve the status quo. He lists the benefits that might follow from making peace for all the Greeks (common peace, freedom, independence and freedom of the seas, **17, 19**), but does not suggest how they would benefit the Athenians in concrete terms in the future. Nor does he explain why the practical gains the Athenians would make from peace (walls, ships and islands, **23**) should be seen as a guarantee of future prosperity. He only, in fact, talks of the future disadvantages of rejecting the peace (**24-32**), so while his opponents will have made use of an appeal to hope, Andocides bases his arguments on a strategy of fear. In **15**, for example, he makes no attempt to justify his rejection of the pro-war arguments, but ends with an alleged, unspecified dreadful consequence that would follow from victory over Sparta. Andocides' method may be compared with the approaches of Archidamus and Nicias in books 1 and 6, respectively, of Thucydides. Their deliberative speeches were also addressed to hostile audiences and they also employed the raising of fear as a weapon, but they did so by rational arguments to explain why their cities did not have the necessary resources to succeed in the proposed enterprise.[98] Andocides is unique in failing to comply with the principle that the speaker must justify his policy. This rhetorical choice then contrasts with his portrayal of the Spartans: in **18** they are willingly promoting the freedom of Greece, and he paints a distorted picture of unbroken Spartan success, thereby revealing his pro-Spartan bias. In other words, Andocides' strategy of fear is designed not simply to show that the Spartans enjoy military supremacy, but to persuade the assembly therefore to preserve the status quo. There is, besides, a theme of Spartan

---

97 Missiou examines the funeral speech and the debates over Corcyra, Mytilene and Plataea.

98 Missiou also examines Demosthenes' use of rational argument in *On the Symmories*.

magnanimity, specifically in **19** and **21-3**. Argos, on the contrary, is depicted as an aggressor (**26-7**) and disastrous ally (**9, 31, 41**), which perhaps stems from the fears of the Athenian propertied class over losing their land.

Finally, in the light of the above interpretation of the *De Pace* we must question the depiction of Andocides as the far-sighted, sound counsellor whose advice was ignored by an irrational assembly.[99] His aim was not simply to win a majority of votes for peace: knowing, in fact, that he had little chance of persuading the assembly to change its mind over continuing the war, which for the lower classes meant empire and its benefits, Andocides delivered a speech which was part of a long-term attempt to transform popular attitudes, in defence of the interests of the rich land-owning class. His was an emotional appeal, based on oligarchic ideology and without substance, and it was therefore unacceptable to the majority of Athenians.

Missiou's approach to the study of political oratory, which draws on modern communications studies, concentrates less on the speaker as the manipulator of his audience's emotions and more on the interaction between speaker and audience. This methodology is clearly sound, although some elements of her thesis as applied to Andocides' actions in 392/1 are questionable. There must, for example, be some doubt over how far Andocides had in mind a long-term strategy rather than an immediate victory, for it is very dangerous to assume that he was speaking on behalf of a united oligarchic group. Nor was there any simple division along oligarchic/democratic lines over attitudes to the war. His fellow-ambassador Epicrates was certainly no oligarch, quite the reverse, and he shared Andocides' fate.[100] But while Missiou's socio-political model may not be entirely convincing, her basic premise is cogent: Andocides was an adherent of oligarchy, and his *De Pace* was essentially subversive.

---

99   For which see, e.g., Jebb 82-3.
100 For an analysis of the political groupings of this period see B. S. Strauss, *Athens after the Peloponnesian War* (London, 1986) chapter 5, especially pp. 138-43.

ΠΕΡΙ ΤΗΣ ΠΡΟΣ ΛΑΚΕΔΑΙΜΟΝΙΟΥΣ ΕΙΡΗΝΗΣ

[1] Ὅτι μὲν εἰρήνην ποιεῖσθαι δικαίαν ἄμεινόν ἐστιν ἢ πολεμεῖν, δοκεῖτέ μοι, ὦ Ἀθηναῖοι, πάντες γιγνώσκειν· ὅτι δὲ οἱ ῥήτορες τῷ μὲν ὀνόματι τῆς εἰρήνης συγχωροῦσι, τοῖς δ' ἔργοις ἀφ' ὧν ἂν ἡ εἰρήνη γένοιτο ἐναντιοῦνται, τοῦτο δὲ οὐ πάντες αἰσθάνεσθε. λέγουσι γὰρ ὡς ἔστι δεινότατον τῷ δήμῳ, γενομένης εἰρήνης, ἡ νῦν οὖσα πολιτεία μὴ καταλυθῇ. [2] εἰ μὲν οὖν μηδεπώποτε πρότερον ὁ δῆμος ὁ Ἀθηναίων εἰρήνην ἐποιήσατο πρὸς Λακεδαιμονίους, εἰκότως ἂν ἐφοβούμεθα αὐτὸ διά τε τὴν ἀπειρίαν τοῦ ἔργου διά τε τὴν ἐκείνων ἀπιστίαν· ὅπου δὲ πολλάκις ἤδη πρότερον εἰρήνην ἐποιήσασθε δημοκρατούμενοι, πῶς οὐκ εἰκὸς ὑμᾶς πρῶτον ἐκεῖνα σκέψασθαι τὰ τότε γενόμενα; χρὴ γάρ, ὦ Ἀθηναῖοι, τεκμηρίοις χρῆσθαι τοῖς πρότερον γενομένοις περὶ τῶν μελλόντων ἔσεσθαι.

[3] Ἡνίκα τοίνυν ἦν μὲν ὁ πόλεμος ἡμῖν ἐν Εὐβοίᾳ, Μέγαρα δὲ εἴχομεν καὶ Πηγὰς καὶ Τροζῆνα, εἰρήνης ἐπεθυμήσαμεν, καὶ Μιλτιάδην τὸν Κίμωνος ὠστρακισμένον καὶ ὄντα ἐν Χερρονήσῳ κατεδεξάμεθα δι' αὐτὸ τοῦτο, πρόξενον ὄντα Λακεδαιμονίων, ὅπως πέμψαιμεν εἰς Λακεδαίμονα προκηρυκευσόμενον περὶ σπονδῶν. [4] καὶ τότε ἡμῖν εἰρήνη ἐγένετο πρὸς Λακεδαιμονίους ἔτη πεντήκοντα, καὶ ἐνεμείναμεν ἀμφότεροι ταύταις ταῖς σπονδαῖς ἔτη τριακαίδεκα. ἓν δὴ τοῦτο, ὦ Ἀθηναῖοι, πρῶτον σκεψώμεθα. ἐν ταύτῃ τῇ εἰρήνῃ ὁ δῆμος ὁ Ἀθηναίων ἔσθ' ὅπου κατελύθη; οὐδεὶς ἀποδείξει. ἀγαθὰ δὲ ὅσα ἐγένετο διὰ ταύτην τὴν εἰρήνην, ἐγὼ ὑμῖν φράσω. [5] πρῶτον μὲν τὸν Πειραιᾶ ἐτειχίσαμεν ἐν τούτῳ τῷ χρόνῳ, εἶτα τὸ μακρὸν τεῖχος τὸ βόρειον· ἀντὶ δὲ τῶν τριήρων αἳ τότε ἡμῖν ἦσαν παλαιαὶ καὶ ἄπλοι, αἷς βασιλέα καὶ τοὺς βαρβάρους καταναυμαχήσαντες ἠλευθερώσαμεν τοὺς Ἕλληνας, ἀντὶ τούτων τῶν νεῶν ἑκατὸν τριήρεις ἐναυπηγησάμεθα, καὶ πρῶτον τότε τριακοσίους ἱππέας κατεστησάμεθα καὶ τοξότας τριακοσίους Σκύθας ἐπριάμεθα. καὶ ταῦτα ἐκ τῆς εἰρήνης τῆς πρὸς Λακεδαιμονίους ἀγαθὰ τῇ πόλει καὶ δύναμις τῷ δήμῳ τῷ Ἀθηναίων ἐγένετο.

[6] Μετὰ δὲ ταῦτα δι' Αἰγινήτας εἰς πόλεμον κατέστημεν, καὶ πολλὰ κακὰ παθόντες πολλὰ δὲ ποιήσαντες ἐπεθυμήσαμεν πάλιν τῆς εἰρήνης, καὶ ἡρέθησαν δέκα ἄνδρες ἐξ Ἀθηναίων ἁπάντων πρέσβεις εἰς Λακεδαίμονα περὶ εἰρήνης αὐτοκράτορες, ὧν ἦν καὶ Ἀνδοκίδης ὁ πάππος ὁ ἡμέτερος. οὗτοι ἡμῖν εἰρήνην

ON THE PEACE WITH THE SPARTANS

[1] That it is better to make a just peace than to make war you all seem to me, Athenians, to understand; but that the public speakers accept the name of peace but are opposed to the actions by which peace might be concluded, this you do not all perceive. For they say that there is a very great danger for the democracy, once peace has been concluded, of the existing constitution being overthrown. [2] Now if the Athenian democracy had never previously made peace with the Spartans, we might reasonably have been afraid of it both through inexperience of the act and through their treachery; but when you have often already previously made peace under the democracy, how is it not reasonable for you firstly to consider the things which happened then? For it is necessary, Athenians, to use past events as indications of the future.

[3] Now, when we were fighting the war in Euboea and were holding Megara, Pegae and Troezen, we longed for peace and recalled Miltiades, son of Cimon, who had been ostracised and was in the Chersonese, for this very reason, since he was an official representative of the Spartans, that we might send him to Sparta to negotiate about a truce. [4] Then a peace was concluded between us and the Spartans for fifty years, and we both abided by this truce for thirteen years. Let us indeed, Athenians, firstly consider this one instance. Was there a time during this peace when the Athenian democracy was overthrown? No one can show that. But I can tell you the benefits which came out of this peace. [5] Firstly we fortified Peiraeus during this period, then built the northern Long Wall; and in place of the old and unseaworthy triremes which we then had, with which we defeated at sea the King and his barbarians and freed the Greeks, in place of these ships we built one hundred triremes, and we firstly then established three hundred cavalry and bought three hundred Scythian archers. From the peace with the Spartans came these benefits for the city and power for the Athenian democracy.

[6] After this we went to war because of the Aeginetans, and after suffering many ills and inflicting many, we again longed for peace, and ten men were chosen from all the Athenians as ambassadors to Sparta with full powers to negotiate about peace, one of whom was Andocides, my

ἐποίησαν πρὸς Λακεδαιμονίους ἔτη τριάκοντα. καὶ ἐν τοσούτῳ χρόνῳ ἔστιν ὅπου, ὦ 'Αθηναῖοι, ὁ δῆμος κατελύθη; τί δε; πράττοντές τινες δήμου κατάλυσιν ἐλήφθησαν; οὐκ ἔστιν ὅστις ἀποδείξει. [7] ἀλλ' αὐτὸ τὸ ἐναντιώτατον· αὕτη γὰρ ἡ εἰρήνη τὸν δῆμον τὸν 'Αθηναίων ὑψηλὸν ἦρε καὶ κατέστησεν ἰσχυρὸν οὕτως ὥστε πρῶτον μὲν ἐν τούτοις τοῖς ἔτεσιν εἰρήνην λαβόντες ἀνηνέγκαμεν χίλια τάλαντα εἰς τὴν ἀκρόπολιν, καὶ νόμῳ κατεκλῄσαμεν ἐξαίρετα εἶναι τῷ δήμῳ, τοῦτο δὲ τριήρεις ἄλλας ἑκατὸν ἐναυπηγησάμεθα, καὶ ταύτας ἐξαιρέτους ἐψηφισάμεθα εἶναι, νεωσοίκους τε ᾠκοδομησάμεθα, χιλίους τε καὶ διακοσίους ἱππέας καὶ τοξότας τοσούτους ἑτέρους κατεστήσαμεν, καὶ τὸ τεῖχος τὸ μακρὸν τὸ νότιον ἐτειχίσθη. ταῦτα ἐκ τῆς εἰρήνης τῆς πρὸς Λακεδαιμονίους ἀγαθὰ τῇ πόλει καὶ δύναμις τῷ δήμῳ τῷ 'Αθηναίων ἐγένετο.

[8] Πάλιν δὲ διὰ Μεγαρέας πολεμήσαντες καὶ τὴν χώραν τμηθῆναι προέμενοι, πολλῶν ἀγαθῶν στερηθέντες αὖθις τὴν εἰρήνην ἐποιησάμεθα, ἣν ἡμῖν Νικίας ὁ Νικηράτου κατηργάσατο. οἶμαι δ' ὑμᾶς ἅπαντας εἰδέναι τοῦτο, ὅτι διὰ ταύτην τὴν εἰρήνην ἑπτακισχίλια μὲν τάλαντα νομίσματος εἰς τὴν ἀκρόπολιν ἀνηνέγκαμεν, [9] ναῦς δὲ πλείους ἢ τριακοσίας ἐκτησάμεθα, καὶ φόρος προσῄει κατ' ἐνιαυτὸν πλέον ἢ διακόσια καὶ χίλια τάλαντα, καὶ Χερρόνησόν τε εἴχομεν καὶ Νάξον καὶ Εὐβοίας πλέον ἢ τὰ δύο μέρη· τάς τε ἄλλας ἀποικίας καθ' ἕκαστον διηγεῖσθαι μακρὸς ἂν εἴη λόγος. ταῦτα δ' ἔχοντες τὰ ἀγαθὰ πάλιν κατέστημεν εἰς πόλεμον πρὸς Λακεδαιμονίους, πεισθέντες καὶ τότε ὑπ' 'Αργείων.

[10] Πρῶτον μὲν οὖν, ὦ 'Αθηναῖοι, τούτου ἀναμνήσθητε, τί ὑμῖν ἐξ ἀρχῆς ὑπεθέμην τῷ λόγῳ. ἄλλο τι ἢ τοῦτο, ὅτι διὰ τὴν εἰρήνην οὐδεπώποτε ὁ δῆμος ὁ 'Αθηναίων κατελύθη; οὐκοῦν ἀποδέδεικται. καὶ οὐδεὶς ἐξελέγξει με ὡς οὐκ ἔστι ταῦτα ἀληθῆ. ἤδη δέ τινων ἤκουσα λεγόντων ὡς ἐκ τῆς τελευταίας εἰρήνης τῆς πρὸς Λακεδαιμονίους οἵ τε τριάκοντα κατέστησαν πολλοί τε 'Αθηναίων κώνειον πιόντες ἀπέθανον, οἱ δὲ φεύγοντες ᾤχοντο. [11] ὁπόσοι οὖν ταῦτα λέγουσιν, οὐκ ὀρθῶς γιγνώσκουσιν· εἰρήνη γὰρ καὶ σπονδαὶ πολὺ διαφέρουσι σφῶν αὐτῶν. εἰρήνην μὲν γὰρ ἐξ ἴσου ποιοῦνται πρὸς ἀλλήλους ὁμολογήσαντες περὶ ὧν ἂν διαφέρωνται· σπονδὰς δέ, ὅταν κρατήσωσι κατὰ τὸν πόλεμον, οἱ κρείττους τοῖς ἥττοσιν ἐξ ἐπιταγμάτων ποιοῦνται, ὥσπερ ἡμῶν κρατήσαντες Λακεδαιμόνιοι τῷ πολέμῳ ἐπέταξαν ἡμῖν καὶ <τὰ> τείχη καθαιρεῖν καὶ τὰς ναῦς παραδιδόναι καὶ τοὺς φεύγοντας καταδέχεσθαι. [12]

grandfather. These made a thirty years' peace between us and the Spartans. Now, was there a time during so long a period when, Athenians, the democracy was overthrown? I ask you, were any people caught working for the overthrow of the democracy? There is no one who can show this. [7] In fact, exactly the opposite; for this peace raised the Athenian democracy so high and rendered it so strong that firstly, during these years after gaining peace, we deposited one thousand talents on the Acropolis and declared them by law to be set apart as a reserve for the people; and besides that we built another hundred triremes and voted they be set apart as a reserve, and we built shipsheds and established twelve hundred cavalry and as many archers, and the southern Long Wall was built. From the peace with the Spartans came these benefits for the city and power for the Athenian democracy.

[8] Then we went to war again because of the Megarians and abandoned our territory to be laid waste, but deprived of many benefits we once more made peace, the one which Nicias, son of Niceratus, achieved for us. I think you all know this, that through this peace we deposited seven thousand talents of coined silver on the Acropolis; [9] and we acquired more than three hundred ships, tribute was coming in each year of more than twelve hundred talents, and we were holding the Chersonese, Naxos and more than two-thirds of Euboea; while to describe our other colonies individually would be a long story. But despite having these benefits we again went to war with the Spartans, persuaded then, as now, by the Argives.

[10] Firstly then, Athenians, recall what I proposed from the beginning to show you by my speech. Was it anything other than this, that the Athenian democracy has never yet been overthrown through peace? Surely then this has been shown. No one will prove against me that this is not true. But I have already heard some people saying that as a result of the last peace with the Spartans the Thirty were established, many Athenians died by drinking hemlock, and others fled into exile. [11] Those who say this do not understand correctly, for a peace and a truce are very different things. A peace is made by men on equal terms, having reached agreement with one another over their differences, a truce is made by injunction by the victors, after winning the war, over the vanquished, just as the Spartans, after defeating us in the war, enjoined us to demolish our walls, surrender our fleet and recall our exiles. [12] A truce then was forcibly concluded by

τότε μὲν οὖν σπονδαὶ κατ' ἀνάγκην ἐξ ἐπιταγμάτων ἐγένοντο· νῦν δὲ περὶ εἰρήνης βουλεύεσθε. σκέψασθε δὲ ἐξ αὐτῶν τῶν γραμμάτων, ἅ τε ἡμῖν ἐν τῇ στήλῃ γέγραπται, ἐφ' οἷς τε νῦν ἔξεστι τὴν εἰρήνην ποιεῖσθαι. ἐκεῖ μὲν γὰρ γέγραπται τὰ τείχη καθαιρεῖν, ἐν δὲ τοῖσδε ἔξεστιν οἰκοδομεῖν· ναῦς ἐκεῖ μὲν δώδεκα κεκτῆσθαι, νῦν δ' ὁπόσας ἂν βουλώμεθα· Λῆμνον δὲ καὶ Ἴμβρον καὶ Σκῦρον τότε μὲν ἔχειν τοὺς ἔχοντας, νῦν δὲ ἡμετέρας εἶναι· καὶ φεύγοντας νῦν μὲν οὐκ ἐπάναγκες οὐδένα καταδέχεσθαι, τότε δ' ἐπάναγκες, ἐξ ὧν ὁ δῆμος κατελύθη. τί ταῦτα ἐκείνοις ὁμολογεῖ; τοσοῦτον οὖν ἔγωγε, ὦ Ἀθηναῖοι, διορίζομαι περὶ τούτων, τὴν μὲν εἰρήνην σωτηρίαν εἶναι τῷ δήμῳ καὶ δύναμιν, τὸν δὲ πόλεμον δήμου κατάλυσιν γίγνεσθαι. περὶ μὲν οὖν τούτων ταῦτα λέγω.

[13] Φασὶ δέ τινες ἀναγκαίως νῦν ἡμῖν ἔχειν πολεμεῖν· σκεψώμεθα οὖν πρῶτον, ὦ ἄνδρες Ἀθηναῖοι, διὰ τί καὶ πολεμήσωμεν. οἶμαι γὰρ ἂν πάντας ἀνθρώπους ὁμολογῆσαι διὰ τάδε δεῖν πολεμεῖν, ἢ ἀδικουμένους ἢ βοηθοῦντας ἠδικημένοις. ἡμεῖς τοίνυν αὐτοί τε ἠδικούμεθα Βοιωτοῖς τε ἀδικουμένοις ἐβοηθοῦμεν. εἰ τοίνυν ἡμῖν τέ ἐστι τοῦτο παρὰ Λακεδαιμονίων, τὸ μηκέτι ἀδικεῖσθαι, Βοιωτοῖς τε δέδοκται ποιεῖσθαι τὴν εἰρήνην ἀφεῖσιν Ὀρχομενὸν αὐτόνομον, τίνος ἕνεκα πολεμήσωμεν; [14] ἵνα ἡ πόλις ἡμῶν ἐλευθέρα ᾖ; ἀλλὰ τοῦτό γε αὐτῇ ὑπάρχει. ἀλλ' ὅπως ἡμῖν τείχη γένηται; ἔστι καὶ ταῦτα ἐκ τῆς εἰρήνης. ἀλλ' ἵνα τριήρεις ἐξῇ ναυπηγεῖσθαι καὶ τὰς οὔσας ἐπισκευάζειν καὶ κεκτῆσθαι; καὶ τοῦτο ὑπάρχει· τὰς γὰρ πόλεις αὐτονόμους αἱ συνθῆκαι ποιοῦσιν. ἀλλ' ὅπως τὰς νήσους κομισώμεθα, Λῆμνον καὶ Σκῦρον καὶ Ἴμβρον; οὐκοῦν διαρρήδην γέγραπται ταύτας Ἀθηναίων εἶναι. [15] φέρε, ἀλλὰ Χερρόνησον καὶ τὰς ἀποικίας καὶ τὰ ἐγκτήματα καὶ τὰ χρέα ἵνα ἀπολάβωμεν; ἀλλ' οὔτε βασιλεὺς οὔτε οἱ σύμμαχοι συγχωροῦσιν ἡμῖν, μεθ' ὧν αὐτὰ δεῖ πολεμοῦντας κτήσασθαι. ἀλλὰ νὴ Δία ἕως ἂν Λακεδαιμονίους καταπολεμήσωμεν καὶ τοὺς συμμάχους αὐτῶν, μέχρι τούτου δεῖ πολεμεῖν; ἀλλ' οὔ μοι δοκοῦμεν οὕτω παρεσκευάσθαι. ἐὰν δ' ἄρα κατεργασώμεθα, τί ποτε αὐτοὶ πείσεσθαι δοκοῦμεν ὑπὸ τῶν βαρβάρων, ὅταν ταῦτα πράξωμεν; [16] εἰ τοίνυν περὶ τούτου μὲν ἔδει πολεμεῖν, χρήματα δὲ ὑπῆρχεν ἡμῖν ἱκανά, τοῖς δὲ σώμασιν ἦμεν δυνατοί, οὐδὲ οὕτως ἔδει πολεμεῖν. εἰ δὲ μήτε δι' ὅ τι μήτε ὅτοισι μήτε ἀφ' ὅτου πολεμήσωμεν ἔστι, πῶς οὐκ ἐκ παντὸς τρόπου τὴν εἰρήνην ποιητέον ἡμῖν;

injunction, but today you are deliberating about a peace. Consider too the actual recorded provisions, both those which have been inscribed for us on the stele and those on which it is possible to make peace today. For there it is prescribed that we demolish the walls, on these we are permitted to build them; there we can have twelve ships, today as many as we wish; then those holding Lemnos, Imbros and Scyros were to have them, today they are to be ours; and today there is no compulsion to recall exiles, whereas then there was compulsion, with the consequence that the democracy was overthrown. What is the correspondence between these provisions and those? Therefore I myself, Athenians, draw the following conclusion about this matter, that peace means safety and power for the democracy, but war means the overthrow of democracy. This, then, is what I have to say about this matter.

[13] Some say that we are today bound to make war; let us therefore consider firstly, men of Athens, why indeed we should make war. For I think that all men would agree that it is necessary to make war for these reasons, either when they are being wronged or to help those wronged. Now, we were both ourselves being wronged and were helping the Boeotians being wronged. If, then, we receive this guarantee from the Spartans, that we will no longer be wronged, and if the Boeotians have decided to make peace by allowing Orchomenus autonomy, for what reason should we make war? [14] That our city may be free? But this is what it already is. That we may build walls? These are also part of the peace. That it may be possible to build triremes, and to repair and keep the ones we have? This too is already the case, since the treaty makes states autonomous. That we may recover the islands, Lemnos, Scyros and Imbros? But it is expressly laid down that these are to be the Athenians'. [15] Well, that we may regain the Chersonese, our colonies, our possessions abroad and our debts? But neither the King of Persia nor our allies allow us, and to acquire them we must make war with their help. Then, by Heaven, must we continue to make war until we have reduced the Spartans and their allies? But we do not seem to me to be equipped for that. Then if we are successful, what do we think we will then suffer ourselves at the hands of the barbarians, when we have done this? [16] Even if we should make war for this reason, and we had sufficient money and enough men, not even then should we make war. But if there is neither any reason for us to make war nor anyone against whom we should do it nor anything with which to sustain it, how should we not do everything possible to make peace?

[17] Σκέψασθε δέ, ὦ Ἀθηναῖοι, καὶ τόδε, ὅτι νυνὶ πᾶσι τοῖς Ἕλλησι κοινὴν εἰρήνην καὶ ἐλευθερίαν πράττετε, καὶ μετέχειν ἅπασι πάντων ἐξουσίαν ποιεῖτε. ἐνθυμήθητε οὖν τῶν πόλεων τὰς μεγίστας, τίνι τρόπῳ τὸν πόλεμον καταλύονται. πρῶτον μὲν Λακεδαιμονίους, οἵτινες ἀρχόμενοι μὲν ἡμῖν καὶ τοῖς συμμάχοις πολεμεῖν ἦρχον καὶ κατὰ γῆν καὶ κατὰ θάλατταν, νῦν δ' αὐτοῖς ἐκ τῆς εἰρήνης οὐδέτερον τούτων ὑπάρχει. [18] καὶ οὐχ ὑφ' ἡμῶν ἀναγκαζόμενοι ταῦτ' ἀφιᾶσιν, ἀλλ' ἐπ' ἐλευθερίᾳ πάσης τῆς Ἑλλάδος. νενικήκασι γὰρ τρὶς ἤδη μαχόμενοι, τοτὲ μὲν ἐν Κορίνθῳ πάντας πανδημεὶ τοὺς συμμάχους παρόντας, οὐχ ὑπολιπόντες πρόφασιν οὐδεμίαν, ἀλλ' ἐν τῷ κρατιστεύειν μόνοι πάντων, αὖθις δ' ἐν Βοιωτοῖς, ὅτ' αὐτῶν Ἀγησίλαος ἡγεῖτο, τὸν αὐτὸν τρόπον καὶ τότε τὴν νίκην ἐποιήσαντο, τρίτον δ' ἡνίκα Λέχαιον ἔλαβον, Ἀργείους μὲν ἅπαντας καὶ Κορινθίους, ἡμῶν δὲ καὶ Βοιωτῶν τοὺς παρόντας. [19] τοιαῦτα δ' ἔργα ἐπιδειξάμενοι τὴν εἰρήνην εἰσὶν ἕτοιμοι ποιεῖσθαι τὴν ἑαυτῶν ἔχοντες, οἳ ἐνίκων μαχόμενοι, καὶ τὰς πόλεις αὐτονόμους εἶναι καὶ τὴν θάλατταν κοινὴν ἐῶντες τοῖς ἡττημένοις. καίτοι ποίας τινὸς ἂν ἐκεῖνοι παρ' ἡμῶν εἰρήνης ἔτυχον, εἰ μίαν μόνον μάχην ἡττήθησαν; [20] Βοιωτοὶ δ' αὖ πῶς τὴν εἰρήνην ποιοῦνται; οἵτινες τὸν μὲν πόλεμον ἐποιήσαντο ἕνεκα Ὀρχομενοῦ, ὡς οὐκ ἐπιτρέψοντες αὐτόνομον εἶναι, νῦν δὲ τεθνεώτων μὲν αὐτοῖς ἀνδρῶν τοσούτων τὸ πλῆθος, τῆς δὲ γῆς ἐκ μέρους τινὸς τετμημένης, χρήματα δ' εἰσενηνοχότες πολλὰ καὶ ἰδίᾳ καὶ δημοσίᾳ, ὧν στέρονται, πολεμήσαντες δὲ ἔτη τέτταρα, ὅμως Ὀρχομενὸν ἀφέντες αὐτόνομον τὴν εἰρήνην ποιοῦνται καὶ ταῦτα μάτην πεπόνθασιν· ἐξῆν γὰρ αὐτοῖς καὶ τὴν ἀρχὴν ἐῶσιν Ὀρχομενίους αὐτονόμους εἰρήνην ἄγειν. οὗτοι δ' αὖ τούτῳ <τῷ> τρόπῳ τὸν πόλεμον καταλύονται. [21] ἡμῖν δέ, ὦ Ἀθηναῖοι, πῶς ἔξεστι τὴν εἰρήνην ποιήσασθαι; ποίων τινῶν Λακεδαιμονίων τυγχάνοντας; καὶ γὰρ εἴ τις ὑμῶν ἀχθεσθήσεται παραιτοῦμαι· <τὰ> γὰρ ὄντα λέξω. πρῶτον μὲν γὰρ ἡνίκα ἀπωλέσαμεν τὰς ναῦς ἐν Ἑλλησπόντῳ καὶ τειχήρεις ἐγενόμεθα, τίνα γνώμην ἔθεντο περὶ ἡμῶν οἱ νῦν μὲν ἡμέτεροι τότε δὲ Λακεδαιμονίων ὄντες σύμμαχοι; οὐ τὴν πόλιν ἡμῶν ἀνδραποδίζεσθαι καὶ τὴν χώραν ἐρημοῦν; οἱ δὲ διακωλύσαντες ταῦτα μὴ γενέσθαι τίνες ἦσαν; οὐ Λακεδαιμόνιοι, τοὺς μὲν συμμάχους ἀποτρέψαντες τῆς γνώμης, αὐτοὶ δ' οὐδ' ἐπιχειρήσαντες διαβουλεύσασθαι περὶ τοιούτων ἔργων; [22] μετὰ δὲ τοῦτο ὅρκους ὀμόσαντες αὐτοῖς καὶ τὴν στήλην εὑρόμενοι <παρ'> αὐτῶν στῆσαι, κακὸν ἀγαπητὸν ἐν ἐκείνῳ τῷ χρόνῳ, σπονδὰς

[17] Consider this too, Athenians, that today you are making a common peace and freedom for all Greeks, and you are giving them all the power to share in everything. Bear in mind in what way the greatest states are ending the war. Firstly the Spartans, who when they began to make war against us and our allies ruled both by land and by sea, but today are left by the peace with neither of these. [18] Nor are they giving these up under compulsion by us, but for the freedom of the whole of Greece. For they have already won three battles, the first at Corinth against all the allies present in full force, and leaving no excuse but their superiority over everyone by themselves; secondly in Boeotia, under the command of Agesilaus, they won a victory in the same manner as then; and thirdly when they took Lechaeum against all the Argives and Corinthians, and those of us and the Boeotians as were present. [19] But after these striking successes they are ready to make peace, keeping their own territory, they who were victorious in battle, and allowing states to be autonomous and the sea to be common to the defeated. Yet what kind of peace would they have obtained from us, if they had been defeated in one single battle? [20] Again, how are the Boeotians making peace? They made war because of Orchomenus, so as not to allow it to be autonomous, but today, with so many of their men dead and a good part of their land laid waste, and having contributed much money both privately and publicly, which they have lost, and having made war for four years, they nevertheless are allowing Orchomenus its autonomy and are making peace, and they have suffered these things in vain; for they could have allowed the Orchomenians their autonomy from the beginning and lived in peace. They are ending the war, then, in this way. [21] Now, Athenians, under what terms can we make peace? Finding what disposition towards us in the Spartans? If any of you is going to feel hurt, I beg his pardon; for I shall be stating the facts. Firstly, when we lost our ships in the Hellespont and became besieged, what proposal did our present allies, who were then on the Spartans' side, make about us? Was it not to enslave our city and lay waste its territory? Who were the ones that prevented this from happening? Was it not the Spartans, dissuading their allies from the proposal and themselves not even attempting to debate about such measures? [22] After this, having sworn oaths to them and being allowed by them to erect the stele, an evil to be acquiesced in at that time, we observed a truce on dictated terms. But then

ἤγομεν ἐπὶ ῥητοῖς. εἶτα δὲ συμμαχίαν ποιησάμενοι Βοιωτοὺς καὶ Κορινθίους ἀποστήσαντες αὐτῶν, 'Αργείους δὲ ἀγαγόντες εἰς τὴν ποτὲ φιλίαν, αἴτιοι τῆς ἐν Κορίνθῳ μάχης ἐγενόμεθα αὐτοῖς. τίνες δὲ βασιλέα πολέμιον αὐτοῖς ἐποίησαν, καὶ Κόνωνι τὴν ναυμαχίαν παρεσκεύασαν, δι' ἣν ἀπώλεσαν τὴν ἀρχὴν τῆς θαλάττης; [23] ὅμως τοίνυν ταῦτα πεπονθότες ὑφ' ἡμῶν συγχωροῦσι ταὐτὰ ἅπερ οἱ σύμμαχοι, καὶ διδόασιν ἡμῖν τὰ τείχη καὶ τὰς ναῦς καὶ τὰς νήσους ἡμῶν εἶναι. ποίαν τιν' οὖν χρὴ εἰρήνην πρεσβεύοντας ἥκειν; οὐ ταὐτὰ παρὰ τῶν πολεμίων εὑρομένους ἅπερ οἱ φίλοι διδόασι, καὶ δι' ἅπερ ἠρξάμεθα πολεμεῖν, ἵνα ἡμῶν γένηται τῇ πόλει ταῦτα; οἱ μὲν τοίνυν ἄλλοι τὴν εἰρήνην ποιοῦνται τῶν ὑπαρχόντων ἀφιέντες, ἡμεῖς δὲ προσλαμβάνοντες αὐτὰ ὧν μάλιστα δεόμεθα.

[24] Τί οὖν ἐστιν ὑπόλοιπον περὶ ὅτου δεῖ βουλεύεσθαι; περὶ Κορίνθου καὶ περὶ ὧν ἡμᾶς 'Αργεῖοι προκαλοῦνται. πρῶτον μὲν περὶ Κορίνθου διδαξάτω μέ τις, Βοιωτῶν μὴ συμπολεμούντων, εἰρήνην δὲ ποιουμένων πρὸς Λακεδαιμονίους, τίνος ἐστὶν ἡμῖν ἀξία Κόρινθος. [25] ἀναμνήσθητε γάρ, ὦ 'Αθηναῖοι, τῆς ἡμέρας ἐκείνης ὅτε Βοιωτοῖς τὴν συμμαχίαν ἐποιούμεθα, τίνα γνώμην ἔχοντες ταῦτα ἐπράττομεν. οὐχ ὡς ἱκανὴν οὖσαν τὴν Βοιωτῶν δύναμιν μεθ' ἡμῶν γενομένην κοινῇ πάντας ἀνθρώπους ἀμύνασθαι; νῦν δὲ βουλευόμεθα, Βοιωτῶν εἰρήνην ποιουμένων πῶς δυνατοὶ Λακεδαιμονίοις πολεμεῖν ἐσμεν ἄνευ Βοιωτῶν. [26] ναί, φασί τινες, ἂν Κόρινθόν τε φυλάττωμεν καὶ συμμάχους ἔχωμεν 'Αργείους. ἰόντων δὲ Λακεδαιμονίων εἰς 'Άργος πότερον βοηθήσομεν αὐτοῖς ἢ οὔ; πολλὴ γὰρ ἀνάγκη ὁπότερον τούτων ἑλέσθαι. μὴ βοηθούντων μὲν οὖν ἡμῶν οὐδὲ λόγος ὑπολείπεται μὴ οὐκ ἀδικεῖν καὶ ποιεῖν 'Αργείους ὁποῖον ἄν τι βούλωνται δικαίως· βοηθούντων δὲ ἡμῶν εἰς 'Άργος οὐχ ἕτοιμον μάχεσθαι Λακεδαιμονίοις; ἵνα ἡμῖν τί γένηται; ἵνα ἡττώμενοι μὲν καὶ τὴν οἰκείαν χώραν ἀπολέσωμεν πρὸς τῇ Κορινθίων, νικήσαντες δὲ τὴν Κορινθίων 'Αργείων ποιήσωμεν. οὐχ ἕνεκα τούτων πολεμήσομεν;

[27] Σκεψώμεθα δὴ καὶ τοὺς 'Αργείων λόγους. κελεύουσι γὰρ ἡμᾶς κοινῇ μετὰ σφῶν καὶ μετὰ Κορινθίων πολεμεῖν, αὐτοὶ δ' ἰδίᾳ εἰρήνην ποιησάμενοι τὴν χώραν οὐ παρέχουσιν ἐμπολεμεῖν. καὶ μετὰ μὲν πάντων τῶν συμμάχων τὴν εἰρήνην ποιουμένους οὐκ ἐῶσιν ἡμᾶς οὐδὲν πιστεύειν Λακεδαιμονίοις· ἃ δὲ πρὸς τούτους μόνους ἐκεῖνοι συνέθεντο, ταῦτα δ' οὐδεπώποτ' αὐτούς φασι παραβῆναι. πατρίαν τε εἰρήνην ὀνομάζοντες ᾗ χρῶνται, τοῖς ἄλλοις

we made an alliance and detached the Boeotians and Corinthians from them, and we resumed our one-time alliance with the Argives, so involving them in the battle of Corinth. Who, again, made the King of Persia hostile towards them and contrived for Conon the sea-battle through which they lost their sovereignty of the sea? [23] Yet in spite of suffering these things at our hands, they are accepting the same terms as our allies and offering to us to keep our walls, ships and islands. What kind of peace, then, should ambassadors bring? If not to obtain the same terms from the enemy as our friends are offering and through which we began to make war, to secure them for our city? Now, others make peace by conceding some of what they had, but we are doing so by gaining the very things which we most want.

[24] What is there remaining, then, about which we must deliberate? About Corinth and about the appeal the Argives are making to us. Firstly about Corinth, let someone inform me, if the Boeotians do not make war alongside us but make peace with the Spartans, of what value is Corinth to us? [25] Recall, Athenians, that day when we made the alliance with the Boeotians, with what purpose we did this. Was it not that the power of the Boeotians being joined with us was sufficient to defend ourselves against the whole world? But today we are deliberating how, with the Boeotians making peace, we are able to continue making war against the Spartans without the Boeotians. [26] Yes we can, some are saying, if we guard Corinth and have the Argives as allies. But if the Spartans attack Argos, shall we go to help them or not? For it will certainly be necessary to choose one of these courses. If we do not help, there is no argument remaining whatsoever that we are not in the wrong and that the Argives can rightly do whatever they wish; but if we do go to help Argos, is not war with the Spartans inevitable? To secure what? To lose our own territory in addition to that of the Corinthians if we are defeated, and to make the Corinthians' territory the Argives' if we are victorious. Are not these the objectives for which we shall be making war?

[27] Let us also consider the words of the Argives. They are urging us to make war together with themselves and with the Corinthians, but they themselves, after making a private peace, are removing their territory from the hostilities. Moreover, they forbid us, in making peace along with all our allies, to put any trust in the Spartans; but the agreements they have made with them alone they say they have never broken. Again, they call the peace

Ἕλλησιν οὐκ ἐῶσι πατρίαν γενέσθαι τὴν εἰρήνην· ἐκ γὰρ τοῦ πολέμου χρονισθέντος Κόρινθον ἑλεῖν προσδοκῶσι, κρατήσαντες δὲ τούτων ὑφ' ὧν ἀεὶ κρατοῦνται, καὶ τοὺς συννικῶντας ἐλπίζουσι παραστήσεσθαι.

[28] Τοιούτων δ' ἐλπίδων μετασχόντας ἡμᾶς δεῖ δυοῖν θάτερον ἑλέσθαι, ἢ πολεμεῖν μετὰ Ἀργείων Λακεδαιμονίοις, ἢ μετὰ Βοιωτῶν κοινῇ τὴν εἰρήνην ποιεῖσθαι. ἐγὼ μὲν οὖν ἐκεῖνο δέδοικα μάλιστα, ὦ Ἀθηναῖοι, τὸ εἰθισμένον κακόν, ὅτι τοὺς κρείττους φίλους ἀφιέντες ἀεὶ τοὺς ἥττους αἱρούμεθα, καὶ πόλεμον ποιούμεθα δι' ἑτέρους, ἐξὸν δι' ἡμᾶς αὐτοὺς εἰρήνην ἄγειν· [29] οἵτινες πρῶτον μὲν βασιλεῖ τῷ μεγάλῳ (χρὴ γὰρ ἀναμνησθέντας τὰ γεγενημένα καλῶς βουλεύσασθαι) σπονδὰς ποιησάμενοι καὶ συνθέμενοι φιλίαν εἰς τὸν ἅπαντα χρόνον, ἃ ἡμῖν ἐπρέσβευσεν Ἐπίλυκος Τεισάνδρου, τῆς μητρὸς τῆς ἡμετέρας ἀδελφός, <μετὰ> ταῦτα Ἀμόργῃ πειθόμενοι τῷ δούλῳ τῷ βασιλέως καὶ φυγάδι τὴν μὲν βασιλέως δύναμιν ἀπεβαλόμεθα ὡς οὐδενὸς οὖσαν ἀξίαν, τὴν δὲ Ἀμόργου φιλίαν εἱλόμεθα, κρείττω νομίσαντες εἶναι· ἀνθ' ὧν βασιλεὺς ὀργισθεὶς ἡμῖν, σύμμαχος γενόμενος Λακεδαιμονίοις, παρέσχεν αὐτοῖς εἰς τὸν πόλεμον πεντακισχίλια τάλαντα, ἕως κατέλυσεν ἡμῶν τὴν δύναμιν. ἓν μὲν βούλευμα τοιοῦτον ἐβουλευσάμεθα· [30] Συρακόσιοι δ' ὅτε ἦλθον ἡμῶν δεόμενοι, φιλότητα μὲν ἀντὶ διαφορᾶς ἐθέλοντες εἰρήνην δ' ἀντὶ πολέμου ποιεῖσθαι, τήν τε συμμαχίαν ἀποδεικνύντες ὅσῳ κρείττων ἡ σφετέρα εἴη τῆς Ἐγεσταίων καὶ Καταναίων, εἰ βουλοίμεθα πρὸς αὐτοὺς ποιεῖσθαι, ἡμεῖς τοίνυν εἱλόμεθα καὶ τότε πόλεμον μὲν ἀντὶ εἰρήνης, Ἐγεσταίους δὲ ἀντὶ Συρακοσίων, στρατεύεσθαι δ' εἰς Σικελίαν ἀντὶ τοῦ μένοντες οἴκοι συμμάχους ἔχειν Συρακοσίους· ἐξ ὧν πολλοὺς μὲν Ἀθηναίων ἀπολέσαντες ἀριστίνδην καὶ τῶν συμμάχων, πολλὰς δὲ ναῦς καὶ χρήματα καὶ δύναμιν ἀποβαλόντες, αἰσχρῶς διεκομίσθησαν οἱ σωθέντες αὐτῶν. [31] ὕστερον δ' ὑπ' Ἀργείων ἐπείσθημεν, οἵπερ νῦν ἥκουσι πείθοντες πολεμεῖν, πλεύσαντες ἐπὶ τὴν Λακωνικὴν εἰρήνης ἡμῖν οὔσης πρὸς Λακεδαιμονίους ἐκτεῖναι τὸν θυμόν, ἀρχὴν πολλῶν κακῶν· ἐξ οὗ πολεμήσαντες ἠναγκάσθημεν τὰ τείχη κατασκάπτειν καὶ τὰς ναῦς παραδιδόναι καὶ τοὺς φεύγοντας καταδέχεσθαι. ταῦτα δὲ πασχόντων ἡμῶν οἱ πείσαντες ἡμᾶς πολεμεῖν Ἀργεῖοι τίνα ὠφέλειαν παρέσχον ἡμῖν; τίνα δὲ κίνδυνον ὑπὲρ Ἀθηναίων ἐποιήσαντο; [32] νῦν οὖν τοῦτο ὑπόλοιπόν ἐστιν ἡμῖν, πόλεμον μὲν ἑλέσθαι καὶ νῦν ἀντ' εἰρήνης, τὴν δὲ συμμαχίαν τὴν Ἀργείων

which they are enjoying ancestral but forbid the other Greeks to conclude an ancestral peace, because by prolonging the war they expect to secure Corinth, and after becoming masters of those by whom they have always been mastered, they hope also to bring to terms their partners in victory.

[28] Committed to such prospects, we must choose one of two courses, either to make war with the Argives against the Spartans or to make peace in common with the Boeotians. What I fear the most is this, Athenians, our accustomed error that we always abandon our stronger friends and choose the weaker, and make war for the sake of others when it is possible for our own sakes to live in peace. [29] We firstly made a truce with the Great King (it is necessary to recall the past to deliberate rightly) and concluded a friendship for all time, negotiated for us by Epilycus, son of Teisander, my mother's brother; but after this we were persuaded by Amorges, the runaway slave of the King, to reject the power of the King as being worth nothing, and we chose the friendship of Amorges, thinking it was stronger; in return for this the King, in his anger at us, became an ally of the Spartans and provided them with five thousand talents to prosecute the war until he had overthrown our power. This is one such resolution we passed. [30] Then when the Syracusans came with a request to us, desiring friendship instead of disagreement and to make peace instead of war, and pointing out how much stronger would be the alliance with themselves than that with the Egestaeans and Catanians, if we were willing to make one with them, we then again chose war instead of peace, the Egestaeans instead of the Syracusans, to send an army to Sicily instead of staying at home and having the Syracusans as allies. The consequences were that we lost many Athenians and allies, the best before the rest, threw away many ships and a great deal of money and resources, and the survivors returned in disgrace. [31] Afterwards, we were persuaded by the same Argives, who are here today to persuade us to make war, to sail against Laconia, while we were at peace with the Spartans, and excite their anger, the beginning of many troubles. The consequence was that we made war and were forced to demolish our walls, surrender our fleet and recall our exiles. But while we were suffering these things, what help did the Argives who persuaded us to make war provide us? What danger did they brave on behalf of the Athenians? [32] This remains for us today, therefore, to choose war again today instead of peace, the alliance with the Argives instead of with the

ἀντὶ τῆς Βοιωτῶν, Κορινθίων δὲ τοὺς νῦν ἔχοντας τὴν πόλιν ἀντὶ Λακεδαιμονίων. μὴ δῆτα, ὦ Ἀθηναῖοι, μηδεὶς ἡμᾶς ταῦτα πείσῃ· τὰ γὰρ παραδείγματα τὰ γεγενημένα τῶν ἁμαρτημάτων ἱκανὰ τοῖς σώφροσι τῶν ἀνθρώπων ὥστε μηκέτι ἁμαρτάνειν.

[33] Εἰσὶ δέ τινες ὑμῶν οἳ τοσαύτην ὑπερβολὴν τῆς ἐπιθυμίας ἔχουσιν εἰρήνην ὡς τάχιστα γενέσθαι· φασὶ γὰρ καὶ τὰς τετταράκονθ᾽ ἡμέρας ἐν αἷς ὑμῖν ἔξεστι βουλεύεσθαι περίεργον εἶναι, καὶ τοῦτο ἀδικεῖν ἡμᾶς· αὐτοκράτορας γὰρ πεμφθῆναι εἰς Λακεδαίμονα διὰ ταῦθ᾽, ἵνα μὴ πάλιν ἐπαναφέρωμεν. τήν τε ἀσφάλειαν ἡμῶν τῆς ἐπαναφορᾶς δέος ὀνομάζουσι, λέγοντες ὡς οὐδεὶς πώποτε τὸν δῆμον τὸν Ἀθηναίων ἐκ τοῦ φανεροῦ πείσας ἔσωσεν, ἀλλὰ δεῖ λαθόντας ἢ ἐξαπατήσαντας αὐτὸν εὖ ποιῆσαι. [34] τὸν λόγον οὖν τοῦτον οὐκ ἐπαινῶ. φημὶ γάρ, ὦ Ἀθηναῖοι, πολέμου μὲν ὄντος ἄνδρα στρατηγὸν τῇ πόλει τε εὔνουν εἰδότα τε ὅ τι πράττῃ, λανθάνοντα δεῖν τοὺς πολλοὺς τῶν ἀνθρώπων καὶ ἐξαπατῶντα ἄγειν ἐπὶ τοὺς κινδύνους, εἰρήνης δὲ πέρι πρεσβεύοντας κοινῆς τοῖς Ἕλλησιν, ἐφ᾽ οἷς ὅρκοι τε ὀμοσθήσονται στῆλαί τε σταθήσονται γεγραμμέναι, ταῦτα δὲ οὔτε λαθεῖν οὔτε ἐξαπατῆσαι δεῖν, ἀλλὰ πολὺ μᾶλλον ἐπαινεῖν ἢ ψέγειν, εἰ πεμφθέντες αὐτοκράτορες ἔτι ἀποδώσομεν ὑμῖν περὶ αὐτῶν σκέψασθαι. βουλεύσασθαι μὲν οὖν ἀσφαλῶς χρὴ κατὰ δύναμιν, οἷς δ᾽ ἂν ὀμόσωμεν καὶ συνθώμεθα, τούτοις ἐμμένειν. [35] οὐ γὰρ μόνον, ὦ Ἀθηναῖοι, πρὸς γράμματα τὰ γεγραμμένα δεῖ βλέποντας πρεσβεύειν ἡμᾶς, ἀλλὰ καὶ πρὸς τοὺς τρόπους τοὺς ὑμετέρους. ὑμεῖς γὰρ περὶ μὲν τῶν ἑτοίμων ὑμῖν ὑπονοεῖν εἰώθατε καὶ δυσχεραίνειν, τὰ δ᾽ οὐκ ὄντα λογοποιεῖν ὡς ἔστιν ὑμῖν ἕτοιμα· κἂν μὲν πολεμεῖν δέῃ, τῆς εἰρήνης ἐπιθυμεῖτε, ἐὰν δέ τις ὑμῖν τὴν εἰρήνην· πράττῃ, λογίζεσθε τὸν πόλεμον ὅσα ἀγαθὰ ὑμῖν κατηργάσατο. [36] ὅπου καὶ νῦν ἤδη τινές λέγουσιν οὐ γιγνώσκειν τὰς διαλλαγὰς αἵτινές εἰσιν, τείχη καὶ νῆες εἰ γενήσονται τῇ πόλει· τὰ γὰρ ἴδια τὰ σφέτερ᾽ αὐτῶν ἐκ τῆς ὑπερορίας οὐκ ἀπολαμβάνειν, ἀπὸ δὲ τῶν τειχῶν οὐκ εἶναι σφίσι τροφήν. ἀναγκαίως οὖν ἔχει καὶ πρὸς ταῦτ᾽ ἀντειπεῖν.

[37] Ἦν γάρ ποτε χρόνος, ὦ Ἀθηναῖοι, ὅτε τείχη καὶ ναῦς οὐκ ἐκεκτήμεθα· γενομένων δὲ τούτων τὴν ἀρχὴν ἐποιησάμεθα τῶν ἀγαθῶν. ὧν εἰ καὶ νῦν ἐπιθυμεῖτε, ταῦτα κατεργάσασθε. ταύτην δὲ λαβόντες ἀφορμὴν οἱ πατέρες ἡμῶν κατηργάσαντο τῇ πόλει δύναμιν τοσαύτην ὅσην οὔπω τις ἄλλη πόλις ἐκτήσατο, τὰ μὲν πείσαντες τοὺς Ἕλληνας, τὰ δὲ λαθόντες, τὰ δὲ πριάμενοι, τὰ δὲ

Boeotians, those who are today holding the city of the Corinthians instead of the Spartans. No, Athenians, let no one persuade us into this course; the examples from the past of our mistakes are sufficient to deter sensible men from making any more mistakes.

[33] There are some of you who have this greatly excessive desire for peace to be concluded as quickly as possible; for they even say that the forty days in which you are allowed to deliberate are superfluous, and we are doing wrong in this: we were sent to Sparta with full powers for this reason, to avoid referring back again. They call the precaution taken by us in making the reference fear, saying that nobody has ever yet saved the Athenian people by open persuasion, but it is necessary to serve it well in secret and by deception. [34] Now, I do not approve of this reasoning. I agree, Athenians, that in wartime a general who both is well-disposed to his state and knows what to do should practise secrecy and deception when leading the majority of men into dangers, but I say that those who are negotiating about a common peace for the Greeks, on matters about which oaths will be sworn and inscribed stelae erected, should practise neither secrecy nor deception in these matters, but we deserve praise far more than blame if, though sent with full powers, we still refer them to you for consideration. Deliberation should be conducted with as much caution as possible, and once we have sworn and made agreements we should abide by them. [35] When negotiating, Athenians, we must look not only to our written instructions but also to your character. For you are accustomed to suspect and be displeased with things ready to hand for you, and to talk idly about things you do not have as if they are ready to hand for you. If you must make war, you long for peace, if someone makes peace for you, you calculate all the benefits the war has brought you. [36] Thus even today there are already some people saying that they do not understand what the value of the reconciliation is, if it is walls and ships that are to come to the city; for they are not regaining their own private property from abroad, and the walls cannot feed them. So it is necessary also to speak in answer to this.

[37] There was once a time, Athenians, when we did not possess walls and ships; but when we had these, we began our successes. If you desire them also today, acquire these things. From this starting-point our fathers acquired for the city such great power as no other state has yet possessed, partly by persuading the Greeks, partly by acting unobserved,

βιασάμενοι· [38] πείσαντες μὲν οὖν Ἀθήνησι ποιήσασθαι τῶν
κοινῶν χρημάτων Ἑλληνοταμίας, καὶ τὸν σύλλογον τῶν νεῶν παρ'
ἡμῖν γενέσθαι, ὅσαι δὲ τῶν πόλεων τριήρεις μὴ κέκτηνται, ταύταις
ἡμᾶς παρέχειν· λαθόντες δὲ Πελοποννησίους τειχισάμενοι τὰ
τείχη· πριάμενοι δὲ παρὰ Λακεδαιμονίων μὴ δοῦναι τούτων δίκην·
βιασάμενοι δὲ τοὺς ἐναντίους τὴν ἀρχὴν τῶν Ἑλλήνων
κατηργασάμεθα. καὶ ταῦτα τὰ ἀγαθὰ ἐν ὀγδοήκοντα καὶ πέντε
ἡμῖν ἔτεσιν ἐγένετο. [39] κρατηθέντες δὲ τῷ πολέμῳ τά τε ἄλλα
ἀπωλέσαμεν, καὶ τὰ τείχη καὶ τὰς ναῦς ἔλαβον ἡμῶν ἐνέχυρα
Λακεδαιμόνιοι, τὰς μὲν παραλαβόντες, τὰ δὲ καθελόντες, ὅπως μὴ
πάλιν ταύτην ἔχοντες ἀφορμὴν δύναμιν τῇ πόλει κατασκευάσαιμεν.
πεισθέντες τοίνυν ὑφ' ἡμῶν Λακεδαιμόνιοι πάρεισι νυνὶ πρέσβεις
αὐτοκράτορες, τά τε ἐνέχυρα ἡμῖν ἀποδιδόντες, καὶ τὰ τείχη καὶ
<τὰς> ναῦς ἐῶντες κεκτῆσθαι, τάς τε νήσους ἡμετέρας εἶναι.

[40] Τὴν αὐτὴν τοίνυν ἀρχὴν ἀγαθῶν λαμβάνοντας ἥνπερ
ἡμῶν ἐλάμβανον οἱ πρόγονοι, ταύτην οὐ πρακτέον φασὶ τὴν
εἰρήνην τινὲς εἶναι. παριόντες οὖν αὐτοὶ διδασκόντων ὑμᾶς
(ἐξουσίαν δ' αὐτοῖς ἡμεῖς ἐποιήσαμεν, προσθέντες τεττεράκοντα
ἡμέρας βουλεύσασθαι) τοῦτο μὲν τῶν γεγραμμένων εἴ τι τυγχάνει
μὴ καλῶς ἔχον (ἔξεστι γὰρ ἀφελεῖν), τοῦτο δ' εἴ τίς <τι>
προσθεῖναι βούλεται, πείσας ὑμᾶς προσγραψάτω. πᾶσί τε τοῖς
γεγραμμένοις χρωμένοις ἔστιν εἰρήνην ἄγειν. [41] εἰ δὲ μηδὲν
ἀρέσκει τούτων, πολεμεῖν ἕτοιμον. καὶ ταῦτ' ἐφ' ὑμῖν πάντ' ἐστίν,
ὦ Ἀθηναῖοι· τούτων ὅ τι ἂν βούλησθε ἕλεσθε. πάρεισι μὲν γὰρ
Ἀργεῖοι καὶ Κορίνθιοι διδάξοντες ὡς ἄμεινόν ἐστι πολεμεῖν,
ἥκουσι δὲ Λακεδαιμόνιοι πείσοντες ὑμᾶς εἰρήνην ποιήσασθαι.
τούτων δ' ἐστὶ τὸ τέλος παρ' ὑμῖν, ἀλλ' οὐκ ἐν Λακεδαιμονίοις, δι'
ἡμᾶς.

Πρεσβευτὰς οὖν πάντας ὑμᾶς ἡμεῖς οἱ πρέσβεις ποιοῦμεν·
ὁ γὰρ τὴν χεῖρα μέλλων ὑμῶν αἴρειν, οὗτος ὁ πρεσβεύων ἐστίν,
ὁπότερ' ἂν αὐτῷ δοκῇ, καὶ τὴν εἰρήνην καὶ τὸν πόλεμον ποιεῖν.
μέμνησθε μὲν οὖν, ὦ Ἀθηναῖοι, τοὺς ἡμετέρους λόγους, ψηφίσασθε
δὲ τοιαῦτα ἐξ ὧν ὑμῖν μηδέποτε μεταμελήσει.

partly by bribing and partly by using force against them. [38] By persuading them that Hellenotamiae of the common funds should be appointed at Athens, that the assembly of ships should take place in our port and that we should provide triremes to such states as did not possess them; by acting unobserved by the Peloponnesians in building the walls; by bribing the Spartans to escape punishment for this; by using force against our enemies, we acquired sovereignty over the Greeks. Moreover, these successes were achieved in eighty-five years. [39] But defeated in the war we lost the rest and the Spartans seized our walls and ships as securities, confiscating the latter and demolishing the former so that we should not have this basis on which to establish power again for the city. Now, persuaded by us, Spartan ambassadors are here today with full powers, both restoring the securities to us, and allowing us to possess the walls and ships, and the islands to be ours.

[40] Now, although we possess the same foundation for success as our ancestors, some say that this peace must not be made. Let them come forward, then, and inform you (we have given them the power to do so, by imposing an additional forty days for deliberation) on the one hand if any of the clauses drafted happens not to be acceptable (for it can be removed), and on the other hand if anyone wishes to add anything, let him persuade you and inscribe it. By applying all the clauses drafted you can live in peace. [41] But if none of them is satisfactory, war is inevitable. This all depends on you, Athenians; choose whichever option you wish. The Argives and Corinthians are present to show you that it is better to make war, the Spartans have come to persuade you to make peace. The decision in the matter rests with you instead of with the Spartans, thanks to us.

Therefore we the ambassadors are making you all ambassadors; for every one of you who is about to raise his hand is negotiating about making both peace and war, whichever option he prefers. So remember my words, Athenians, and vote in such a way as will never cause you regret.

INTRODUCTION 4: *AGAINST ALCIBIADES*

The *Against Alcibiades* purports to be a speech delivered to the assembly by one of the candidates at an ostracism. Every year the assembly decided whether to hold a ballot, in which citizens could vote against a political leader by inscribing his name on a piece of broken pottery (*ostrakon*). If a quorum of 6000 exercised their right, the man with the most votes was exiled for ten years, without further penalty. The institution seems to have fallen into abeyance after 443, except in the case of Hyperbolus (see below), which would appear to be the one we are concerned with here. The speaker is ostensibly Andocides himself, but a number of historical difficulties make the occasion and Andocides' part in it virtually impossible. Most modern scholars have therefore concluded that the *Against Alcibiades* was not the work of Andocides at all, but was composed later, as a political pamphlet or a literary exercise, though a few have attempted to defend his authorship.[101] The approach on both sides has largely been based on the content of the work, but stylistic grounds have also been adduced in support of the proposition that the speech is spurious.[102] The main arguments against the work being a genuine speech, in the sense of actually being delivered, are as follows.

The first question we must ask is whether the ostracism being envisaged can actually have taken place. Since the speaker talks of Alcibiades' conduct at the Olympics in summer 416 (25-33) and the capture of Melos in October/November of the same year (22), and since he names Nicias and Alcibiades as his two opponents, it can only have been held in the eighth prytany of 416/15 (i.e. spring 415), before the assembly voted to send the expedition to Sicily led by Nicias, Alcibiades and

---

101 Blass, *Die attische Beredsamkeit* 325-331 regarded the speech as a fourth-century forgery, used by Plutarch in his biography of Alcibiades, and Dalmeyda 103-10 suggested it was composed by the pupil of a sophist as a school exercise early in the same century; whereas Jebb 131-6 thought it a late forgery which drew on Plutarch. A. R. Burn, 'A biographical source on Phaiax and Alkibiades?', *CQ* 4 (1954) 138-42 argued that both works derive from a lost independent source, possibly Theophrastus. Dover, in *Lysias and the Corpus Lysiacum* 191-2 and *HCT* 4.287-8, accepted the speech as a fourth-century piece of historical fiction, but his suggestion that it may still have been written by Andocides (with his father cast in the role of Alcibiades' opponent) was withdrawn in *Greek Popular Morality* 8 n. 1. On the other hand, A. Schroff, *Zur Echtheitsfrage der vierten Rede des Andokides* (Diss. Erlangen, 1901) took the extreme view of authenticity, that Andocides wrote the *Against Alcibiades* and delivered it himself on the occasion in question; and A. E. Raubitschek, 'The case against Alcibiades (Andocides IV)', *TAPA* 79 (1948) 191-210 contended that the speech was composed in its historical context, possibly by Andocides. W. D. Furley, 'Andokides IV ("Against Alcibiades"), fact or fiction?', *Hermes* 117 (1989) 138-56 ingeniously argued that the speech was written as a political pamphlet after Alcibiades' departure for Sicily and before his recall.

102 See especially Feraboli (1972) and 'Ancora sulla iv. orazione del Corpus Andocideum', *Maia* 26 (1974) 245-6.

Lamachus. But Plutarch (*Alcibiades* 13.3-5, cf. *Nicias* 11:4) relates the story of the last known ostracism at Athens, that of Hyperbolus in 417 or (more likely) 416.[103] Further, the speaker says in 22 that Alcibiades has had a son by a woman purchased from among the prisoners captured at Melos, and the interval between the capture and the ostracism is insufficient to accommodate her pregnancy.[104]

Clearly, then, the ostracism referred to in the *Against Alcibiades* is fictitious, and the same must also apply to Andocides' participation in it. He was far too young in 415 to have had the distinguished public career described in 41-2 and to have himself been a candidate for ostracism at this time.[105] Furthermore, it is unlikely that set speeches were made either at the preliminary meeting which voted for an ostracism to be held or at the ostracism itself, as the speaker himself seems to confirm at 3.

But if the circumstances of the *Against Alcibiades* are not historical, does this also imply that it was not written by Andocides? In addition to the above anomalies, two more arguments based on content that have been adduced against authenticity may be noted here, though these are by no means conclusive. Firstly, the statement in 13 that Hipponicus died **as a general at Delium** seems to conflict with the version of Thucydides (4.101.2), who says the fallen general was Hippocrates. But given the gross historical errors in Andocides' other speeches, this confusion of the names can hardly be taken as evidence of authorship either way, and besides there is no certain proof that Hipponicus did not die at Delium. Secondly, it has been argued that the author of the *Against Alcibiades* appears to write with prescience of events later than 415. He says in **12, the enmity of the allies will show itself as soon as there is a war at sea between us and the Spartans,** which seems to foreshadow the Ionian War; and in **24, I think that the city will suffer the greatest evils through this man and that he will be thought responsible in the future for events so terrible that nobody will remember his past wrongs.** Furley contends that the first of these remarks in fact reflects the arguments used by opponents of the Sicilian expedition;[106] and he rightly points out that the prediction of Alcibiades' future career resembles a forensic commonplace, in which prosecutors predict that the defendant, if acquitted, will commit further crimes,[107] while defendants claim

---

103 For the date see *HCT* 5.259-63.
104 Unless she was already pregnant when bought by Alcibiades, or the purchase in fact took place earlier in the campaign, but both these alternatives undermine the point of the story (Alcibiades' tyrannical cynicism).
105 We might also have expected Andocides to mention a vote in his favour in his *Return* and *Mysteries* speeches.
106 Cf. Nicias at Thuc. 6.10-11. Furley notes that Athenagoras makes the same point as Nicias in the Syracusan assembly (Thuc. 6.36.4), but the similarity might suggest that Thucydides himself is guilty of prescience in composing these speeches.
107 E.g. Lys. 14.2, 43.

that after their acquittal they will confer benefits on the city.[108] So again, these passages are not compelling evidence of spuriousness.

On the other hand, the arguments from content adduced in favour of authenticity, in particular by Raubitschek and Furley, are themselves unconvincing. Raubitschek notes that the author refers to Alcibiades' part in a reassessment of tribute, apparently that of 425/4, which is not known from other literary sources but is confirmed by epigraphical evidence.[109] But Alcibiades was very young at this time to have been involved in such activity, and the *argumentum ex silentio* over the sources is very dangerous. Furthermore, there was clearly a vogue for pamphlet literature in the last two decades of the fifth century,[110] in which Alcibiades certainly featured,[111] and this could be the source for many of the stories connected with him, including the one about his part in the Olympics.[112] Again, the author's knowledge of ostracism is a tenuous indication of authenticity. Furley remarks on the similarity in tone and content of the passages in which the birth of a boy is compared to that of Aegisthus (**1.128-9, 4.22**), arguing that a later forger would not have written the version in the *Against Alcibiades* as if it were by Andocides for another to deliver. But closer inspection in fact reveals no verbal similarities between the two passages, and once more the anti-Alcibiades literature may have inspired the comparison. In addition, this literature clearly can have lain behind the resentment that Furley notices in various sections of the *Against Alcibiades*,[113] which compares with that in Thuc. 6.28.2; and behind the details of the audience's reaction to the Taureas episode (**20**)[114] and of his behaviour at Olympia (**29**).[115] Finally, Furley notes various indications that the author had oligarchic

---

108 As Andocides does himself at **1.144-5, 2.19**.

109 See **11**n.

110 See W. R. Connor, *Theopompus and Fifth-Century Athens* (Washington, 1968) 103-6.

111 An *Abuse of Alcibiades* was in circulation under the name of Antiphon (frgs 66-7 Thalheim), and he was clearly still a favourite target of attack in the fourth century (cf. Lys. 14.30-40; Isoc. 16, *Concerning the Team of Horses*). See Hatzfeld 59-60.

112 This is also noted at Thuc. 6.16.2.

113 See **13**n.

114 Additionally, the reference in **23** to the audience's reaction to tragedy is merely a general reflection.

115 Alcibiades' abuse of the processional vessels was paralleled by the Segestans in the following winter, when they convinced the Athenian envoys of their wealth by collecting gold and silver vessels and using them at successive banquets (Thuc. 6.46.3-4). Furley argues this was done on Alcibiades' instructions, but admits this hardly proves that a later author did not have a source unknown to us for the episode at Olympia.

affiliations,[116] but a good deal of early fourth-century literature, for instance, was oligarchic.[117]

A different approach to the question of authenticity is provided by stylistic analysis. The verdicts of modern scholars were largely subjective and influenced by the content arguments until a more detailed analysis was undertaken by Feraboli. A detailed summary of Feraboli's observations is reserved for Appendix C, and we may simply note here her conclusions, on the basis of the cumulative weight of small factors, that the style of the *Against Alcibiades* is more formal, studied and symmetrical than that of the other speeches. This by itself is inconclusive, and there are various difficulties which make stylistic analysis problematic, not least the small volume of data with which we have to work.[118] In addition, such analysis cannot decide for us whether a work was written in the fourth century rather than much later, since the very purpose of later rhetorical instruction was to produce as closely as possible imitations of classical models and style (see below). But just as Feraboli's small factors, when put together, build into a strong case against Andocides' authorship, so is the combined weight of the arguments from content and style compelling, all the more so when we consider what, if it was not a real speech, the *Against Alcibiades* can have been.

Two possibilities have been suggested, firstly that it was a kind of political pamphlet. If so, it can hardly have been written in the fourth century as some scholars have suggested, for the simple reason that no mention is made of Alcibiades' defection to the Spartans by the end of summer 415. Furley uses this argument in connection with the Melian woman, contending that the moral issue of Alcibiades' child by her would only have been of weight as a ground for political calumny in the period between the birth and Alcibiades' defection, but it in fact applies to the work as a whole. It is highly unlikely that Andocides or any other author would have omitted Alcibiades' treason in a fourth-century political pamphlet directed against him (compare, for example, Lys. 14.30; Isoc. 16.10). It is also strange that no mention is made of Alcibiades' aggressive foreign policy, which culminated in the Sicilian disaster. Furley himself, in defending Andocides' authorship, dates the tract to the summer of 415, after Alcibiades' departure for

---

116 He is opposed to the tribute reassessment (**11-12**), praises Spartan mores at the games (**28**) and defends thriftiness (**32**), the last of which reflects the reluctance of the upper-classes to squander their wealth on the war.

117 See, e.g., Missiou 182.

118 Furley argues that small differences in style are explicable as reflecting the different purpose and circumstances of the *Against Alcibiades* from in particular speeches 1 and 2, though this depends on the questionable premise that the work was really a political pamphlet. If so, it was composed for reading rather than oral delivery like the speeches, which in addition were concerned with Andocides' very life and citizenship. But while Andocides may well have been capable of adapting his style to suit different occasions, we should bear in mind that the *Against Alcibiades* does after all purport to be a speech in defence of the speaker's continued residence in Athens.

Sicily and before Andocides' imprisonment. At this point the Melian woman could possibly have had her baby,[119] and Alcibiades' enemies could hardly attack what was a popular policy, but instead concentrated on impugning his political ideology.[120] But just as it would be very strange for a fourth-century pamphlet to make no mention of Alcibiades' failed foreign policy and treason, so is it even stranger for a pamphlet written in the summer of 415 not to mention Alcibiades' alleged part in the Mysteries and Hermae affairs, for which he was charged before leaving Athens. Why, instead, set the scene at an imaginary ostracism in the spring? Even if Andocides was afraid to bring up a crime of which he knew he might soon be accused himself, he must have realised that any attack on Alcibiades at this time which did not mention the sacrilege lost all its sting. So the theory that the *Against Alcibiades* was a political pamphlet is barely tenable.

The only alternative which can at all account for these inconsistencies is that the *Against Alcibiades* was an historical exercise of the kind undertaken in schools of rhetoric.[121] But where could a later student have found his information? Plutarch, it seems,[122] knew of a speech written *Against Alcibiades* either by or on behalf of the politician Phaeax, and although the example he cites from it of Alcibiades' behaviour could derive from 29, there are some differences between the two versions.[123] Plutarch goes on to tell the story of Hyperbolus' ostracism. He says that Alcibiades and Nicias temporarily halted their feuding and joined forces to ensure that the vote went against Hyperbolus, but also records the version of Theophrastus, that the feud and deal were between Alcibiades and Phaeax.[124] Since the speaker of our *Against Alcibiades* bears some similarity to the Phaeax of Aristophanes, Thucydides and Plutarch,[125] it has been suggested that the two are identical, and that the *Against Alcibiades* was the speech of Phaeax known to Plutarch. But the

---

119 See also 23n. on the possible significance of the sequence of tenses there.

120 See 13n.

121 Cf. the 'speech of Nicias to his Syracusan captors', Dion. Hal. *Lysias* 14. Further on this type of exercise see D. A. Russell, *Greek Declamation* (Cambridge, 1983) 16-17.

122 This depends on a textual emendation at *Alcibiades* 13.2: φέρεται δὲ καὶ λόγος τις κατ' Ἀλκιβιάδου καὶ (καὶ om. N) Φαίακος γεγραμμένος. The second καί has been variously emended, to ὑπό (Xylander: i.e. a speech against Alcibiades 'written by Phaeax'), ὡς (Meier: 'attributed to Phaeax') and ὑπέρ (Blass: 'on behalf of Phaeax'). Raubitschek wished to read φέρεται δὲ καὶ Φαίακος λόγος τις κατ' Ἀλκιβιάδου γεγραμμένος ('there is also a speech by Phaeax written against Alcibiades').

123 Plutarch says ἐν ᾧ μετὰ τῶν ἄλλων γέγραπται καὶ ὅτι τῆς πόλεως πολλὰ πομπεῖα χρυσᾶ καὶ ἀργυρᾶ κεκτημένης Ἀλκιβιάδης ἐχρῆτο πᾶσιν αὐτοῖς ὥσπερ ἰδίοις πρὸς τὴν καθ' ἡμέραν δίαιταν ('in which it is written, among other things, that Alcibiades used all the city's many processional vessels of gold and silver at his regular table as though they were his own').

124 Ostraka bearing the name of Phaeax have been found.

125 Phaeax came from an illustrious family, was sent as an Athenian ambassador to Italy and Sicily, and was tried for his life at least once. Cf. Ar. *Knights* 1377-80; Thuc. 5.4-5; Plut. *Alc.* 13.1-2 (compare these details with 8, 41-2).

historical problems outlined above apply equally in the case of Phaeax's authorship, and the details in Plutarch's account of Phaeax must derive from another source, which may have been common to both the *Against Alcibiades* and Plutarch.[126]

It is likely, then, that what we possess is a literary exercise, perhaps composed during the fourth century but possibly later, drawing on an unknown source and written in imitation of the style of Phaeax. If this was the speech known to Plutarch, it is possible, as Dover suggested,[127] that in the Hellenistic period it was ascribed to Andocides by the great librarian of Alexandria, Callimachus, but to Phaeax in the Pergamene catalogue.[128] Such a faulty ascription should occasion little surprise. The Augustan critics Dionysius and Caecilius spent much time re-examining Callimachus' catalogue and pronounced many speeches in the oratorical corpus spurious, with good reason.[129] One excellent, but unusually straightforward example adduced by Dover, is that Callimachus ascribed to Demosthenes the speech *Against Theocrines*, which contains hostile references to Demosthenes himself.[130] Modern scholars have likewise questioned the authenticity of numerous speeches in the manuscripts,[131] and the *Against Alcibiades* is a prime candidate. Another, as it were inverse, example will serve both as a close parallel to our case and to underline the difficult nature of the problem: some scholars regard the speech *On the Constitution*, (perhaps wrongly) ascribed in the tradition to the second century A.D. rhetorician Herodes Atticus, as a genuine work from the year 404 B.C.[132]

---

126 Plutarch gives the name of his father, Erasistratus, and says that Phaeax's oratorical ability was greater in private than public, citing a line of Eupolis (λαλεῖν ἄριστος, ἀδυνατώτατος λέγειν, 'highly good at talking, but highly incapable at speaking'). See further *IICT* 5.258-9.

127 Dover (1968) 191.

128 It should be noted, however, that with the possible exception of Plut. *Alc.* 13.2 (see n. 122 above) none of the extant ancient sources doubts Andocides' authorship of the *Against Alcibiades*. Harpocration cites Andocides' speech against Alcibiades twice (s.v. ἐμποδών, εὐανδρία); and Athenaeus (9.408c) quotes a few words from it which he wrongly attributes to Lysias. The *Life of And.* 835A refers to an Ἀπολογία πρὸς Φαίακα or *Defence against Phaeax*, perhaps by confusion.

129 E.g. ps.-Plutarch in the *Lives of the Ten Orators* records that Caecilius pronounced 25 of the 60 speeches attributed to Antiphon spurious (833C), while Caecilius and Dionysius only accepted 233 of the 425 speeches in the Lysianic corpus as genuine (836A).

130 Cf. ps.-Dem. 58.35-6, 41-4; Dover (1968) 23-6.

131 E.g. the speech *On the Twelve Years*, attributed to Demades in the MSS, is clearly a declamatory exercise. See Russell, *op. cit.* 111.

132 See Russell, *op. cit.* 111, with the review by M. J. Edwards in *JHS* 105 (1985) 202.

[ΑΝΔΟΚΙΔΟΥ]

ΚΑΤΑ ΑΛΚΙΒΙΑΔΟΥ

[1] Οὐκ ἐν τῷ παρόντι μόνον γιγνώσκω τῶν πολιτικῶν πραγμάτων ὡς σφαλερόν ἐστιν ἅπτεσθαι, ἀλλὰ καὶ πρότερον χαλεπὸν ἡγούμην, πρὶν τῶν κοινῶν ἐπιμελεῖσθαί τινος. πολίτου δὲ ἀγαθοῦ νομίζω προκινδυνεύειν ἐθέλειν τοῦ πλήθους, καὶ μὴ καταδείσαντα τὰς ἔχθρας τὰς ἰδίας ὑπὲρ τῶν δημοσίων ἔχειν ἡσυχίαν· διὰ μὲν γὰρ τοὺς τῶν ἰδίων ἐπιμελουμένους οὐδὲν αἱ πόλεις μείζους καθίστανται, διὰ δὲ τοὺς τῶν κοινῶν μεγάλαι καὶ ἐλεύθεραι γίγνονται. [2] ὧν εἷς ἐγὼ βουληθεὶς ἐξετάζεσθαι μεγίστοις περιπέπτωκα κινδύνοις, προθύμων μὲν καὶ ἀγαθῶν ἀνδρῶν· ὑμῶν τυγχάνων, δι' ὅπερ σῴζομαι, πλείστοις δὲ καὶ δεινοτάτοις ἐχθροῖς χρώμενος, ὑφ' ὧν διαβάλλομαι. ὁ μὲν οὖν ἀγὼν ὁ παρὼν οὐ στεφανηφόρος, ἀλλ' εἰ χρὴ μηδὲν ἀδικήσαντα τὴν πόλιν δέκα ἔτη φεύγειν· οἱ δ' ἀνταγωνιζόμενοι περὶ τῶν ἄθλων τούτων ἐσμὲν ἐγὼ καὶ Ἀλκιβιάδης καὶ Νικίας, ὧν ἀναγκαῖον ἕνα τῇ συμφορᾷ περιπεσεῖν.

[3] Ἄξιον δὲ μέμψασθαι τὸν θέντα τὸν νόμον, ὃς ἐναντία τῷ ὅρκῳ τοῦ δήμου καὶ τῆς βουλῆς ἐνομοθέτησεν· ἐκεῖ μὲν γὰρ ὄμνυτε μηδένα μήτε ἐξελᾶν μήτε δήσειν μήτε ἀποκτενεῖν ἄκριτον, ἐν δὲ τῷδε τῷ καιρῷ οὔτε κατηγορίας γενομένης οὔτε ἀπολογίας ἀποδοθείσης οὔτε διαψηφισαμένων κρύβδην τὸν ὀστρακισθέντα τοσοῦτον χρόνον δεῖ στερηθῆναι τῆς πόλεως. [4] εἶτα ἐν τοῖς τοιούτοις οἱ τοὺς ἑταίρους καὶ συνωμότας κεκτημένοι πλέον φέρονται τῶν ἄλλων· οὐ γὰρ ὥσπερ ἐν τοῖς δικαστηρίοις οἱ λαχόντες κρίνουσιν, ἀλλὰ τούτου τοῦ πράγματος ἅπασιν Ἀθηναίοις μέτεστι. πρὸς δὲ τούτοις τῷ μὲν ἐλλείπειν τῷ δ' ὑπερβάλλειν ὁ νόμος μοι δοκεῖ· τῶν μὲν γὰρ ἰδίων ἀδικημάτων μεγάλην τιμωρίαν ταύτην νομίζω, τῶν δὲ δημοσίων μικρὰν καὶ οὐδενὸς ἀξίαν ἡγοῦμαι ζημίαν, ἐξὸν κολάζειν χρήμασι καὶ δεσμῷ καὶ θανάτῳ. [5] ἔτι δ' εἴ τις διὰ τοῦτο μεθίσταται ὅτι <πονηρὸς> πολίτης ἐστίν, οὗτος οὐδ' ἀπελθὼν ἐνθένδε παύσεται, ἀλλ' ὅπου ἂν οἰκῇ, ταύτην τὴν πόλιν διαφθερεῖ, καὶ τῇδε οὐδὲν ἧττον ἐπιβουλεύσει, ἀλλὰ καὶ μᾶλλον <καὶ> δικαιότερον ἢ πρὶν ἐκβληθῆναι. οἶμαι δὲ καὶ τοὺς φίλους ὑμῶν ἐν ταύτῃ μάλιστα τῇ ἡμέρᾳ λυπεῖσθαι καὶ τοὺς ἐχθροὺς ἥδεσθαι, συνειδότας ὡς, ἂν ἀγνοήσαντες ἐξελάσητε τὸν βέλτιστον, δέκα ἐτῶν ἡ πόλις οὐδὲν ἀγαθὸν ὑπὸ τούτου τοῦ ἀνδρὸς πείσεται.

[ANDOCIDES]

AGAINST ALCIBIADES

[1] It is not only on the present occasion that I have recognised how perilous it is to engage in political affairs, but I also thought it dangerous previously, before concerning myself in any way with state affairs. But I consider it the duty of a good citizen to be willing to brave danger for the people and not to keep silent concerning public matters through fear of private enmities; for states do not become greater in any way through those who are concerned with their private affairs, they become great and free through those concerned with state affairs. [2] I wanted to be counted as one of these and have now fallen into the greatest dangers, meeting in you men who are well-wishing and fine, whereby I am saved, but having very many and very dangerous enemies by whom I am being slandered. The present contest is not for the prize of a crown, but whether someone who has done no wrong must live in exile from the city for ten years. The competitors for this prize are myself, Alcibiades and Nicias, one of whom must suffer this disaster.

[3] It is just to blame the author of the law, since he framed it contrary to the oath of the people and council. For by this you swear neither to exile nor to imprison nor to put to death anybody without trial, but on this occasion the one ostracised must be deprived of his city for so long with no accusation made nor defence allowed nor with the voting in secret. [4] Moreover, in such circumstances those who have political friends and confederates have an advantage over the others; for it is not men appointed by lot who are judging, as in the courts, but all Athenians have a say in this matter. In addition to this, the law seems to me on the one hand not to go far enough and on the other to go too far; for I consider this a severe punishment for private wrongs, but I think it a light and valueless penalty for public wrongs, when it is possible to punish with a fine, imprisonment or death. [5] Further, if someone is banished because he is a bad citizen, he will not cease to be so by leaving here, but wherever he is living he will harm this city and intrigue against it no less, but in fact more so and more justly than before his expulsion. I think also that on this day more than ever your friends are distressed and your enemies joyful, knowing that if you by mistake banish your best citizen, for ten years the city will derive no benefit from this man.

[6] ῥᾴδιον δὲ καὶ ἐντεῦθεν γνῶναι τὸν νόμον πονηρὸν ὄντα· μόνοι γὰρ αὐτῷ τῶν Ἑλλήνων χρώμεθα, καὶ οὐδεμία τῶν ἄλλων πόλεων ἐθέλει μιμήσασθαι. καίτοι ταῦτα διέγνωσται ἄριστα τῶν δογμάτων, ἃ καὶ τοῖς πολλοῖς καὶ τοῖς ὀλίγοις ἁρμόττοντα μάλιστα τυγχάνει καὶ πλείστους ἐπιθυμητὰς ἔχει.

[7] Περὶ μὲν οὖν τούτων οὐκ οἶδ' ὅ τι δεῖ μακρότερα λέγειν· πάντως γὰρ οὐδὲν ἂν πλεῖον εἰς τὸ παρὸν ποιήσαιμεν· δέομαι δ' ὑμῶν τῶν λόγων ἴσους καὶ κοινοὺς ἡμῖν ἐπιστάτας γενέσθαι, καὶ πάντας ἄρχοντας περὶ τούτων καταστῆναι, καὶ μήτε τοῖς λοιδορουμένοις μήτε τοῖς ὑπὲρ καιρὸν χαριζομένοις ἐπιτρέπειν, ἀλλὰ τῷ μὲν θέλοντι λέγειν καὶ ἀκούειν εὐμενεῖς εἶναι, τῷ δὲ ἀσελγαίνοντι καὶ θορυβοῦντι χαλεπούς. ἀκούσαντες γὰρ ἕκαστον τῶν ὑπαρχόντων ἄμεινον βουλεύσεσθε περὶ ἡμῶν.

[8] Ἔστι δὲ περὶ τῆς μισοδημίας καὶ τῆς στασιωτείας βραχύς μοι λόγος καταλελειμμένος. εἰ μὲν γὰρ ἄκριτος ἦν, εἰκότως ἂν τῶν κατηγορούντων ἠκροᾶσθε καὶ ἐμοὶ ἀναγκαῖον ἦν ἀπολογεῖσθαι περὶ τούτων· ἐπειδὴ δὲ τετράκις ἀγωνιζόμενος ἀπέφυγον, οὐκέτι δίκαιον ἡγοῦμαι λόγον οὐδένα περὶ τούτου γίγνεσθαι. πρὶν μὲν γὰρ κριθῆναι οὐ ῥᾴδιον εἰδέναι τὰς αἰτίας, οὔτ' εἰ ψευδεῖς εἰσιν οὔτ' εἰ ἀληθεῖς· ἀποφυγόντος δὲ ἢ καταγνωσθέντος τέλος ἔχει καὶ διώρισται τούτων ὁπότερόν ἐστιν. [9] ὥστε δεινὸν νομίζω τοὺς μὲν ἁλόντας μιᾷ ψήφῳ μόνον ἀποθνήσκειν, καὶ τὰ χρήματα δημεύεσθαι αὐτῶν, τοὺς δὲ νικήσαντας πάλιν τὰς αὐτὰς κατηγορίας ὑπομένειν, καὶ τοὺς δικαστὰς ἀπολέσαι μὲν κυρίους εἶναι, σῶσαι δ' ἀκύρους καὶ ἀτελεῖς φαίνεσθαι, ἄλλως τε καὶ τῶν νόμων ἀπαγορευόντων δὶς περὶ τῶν αὐτῶν πρὸς τὸν αὐτὸν μὴ ἐξεῖναι δικάζεσθαι, καὶ ὑμῶν ὀμωμοκότων χρῆσθαι τοῖς νόμοις. [10] ὧν ἕνεκα περὶ ἐμαυτοῦ παραλιπὼν Ἀλκιβιάδου τὸν βίον ἀναμνῆσαι βούλομαι. καίτοι ἀπορῶ γε διὰ τὸ πλῆθος τῶν ἁμαρτημάτων πόθεν ἄρξωμαι, ἐμποδὼν ἁπάντων ὄντων. περὶ μὲν οὖν μοιχείας καὶ γυναικῶν ἀλλοτρίων ἁρπαγῆς καὶ τῆς ἄλλης βιαιότητος καὶ παρανομίας καθ' ἕκαστον εἰ δεήσειε λέγειν, οὐκ ἂν ἐξαρκέσειεν ὁ παρὼν χρόνος, ἅμα δὲ καὶ πολλοῖς ἀπεχθοίμην τῶν πολιτῶν, φανερὰς τὰς συμφορὰς ποιῶν αὐτῶν. ἃ δὲ περὶ τὴν πόλιν εἴργασται καὶ τοὺς προσήκοντας καὶ τῶν ἄλλων ἀστῶν καὶ ξένων τοὺς ἐντυγχάνοντας, ἀποδείξω.

[11] Πρῶτον μὲν οὖν πείσας ὑμᾶς τὸν φόρον ταῖς πόλεσιν ἐξ ἀρχῆς τάξαι τὸν ὑπ' Ἀριστείδου πάντων δικαιότατα τεταγμένον, αἱρεθεὶς ἐπὶ τούτῳ δέκατος αὐτὸς μάλιστα διπλάσιον

[6] It is also easy to recognise that the law is bad from this: we alone of the Greeks use it, and none of the other states wishes to imitate us. Yet these are perceived to be the best ordinances which prove especially suited to both democracy and oligarchy, and have the most people desiring them.

[7] I do not see any necessity to speak further about this; for I would achieve absolutely nothing more for the present. But I do ask you to be fair and impartial presidents over our speeches, and all of you to act as archons concerning them; and not to give way either to those using abuse or to those using flattery to excess, but to be well-disposed towards the one who is willing to speak and to listen, but stern towards the one who is insolent and disorderly. For if you listen to each of the circumstances, you will come to a better decision about us.

[8] It remains for me to say a few words about my hatred of democracy and my membership of a faction. If I had not been tried, you would reasonably have listened to my accusers, and it would have been necessary for me to reply to these points; but since I have been tried and acquitted four times, I think it is no longer just for there to be any discussion about this. Before a man is tried, it is not easy to know whether the charges are false or true; but when he has been acquitted or convicted, the matter is finished and is settled whichever of these is the case. **[9]** So I think it strange that those who are convicted by merely a single vote are put to death and their property is confiscated, but those who win face the same charges again, and that the jurors have the power to destroy but seem powerless and ineffectual at saving, especially since the laws forbid the possibility of the same man being tried twice on the same charge, and you have sworn to employ the laws. **[10]** For these reasons I shall not speak about myself, but I wish to remind you of the life of Alcibiades. Yet I am at a loss where to begin, because of the large number of his misdeeds, all of them crowding before me. If I had to speak in detail of his adultery, stealing of other men's wives, his other violence and illegal behaviour, the time allotted me would not suffice, and furthermore I would incur the hatred of many of my fellow-citizens by making their misfortunes public. But what he has done with regard to the state, his relatives and the other citizens and foreigners who have crossed his path, I shall make known to you.

[11] Firstly, then, he persuaded you to assess anew the tribute from the allied states which was set by Aristeides with extreme fairness; chosen for this task with nine others he practically doubled the tribute for each of the

αὐτὸν ἑκάστοις τῶν συμμάχων ἐποίησεν, ἐπιδείξας δ' αὐτὸν
φοβερὸν καὶ μέγα δυνάμενον ἰδίας ἀπὸ τῶν κοινῶν προσόδους
κατεσκευάσατο. σκέψασθε δὲ πῶς ἄν τις κακὰ μείζω τούτων
κατασκευάσειεν, εἰ τῆς σωτηρίας ἡμῖν πάσης διὰ τῶν συμμάχων
οὔσης, ὁμολογουμένως νῦν κάκιον ἢ πρότερον πραττόντων, τὸν
φόρον ἑκάστοις διπλασιάσειεν. [12] ὥστ' εἴπερ ἡγεῖσθε πολίτην
ἀγαθὸν Ἀριστείδην καὶ δίκαιον γεγονέναι, τοῦτον προσήκει
κάκιστον νομίζειν, ὡς τἀναντία περὶ τῶν πόλεων ἐκείνῳ
γιγνώσκοντα. τοιγάρτοι διὰ ταῦτα πολλοὶ τὴν πατρίδα τὴν αὐτῶν
ἀπολιπόντες φυγάδες γίγνονται καὶ εἰς Θουρίους οἰκήσοντες
ἀπέρχονται. δηλώσει δὲ ἡ τῶν συμμάχων ἔχθρα, ὅταν πρῶτον ἡμῖν
καὶ Λακεδαιμονίοις γένηται ναυτικὸς πόλεμος. ἐγὼ δὲ νομίζω τὸν
τοιοῦτον πονηρὸν εἶναι προστάτην, ὅστις τοῦ παρόντος χρόνου
ἐπιμελεῖται, ἀλλὰ μὴ καὶ τοῦ μέλλοντος προνοεῖται, καὶ τὰ ἥδιστα
τῷ πλήθει, παραλιπὼν τὰ βέλτιστα, συμβουλεύει.

[13] Θαυμάζω δὲ τῶν πεπεισμένων Ἀλκιβιάδην δημοκρατίας
ἐπιθυμεῖν, τοιαύτης πολιτείας ἢ μάλιστα κοινότητα δοκεῖ ἡρῆσθαι,
οἳ οὐδ' ἀπὸ τῶν ἰδίων αὐτὸν θεῶνται, ὁρῶντες τὴν πλεονεξίαν καὶ
τὴν ὑπερηφανίαν, ὃς τὴν Καλλίου γήμας ἀδελφὴν ἐπὶ δέκα
ταλάντοις, τελευτήσαντος Ἱππονίκου στρατηγοῦντος ἐπὶ Δηλίῳ
ἕτερα τοσαῦτα προσεπράξατο, λέγων ὡς ὡμολόγησεν ἐκεῖνος, ὁπότε
παῖς αὐτῷ ἐκ τῆς θυγατρὸς γένοιτο, προσθήσειν ταῦτα. [14] λαβὼν
δὲ τοσαύτην προῖκα ὅσην οὐδεὶς τῶν Ἑλλήνων, οὕτως ὑβριστὴς ἦν,
ἐπεισάγων εἰς τὴν αὐτὴν οἰκίαν ἑταίρας, καὶ δούλας καὶ
ἐλευθέρας, ὥστ' ἠνάγκασε τὴν γυναῖκα σωφρονεστάτην οὖσαν
ἀπολιπεῖν, ἐλθοῦσαν πρὸς τὸν ἄρχοντα κατὰ τὸν νόμον. οὗ δὴ
μάλιστα τὴν αὐτοῦ δύναμιν ἐπεδείξατο· παρακαλέσας γὰρ τοὺς
ἑταίρους, ἁρπάσας ἐκ τῆς ἀγορᾶς τὴν γυναῖκα ᾤχετο βίᾳ, καὶ
πᾶσιν ἐδήλωσε καὶ τῶν ἀρχόντων καὶ τῶν νόμων καὶ τῶν ἄλλων
πολιτῶν καταφρονῶν. [15] οὐ τοίνυν ταῦτα μόνον ἐξήρκεσεν, ἀλλὰ
καὶ λαθραῖον θάνατον ἐπεβούλευσε Καλλίᾳ, ἵνα τὸν οἶκον τὸν
Ἱππονίκου κατάσχοι, ὡς ἐναντίον πάντων ὑμῶν ἐν τῇ ἐκκλησίᾳ
κατηγόρει· καὶ τὰ χρήματα τῷ δήμῳ ἔδωκεν, εἴ πως τελευτήσειεν
ἄπαις, φοβούμενος μὴ διὰ τὴν οὐσίαν ἀπόλοιτο. ἀλλὰ μὴν οὐδ'
ἔρημος οὐδ' εὐαδίκητός ἐστιν, ἐπεὶ διὰ τὸν πλοῦτον ἔχει πολλοὺς
τοὺς βοηθήσοντας. καίτοι ὅστις ὑβρίζει γυναῖκα τὴν ἑαυτοῦ καὶ τῷ
κηδεστῇ θάνατον ἐπιβουλεύει, τί χρὴ προσδοκᾶν τοῦτον περὶ τοὺς
ἐντυχόντας τῶν πολιτῶν διαπράττεσθαι; πάντες γὰρ ἄνθρωποι τοὺς
οἰκείους τῶν ἀλλοτρίων ποιοῦνται περὶ πλείονος.

allies, and by showing himself to be formidable and powerful he procured private revenue out of public revenue. But consider how anyone could procure troubles greater than these, if, with our whole safety depending on our allies and with them by common consent faring worse today than previously, he doubled the tribute of each. [12] If, then, you think Aristeides was a fine and just citizen, this one it is fitting to consider the worst, as he makes the opposite judgments to him about the allied states. Indeed, because of this many are leaving their own country as exiles and going off to settle at Thurii. The enmity of the allies will show itself as soon as there is a war at sea between us and the Spartans. But I think a man is a bad leader who is concerned with the present time but does not also provide for the future, and counsels the measures most pleasing to the people while saying nothing about their best interests.

[13] I am amazed, too, at those who have been persuaded that Alcibiades is a lover of democracy, that form of constitution which above all seems to have chosen equality - they are not looking at him from the point of view of his private life, although his greed and arrogance are plain to them. He married the sister of Callias with a dowry of ten talents but, after the death of Hipponicus as a general at Delium, exacted another ten, saying that Hipponicus had agreed to add this when Alcibiades had had a child by his daughter. [14] But after receiving such a dowry as no other Greek ever had, he was so licentious, bringing mistresses both slave and free into the same house, that he compelled his wife, a very chaste woman, to desert him and go to the archon, in accordance with the law. At that point, indeed, he really showed his power, for he summoned his friends, seized and carried off his wife from the agora by force, and showed to everybody his contempt for the magistrates, the laws and the rest of the citizens. [15] Moreover, this did not suffice for him, but he also plotted the murder of Callias in order to gain possession of Hipponicus' estate, as he accused him of doing before all of you in the assembly; and he made over his property to the people in the event of his dying childless, afraid that he might be destroyed by his wealth. But truly Callias is neither friendless nor vulnerable, since through his wealth he has many to protect him. Yet a man who maltreats his own wife and plots the death of his brother-in-law, how should he be expected to behave towards those citizens who cross his path? For all men value their relatives above strangers.

[16] Ὁ δὲ πάντων δεινότατόν ἐστι, τοιοῦτος ὢν ὡς εὔνους τῷ δήμῳ τοὺς λόγους ποιεῖται, καὶ τοὺς ἄλλους ὀλιγαρχικοὺς καὶ μισοδήμους ἀποκαλεῖ. καὶ ὃν ἔδει τεθνάναι διὰ τὰ ἐπιτηδεύματα, κατήγορος τῶν διαβεβλημένων ὑφ᾽ ὑμῶν αἱρεῖται, καί φησι φύλαξ εἶναι τῆς πολιτείας, οὐδενὶ τῶν ἄλλων Ἀθηναίων οὔτ᾽ ἴσον οὔτ᾽ ὀλίγῳ πλέον ἀξιῶν ἔχειν· ἀλλ᾽ οὕτω σφόδρα καταπεφρόνηκεν ὥστε διατετέλεκεν ἀθρόους μὲν ὑμᾶς κολακεύων, ἕνα δ᾽ ἕκαστον προπηλακίζων. [17] ὃς εἰς τοσοῦτον ἐλήλυθε τόλμης ὥστε πείσας Ἀγάθαρχον τὸν γραφέα συνεισελθεῖν τὴν οἰκίαν ἐπηνάγκασε γράφειν, δεομένου δὲ καὶ προφάσεις ἀληθεῖς λέγοντος, ὡς οὐκ ἂν δύναιτο ταῦτα πράττειν ἤδη διὰ τὸ συγγραφὰς ἔχειν παρ᾽ ἑτέρων, προεῖπεν αὐτῷ δήσειν, εἰ μὴ πάνυ ταχέως γράφοι. ὅπερ ἐποίησε· καὶ οὐ πρότερον ἀπηλλάγη, πρὶν ἀποδρὰς ᾤχετο τετάρτῳ μηνί, τοὺς φύλακας λαθών, ὥσπερ παρὰ βασιλέως. οὕτω δ᾽ ἀναίσχυντός ἐστιν, ὥστε προσελθὼν ἐνεκάλει αὐτῷ ὡς ἀδικούμενος, καὶ οὐχ ὧν ἐβιάσατο μετέμελεν αὐτῷ, ἀλλ᾽ ὅτι κατέλιπε τὸ ἔργον ἠπείλει, καὶ οὔτε τῆς δημοκρατίας οὔτε τῆς ἐλευθερίας οὐδὲν ἦν ὄφελος· οὐδὲν γὰρ ἧττον ἐδεδέκει τῶν ὁμολογουμένων δούλων. [18] ἀγανακτῶ δ᾽ ἐνθυμούμενος ὑμῖν μὲν οὐδὲ τοὺς κακούργους ἀσφαλὲς εἰς τὸ δεσμωτήριον ὂν ἀπάγειν, διὰ τὸ χιλίας δραχμὰς τετάχθαι ἀποτεῖσαι ὃς ἂν τὸ πέμπτον μέρος μὴ μεταλάβῃ τῶν ψήφων· ὁ δὲ τοσοῦτον χρόνον εἴρξας καὶ ἐπαναγκάζων γράφειν οὐδὲν κακὸν πέπονθεν, ἀλλὰ διὰ ταῦτα σεμνότερος δοκεῖ καὶ φοβερώτερος εἶναι. καὶ πρὸς μὲν τὰς ἄλλας πόλεις ἐν τοῖς συμβόλοις συντιθέμεθα μὴ ἐξεῖναι μήθ᾽ εἷρξαι μήτε δῆσαι τὸν ἐλεύθερον· ἐὰν δέ τις παραβῇ, μεγάλην ζημίαν ἐπὶ τούτοις ἔθεμεν· τούτου δὲ τοιαῦτα πράξαντος οὐδεμίαν οὐδεὶς οὔτ᾽ ἰδίαν οὔτε δημοσίαν τιμωρίαν ποιεῖται. [19] νομίζω δὲ ταύτην εἶναι σωτηρίαν ἅπασι, πείθεσθαι τοῖς ἄρχουσι καὶ τοῖς νόμοις· ὅστις δὲ ὑπερορᾷ ταῦτα, τὴν μεγίστην φυλακὴν ἀνῄρηκε τῆς πόλεως. δεινὸν μὲν οὖν ἐστι καὶ ὑπὸ τῶν ἀγνοούντων τὰ δίκαια πάσχειν κακῶς, πολὺ δὲ χαλεπώτερον, ὅταν τις ἐπιστάμενος τὰ διαφέροντα παραβαίνειν τολμᾷ· φανερῶς γὰρ ἐνδείκνυται, ὥσπερ οὗτος, οὐκ αὐτὸς τοῖς νόμοις τοῖς τῆς πόλεως, ἀλλ᾽ ὑμᾶς τοῖς αὑτοῦ τρόποις ἀκολουθεῖν ἀξιῶν.

[20] Ἐνθυμήθητε δὲ Ταυρέαν, ὃς ἀντιχορηγὸς ἦν Ἀλκιβιάδῃ παισί. κελεύοντος δὲ τοῦ νόμου τῶν χορευτῶν ἐξάγειν ὃν ἄν τις βούληται ξένον ἀγωνιζόμενον, οὐκ ἐξὸν ἐπιχειρήσαντα κωλύειν, ἐναντίον ὑμῶν καὶ τῶν ἄλλων Ἑλλήνων τῶν θεωρούντων καὶ τῶν ἀρχόντων ἁπάντων παρόντων ἐν τῇ πόλει τύπτων ἐξήλασεν αὐτόν,

[16] But what is most terrible of all is that such a man should talk as if he were well-disposed towards the people, and call others oligarchs and haters of democracy. Moreover, one who should have died for his way of life is chosen by you as an accuser of those at variance with you, and he says he is a guardian of the constitution, although he refuses to be either the equal or only a little superior to any other Athenian; but he holds you in such exceeding contempt that he lives his life flattering you in a body and insulting you individually. [17] He has reached such a pitch of daring that he persuaded Agatharchus the painter to go into his house with him and constrained him to paint, and when he begged and pleaded what was in fact true, that he could not do this now because he had contracts with others, Alcibiades threatened to imprison him if he did not start painting right away. Which Alcibiades did, and Agatharchus did not escape until, three months later, he slipped past his guards and ran away, as if from the King of Persia. But Alcibiades is so shameless that he went to Agatharchus and accused him of doing him a wrong, and he did not repent for the force he had used but threatened him for leaving his work unfinished: democracy and freedom were of no help to him, he had been put in chains just like acknowledged slaves. [18] But I am annoyed to think that it is not safe for you to carry even malefactors off to prison through the enactment that he who fails to gain one-fifth of the votes is to pay a fine of a thousand drachmas, while the one who shut up a man for so long and constrained him to paint paid no penalty, but through this seems to be even more haughty and feared. In our treaties with other states we agree that it is forbidden to shut up or imprison a free man; and if anyone should break this, we imposed a heavy fine on them; but when this man has done such things, nobody is exacting any private or public vengeance. [19] I think this means safety for all, obeying the magistrates and the laws; and he who takes no notice of them has destroyed the city's greatest safeguard. So while it is a terrible thing to be ill treated by those who are ignorant of what is right, it is far harder to bear when someone who knows what is vital to the state dares to offend against it; for he is showing clearly, like this man, that he thinks not that he should obey the laws of the state, but that you should obey his own ways.

[20] Remember also Taureas, who was a rival choregus of boys to Alcibiades. The law allows anyone who wishes to expel any of the competing choral dancers who is a foreigner, and it is not allowed to prevent the one attempting to do so, but before you and the rest of the Greeks who were spectating and all the magistrates present in the city Alcibiades drove

καὶ τῶν θεατῶν συμφιλονικούντων ἐκείνῳ καὶ μισούντων τοῦτον, ὥστε τῶν χορῶν τὸν μὲν ἐπαινούντων, τοῦ δ' ἀκροάσασθαι οὐκ ἐθελόντων, οὐδὲν πλέον ἔπραξεν· [21] ἀλλὰ τῶν κριτῶν οἱ μὲν φοβούμενοι οἱ δὲ χαριζόμενοι νικᾶν ἔκριναν αὐτόν, περὶ ἐλάττονος ποιούμενοι τὸν ὅρκον ἢ τοῦτον. εἰκότως δέ μοι δοκοῦσιν οἱ κριταὶ ὑπέρχεσθαι Ἀλκιβιάδην, ὁρῶντες Ταυρέαν μὲν τοσαῦτα χρήματα ἀναλώσαντα προπηλακιζόμενον, τὸν δὲ τοιαῦτα παρανομοῦντα μέγιστον δυνάμενον. αἴτιοι δ' ὑμεῖς, οὐ τιμωρούμενοι τοὺς ὑβρίζοντας, καὶ τοὺς μὲν λάθρᾳ ἀδικοῦντας κολάζοντες, τοὺς δὲ φανερῶς ἀσελγαίνοντας θαυμάζοντες. [22] τοιγάρτοι τῶν νέων αἱ διατριβαὶ οὐκ ἐν τοῖς γυμνασίοις, ἀλλ' ἐν τοῖς δικαστηρίοις εἰσί, καὶ στρατεύονται μὲν οἱ πρεσβύτεροι, δημηγοροῦσι δὲ οἱ νεώτεροι, παραδείγματι τούτῳ χρώμενοι, ὃς τηλικαύτας ποιεῖται τῶν ἁμαρτημάτων ὑπερβολάς, ὥστε περὶ τῶν Μηλίων γνώμην ἀποφηνάμενος ἐξανδραποδίζεσθαι, πριάμενος γυναῖκα τῶν αἰχμαλώτων υἱὸν ἐξ αὐτῆς πεποίηται, ὃς τοσούτῳ παρανομωτέρως Αἰγίσθου γέγονεν, ὥστ' ἐκ τῶν ἐχθίστων ἀλλήλοις πέφυκε, καὶ τῶν οἰκειοτάτων ὑπάρχει αὐτῷ τὰ ἔσχατα τοὺς μὲν πεποιηκέναι τοὺς δὲ πεπονθέναι. [23] ἄξιον δὲ τὴν τόλμαν αὐτοῦ σαφέστερον ἔτι διελθεῖν. ἐκ ταύτης γὰρ παιδοποιεῖται τῆς γυναικός, ἣν ἀντ' ἐλευθέρας δούλην κατέστησε, καὶ ἧς τὸν πατέρα καὶ τοὺς προσήκοντας ἀπέκτεινε, καὶ τὴν πόλιν ἀνάστατον πεποίηκεν, ὡς ἂν μάλιστα τὸν υἱὸν ἐχθρὸν ἑαυτῷ καὶ τῇ πόλει ποιήσειε· τοσαύταις ἀνάγκαις κατείληπται μισεῖν. ἀλλ' ὑμεῖς ἐν μὲν ταῖς τραγῳδίαις τοιαῦτα θεωροῦντες δεινὰ νομίζετε, γιγνόμενα δ' ἐν τῇ πόλει ὁρῶντες οὐδὲν φροντίζετε. καίτοι ἐκεῖνα μὲν οὐκ ἐπίστασθε πότερον οὕτω γεγένηται ἢ πέπλασται ὑπὸ τῶν ποιητῶν· ταῦτα δὲ σαφῶς εἰδότες οὕτω παρανόμως πεπραγμένα ῥᾳθύμως φέρετε.

[24] Πρὸς δὲ τούτοις τολμῶσί τινες περὶ αὐτοῦ λέγειν ὡς οὐδὲ γεγένηται οὐδεὶς πώποτε τοιοῦτος. ἐγὼ δὲ νομίζω μέγιστα κακὰ τὴν πόλιν ὑπὸ τούτου πείσεσθαι, καὶ τηλικούτων πραγμάτων εἰς τὸν λοιπὸν χρόνον αἴτιον δόξειν, ὥστε μηδένα τῶν προτέρων ἀδικημάτων μεμνῆσθαι· ἀνέλπιστον γὰρ οὐδέν, τὸν τὴν ἀρχὴν τοῦ βίου τοιαύτην κατασκευασάμενον καὶ τὴν τελευτὴν ὑπερβάλλουσάν ποιήσασθαι. ἔστι δὲ σωφρόνων ἀνδρῶν φυλάττεσθαι τῶν πολιτῶν τοὺς ὑπεραυξανομένους, ἐνθυμουμένους ὑπὸ τῶν τοιούτων τὰς τυραννίδας καθισταμένας.

[25] Ἡγοῦμαι δ' αὐτὸν πρὸς ταῦτα μὲν οὐδὲν ἀντερεῖν, λέξειν δὲ περὶ τῆς νίκης τῆς Ὀλυμπίασι, καὶ περὶ πάντων μᾶλλον

him out with his fists; and the spectators, who sided with Taureas and showed hatred of Alcibiades, applauded the one chorus and refused to listen to the other, but Taureas did not gain anything from that. [21] Of the judges some in fear, others in complaisance judged Alcibiades the winner, valuing their oath less than him. But it seems reasonable to me that the judges fawned on Alcibiades, seeing that Taureas, who had spent so much money, was being insulted, but the other, who was committing a crime, was all-powerful. You are to blame, for not punishing the outrageous, and for chastising those who secretly do wrong but admiring those who are openly insolent. [22] That is why the young pass their time not in the gymnasia but in the courts, and why the old serve in the army while the young make public speeches, using this man as their model, who goes so far in his misdeeds that, after declaring his opinion about the Melians that they should be reduced to slavery, he bought a woman from among the captives and has had a son by her, whose birth was more illegal than that of Aegisthus, since he is born of the bitterest enemies, and of his closest relatives he has one who has committed and the other who has suffered the worst of wrongs. [23] But it is worth going through his daring more clearly still. For he begat a child from the very woman whom he had turned from free to slave, whose father and relatives he had killed and whose city he has devastated, that he might make his son the bitterest enemy of himself and his city; he has been compelled by such necessities to hate them. But you, although when you watch such things in tragedies you consider them terrible, when you see them happening in the city you think nothing of them. Yet you do not know whether the former are real or invented by the poets, but knowing well that the latter have been done so illegally, you bear them lightly.

[24] In addition to this, some are daring to say about Alcibiades that there has never been the like of him. But I think that the city will suffer the greatest evils through this man and that he will be thought responsible in the future for events so terrible that nobody will remember his past wrongs; for it is only reasonable to expect that one who has achieved such a beginning to his life will also make its end excessive. It is a mark of sensible men to be on guard against those citizens who are becoming over-powerful, remembering that by such men are tyrannies established.

[25] I believe that he will not reply to any of this, but will talk about his victory at Olympia and defend himself on anything rather than the actual

ἢ τῶν κατηγορηθέντων ἀπολογήσεσθαι. ἐξ αὐτῶν δὲ τούτων ἐπιδείξω αὐτὸν ἐπιτηδειότερον τεθνάναι μᾶλλον ἢ σώζεσθαι. διηγήσομαι δ' ὑμῖν. [26] Διομήδης ἦλθε ζεῦγος ἵππων ἄγων Ὀλυμπίαζε, κεκτημένος μὲν οὐσίαν μετρίαν, στεφανῶσαι δὲ ἀπὸ τῶν ὑπαρχόντων τὴν πόλιν καὶ τὴν οἰκίαν βουλόμενος, λογιζόμενος τοὺς ἀγῶνας τοὺς ἱππικοὺς τύχῃ τοὺς πλείστους κρινομένους. τοῦτον Ἀλκιβιάδης πολίτην ὄντα καὶ τὸν ἐπιτυχόντα, δυνάμενος παρὰ τοῖς ἀγωνοθέταις τῶν Ἠλείων, ἀφελόμενός αὐτὸς ἠγωνίζετο. καίτοι τί ἂν ἐποίησεν, εἴ τις τῶν συμμάχων τῶν ὑμετέρων ἀφίκετο ζεῦγος ἵππων ἔχων; [27] ἦ που ταχέως ἐπέτρεψεν ἂν ἀνταγωνίζεσθαι ἑαυτῷ, ὃς Ἀθηναῖον ἄνδρα βιασάμενος τοῖς ἀλλοτρίοις ἐτόλμησεν ἵπποις ἁμιλλᾶσθαι, δηλώσας τοῖς Ἕλλησι μηδὲν θαυμάζειν ἄν τινα αὐτῶν βιάσηται, ἐπεὶ καὶ τοῖς πολίταις οὐκ ἐξ ἴσου χρῆται, ἀλλὰ τοὺς μὲν ἀφαιρούμενος, τοὺς δὲ τύπτων, τοὺς δὲ εἰργνύων, τοὺς δὲ χρήματα πραττόμενος, οὐδενὸς ἀξίαν τὴν δημοκρατίαν ἀποφαίνει, τοὺς μὲν λόγους δημαγωγοῦ τὰ δ' ἔργα τυράννου παρέχων, καταμαθὼν ὑμᾶς τοῦ μὲν ὀνόματος φροντίζοντας, τοῦ δὲ πράγματος ἀμελοῦντας. [28] τοσοῦτον δὲ διαφέρει Λακεδαιμονίων, ὥστ' ἐκεῖνοι μὲν καὶ ὑπὸ τῶν συμμάχων ἀνταγωνιζομένων ἀνέχονται ἡττώμενοι, οὗτος δὲ οὐδ' ὑπὸ τῶν πολιτῶν, ἀλλὰ φανερῶς εἴρηκεν οὐκ ἐπιτρέψειν τοῖς ἀντεπιθυμοῦσί τινος. εἶτ' ἐκ τῶν τοιούτων ἀναγκαῖον τὰς πόλεις τῶν ἡμετέρων πολεμίων ἐπιθυμεῖν, ἡμᾶς δὲ μισεῖν.

[29] Ἵνα δὲ μὴ μόνον Διομήδην, ἀλλὰ καὶ τὴν πόλιν ὅλην ὑβρίζων ἐπιδείξειε, τὰ πομπεῖα παρὰ τῶν ἀρχιθεώρων αἰτησάμενος, ὡς εἰς τἀπινίκια τῇ προτεραίᾳ τῆς θυσίας χρησόμενος, ἐξηπάτησε καὶ ἀποδοῦναι οὐκ ἤθελε, βουλόμενος τῇ ὑστεραίᾳ πρότερος τῆς πόλεως χρήσασθαι τοῖς χρυσοῖς χερνιβίοις καὶ θυμιατηρίοις. ὅσοι μὲν οὖν τῶν ξένων μὴ ἐγίγνωσκον ἡμέτερα ὄντα, τὴν πομπὴν τὴν κοινὴν ὁρῶντες ὑστέραν οὖσαν τῆς Ἀλκιβιάδου τοῖς τούτου πομπείοις χρῆσθαι ἐνόμιζον ἡμᾶς· ὅσοι δὲ ἢ παρὰ τῶν πολιτῶν ἤκουον ἢ καὶ ἐπεγίγνωσκον τὰ τούτου, κατεγέλων ἡμῶν, ὁρῶντες ἕνα ἄνδρα μεῖζον ἁπάσης τῆς πόλεως δυνάμενον.

[30] Σκέψασθε δὲ καὶ τὴν ἄλλην ἀποδημίαν τὴν εἰς Ὀλυμπίαν ὡς διέθετο. τούτῳ σκηνὴν μὲν Περσικὴν Ἐφέσιοι διπλασίαν τῆς δημοσίας ἔπηξαν, ἱερεῖα δὲ καὶ τοῖς ἵπποις ἐφόδια Χῖοι παρεσκεύασαν, οἶνον δὲ καὶ τὰ ἄλλα ἀναλώματα Λεσβίοις προσέταξε. καὶ οὕτως εὐτυχής ἐστιν ὥστε τοὺς Ἕλληνας τῆς παρανομίας καὶ τῆς δωροδοκίας μάρτυρας κεκτημένος οὐδεμίαν

charges. But I shall show from these very things that he deserves to die rather than be acquitted. I shall explain why. [26] Diomedes went with a chariot-team to Olympia, possessing moderate means but desiring to win glory for the city and his family from those he had, reckoning the chariot-races were mostly decided by chance. This man was a citizen and the first person he met, but Alcibiades, who had influence with the Elean presidents of the games, deprived him of his team and competed with it himself. Yet what would he have done if one of your allies had arrived with a chariot-team? [27] Do you think he would have eagerly left him to compete against himself - who used force against an Athenian and then had the audacity to race with another man's horses, having shown the Greeks that they should not be at all surprised if he used force against any of them, since he does not treat even his fellow-citizens as equals, but by robbing some, hitting others, shutting up others in prison and extorting money from others still, he shows democracy is worth nothing, employing the words of a popular leader but the deeds of a tyrant after perceiving that you heed the name but do not care about the thing itself. [28] He differs so much from the Spartans that while they endure defeat even by their allies, when they contend against them, he does not endure it even by his fellow-citizens but has openly stated that he will not suffer those desiring anything in rivalry to himself. With such behaviour, then, it is inevitable that our allied states covet our enemies and hate us.

[29] In order to show, however, that he was insulting not only Diomedes but also the whole city, he asked for the processional vessels from the leaders of the delegation, to use them, he said, for his victory celebration on the day before the sacrifice, but deceived them and refused to return the vessels, wanting to use the golden basins and censers the next day before the city did. Therefore when those foreigners who did not know they were ours saw the state-procession taking place after that of Alcibiades, they thought we were using his vessels; but those who had either heard from his fellow-citizens or indeed recognised the ways of this man laughed at us, seeing that one man was more powerful than the whole state.

[30] Consider also how he arranged the rest of his trip abroad to Olympia. The Ephesians pitched for him a Persian tent twice the size of the state tent, the Chians provided sacrificial victims and fodder for his horses, and he requisitioned wine and the rest of his expenses from the Lesbians. Indeed he is so lucky that although he has the Greeks as witnesses of his illegal behaviour and taking of bribes, he has suffered no punishment, but

δέδωκε δίκην, ἀλλὰ ὁπόσοι μὲν ἄρχοντες ἐν μιᾷ πόλει γεγένηνται, ὑπεύθυνοί εἰσιν, [31] ὁ δὲ πάντων τῶν συμμάχων <ἄρχων> καὶ χρήματα λαμβάνων οὐδενὸς τούτων ὑπόδικός ἐστιν, ἀλλὰ τοιαῦτα διαπεπραγμένος σίτησιν ἐν Πρυτανείῳ ἔλαβε, καὶ προσέτι πολλῇ τῇ νίκῃ χρῆται, ὥσπερ οὐ πολὺ μᾶλλον ἠτιμακὼς ἢ ἐστεφανωκὼς τὴν πόλιν. εἰ δὲ βούλεσθε σκοπεῖν, εὑρήσετε τῶν πολλάκις τούτῳ πεπραγμένων ἕκαστον ὀλίγον χρόνον πράξαντάς τινας ἀναστάτους τοὺς οἴκους ποιήσαντας· οὗτος δ' ἐπιτηδεύων ἅπαντα πολυτελέστατα διπλασίαν οὐσίαν κέκτηται. [32] καίτοι ὑμεῖς γε νομίζετε τοὺς φειδομένους καὶ τοὺς ἀκριβῶς διαιτωμένους φιλοχρημάτους εἶναι, οὐκ ὀρθῶς γιγνώσκοντες· οἱ γὰρ μεγάλα δαπανώμενοι πολλῶν δεόμενοι αἰσχροκερδέστατοί εἰσιν. αἴσχιστον δὲ φανήσεσθε ποιοῦντες, εἰ τοῦτον μὲν ἀγαπᾶτε τὸν ἀπὸ τῶν ὑμετέρων χρημάτων ταῦτα κατεργασάμενον, Καλλίαν δὲ τὸν Διδυμίου, τῷ σώματι νικήσαντα πάντας τοὺς στεφανηφόρους ἀγῶνας, ἐξωστρακίσατε πρὸς τοῦτο οὐδὲν ἀποβλέψαντες, ὃς ἀπὸ τῶν ἑαυτοῦ πόνων ἐτίμησε τὴν πόλιν. [33] ἀναμνήσθητε δὲ καὶ τοὺς προγόνους, ὡς ἀγαθοὶ καὶ σώφρονες ἦσαν, οἵτινες ἐξωστράκισαν Κίμωνα διὰ παρανομίαν, ὅτι τῇ ἀδελφῇ τῇ ἑαυτοῦ συνῴκησε. καίτοι οὐ μόνον αὐτὸς ὀλυμπιονίκης ἦν, ἀλλὰ καὶ ὁ πατὴρ αὐτοῦ Μιλτιάδης. ἀλλ' ὅμως οὐδὲν ὑπελογίζοντο τὰς νίκας· οὐ γὰρ ἐκ τῶν ἀγώνων ἀλλ' ἐκ τῶν ἐπιτηδευμάτων ἔκρινον αὐτόν.

[34] Ἀλλὰ μὴν εἰ δεῖ κατὰ γένος σκοπεῖν, ἐμοὶ μὲν οὐδαμόθεν προσήκει τούτου τοῦ πράγματος οὐδὲ ἔστιν οὐδεὶς ὅστις ἂν ἀποδείξειε τῶν ἡμετέρων οὐδένα τῇ συμφορᾷ ταύτῃ χρησάμενον, Ἀλκιβιάδῃ δὲ μάλιστα πάντων Ἀθηναίων. καὶ γὰρ ὁ τῆς μητρὸς πατὴρ Μεγακλῆς καὶ ὁ πάππος Ἀλκιβιάδης ἐξωστρακίσθησαν ἀμφότεροι, ὥστ' οὐδὲν θαυμαστὸν οὐδ' ἄτοπον πείσεται τῶν αὐτῶν τοῖς προγόνοις ἀξιούμενος. καὶ μὴν οὐδ' ἂν αὐτὸς ἐπιχειρήσειεν ἀντειπεῖν, ὡς οὐ τῶν ἄλλων ἐκεῖνοι παρανομώτατοι ὄντες τούτου σωφρονέστεροι καὶ δικαιότεροι ἦσαν, ἐπεὶ τῶν γε τούτῳ πεπραγμένων οὐδ' ἂν εἷς ἀξίως κατηγορῆσαι δύναιτο.

[35] Νομίζω δὲ καὶ τὸν θέντα τὸν νόμον ταύτην τὴν διάνοιαν ἔχειν· ἀποβλέψαντα τῶν πολιτῶν πρὸς τοὺς κρείττους τῶν ἀρχόντων καὶ τῶν νόμων, ἐπειδὴ παρὰ τῶν τοιούτων οὐκ ἔστιν ἰδίᾳ δίκην λαβεῖν, δημοσίαν τιμωρίαν ὑπὲρ τῶν ἀδικουμένων κατασκευάσαι. ἐγὼ <μὲν> τοίνυν ἔν τε τῷ κοινῷ κέκριμαι τετράκις, ἰδίᾳ τε οὐδένα διεκώλυσα δικάζεσθαι βουλόμενον· Ἀλκιβιάδης δὲ τοιαῦτα ἐργασάμενος οὐδεμίαν πώποτε δίκην

while those who are magistrates in a single city have to render an account of their term, [31] he, who is holding a magistracy over all the allies and receiving money from them, is not liable to trial for any of this, but after accomplishing such things, he received public maintenance in the Prytaneum, and besides he is taking great credit for the victory as though he had not so much brought dishonour to as won glory for the city. But if you will only reflect, you will find that men who have even for a short time done any single one of the things done time and again by this man have ruined their houses; but Alcibiades, who has practised all the most extravagant vices, has doubled his wealth. [32] Yet you think that those who are thrifty and live parsimoniously are money-lovers, but you are mistaken; for those who spend large amounts and have great needs are the most sordidly greedy. You will manifestly have done the most disgraceful thing if you tolerate this man, who has achieved this with your money, when you ostracised Callias, son of Didymius, who was victorious through his personal prowess at all the games where the prize is a crown, paying no attention to this - although by his own efforts he brought honour to the city. [33] Recall too your ancestors, how fine and sensible they were when they ostracised Cimon for illegality, because he married his own sister. Yet not only was he himself an Olympic victor, but so also was his father Miltiades. But nevertheless, they took no account of his victories; for they were judging him not on the games but on his way of life.

[34] Further, if it is necessary to take our families into consideration, this matter has nothing to do with me from any side, nor is there anyone who could prove that any of my relatives has ever suffered this disaster, but it has more to do with Alcibiades than any other Athenian. For his mother's father Megacles and his grandfather Alcibiades were both ostracised, so he will suffer nothing surprising or paradoxical if he is thought worthy of the same treatment as his ancestors. Indeed, not even Alcibiades himself would attempt to gainsay that those men, although being the most lawless men of their day, were more decent and civilised than himself, since there is not a single man who could frame an accusation worthy of his misdeeds.

[35] I think also that the author of the law had this intention: noticing that whenever citizens are more powerful than the magistrates and the laws, it is not possible to obtain private redress from such men, he arranged state punishment for their misdeeds. Now I have been tried four times in a public case, and I have never prevented anyone who wished from going to law against me privately; but Alcibiades, who has done all these

ὑποσχεῖν ἐτόλμησεν. [36] οὕτω γὰρ χαλεπός ἐστιν, ὥστε οὐ περὶ τῶν παρεληλυθότων ἀδικημάτων αὐτὸν τιμωροῦνται, ἀλλ' ὑπὲρ τῶν μελλόντων φοβοῦνται, καὶ τοῖς μὲν πεπονθόσι κακῶς ἀνέχεσθαι λυσιτελεῖ, τούτῳ δὲ οὐκ ἐξαρκεῖ, εἰ μὴ καὶ τὸ λοιπὸν ὅ τι ἂν βούληται διαπράξεται. καίτοι οὐ δήπου, ὦ Ἀθηναῖοι, ὀστρακισθῆναι μὲν ἐπιτήδειός εἰμι, τεθνάναι δὲ οὐκ ἄξιος, οὐδὲ κρινόμενος μὲν ἀποφυγεῖν, ἄκριτος δὲ φεύγειν, οὐδὲ τοσαυτάκις ἀγωνιζόμενος νικήσας δικαίως <ἂν> πάλιν δόξαιμι δι' ἐκεῖνα ἐκπεσεῖν. [37] ἀλλὰ γὰρ ἴσως μετὰ μικρᾶς διαβολῆς ἢ φαύλων κατηγόρων ἢ διὰ τῶν ἐπιτυχόντων ἐχθρῶν ἐκινδύνευον, ἀλλ' οὐ διὰ τῶν ἐρρωμενεστάτων καὶ λέγειν καὶ πράττειν, οἵ τινες δύο τῶν τὴν αὐτὴν αἰτίαν ἐχόντων ἐμοὶ ἀπέκτειναν. οὔκουν τοὺς τοιούτους δίκαιον ἐκβάλλειν, οὓς πολλάκις ἐλέγχοντες εὑρίσκετε μηδὲν ἀδικοῦντας, ἀλλὰ τοὺς μὴ θέλοντας ὑποσχεῖν τῇ πόλει περὶ τοῦ βίου λόγον. [38] δεινὸν δέ μοι δοκεῖ εἶναι, εἰ μέν τις ἀπολογεῖσθαι ἀξιώσειεν ὑπὲρ τῶν ἀποθανόντων ὡς ἀδίκως ἀπολώλασιν, οὐκ <ἂν> ἀνασχέσθαι τῶν ἐπιχειρούντων· εἰ δέ τις τῶν ἀποφυγόντων πάλιν περὶ τῆς αὐτῆς αἰτίας κατηγορεῖ, πῶς οὐ δίκαιον περὶ τοὺς ζῶντας καὶ τοὺς τεθνηκότας τὴν αὐτὴν γνώμην ἔχειν; [39] ἔστι μὲν οὖν Ἀλκιβιάδου μήτε αὐτὸν τῶν νόμων καὶ τῶν ὅρκων φροντίζειν, ὑμᾶς τε παραβαίνειν ἐπιχειρεῖν διδάσκειν, καὶ τοὺς μὲν ἄλλους ἐκβάλλειν καὶ ἀποκτείνειν ἀνηλεῶς, αὐτὸν δὲ ἱκετεύειν καὶ δακρύειν οἰκτρῶς. καὶ ταῦτα μὲν οὐ θαυμάζω· πολλῶν γὰρ αὐτῷ κλαυμάτων ἄξια εἴργασται· ἐνθυμοῦμαι δὲ τίνας ποτὲ καὶ πείσει δεόμενος, πότερα τοὺς νεωτέρους, οὓς πρὸς τὸ πλῆθος διαβέβληκεν ἀσελγαίνων καὶ τὰ γυμνάσια καταλύων καὶ παρὰ τὴν ἡλικίαν πράττων, ἢ τοὺς πρεσβυτέρους, οἷς οὐδὲν ὁμοίως βεβίωκεν, ἀλλὰ τῶν ἐπιτηδευμάτων αὐτῶν καταπεφρόνηκεν; [40] οὐ μόνον δὲ αὐτῶν ἕνεκα τῶν παρανομούντων, ἵνα δίκην διδῶσιν, ἐπιμελεῖσθαι ἄξιον, ἀλλὰ καὶ τῶν ἄλλων, ὅπως τούτους ὁρῶντες δικαιότεροι καὶ σωφρονέστεροι γίγνωνται. ἐμὲ μὲν τοίνυν ἐξελάσαντες τοὺς βελτίστους περιδεεῖς καταστήσετε, τοῦτον δὲ κολάσαντες τοὺς ἀσελγεστάτους νομιμωτέρους ποιήσετε.

[41] Βούλομαι δ' ὑμᾶς ἀναμνῆσαι τῶν ἐμοὶ πεπραγμένων. ἐγὼ γὰρ πρεσβεύσας εἰς Θετταλίαν καὶ εἰς Μακεδονίαν καὶ εἰς Μολοσσίαν καὶ εἰς Θεσπρωτίαν καὶ εἰς Ἰταλίαν καὶ εἰς Σικελίαν τοὺς μὲν διαφόρους ὄντας διήλλαξα, τοὺς δ' ἐπιτηδείους ἐποίησα, τοὺς δ' ἀπὸ τῶν ἐχθρῶν ἀπέστησα. καίτοι εἰ τῶν πρεσβευόντων ἕκαστος τὰ αὐτὰ ἐποίησεν, ὀλίγους ἂν πολεμίους εἴχετε καὶ

things, has never yet dared to undergo trial. [36] For he is so difficult to deal with that they do not punish him for his past wrongs but fear him for his future ones, and while it is better for those who have been ill treated by him to suffer in silence, it is not sufficient for him unless he can accomplish whatever he wishes also in the future. Yet surely, Athenians, I do not deserve to be ostracised when I do not warrant being put to death, nor after being tried and acquitted to be exiled without trial, nor after being victorious in court so many times can I justly be thought to deserve banishment on those grounds again. [37] But perhaps I faced danger with a weak charge or indifferent accusers, or through casual enemies and not through the most formidable men of speech and action who caused the deaths of two of those on the same charge as me. I say that it is just to banish not those such as, after repeated questioning, you find are not guilty, but those who are unwilling to render to the state an account of their life. [38] This seems strange to me - if somebody resolved to speak in defence of those who have been put to death that they were unjustly destroyed, their attempt would not be tolerated; but if somebody accuses those who have been acquitted on the same charge again, how is it not just to hold the same opinion concerning the living and the dead? [39] It is typical of Alcibiades to think nothing of the laws or oaths himself, and to attempt to teach you to offend against them, and to cause the banishment and death of others unmercifully, but himself to beg and cry piteously. I am not indeed surprised at this, for he has done things worthy of much weeping; but I ask myself whom he will persuade by his entreaties - the young, whom he has brought into discredit with the people by his insolence, his emptying of the gymnasia and his behaviour out of line with his age, or the old, to whom he has lived a completely opposite life and whose way of life he has held in contempt? [40] However, you should be concerned not only about those who have committed a crime, that they be punished, but also about everybody else, that seeing these punished they become more civilised and decent. By banishing me, then, you will render the best men very fearful, but by punishing this man you will make the most insolent men more observant of law.

[41] I also wish to remind you of what I have done. As an ambassador to Thessaly, Macedonia, Molossia, Thesprotia, Italy and Sicily I reconciled some who were at variance with you, made others friendly and detached others from your enemies. If every one of your ambassadors had done the same, you would have few enemies, and you would have gained

πολλοὺς συμμάχους ἐκέκτησθε. [42] περὶ δὲ τῶν λῃτουργιῶν οὐκ ἀξιῶ μεμνῆσθαι, πλὴν κατὰ τοσοῦτον, ὅτι τὰ προσταττόμενα δαπανῶ οὐκ ἀπὸ τῶν κοινῶν ἀλλ' ἀπὸ τῶν ἰδίων. καίτοι τυγχάνω νενικηκὼς εὐανδρίᾳ καὶ λαμπάδι καὶ τραγῳδοῖς, οὐ τύπτων τοὺς ἀντιχορηγοῦντας, οὐδ' αἰσχυνόμενος εἰ τῶν νόμων ἔλαττον δύναμαι. τοὺς οὖν τοιούτους τῶν πολιτῶν πολὺ μᾶλλον ἐπιτηδείους ἡγοῦμαι μένειν ἢ φεύγειν.

many allies. [42] I do not propose to recall my public services, save only this that I meet the expenditure required of me not from state funds but from private funds. Yet I have gained victories in the physical fitness contest, in the torch-race and in the tragic competitions, without hitting my rival choregi nor being ashamed that I am less powerful than the laws. Citizens of this kind deserve far more, I think, to remain here than to live in exile.

Apparatus Criticus

A fuller *apparatus* may be consulted in the Teubner edition. The abbreviation 'ap.' refers to the 'apographa' (later manuscripts, all deriving from A); 'Ald.' refers to the Aldine edition.

1. *De Mysteriis*

3. ἥνπερ Ald.: ἥπερ | οἷα Markland: ὅσα
4. γῆ Valckenaer: ἤ
7. γεγένηται Dobree: γεγένηνται
9. αὐτοὺς Emperius: λόγους
11. ἀρεῖσθαι Bekker: αἱρεῖσθαι | ᾧ add. Bekker
12. πολέμαρχον del. MacDowell
16. ἔφυγον Blass: ἔφευγον (it. 18 bis, 25)
19. ὑμῖν ap.: ἡμῖν | οὕτω Reiske: οὐ | ἀναμιμνήσκοντα Reiske: ἀναμιμνήσκοντας
22. ἔλθοι ap.: ἔλθῃ
23. ἀνοσιώτερον καὶ ἀπιστότερον Reiske: ἀνοσιώτατον καὶ ἀπιστότατον
24. μου κατηγόρησαν Dobree: μ' ἐκατηγόρησαν
25. φυγόντων Blass: φευγόντων | ἐπὶ Reiske: ἐν
26. βούλεται Bekker: βούληται
32. τῶν μηδὲν ἠδικηκότων Lipsius: τοὺς μηδὲν ἠδικηκότας
34. καὶ τῶν Ald.: ἐκ
36. ἀνείποι Schoemann: ἀνείπῃ | ἔφευγον Baiter: ἔφυγον
37. Διοκλείδης Ald.: διὸ καὶ δὶς
38. μὲν et μάλιστα add. Sluiter e Galeno
40. ἴδοι ἡμᾶς Ald.: ἴδοι ὑμᾶς
41. αὐτὸν Reiske: αὐτῶν
43. αὐτῷ Reiske: αὐτῶν
44. ἐξεγγυηθέντες Sluiter: ἐξεγγυηθέντας | ἐν add. Weidner
45. στεφανώσαντες Bekker: στεφανώσοντες
47. Εὐκράτης. sic interpunxit Maidment (verba ὁ Νικίου ἀδελφός in A cum Εὐκράτης coniuncta sunt) | Post Κριτίας ἀνεψιὸς legebantur Εὐκρατίας ὁ Νικίου ἀδελφός, quae del. Reiske | ἀπέγραψεν Stephanus: ἐπέγραψεν
48. συνεκέκλητο Sauppe: συνεκέκλειστο
49. Habet A lacunam post ἀδικεῖν
50. δέη Bekker: δέοι
53. ὁ add. Reiske
55. δεῖ δοῦναι Dobree: διδόναι | λέγω...56. εἶτα δὲ sic interpunxit MacDowell: punctum post γενόμενα
56. δὲ Reiske: lacuna
57. γενόμενα Reiske: λεγόμενα
59. τῶν δ' ἄλλων οἳ Dobree: τῶν δ' ἄλλων οἱ λοιποὶ
61. ἐξέδειξα MacDowell: ἐξήλεγξα | βουλὴν Εὐφίλητος Bekker: βουλὴν γενέσθαι Εὐφίλητος
62. ποιήσοντος Valckenaer: ποιήσαντος
66. ἀπῆτε Weidner: ἀπίητε

67. ἂν add. Reiske | ἐκεῖνον Naber: ἐκείνῳ
69. ΜΑΡΤΥΡΕΣ add. Markland
71. Ἰσοτιμίδης οὗ Reiske: εἰς ὅτι μὴδ᾽ ἴσου
73. ὤφλον Reiske: ὤφειλον | ἐπιβολὰς Stephanus: ἐπιβουλὰς
74. εἶχον Bekker: ἔσχον | ἀναυμαχίου Suda: ναυμαχίου
77. τῶν ἀτίμων καὶ add. Sauppe
78. ὅσων ap.: ὅσον | καὶ τῶν Boeckh: ἢ τῶν | οἷς add. Lipsius | δικασθεῖσιν Lipsius: ἐδικάσθη ἢ
79. ἔχῃ Hermann: ἔχει
81. ἄλλοι Stahl: ἂν οἱ
82. καὶ τῶν ap.: καὶ τοῦ | νόμους ap.: ἀνόμους
83. ΨΗΦΙΣΜΑ add. Ald. | προσδέῃ Bekker: προσδέοι | ἀναγραφέντας Naber: ἀναγράφοντας
84. ἐπειδὰν ὀμωμόκωσιν Dobree: ἐπειδὴ ὀμωμόκασιν
86. ἔστιν οὕτως MacDowell: ἐστι τοῦτο | δὴ MacDowell: ἂν | ἢ που ἀγράφῳ Bekker: ἢ που ἂν ἀγράφῳ
87. ΝΟΜΟΣ add. Ald.
88. τῇ add. ap. | ἐφ᾽ add. Blass
89. μηδὲν add. Blass | νόμου add. Reiske
90. ὤμνυτε Ald.: ὤμινται | μεγίστων Reiske: μεγίστοις
91. αὖ ἡ Reiske: αὕτη | φυγόντων Sauppe: φευγόντων | ὑμῶν ap.: ἡμῶν
92. ὑπάρχοι Emperius: ὑπαρχόντων
93. τὴν βουλήν Stephanus: τήν τε βουλήν | ἐψηφίσασθε Reiske: ἀπεψηφίσασθε
94. καὶ add. Baiter
95. οὑτοσί Blass: οὗτος | ἄλλο τι Canter: ἀλλ᾽ ὅτι | ἢ Ald.: εἰ
96. οἷς Droysen: ὅτε | καταλύῃ Ald.: καταλύει | ἄρχῃ Ald.: ἄρχει | ἔσται Stephanus: ἔσται
97. ἀποκτενεῖν Droysen: ἀποκτείνειν | καὶ λόγῳ καὶ ἔργῳ καὶ ψήφῳ transtulit, καὶ add. Sauppe | τιν᾽ Reiske: τὴν | τὸν ap.: τῶν
98. ἀποθάνῃ Ald.: ἀποθάνοι | τῷ Ἀθηναίων Osann: τῶν Ἀθηναίων
100. ἑτέρων Reiske: ἑταιρῶν
101. σεαυτοῦ ap.: ἑαυτοῦ
102. ἂν add. Dobree | ὑμᾶς Reiske: ἡμᾶς | ὑμῖν ap.: ἡμῖν
103. καὶ ψηφίσματα Bekker: καὶ τὰ ψηφίσματα
104. πρότερον Stephanus: προτέρων (it. infra)
106. ἔφευγε Sauppe: ἔφυγε | τῶν ap.: τοὺς
107. τὴν βασιλέως Bekker: τοῦ βασιλέως | φεύγοντας Baiter et Sauppe: φυγόντας
110. δ᾽ εἴη Bekker: δὲ ἦν
111. ἐπαγγεῖλαι Bekker: ἀπαγγεῖλαι
112. ΜΑΡΤΥΡΙΑ add. Ald.
113. ὃ add. MacDowell
115. ἀναστὰς Baiter: στὰς
116. ὤν Reiske: ὦν | ὄν add. Frohberger
117. βούλοισθε Dobree: βούλεσθε
120. λέγων hic addidi, πρότερον μὲν λέγων Λεάγρῳ MacDowell: προτέρῳ μὲν Λεάγρῳ ὅτι
121. πείσας Scaliger: πείσων
122. οὐδ᾽ add. Reiske
123. ἀποφεύξομαι Valckenaer: ἀποφεύξαιμι
125. ἀποδρᾶσα Bekker: ἀποδράσασα

126. οἱ add. Muretus
127. αὐτοῦ Baiter: αὐτοῦ | Καλλικλῆς MacDowell: καλλίδης | ὅς Ald.: ὅ | αὐτοῖς Bekker: αὐτὸς | πρότερον add. MacDowell / ΜΑΡΤΥΡΕΣ add. Ald.
130. κατεῖχεν Blass: κατέσχεν
132. 'Α....Δελφόν Bekker: ἀδελφὸν
133. ἀρχώνης Valckenaer: ἄρχων, εἰς | αὐτῷ Reiske: αὐτοὶ | λεύκην, οὓς Muretus: λευκὴν τὸ πόσους | ὑπερβάλλουσι Stephanus: ὑπερβάλλωσι
135. τὸ Ἀθηναίων Fuhr: τῶν Ἀθηναίων | ἡμῖν Reiske: ὑμῖν
136. τὸ add. Valckenaer | ὡς Blass: τοὺς | ὑμῖν Reiske: ἡμῖν | μὲν add. Reiske
138. οὐκ ἐξῆν Stephanus: οὐ πεζὴν
139. πάνυ Reiske: πολὺ
140. βούλεσθε Taylor: βουλεύεσθε
141. ὑμῶν add. Reiske | γένοιτο Dobree: γένηται
142. μεμνῆσθε Schneider: μεμνῆσθαι | ὑμετέρων Reiske: ἡμετέρων (it. 143)
143. κἀμοὶ Ald.: καί μοι
144. καινὸν Emperius: καὶ | τοῖν (bis) Marchant: ταῖν
145. lacunam Reiske
146. ὄνειδος ὑμῖν ap.: ὄνειδος ἡμῖν
147. οὐδὲν πώποτε Sluiter: οὐδὲν ἂν πώποτε
149. παρ' ὑμῶν ap.: παρ' ὑμῖν
150. ᾑρημένοι Valckenaer: εἰρημένοι

2. De Reditu

1. ἕτερος Reiske: ἑτέρως
3. ἐλέγχοντες Emperius: ἐλέγξοντες
7. βουληθέντι Ald.: βουληθέντα
11. τέμνεσθαί Dobree: γένεσθαί
12. αἴτια Blass: ἄξια
15. ἐπειδὴ Reiske: καὶ ἐπειδὴ | ἔχοντα ὀνείδη οὗτοί με Sauppe: εἶχον τὰ ὀνείδη οὗτοι, οἵ με
16. εὖ hic addidi, post ἐφαίνετο Ald. | ἀπωλλύμην Bekker: ἀπολοίμην ὅποι Reiske: ὅπου
19. post ἴσασιν ἡ βουλή del. Valckenaer | εἰκὸς Ald.: εἰς | ἂν add. Dobree
20. οἷόν τέ Stephanus: οἷόν γέ | ἠγγέλθη ὑμῖν Valckenaer: ἠγγέλθη ἡμῖν | αὐτῶν Baiter et Sauppe: αὐτῶν
21. τάδε δὲ Gebauer: τὰ δὲ | ἂν add. Dobree | προῄδετε Blass: προειδῆτε
23. παντοδαποῖς Stephanus: παντοδαπῆς | πολιτείαν Reiske: πολιτείας
24. ἐμοῦ τὸ Reiske: ὁμοῦ τὸ | ταὐτὸν ἔτι ὄν Bekker: τοῦτ' ἀναίτιον | διαβεβλῆσθε Bekker: διαβεβλῆσθαι
26. ἀλλὰ Reiske: ἄλλο
27. θαυμάζοι Ald.: θαυμάζει

3. De Pace

1. ἂν ἡ εἰρήνη Lipsius: ἂν εἰρήνη Q, ἡ εἰρήνη Α
2. ὁ Ἀθηναίων Spengel: ὁ τῶν Ἀθηναίων (it. 4, 10) | ἐποιήσασθε Reiske:

ἐποιήσατε

3. πέμψαιμεν A, πέμψωμεν Q
4. πεντήκοντα Meursius cum Aeschine 2.172: πέντε | ὑμῖν edd.: ἡμῖν
5. τῷ Ἀθηναίων Spengel: τῶν Ἀθηναίων (it. 7)
6. ἡμῖν Q: ὑμῖν A | ἐποίησον Bekker: ἐποιήσαντο
7. τὸν Ἀθηναίων Bekker: τῶν Ἀθηναίων
9. τριακοσίας Markland cum Aeschine 2.175: τετρακοσίας
10. ἐξελέγξει Taylor: ἐξελέγχει
11. τὰ add. Reiske
12. δήμου Canter: δήπου
13. ἀδικουμένους A corr.: ἠδικημένους A pr.: ἀδικοῦντας Q | ἠδικημένοις A: ἀδικουμένοις Q | ἀφεῖσιν Reiske: ἀφήσειν
15. ἐγκτήματα Valckenaer: ἐγκλήματα
18. δ' ἐν Βοιωτοῖς Sauppe: δὲ βοιωτοῖς | τότε Sluiter: ὅτε
20. τῷ add. ap.
21. τὰ add. Ald.
22. παρ' add. Ald.
23. ταὐτὰ (bis) Osann: ταῦτα
24. ἡμᾶς Dobree: ἂν ἡμᾶς
26. ἰόντων Ald.: ὄντων | καὶ ποιεῖν Ἀργείους Sluiter: Ἀργείους καὶ ποιεῖν | ποιήσωμεν ap.: ποιήσομεν | πολεμήσομεν Ald.: πολεμήσωμεν
27. ποιουμένους Reiske: ποιουμένοις | τοῖς ἄλλοις Reiske: τοῖς δὲ ἄλλοις | παραστήσεσθαι Reiske: ἀποστήσεσθαι
29. μετὰ add. Reiske | τῷ βασιλέως Q: τοῦ βασιλέως A | οὐδενὸς Reiske: οὐδὲν
30. τῆς Ἐγεσταίων καὶ Καταναίων Francke: τῶν Ἐγεσταίων καὶ τῶν Καταναίων | βουλοίμεθα Reiske: βουλόμεθα | μένοιτες Blass: μένοιτας
31. ὑπὲρ Ἀθηναίων Pertz: ὑπὲρ τῶν Ἀθηναίων
33. ὑμῖν Bekker: ἡμῖν | ταῦθ' Reiske: ταύτην | τὸν Ἀθηναίων Spengel: τῶν Ἀθηναίων
34. πράττῃ Ydén: πράττοι | ἔτι Reiske: τι | ὑμῖν ap.: ἡμῖν
37. ἐκεκτήμεθα Hirschig: κεκτήμεθα
38. τειχισάμενοι Emperius: ἐτειχίσαμεν
39. τὰς μὲν Reiske: τὰ μὲν | ταύτην Hirschig: ταῦτ' | τὰς add. Fuhr
40. οὐ πρακτέον Albini: οὐκ ἀκτέον | εἴ τι Ald.: ἔτι | τι add. Blass
41. ἔλεσθε edd.: ἐλέσθαι

4. In Alcibiadem

2. ὧν εἰς Valckenaer: ὧν τῶν ἀγαθῶν εἰς
3. ἀποκτενεῖν Stephanus: ἀποκτείνειν | οὔτε ante διαψηφισαμένων del. Schleiermacher
5. πονηρὸς add. Emperius | διαφθερεῖ Ald.: διαφθείρη A: διαφθείρει Q | καὶ add. Reiske | ὑμῶν Stephanus: ἡμῶν | ὑπὸ Bekker: ἀπὸ
7. ἕκαστον Maidment: ἑκάστου
8. στασιωτείας Ald.: στασιωτίας A: ἀσωτίας Q | οὐ ῥάδιον εἰδέναι Blass: οὐ ῥάδιον ἦν εἰδέναι | ἀποφυγόντος Ald.: ἀποφεύγοντος
9. ὥστε Stephanus: ὡς | δημεύεσθαι Muretus: δημεύειν | τοὺς δὲ νικήσαντας Muretus: τῶν δὲ νικησάντων
10. ἄρξωμαι Blass: ἄρξομαι | δεήσειε Baiter: δεήσει

11. ἑκάστοις τῶν Blass: ἑκάστῳ τῶν | ἑκάστοις Baiter et Sauppe: ἑκάστης
12. ὅταν πρῶτον Reiske: πρῶτον ὅταν
13. ᾑρῆσθαι Valckenaer: εὑρῆσθαι | θυγατρὸς γένοιτο Α: θυγατρὸς αὐτοῦ γένοιτο Q
15. κατηγόρει Stephanus: κατηγορεῖ | verba ἀλλὰ μὴν...βοηθήσοιτας, quae post περὶ πλείονος habent codd., huc transposuit Fuhr
16. καὶ τοὺς Dobree: αὐτὸς | ἔδει Dobree: δεῖ | ὑμῶν Emperius: ἡμῶν
17. τὴν οἰκίαν Hirschig: οἴκαδε τὴν οἰκίαν | ἐδεδέκει Emperius: ἐδεδοίκει
19. αὐτοῦ Baiter et Sauppe: αὐτοῦ
22. παρανομωτέρως Reiske: παρανομώτατος Α: παρανομώτερος Q
23. καὶ τὴν πόλιν Α pr.: καὶ ἧς τὴν πόλιν Α corr. Q
25. ταῦτα Meier: τοῦτο | ἀπολογήσεσθαι Ald.: ἀπολογήσασθαι
27. ἀποφαίνει Reiske: ἀποφαίνων
29. ἐπιδείξειε Emperius: ἐπιδόξειε | τἀπινίκια Meursius: τὰ πινάκια | προτεραίᾳ Canter: προτέρα | θυσίας Scaliger: οὐσίας | χερνιβίοις Taylor ex Athen. 9.408c: χερνίβοις | μεῖζον ἁπάσης Sluiter: μείζονα πάσης
30. διέθετο. τούτῳ Reiske: διέθετο (διετίθετο Q) τοῦτο.
31. ἄρχων add. Meier | τῶν πολλάκις τούτῳ Lipsius: πολλὰ τῶν τούτω
32. τοῦτο Stephanus: τοῦτον
34. Ἀλκιβιάδῃ Valckenaer: Ἀλκιβιάδης Α: Ἀλκιβιάδην Q
35. μὲν add. Bekker
36. διαπράξεται Bekker: διαπράξηται | νικήσας καὶ δικαίως Reiske, καὶ del. Blass: δικαίως καὶ νικήσας | ἂν add. Baiter et Sauppe
38. ἂν add. Reiske
40. ἀσελγεστάτους Emperius: ἀσελγεστέρους
41. πρεσβευόντων Luzac: πρωτευόντων

Commentary

SPEECH 1: *ON THE MYSTERIES*

1-10: proem
The aims of the προοίμιον, or introductory remarks, were to render the listeners well-disposed, attentive and docile. The methods employed to achieve this *captatio benevolentiae* by a defendant in a forensic case included, respectively, praising or flattering the jurors and highlighting the disadvantages under which he was speaking; direct appeal to the jurors and stressing the importance or improbability of the case, and its interest both for the defendant and for the jurors and the state itself; enabling the jurors to follow intelligently the narrative of events. Examples of these elements here are: **I trusted...in you (2), the defendant is necessarily at a disadvantage (6); I shall instead ask of you, gentlemen (1, cf. 6), I left it to you to give judgment on my life (5); So I think the best thing is...to omit nothing (8).** Additionally, speakers use stock themes (*topoi*): parts of **1, 6, 7** and **9** recur with variations in Lys. 19.2-5, 11, suggesting derivation from a collection of proems. These commonplaces considerably lengthen the proem, as is also the case with the speeches of Andocides' older contemporary Antiphon (e.g. 5.1-7).

1. **The preparation:** hinting at the use of bribery to shore up a weak case (cf. **105, 123**; Is. 8.3). Speakers frequently accuse their opponents of caballing (e.g. Ant. 5.79; Is. 4.5; Dem. 30.3; Aesch. 2.1); and another element of the *topos* was to contrast the opponent's elaborate artifice with one's own lack of time for preparation (**6**; Ant. 5.19; Lys. 7.3, 19.3; cf. Isoc. 4.13) or inexperience (Lys. 19.2; Is. 8.5; Dem. 27.2). The plot theme is developed in **121-3**.

Andocides' version of the *topos* is carefully arranged to make the maximum impact on the jurors. Note the frequency of the letters tau and pi; the positioning of τὴν παρασκευήν at the beginning (sim. Aesch. 3.1) and the delaying of the first main verb ἐπίστασθε; the etymological figure (δικαίως καὶ ἀδίκως); the periphrasis πολλοὺς λόγους ποιεῖσθαι (simply λέγειν in Lys. 19.2). Note also how τὴν μὲν παρασκευήν is only loosely contrasted with ἐγὼ δέ, and how μέν is used at the beginning of the speech ('inceptive' μέν): both are features of the speeches of Antiphon and Andocides. See Denniston 371-2, 380-4.

the very moment...city: in 403.

almost all of you know...about this: an element of the *captatio benevolentiae*, but a common form of expression in other parts of speeches (e.g. **20, 2.20**; see also **37n**.). Sometimes (as in **22**, cf. Dem. 40.53) it appears to gloss over the fact that no witnesses are being produced in support of a contention. Similar remarks are also made when speakers are adducing historical examples, to avoid giving the impression that they are lecturing their audience. See Pearson 212.

2. **having neither given sureties...prison:** Andocides was accused by the procedure *endeixis*, in which the alleged criminal was denounced in writing to a public official before being arrested by his accuser. If Andocides' statement here is true, it indicates that a man accused by *endeixis* could be allowed bail if he provided sureties, i.e. three persons of the same property-class as the accused who guaranteed his appearance at his trial (cf. Dem. 24.144). There is insufficient evidence to decide whether the accused had the right to bail (except in certain cases) or whether bail depended on the will of the prosecutor. See Hansen (1976) 11-13; Edwards and Usher 26. Andocides intimates in **4** that his accusers wanted him to be at liberty, so that he could flee and thereby allow Callias to win his claim to the heiress. Possibly Andocides' sureties would then have suffered the punishment due to him if he stayed and lost (but see **44**n.).

I trusted...cast: another *topos*, repeated in **9** (cf. Ant. 5.8; Lys. 3.2; Isoc. 15.169-70; Aesch. 2.24; for the unjustly/justly antithesis cf. Ant. 5.73; Lys. 19.54).

the oaths you have sworn: in fact, members of the Heliaea probably only swore one, annual heliastic oath. See Harrison 2.48.

3.   **those who are unwilling to stay...admit their guilt:** the first part of this *topos* (cf. Ant. 5.13, 93; ps.-Lys. 20.21-2; Aesch. 2.6) was a natural assumption; the speciousness of the second part is evident from Lys. 12.84; Lyc. 1.90.

4.   **For example...exile:** see **2**n.

being offered: it may have been common knowledge in Athens that Euagoras, the ruler of Salamis, had opened up his previously hostile kingdom to Greek settlers (Isoc. 9.49-51), and Andocides asserts his foreign connections in **145**. His opponents alleged, however, that Andocides had been in trouble with Euagoras and the king of Citium (*Ag. And.* 26, 28; cf. *Life of And.* 834F).

a gift: presumably of money.

the state of our city: i.e. Athens was not the place for a trader after the ruinous Peloponnesian War or for a *kalos kagathos* ('gentleman') in the current anti-oligarchic climate (cf. Isoc. 18.2).

5.   **I would never accept...country:** for a Greek, exile and the consequent denial of burial in his homeland (cf. Hyp. 1.20) were worse than death. See Lacey 80-1.

6.   **So I ask you...disadvantage:** sim. Ant. 5.6-7; Lys. 19.2-3. See **1**n.

It is therefore reasonable..(7)..my defence: the repetition in **9** could be taken to reflect Andocides' amateurism, but it adds weight to the *captatio benevolentiae*. Repetition is also a feature of Antiphon's style (e.g. 5.4).

7.   **many before...the accused:** the rhetorical nature of this statement obscures the fact that prosecutors in most public cases who failed to win one-fifth of the votes were liable to a fine of 1000 drachmas and partial loss of rights (*atimia*), as Andocides was well aware (**33**). They could also be prosecuted as sycophants (on whom see **86**n.). See MacDowell (1978) 64-5.

Others again...victims: this element of the *topos*, which is designed to impress on the jurors the gravity of their decision, is also found in Ant. 5.95. The argument clearly implies the possibility of prosecuting witnesses for false testimony after the sentence passed in the original trial had been carried out (except in connection with homicide trials). When this sentence was death or exile, the trial of the witnesses must have been initiated by a third party (n.b. 'his friends' in Antiphon), and the case was therefore a *graphe* (public suit). See MacDowell (1978) 244; **9**n. This was different from the (later) *dike pseudomartyrion*, in which the prosecution had to be initiated before the voting in the original trial (*Ath. Pol.* 68.4). See further Harrison 2.192-7; S. C. Todd in *Nomos* 36-8.

before you: the orators regularly use ὑμεῖς ('you') to mean the people as a whole or a body representing it (e.g. **13** the jury, **81** the democrats). See MacDowell (1978) 40.

8.   **8-10** form the *prothesis*, or explanatory introduction to the narrative.

the end of the story: i.e. events after Andocides' return to Athens, which he does not begin to relate until **71**.

9.   **I trusted in you:** see **2**n.

in both private and public cases: the basic distinction between cases in Athenian law, according to whether the offence concerned only the individuals involved (*dike idia*) or the state as a whole (*dike demosia*). In the latter any free adult male (with certain exceptions) could prosecute, commonly by a *graphe*, and *endeixis* was another type of public suit. See MacDowell (1978) 57-61.

and indeed...together: others stress the importance of the laws (Eur. *Suppl.* 312-13) and law-courts (Dem. 24.2) in preserving the state.

I do, however, ask this...oaths: picking up the *topos* in **6-7**.

nor view what I say...words: cf. Ant. 5.5. The opposite point, that what the parties in a suit say must be closely scrutinised and suspected (especially in a homicide trial), is made in similar fashion at Ant. 6.18. For the metaphorical use of θηρεύειν cf. Pl. *Gorg.* 489b.

10. **turned informer:** any man or woman, of whatever status, had the right to reveal the name of a traitor or serious criminal to the council or assembly, as we see in the following sections. Further on *menysis* see MacDowell (1978) 181-3.

11-33: the profanation of the Mysteries
This part of the speech divides clearly into a narrative (**11-18**) followed by a proof (**19-33**). The διήγησις is the section in which the facts of the case are recited, and according to rhetorical theory it should be brief, clear and credible. Its beginning is regularly marked by the particle γάρ; and it usually follows the proem and precedes the proofs, though sometimes it is divided into two or more parts, and on other occasions (especially in non-forensic speeches) it is blended with the proofs. This speech also has a combined narrative and proof section (**34-70**).

11. **Nicias:** see Davies 403-4; Develin 2116. Nicias, son of the extremely wealthy Niceratus, was himself famed for his wealth (which derived mainly from silver-mining and investments in slave-miners) and conspicuous consumption. His political opinions were moderate, and his opposition to the Sicilian expedition is recorded by Thucydides (6.8-14). Left in sole command after the recall of Alcibiades and death of Lamachus, Nicias' irresolute leadership was a major factor in the Athenians' disastrous defeat, which led to his surrender and execution. For the Peace of Nicias see **3.8n**.

    Lamachus: see Develin 1770. He may by this time have been in his fifties, and he died in Sicily in 414. Lamachus is perhaps best known for being the butt of Dicaeopolis' ridicule in Aristophanes' *Acharnians*.

    Alcibiades: see Davies 17-21; Develin 84. Alcibiades was the son of Cleinias and Deinomache, daughter of the Alcmaeonid Megacles (see **4.34n.**). After his father's death at Coronea in 446, he was brought up by Pericles and became a follower of Socrates. Service at Potidaea (432-30) and Delium (424) was followed by his election as general in 420, probably at the minimum legal age of thirty. Alcibiades led the extreme democrats and favoured a policy of aggressive imperialism, which culminated in the launching of the Sicilian expedition. Recalled to Athens in connection with his alleged part in the Mysteries and Hermae scandals, Alcibiades escaped to Sparta and fomented the Ionian revolt against Athens in 412, but he then fell out of favour with the Spartans and was made general by the Athenian fleet at Samos in 411. He went on to direct the Athenian war operations brilliantly until 406, when he lost his position after the defeat at Notium. Alcibiades retired to the Thracian Chersonese and was assassinated in 404.

    in a house: instead of in the temple at Eleusis. For an explicit contrast between a private house and a sacred place cf. Dem. 21.73-4.

    if you vote immunity: to prevent Andromachus being charged as an accomplice. The penalty for false information given under immunity was death (**20**).

12.   **Alcibiades...denied the charge:** he also insisted on standing trial at once, but the case was postponed until after his departure for Sicily (Thuc. 6.29; Plut. *Alc.* 19.3-5).

the prytaneis: the fifty 'presidents' who represented their tribe in the Boule (council of 500, consisting of fifty members from each of the ten tribes). Each of the groups served for one-tenth of the year (a *prytaneia*) as the convenors and executive committee of the council and assembly. In the fifth century they also presided over meetings of these bodies, with a chairman (*epistates*) who was elected by lot and served for one day only. They met in the circular-shaped Tholos.

a slave of Alcibiades: the text here is corrupt, and I hesitantly follow MacDowell in bracketing πολέμαρχον as a gloss on Ἀλκιβιάδου. The best alternative reading is Marchant's Ἀρχεβιάδου <τοῦ> Πολεμάρχου ('a slave of Archebiades, son of Polemarchus').

the house of Pulytion: a grand property on the road to the Dipylon gate (Pl. *Eryx.* 400b; Paus. 1.2.5), which is referred to as being under mortgage by Pherecrates (frg. 58K). Alcibiades' son later attempted to minimise the significance of this performance by saying it took place during a dinner party (Isoc. 16.6; cf. Thuc. 6.28.1). See *HCT* 4.283.

Meletus: presumably the same man as the one denounced by Teucrus (**35**, cf. **63**), but not the prosecutor of Andocides and Socrates (see **94**n.).

the actual performers: in the roles of hierophant ('shower of the sacred things'), dadouchos ('torch-bearer') and herald.

13.   **the rest fled into exile...by you:** Alcibiades for one did not go into exile immediately (cf. Thuc. 6.29) - Andocides telescopes events here, in order to deal with each denunciation separately.

NAMES: many of the names given in this speech by Andocides (and their correct spelling) are confirmed by fragments of stone pillars (*stelai*) set up in the Eleusinium by the *poletai*, the officials who were responsible for selling the property of the condemned (the so-called Hermocopid inscription). Cf. Pollux 10.97; ML 79 (= Fornara 147; AVN 75; CW 162B); D. M. Lewis in *Ancient Society and Institutions: Studies Presented to Victor Ehrenberg* (Oxford, 1966) 177-91. Ostwald's analysis of the names (329-30, App. C) shows that one-third of the twenty-seven men about whom we have further information were followers of the sophists, and about half were antipathetic towards the democracy.

Their names are frequently all we know about those involved, but **Nicides** was wealthy (see Davies 408) and **Oeonias** was one of the richest men known in Athens at any period (see Davies 419); for **Archebiades** cf. Lys. 14.27. **Archippus**, prosecuted by Andocides for mutilating a Hermes (*Ag. And.* 11-12), may have been the comic poet, so too **Aristomenes** (see MacDowell App. N). **Panaetius** will not have been the man denounced by Andocides himself (**52**, **67-8**; *contra* Ostwald 539 n. 14).

Note that Pulytion's name appears to have been omitted from this list. Marr 329 n. 1 suggests he may have given information, which was then used by Thessalus in his prosecution of Alcibiades.

14.   **Diognetus:** either this man or more likely the one denounced by Teucrus (**15**; or just possibly both) was the son of Niceratus, brother of Nicias and Eucrates, and a distant relation of Andocides. See Davies 405; Develin 863; Ostwald 544. He may have been exiled for being a member of the Four Hundred, returning to Athens after the amnesty of 404 (Lys. 18.9-11). Another possibility is the secretary of 409/8 (= Develin 865).

Were you...They are: the only extant example of the questioning of a witness (but cf. Ar. *Wasps* 962-6). Lysias provides some instances of the opponent being questioned (12.25, 13.30-3, 22.5).

a commissioner of inquiry: already appointed to investigate the Hermae affair (cf. **40**). Peisander and Charicles were also commissioners (**36**), and possibly Androcles (see Ellis 58). Peisander was a member of the council in 415/4 (cf. **43**), which may indicate that all the commissioners were councillors (*contra* MacDowell).

impeached: MacDowell takes εἰσήγγειλεν in its non-technical sense of 'report', because Plutarch (*Alc.* 22.3) records the impeachment brought against Alcibiades after his departure for Sicily by Thessalus. Andocides certainly does use the verb in this sense in **2.3, 19, 21**, but it may be that Pythonicus' impeachment was withdrawn, and Thessalus brought his impeachment after new denunciations sponsored by Androcles. See Hansen (1975) 74-7, esp. 75 n. 10; also Ostwald 534 n. 29. Doubt over the precise meaning of the verb recurs in **27, 37**. Further on *eisangelia* see MacDowell (1978) 183-6; Ostwald, Index s.v.

15. **a second information followed:** after Alcibiades' departure.

Teucrus, a metic resident in Athens: just possibly the stonemason mentioned in the Erechtheum accounts (AVN 73; this was suggested by Hatzfeld 167 n. 5). Further on metics (free non-citizens living in Athens) see AVN p. 99-101.

which had full power to act: including the granting of immunity (cf. **12**), which would normally have been conferred by the assembly. See Rhodes (1972) 186-8. The council's extraordinary powers will originally have been granted in connection with the mutilation of the Hermae and later extended to cover the profanation of the Mysteries.

they went...to fetch him: i.e. officials acting for the council.

NAMES: the Hermocopid inscription (**13n.**) lists **Phaedrus**, the son of Pythocles of Myrrhinous. He is therefore the friend of Socrates and eponym of Plato's dialogue; and also a friend of Acumenus (**18**) and his son Eryximachus (**35**; cf. Pl. *Phdr.* 227a, 268a, *Prot.* 315c; the identification of Eryximachus as Acumenus' son is doubted by *HCT* 4.284). Phaedrus' involvement explains his later poverty (Lys. 19.15) and why Diogeiton could move into his house (Lys. 32.14). See further Davies 201. **Cephisodorus**, a metic, was probably the son-in-law of **Isonomus** and a comic dramatist (see MacDowell App. N). For **Diognetus** see **14n.** MacDowell rightly argues that **Antiphon** was not one of the Antiphons known to us from other sources (similarly with **Philocrates** and **Pantacles**). The son of **Teisarchus** is named in a lawsuit of c. 380 (see Davies 501).

all this is also being admitted to you: there was, of course, no reason for Andocides' opponents to question what is said here, unless Teucrus had denounced him too.

16. **The wife of Alcmaeonides...Agariste:** Agariste's knowledge of these events and the names strongly hint at a family connection between Alcibiades (whose mother Deinomache was an Alcmaeonid) and Agariste (the two famous women of this name in the Alcmaeonid family were the wife of Megacles in the sixth century and of Xanthippus, the father of Pericles). The suspicion is strengthened if Damon was the musician and friend of Pericles (Plut. *Per.* 4.1-2). See Davies 382-3; R. W. Wallace, 'Charmides and Damon. Andokides 1.16' (cf. *L'Année philologique* 60 [1989] s.v. Andocides).

Axiochus: Alcibiades' uncle, after whom the dialogue attributed to Plato is named. He will have returned to Athens in 411 (see Davies 16-17) or with Alcibiades in 408/7, since he proposed the second decree honouring Neapolis at this time (ML 89, = Fornara 156) and defended the Arginusae generals in 406 (*Axioch.* 369a). See further Ostwald 541-2.

Adeimantus: a friend of Alcibiades, who also returned early to serve as a general in the Ionian War (Xen. *Hell.* 1.4.21, 1.7.1). Spared by Lysander after Aegospotami, he was suspected of betraying the fleet. See Develin 31; Ostwald 545.

Charmides: possibly Andocides' cousin (**47-51**), or the son of Glaucon, Plato's uncle. See Wallace, *op. cit.*; Ostwald 545.

These too all fled: in most reconstructions Alcibiades had already left for Sicily, presumably accompanied by Adeimantus.

17. **Pherecles:** Teucrus had already denounced him over the Hermae affair (**35**).

gave sureties: see **2n.**

prosecuted Speusippus for illegality: in order to postpone his own trial, but on what charge is unclear. This is perhaps our earliest example of a *graphe paranomon*. See MacDowell (1978) 50-2; Ostwald 126.

before 6000 Athenians: i.e. the whole panel of jurors, reflecting the seriousness of the situation. This is the only known occasion on which all 6000 heard a case, though there are other examples of exceptionally large juries (cf. Lys. 13.35; Dem. 21.223, 24.9; Din. 1.52, 107; *Ath. Pol.* 68.1).

The man principally responsible...was I myself: preparing the ground for the argument of **19-24**. An important theme of Andocides' defence is that he was a good son both to his father and to his country, since his involvement in the mutilation would have given him the image of being an arrogant and dissolute young aristocrat. He has already indignantly denied in **5** that he might have preferred exile to standing trial; he now counters the charge that he had denounced his father, a theme resumed in **48-68**, where he equates the interests of himself, his father and his kinsmen with those of the city. He goes on to attack his accusers as enemies of fatherhood, especially Callias (**124-31**); and he emphasises the role his forefathers have played in Athens' past (**106-9, 141-3**) and how his execution will mean the end of his family (**146-9**). See further on this paternal theme B. S. Strauss, *Fathers and Sons in Athens* (London, 1993) 187-99.

18. **Call Callias and Stephanus:** to support the contention of the previous sentence. Callias was either Andocides' brother-in-law (**42**) or Leogoras' cousin (**47**). Stephanus is presumably one of Leogoras' **other** relatives. For the use of kin as supporting witnesses (cf. possibly the Diognetus of **14**) see S. C. Humphreys, 'Kinship patterns in the Athenian courts', *GRBS* 27 (1986) 57-91.

Call as well Philippus and Alexippus: to support Andocides' account of Lydus' information. That Andocides calls the nephew of **Acumenus** (see **15n.**) rather than his son Eryximachus may suggest that the latter was by now dead. See Davies 462-3.

19-33: proof

Aristotle (*Rhet.* 1.2) recognised two main types of proof (πίστις): *pisteis atechnoi*, i.e. ready-made proofs such as laws, witnesses, contracts, torture-evidence and oaths; and *pisteis entechnoi*, i.e. artificial proofs based on logic. Andocides begins in **19** with the *pistis atechnos* of witnesses, that Lydus was the one who denounced Leogoras and Andocides himself entreated Leogoras to stay in Athens. He moves on in **20-24** to *pisteis entechnoi* to show what would have happened if he had been the informer.

19. **by grasping his knees:** in supplication.

20. **because the law ran:** as MacDowell notes, the imperfect tense implies that this law had since been annulled (possibly during the revision of the laws undertaken in 410). See further MacDowell (1978) 181.

you all indeed know this: see **1n.**

one of us would have had to die: see Introd. 1.vi.I.b.

22. **He urged Speusippus to torture his slaves:** slaves could not appear in court as witnesses, but a statement made under torture was admissible as evidence (a *pistis atechnos*). Often, however, either the owner would offer his slave for torture, or a

litigant would challenge his opponent to give permission for his slaves to be tortured (*proklesis*). Such offers and challenges allegedly revealed a litigant's confidence in his case, while their refusal indicated his opponent's lack of confidence, hence they were used as *pisteis entechnoi*. Normally the owner had to give his consent to a slave's torture, and Speusippus' special power, as a member of the council of 415, to torture the slaves of owners who refused (those of 64?) again reflects the exceptional circumstances of that year. See further MacDowell (1978) 245-7; G. Thür, *Beweisführung vor den Schwurgerichtshöfen Athens: die Proklesis zur Basanon* (Vienna, 1977).

as you all know he did: see 1n. It hardly needs to be noted that not all the present jurors would have known what had been said some fifteen years previously.

23. **a more outrageous and unbelievable story:** cf. **the most abominable and outrageous story imaginable** in 19. Andocides' high dudgeon is perhaps designed to hide the fact that he cannot actually disprove the allegation.

24. This section contains a variant of the *topos* of 'hypothetical inversion' (**just as you would have been angry...so do I think it right that you...**), for which cf. Ant. 5.38 (with Edwards); Lys. 7.36 (with Carey).

25. **four in number:** see Introd. 1.vi.I.a.
     I had the names...read to you: but not those denounced by Lydus. See **Introd. 1.vi.I.a.** Similarly, **the witnesses have given their evidence** does not apply to Agariste's information.

26. **anyone who wishes to stand up:** the offer is repeated in 35, 55. A litigant was not allowed to interrupt his opponent's speech unless such an offer was made.

27. **the rewards:** presumably the larger reward was offered when the smaller one failed to induce sufficient informers to come forward.
     Cleonymus: one of Aristophanes' favourite targets in his earlier plays (see MacDowell and Sommerstein on *Wasps* 19), this demagogue is elsewhere mentioned as the proposer of the second Methone decree (ML 65.34, = Fornara 128) and of another decree concerning the collection of tribute (ML 68.5, = Fornara 133).
     Peisander: also satirised by the comic poets, Peisander was one of the *zetetai* into the Hermae affair, but changed from being **very well-disposed towards the democracy** in 415 (**36**) to being the leader of the oligarchic revolution in 411. He was even one of those negotiating for Alcibiades' recall (Thuc. 8.49), but he opposed the return of Andocides (**2.14**).
     Androcles: the demagogue who played a prominent role in securing the exile of Alcibiades (Plut. *Alc.* 19.1-2), for which he was murdered in 411 (Thuc. 8.65.2). He too was ridiculed by the comedians (see Sommerstein on Ar. *Wasps* 1187).
     on behalf of the council: i.e. the council produced Teucrus and so claimed the reward. The implication is that Androcles was a council member.

28. **those who had been initiated:** jurors were allocated to one court for a year, so all non-initiates who had been assigned to the Heliaea (**the court of the thesmothetae,** the six minor archons) were excluded. On the courts and allotments see MacDowell (1978) 35-40; Ostwald 75-6.
     decide between them: by the process *diadikasia*, employed when two or more persons disputed a claim (as in inheritance cases; see **119n.**).
     the Panathenaea: i.e. the Lesser Panathenaea of 415. Some scholars have maintained that 'Panathenaea' without qualification always refers to the Greater festival, but this would mean that the rewards were not handed out until 414, and it is hard to imagine that the investigations went on so long, despite *Ag. And.* 23 (see **Introd. 1.vi.I.f**). Further on the Panathenaea see Parke 33-50.

29. **I have shown...about them:** fulfilling the promise made in **10**.

   the two goddesses: see Introd. **1.1.a**.

   told stories: like that in *Ag. And.* 1.

30. **they have committed impiety:** by lying about Andocides' involvement in the profanation.

   men who know the truth: more flattery (cf. **22n.**).

31. **men who have sworn...votes:** see **2n**.

33. **one-fifth of the votes:** see **7n**.

   he is forbidden...death: this appears to be an additional form of disfranchisement applied in the context of *asebeia*.

   show this to me: by some form of audible approbation - Athenian juries would applaud or heckle, not sit in silent judgment.

34-70: the mutilation of the Hermae
In this section of the speech Andocides mixes elements of narrative and proof. See **Introd. 1.v**.

34. **he gave the information...images:** *pace* R. Seager, 'Andocides' Confession: A Dubious Note', *Historia* 27 (1978) 221-3, a comparison of this sentence with **15** leaves no room for doubt that Teucrus' information concerned the mutilation of the Hermae, not of other 'images'.

35. **NAMES:** once again, most of these men are obscure. For the role of **Theodorus** in the profanation cf. Plut. *Alc.* 19.1, 22.3, of **Pherecles** cf. **17** and of **Meletus** cf. **12**; for that of **Euphiletus** in the mutilation cf. **51, 56, 61-4**. **Menestratus** was perhaps the Thirty's informer (Lys. 13.55-7); for **Eryximachus** see **15n**. **Timanthes** was pardoned soon after, if he is the same Timanthes as the one in *IG* i^2 106.21-3.

   any one of these...speak: see **26n.**

36. **Peisander:** see **27n.**

   Charicles: see Davies 502-3; Develin 644. General in 414/3, Charicles was probably one of the 400, and then went into exile (Isoc. 16.42; *pace* MacDowell, his membership is not proved by Lys. 13.74; see Rhodes [1981] 435). He later became one of the Thirty (**101**; Lys. 12.55; Xen. *Hell.* 2.3.2).

   was an attempt to overthrow the democracy: which Peisander himself then did in 411. The Athenians seized on the accusation (cf. Thuc. 6.27.3, 28.2, 53.3, 60.1), one such as was commonly made against political rivals during the war (see MacDowell and Sommerstein on Ar. *Wasps* 345). See further **3.1n**.

   the signal: clearly connected with the beginning or ending of meetings of the assembly or council, but precise details are lacking.

   in fear of arrest: since the council had extraordinary powers (cf. **15, 45**).

37. **Diocleides:** his name evidently became synonymous with false accusation (**65-6**); cf. Plut. *Alc.* 20.4.

   three hundred: Andocides makes the figure his own in **51, 58**.

   I ask you...witnesses to these things: a variation on the 'you all know' *topos* (see **1n.**). For similar requests cf. **46, 69**; Dem. 47.44, 50.3. The exaggeration of the jurors' powers of recall is even greater here than in **22**, since these events took place **before the council** and possibly in secret (cf. **45**). Therefore, as MacDowell notes, **before you** is to be taken either as reflecting that both the council and the present jury represent the people (see **7n.**), or as indicating that Diocleides also reported to the assembly (**38** may be parodied in Ar. *Birds* 496). Andocides, of course, was not himself present at the council meeting.

38.   **a slave at Laurium...fee:** on Athens' silver-mines in south-east Attica, which were
      mainly worked, in appalling conditions, by hired slaves, see Hopper 170-89; AVN 95-
      6. In this period the fee was an obol a day, which produced a healthy income for large-
      scale owners such as Nicias (1000 slaves) and Hipponicus, the father of Callias (600
      slaves).
      He got up early: it was over twenty miles to Laurium.
      mistaking the time: explaining what Diocleides was doing up in the dead of night.
      there was a full moon: 'a detail which gave away his whole story, since the night in
      question had been the last of the lunar month, when there was no moon' (Plut. *Alc.*
      20.5). Plutarch's version is accepted by MacDowell App. F, but rejected by *IICT*
      4.274-6.
      When he was by the gateway...orchestra: i.e. the gateway into the complex on the
      south-eastern slope of the Acropolis, which included the sanctuary and theatre of
      Dionysus Eleuthereus. Pericles' immense Odeum (music hall) was adjacent to the
      eastern end of the theatre. The round, open-air orchestra was where the plays were
      performed.
      the bronze statue of the general: there were two such statues near the entrances to
      the theatre, of Miltiades and Themistocles. Either could be meant here.

40.   **a reward of 100 minas:** one mina = 100 drachmas. Therefore, unless there was a
      separate reward for information about the mutilation from the ones mentioned in 27 in
      connection with the profanation, either this is a round figure (the two rewards
      amounted to 11000 drachmas = 110 minas), or it only refers to Peisander's proposal.
      The latter is perhaps more likely (*pace* MacDowell), since Andocides is reporting what
      Diocleides said.
      Callias, son of Telocles: Andocides' brother-in-law (**42, 47, 50, 68**). See Davies 253.
      the temple of Hephaestus: the so-called Theseum (not, of course, that of **45**).
      Hephaestus was the god of fire, and the area around his temple is known to have
      contained smithies.

41.   **You certainly...like them:** because they might offer Diocleides a good deal of money.
      The Greek could mean 'we certainly must not turn away friends like you' (i.e. because
      Diocleides might reveal the conspiracy).
      two talents: = 120 minas.
      he should be one of us: i.e. one of the group (see **49n.**). Marchant and Maidment go
      too far in detecting an implication that he would be one of the oligarchic government
      the group was allegedly trying to set up.

42.   **made a pledge to us on the Acropolis:** cf. similarly **76**.
      in the incoming month: as MacDowell, or 'in the next month', following the dating
      scheme of *IICT* 4.276.

43.   **Mantitheus:** probably the later envoy (409/8) and officer (408/7) in Asia. See Develin
      1909; Ostwald 548.
      Peisander: see **27n.**
      the decree...of Scamandrius: forbidding the torture of Athenian citizens (cf. Lys.
      13.27, 59). The decree itself is only referred to here, and the date of the archonship is
      uncertain (perhaps 510/9). See Develin 2718 and p. 51.

44.   **at the altar:** of Zeus (cf. schol. Aesch. 2.45).
      leaving behind their sureties...bail: see **2n.** This may have been the general rule,
      though the clause only applies to these particular sureties.

45.   **in the area between the Long Walls:** the original walls connected Athens with
      Peiraeus and Phalerum, but in the mid-440s a third, middle wall was built south of the
      Peiraeus wall and parallel to it, and the Phaleric wall fell into disrepair.

the Theseum: on the north side of the Acropolis, along with **the Anaceum** (i.e. the temple of the Anaces, another name for the Dioscuri Castor and Polydeuces). Both are described by Pausanias (1.17.2-6, 18.1).

Hippodamus: the Milesian architect who designed Peiraeus.

the prytaneis in the Tholos: see 12n.

The Boeotians...frontier: Thucydides (6.61.2) tells us that the Spartans had at the same time marched up to the Isthmus of Corinth 'on some business which concerned them and the Boeotians' (we do not know what business), but Alcibiades was suspected of plotting to betray Athens to them. So the Boeotians may in fact have taken the field against the Spartans, but Andocides emphasises the alarm felt in Athens to make his own subsequent actions appear all the more patriotic (**51-68**), while glossing over his betrayal of his friends. Furthermore, Andocides places this episode earlier than Thucydides (who puts it after the conclusion of the Hermae investigation), perhaps deliberately to heighten the effect, though the historian may be in error here.

where he dined: the exceptional honour of σίτησις ἐν πρυτανείῳ, a reward for public benefaction (cf. Pl. *Ap.* 36d; *IG* i² 77).

46.   **those of you who were present...inform the others:** see 37n.

47.   **Read them out to the court:** two names appear to be missing, if the text of **68** is sound (see n.). MacDowell compares Dem. 45.24-5 for another example of a commentary on a document, though there the comments are much fuller.

Charmides: see 16n. *Pace* MacDowell, his father **Aristoteles** cannot be the general of 426/5 and member of the Thirty (= Develin 469), if Charmides was an orphan (see **48n.**). See Davies 30; D. Whitehead, 'The Tribes of the Thirty Tyrants', *JHS* 100 (1980) 208-13.

Taureas: possibly the rival of Alcibiades in **4.20-1**; Dem. 21.147. See Ostwald 120-1.

Alcmaeon: the son or son-in-law of Andocides' great-grandfather Leogoras, and in some way related to the Alcmaeonids. See Davies 382.

Euphemus: cf. **40**.

Phrynichus the former dancer: the appearance in an official list of the words **the former dancer** looks suspiciously like a gloss, but they are possibly part of Andocides' commentary (just as **the brother of Nicias** is wrongly joined with **Eucrates** in the MS. - see app. crit.). If the text is retained, it suggests there was a famous dancer who had recently retired, but the dancer of Ar. *Wasps* 1490 is identified by MacDowell *ad loc.* with the much earlier tragedian, who was well-known for his high kick. Aurenche 75-6 suggests the comic poet; the oligarch of 411 is unlikely. See further A. H. Sommerstein, 'Phrynichus the dancer', *Phoenix* 41 (1987) 189-90; Ostwald 548-9.

Eucrates: brother of Diognetus and Nicias (see **14n.**), and general in 412/11, 405/4 (see Davies 404-5; Develin 1157; Ostwald 547-8). He was executed by the Thirty (Lys. 18.4-5).

Critias: the leader of the Thirty. See Davies 326-7; Ostwald 542-3.

the forty: not including Mantitheus and Apsephion (**43-4**).

48.   **Charmides...said to me:** on the dissimilarity between the accounts of Andocides and Plutarch see **Introd. 1.vi.I.c, f**.

who had been brought up with me...from childhood: implying that he was an orphan (see **47n.**).

49.   **your friends and associates:** Euphiletus (see **35n.**), Meletus (see **12n.**) and others who met for **drinking-parties** (**61**). MacDowell (App. G) argues that the meetings of these oligarchs probably also had a political purpose, of stopping the fleet sailing to Sicily (but not necessarily of overthrowing the democracy). The mutilation was planned (**61**), and Euphiletus proposed that the conspirators bind themselves together by a pledge

(67). Further on such *hetaireiai* see Aurenche; D. Kagan, *The Peace of Nicias and the Sicilian Expedition* (Ithaca and London, 1981) 204-6.

51-3: Andocides pulls out the rhetorical stops in these sections, in order to emphasise how dire the straits were from which he saved not only his relatives, but the city itself (see **17n.**). An especially noteworthy feature is tricolon (three-unit pattern): note the genitive absolutes at the start of **51** (with successive rough breathings in the third limb); also in **51** the tricolon, with increasing numbers of people involved in each limb, **my own relatives/three hundred Athenians/the city**, and within this the tricolon concerning Andocides' relatives, **who are perishing unjustly/are executed and are having their goods confiscated/are having their names inscribed on stelae**...gods (with the length of the clauses increasing - a tricolon *crescens*); in **52** some/others/four (building to a climax in the third limb); in **53** men who are alive today/have been restored/are in possession of their property. Also to be noted are the effective dialogismos (thinking aloud) in **51**; exclamation (**51**, with the superlative δεινοτάτῃ and pi alliteration in πάντων...περιίδω); emotive vocabulary (e.g. **51** ἀπολλυμένους ἀδίκως, repeated in ἀδίκως ἀπολεῖσθαι, cf. ἀπολωλότων and ἀδίκως in **53**; **51** κακοῖς, ὑποψίαν; **53** ὄλεθρος); repetition (**52** ἐνεθυμήθην repeated from **51** and followed by the largely pleonastic ἐλογιζόμην πρὸς ἐμαυτὸν; **53** περιιδεῖν with ἀποθανόντας ἀδίκως completes the circle of thought begun in **51**, περιίδω...ἀπολλυμένους ἀδίκως); etymological figure (**52** ἔργον εἰργασμένους); argument from probability (εἰκός, **53**; the word is only elsewhere found in Andocides with this sense at **2.19**).

51. **having their names inscribed on stelae:** these pillars of stone or bronze would be a lasting record of their crime and disgrace (cf. the condemnation of Antiphon, ps.-Plut. *Life of Antiphon* 834A-B).
    what I heard from Euphiletus: cf. **56, 61-4, 67, 35n.**
52. **Panaetius:** see **13n.**
    Lysistratus: possibly the hungry joker of Aristophanes and/or the man prosecuted by Philinus (Ant. 6.36), but as with other persons mentioned in the speech there are a number of men of this name known to us who could be meant. See Sommerstein on Ar. *Wasps* 787 (more cautious than MacDowell *ad loc.*); Ostwald 546.
55. **they may refute me...permission:** see **26n.**
57. **you should consider the case...trouble:** for such appeals to jurors to put themselves in the position of the speaker (cf. **2.6**) see Dover (1974) 272.
61. **that Euphiletus...drinking-parties:** see **49n.**
    Cynosarges: a gymnasium outside the city, sacred to Heracles, for those not of pure Athenian blood.
62. **the shrine of Phorbas:** we would expect this to refer to a local hero like the charioteer of Theseus, but Harpocration s.v. says the shrine was named after the son of Poseidon killed by Erechtheus.
    our family house: according to Andocides the oldest of all houses (**147**). It will have been in or near the deme Cydathenaeum.
    the only one: and thereafter called 'the Hermes of Andocides' (Aesch. 1.125; Plut. *Nic.* 13.2, *Alc.* 21.1-2). This version (cf. Philochorus F133; Plut. *Nic. ibid.*; Nepos, *Alc.* 3.2) is necessary for Andocides' story here, but Thucydides (6.27.1) says 'nearly all' the images were mutilated (cf. Plut. *Alc.* 18.3, 21.2; *Life of And.* 834D).
63. **Meletus:** see **12n.**
64. **I handed over...house:** see **22n.** This passage is clear evidence that slaves were in fact tortured. See MacDowell (1978) 246 (but n.b. S. C. Todd in *Nomos* 34 n. 26). On the **prytaneis:** see **12n.**

65.   **the men who had induced him...story:** for a possible motive see **Introd. 1.vi.I.a.**
        Alcibiades of Phegus: probably a cousin of *the* Alcibiades (cf. Xen. *Hell.* 1.2.13). See
        Davies 17; Ostwald 549. Phegus was near Marathon.
66.   **you:** see **7n.**
        put him to death: MacDowell suggests for deceiving the people, since Diocleides was
        innocent of the mutilation, and the penalty for perjury was not normally death. He may
        be right, but these were exceptional circumstances.
        recalled the exiles: i.e. Mantitheus and Apsephion (**44**), plus any others who may
        have left on Diocleides' information.
67.   **one of the most treacherous pledges:** i.e. if all members of the group joined in, none
        could betray the others. For the implications of this see **49n.** Note the oxymoron
        (collocation of opposites), which is especially striking in the Greek
        (πίστιν...ἀπιστοτάτην).
68.   **three cousins and seven other relatives:** only eight names are given in **47**, and in
        view of the textual problems there, it is possible that two have dropped out of the list.
        The alternative is to emend the text here, either to 'one cousin' (making Phrynichus a
        cousin of Callias, son of Telocles) or rather to 'five other relatives' (taking Charmides,
        Nisaeus and Phrynichus as the three cousins).
        who still see the light of day: Leogoras was by now dead (**148**), but a number or all of
        the rest are called as witnesses in **69**.
        those of you: see **37n.**

71-91: the amnesties and revision of the laws (405-3)
In this section of the speech Andocides argues that the recent amnesties and legal revision
invalidated Cephisius' denunciation, since it was based on the decree of Isotimides passed in
415 which did not apply to him and had in any case now been repealed. It is clear, however,
that not all of these measures (if any) were in fact relevant to Andocides' situation in 400. See
MacDowell App. I; Hansen (1976) 82-90. Four measures are referred to by Andocides:
(i) The decree of Patrocleides (405), which restored rights to **the disfranchised and state
debtors** (**77**; i.e. *atimoi* and *opheilontes*). Andocides had probably left Athens after the events
of 415 under a form of disfranchisement (*atimia*) due to the decree of Isotimides, which
excluded from the agora and temples **those who had committed impiety and confessed** (**71**).
He can now deny that the decree applied to him, and it may be true that he had not actually
mutilated a Hermes, profaned the Mysteries or admitted to doing so (see **Introd. 1.vi**). At the
very least, however, Andocides was involved with the group that had carried out the
mutilation, he knew the details and had given information to this effect, and at the time he was
forced to go into exile by the decree. MacDowell 4 argues it may even have been directed
specifically against him (cf. *Ag. And.* 9, 24-5). In **73-9** Andocides discusses various types of
atimoi and the restoration of their rights by the decree of Patrocleides. But he does not state
that the decree restored rights to the impious, as we might have expected if it did; nor is there
any explicit reference in the decree to the impious, given that the preserved text is genuine
and largely intact. MacDowell's conclusion is that the impious were not in fact included
among those whose rights were restored by this decree (Andocides quotes it to create the
impression that rights in general were restored); and it does seem to refer to those who had
been (or were about to be) legally condemned, which Andocides was not. Nevertheless,
Hansen shows that the decree does not so much specify the group of *atimoi* it covered as
prescribe that the documents containing the names of *atimoi* are to be destroyed, and a general
amnesty is recorded in the first sentence of the decree. For Hansen (who regards Andocides as
an exile, not an *atimos*) this explains why the group of *atimoi* discussed in **74** do not appear in
the text of the decree, since there was no public record of the decisions concerning them to be

destroyed; but this may also explain the absence of the impious from the decree - or at least give Andocides the opportunity to claim it applied to him. In addition, Andocides *does* mention his own type of *atimia*, at the very end of his list of those who were *atimoi* according to limitations (**76, others still not to enter the agora**). There may, therefore, have been a loophole in the law which both sides were trying to exploit, and it was left to the jury to decide the matter.

(ii) The recall of exiles in 404 (**80**). If, as MacDowell contends, Andocides had not actually been condemned to exile, the recall of exiles was irrelevant, and this explains why Andocides dismisses it so briefly. For Hansen, Andocides probably had been exiled after his second failed attempt to return to Athens, which then makes the discussion of Patrocleides' decree irrelevant (since it excluded exiles). But again, if Andocides' recall from exile brought with it pardon for his previous impiety, we should have expected him to say so.

(iii) The amnesty of 403 (**81, 87**). This was also strictly irrelevant to Andocides' case, because it concerned offences committed before 403: if Andocides could not be prosecuted for impiety committed in 415, this did not make him innocent of that impiety and therefore immune from prosecution in 400 for illegally entering temples. Besides, the amnesty seems to have applied to events during the civil war (cf. *Ag. And.* 37-41). So in this matter Andocides was probably trying to take advantage of the spirit of forgiveness prevalent at the time.

(iv) The decree of Teisamenus (**83-4**) and other laws (at the beginning of **87**). What appears to be Andocides' strongest argument here (cf. **86**) is that, given the decree of Isotimides was not inscribed during the legal revision, it should have been invalidated by the decree of Teisamenus and the laws in **87**. MacDowell counters by arguing not only that Andocides' was a religious offence which for many Athenians could not be excused by man-made laws (cf. *Ag. And.* 10); but also that Isotimides' decree (*psephisma*) might be unwritten (*agraphon*, i.e. not inscribed on stone) but still valid (it was not a law, *nomos*, though it is referred to as such in *Ag. And.* 9, 29, 52). So the accumulated effect of Andocides' arguments, rounded off by an appeal to the jurors to remember their oaths, may well have deceived all but the most attentive of them. Once more, however, the precise legal position may have been unclear, giving Andocides the chance to challenge his opponents' position.

This last point may reflect a change in practice in forensic oratory of this period. The arguments in **71-91** are reminiscent of the προκατασκευή section in Antiphon's *Herodes* speech (5.8-19), in which the defendant claims he has been illegally put on trial for homicide by *endeixis*, instead of by the regular *dike phonou*. Andocides in **8** hesitates as to whether he should begin his defence with the illegality of the prosecution, but decides against doing so for the time being (n.b. in **8** the denunciation itself is illegal, but in **71** and **103** it is lodged **according to the established law**). So Andocides may, on the worst interpretation, be adducing arguments which are fallacious in order to deceive the jurors, but he is nevertheless employing a recognised tactic of the defence.

72. **If I do convince you...opponents:** because prosecution for their offences before 403 (**92-9**) will also be invalid.

73. **you deliberated about unity:** cf. **106-9, 140.** Unity was vital in the aftermath of the Aegospotami disaster (405, **when the fleet was destroyed**), with memories of the oligarchic revolution of 411 still fresh. Restoration of citizen-rights had been advocated early in 405 by Aristophanes (*Frogs* 686-705).

Patrocleides: see Develin 2268. He may be the Patrocleides of Ar. *Birds* 790. For the decree cf. **77-9**; Lys. 25.27; Xen. *Hell.* 2.2.11.

Who were the disfranchised...I will tell you: see in general on Andocides' survey of *atimoi* Hansen (1976) 82-90. It falls into two parts (**73-6, 77-9**), the first being a commentary on the second in three sections: state debtors (**73**), those subject to permanent and total *atimia* (74), those subject to permanent but partial *atimia* (75-6). In Hansen's view these sections are based not on the severity of the penalty (since the rights of the first group, those owing money to the treasury, were restored when they paid their fines), but on who gained most from the amnesty (the first group had their debts cancelled as well as recovering their rights, the second recovered all their rights, the third the rights lost according to limitations).

people owing money to the treasury: state debtors were regarded as being disfranchised until they settled their debt, and were liable to prosecution by *endeixis* if they entered prohibited places or performed functions from which they were debarred. See Hansen (1976) 90-8; MacDowell (1978) 74-5, 165.

the examinations of their conduct: the *euthyna*, on which see MacDowell (1978) 170-2; Ostwald 55-62. First the accounts of officials were examined by the *logistai*, then the rest of their conduct was investigated by the ten examiners (*euthynoi*) with their assessors (*paredroi*; cf. **78**). Those found guilty at the first stage of malefaction (*adikion*), i.e. loss of public money through incompetence rather than **theft or bribery** (see **74n.**), had to repay the simple amount involved (cf. *Ath. Pol.* 54.2 with Rhodes), and thereby became debtors to the treasury.

ejectment cases: the *dike exoules*, in which the plaintiff claimed he had the right of possession of a property which the defendant refused to give up. See MacDowell (1978) 153-4. If found guilty, the defendant had to hand over the property and pay a fine to the state equal to its value, thereby becoming a state debtor.

public cases: i.e. those *graphai* (see **9n.**) in which the penalty was a fine to be paid to the treasury.

those who bought privileges of tax-collection: at annual auctions held by the *poletai* ('sellers') in the presence of the council (cf. *Ath. Pol.* 47.2 with Rhodes). An individual (cf. **92-3**) or a group led by an ἀρχώνης (cf. **133-6**) would bid for the right to collect a certain tax (e.g. customs dues), provide sureties and then collect it. During the year **the money due** was paid to the treasury, and any surplus was profit. See MacDowell (1978) 165; Todd (1993) 143.

in the ninth prytany: early summer. *Ath. Pol.* 54.2 says 'before the ninth prytany' (cf. Dem. 24.98).

they were to pay double: cf. Dem. 58.1

74.   **These were persons...disfranchised:** the offering and accepting of bribes was evidently rife in Athens, not only among officials, and death was a possible penalty for this offence. See further D. Cohen, *Theft in Athenian Law* (Munich, 1983; but with no discussion of this passage); F. D. Harvey in *Crux* 76-117.

those who deserted their posts...shields: along with desertion of one's ship (Pollux 8.42) these may have been offences covered by a single law on military derelictions, though the sources only give partial lists (cf. Lys. 14.5 with Carey 143-4; Aesch. 3.175-6). The various terms were not clearly distinguished, and a man who deserted his post, e.g., might be charged with either *lipotaxion* or *deilia*; but the penalty was the same. See MacDowell (1978) 159-61. Throwing away one's shield is frequently derided by, among others, Aristophanes (e.g. *Wasps* 19).

giving false evidence three times: see MacDowell (1978) 245; **7n.** Briefly on such recidivism see Saunders 111.

falsely acting as summons-witnesses three times: when a summons was served to initiate a suit, this had to be done in the presence of (by the late fifth century) two witnesses. See MacDowell (1978) 238.

those who maltreated their parents: a law attributed to Solon required children to care for their parents and grandparents, and to give them a proper burial. See MacDowell (1978) 92.

75. **In the time of the tyrants:** i.e. during the revolution of 411. On the differences between total and partial *atimia* see Hansen (1976) 61-6; MacDowell (1978) 74-5.

76. **Others were not allowed...denunciation:** including prosecutors who secured less than one-fifth of the votes (see 7n.).

to the Hellespont: leading to the Black Sea and Athens' vital source of grain. There was also a Persian Hellespontine satrapy.

to Ionia: and thence the Persian empire.

not to enter the agora: this was one of the limitations in the decree of Isotimides (*Ag. And.* 9, 24), and (*pace* MacDowell 201) the one which Andocides will have claimed was relevant to his situation. The weakness of his claim (and hence his lack of emphasis on it) may lie in the fact that the decree here (**78**) refers to those whose names were set up in public, but Andocides' presumably was not.

to exchange a pledge of unity on the Acropolis: this is not in the decree as preserved.

77. **DECREE:** usually accepted as a genuine transcript (sim. **83-4, 96-8**).

since the Athenians voted immunity...state debtors: this clause might be taken to include Andocides. The putting of any proposal concerning *atimoi* and *opheilontes* required first the permission of 6000 Athenians (cf. Dem. 24.45-6).

the one passed during the Persian Wars: presumably that of 481/0 (cf. *Ath. Pol.* 22.8; Plut. *Them.* 11.1), which recalled those who had been ostracised, but in **107** Andocides talks of a recall of exiles before Marathon in 490. Nouhaud 160-1 assumes confusion.

those registered...basileus: this formula covers all public debtors. **The revenue-collectors** (the ten *praktores*) were agents of the council (see Rhodes [1972] 150-1); the ten **treasurers of the Goddess** (Athena) and ten of **the other gods** became a single board of ten in 406 (see Rhodes [1981] 391); **the basileus** was the archon in charge of religious matters and hence the rent on sacred land (see Rhodes [1981] 556-7).

anyone else...not deleted: i.e. those who had paid their debts, but whose names had not yet been erased. MacDowell translates 'not recorded', on the grounds that 'not deleted' merely repeats 'those registered', but the main verb is 'obliterate' (**79**).

the archonship of Callias: 406/5 (ending in the summer). For this Callias see Develin 1503.

78. **all who were disfranchised:** for debt.

condemned for misconduct in office: see 73n.

limitations: cf. **75-6**. The decree has moved away from state debtors to other kinds of *atimoi*.

fulfil guarantees: those who, because the defendant in a case involving *atimia* had not attended, became *atimoi* themselves. See further **2, 44**nn.

the Four Hundred...oligarchy: referring to the events of 411.

those who did not remain in Athens: in order to escape punishment, such as those who fled in 415 and the members of the Four Hundred who had gone into exile (Lys. 13.73-4; Thuc. 8.98.1).

after trial...tyrants: very similar wording to that of the Solonian law quoted by Plutarch (*Sol.* 19.3). Different kinds of homicide were tried in different courts, not all of which are mentioned here. **The Areopagus** heard cases of intentional homicide; the fifty-one **ephetae** tried other cases, including ones of lawful homicide at **the Delphinium**, but probably not cases at **the Prytaneum** (involving homicide by an unknown person, or by an animal or inanimate object), which were heard by **the**

basileis (who presided over all homicide trials) and the four phylobasileis. Additionally, those accused of unintentional homicide, or of planning (*bouleusis*) homicide or of homicide of an alien or slave were tried by the ephetae at the Palladium; and those already exiled for unintentional homicide who were accused of committing another homicide intentionally, because they could not enter Attica were allowed to make their defence from a boat offshore at Phreatto, with the ephetae sitting on the beach. The provision against **tyrants** (cf. *Ath. Pol.* 16.10 with Rhodes) had recently been reasserted in the decree of Demophantus (**96-8**).

in some kind of exile: if the text is sound, this presumably refers to the differences between exile for intentional homicide, which was perpetual, and for unintentional homicide, which might be ended by a pardon. See MacDowell (1963) 113-25; M. Gagarin, *Drakon and Early Athenian Homicide Law* (New Haven, 1981) 123-4.

79.   **to obliterate:** for this practice cf. Tod 123, ll. 31-5.

80.   **When the peace was made..(81)..returned from Peiraeus:** a summary of the events of 404/3, including the seizure of **Phyle** by the democratic party under Thrasybulus, which was followed by the capture of **Peiraeus** and fortification of **Munychia**, and the overthrow of **the Thirty**.

81.   **you decided to let bygones be bygones:** cf. *Ath. Pol.* 39. 'You' refers to the democrats.

you elected twenty men: as an interim government, while officials were appointed for 403/2 (such as the council, cf. **82**). These may be the same men as the nomothetae of **82** and **83** (see **83n.**). Indeed, the events described in **81-5** are confused and in all probability deliberately distorted, since it was in Andocides' interests to make out that Athens made a completely fresh start in 403. For recent discussions of the complex problems involved see N. Robertson, 'The Laws of Athens, 410-399 BC: The Evidence for Review and Publication', *JHS* 110 (1990) 43-75; P. J. Rhodes, 'The Athenian Code of Laws, 410-399 B.C.', *JHS* 111 (1991) 87-100; Todd (1993) 57-8 (our other major source for these events is Lysias 30, *Against Nicomachus*).

the laws of Solon and the ordinances of Draco: Solon (in 594/3) was said to have repealed all the laws of Draco (621/0) except those concerning homicide, which were later called 'the ordinances of Draco'. 'The laws of Solon' became a convenient term for the Athenian law-code as a whole, including subsequent legislation (see **95n.**).

82.   **elected nomothetae:** 'lawgivers'. Their task, as is shown by the decree (**83**), was to make proposals for additional laws, rather than to revise the whole code of law. See Robertson, *art. cit.* 62-3.

you voted to examine all the laws: commissioners (*anagrapheis*) had in fact already begun the complicated task of republishing the laws in 410/09, but their work was halted by the Thirty (Lys. 30.2-3; ML 86, = Fornara 15; CW 65C). They resumed in 403, and the revised code was finally published in 400/399.

in the stoa: see **84n.**

83.   **Teisamenus:** the son of Mechanion and one of the *anagrapheis* (Lys. 30.28).

in the traditional manner: i.e. democratically, though in other contexts the phrase could be taken by oligarchs to mean the opposite.

his weights and measures: on these see Rhodes (1981) 164-8.

additions: i.e. laws additional to those already assembled (the laws of Solon and Draco), and needed to make the amnesty of 403/2 work (**85, 87**).

are to be inscribed on boards: a regular form of temporary publication.

the nomothetae elected by the council: and perhaps from the council. The text is doubtful here: Robertson, *art. cit.* 60 n. 60 suggests the addition of 'twenty' (reading οἱ εἴκοσι for οἵδε), equating these with the twenty of **81** (who Andocides says were elected by the assembly) and with the nomothetae of **82**.

in front of the tribal heroes: the statues of the ten eponymous heroes of the Athenian tribes. Their bases were used as state notice boards.

the magistrates: probably the prytaneis (as Rhodes, *art. cit.* 98) rather than the archons (MacDowell).

84.   **first:** before they became law. The assembly plays no part in their ratification.

  the five hundred nomothetae: a different group of lawgivers from those of **83**. See R. Sealey, *The Athenian Republic* (Pennsylvania, 1987) 35-7.

  the council of the Areopagus...laws: the meaning of this is unclear (despite Robertson, *art. cit.* 61-2). The Areopagus had lost its role as guardian of the laws through the reforms of Ephialtes (462/1), but recovered some prestige under the Thirty. The restored democracy, however, is unlikely to have allowed the Areopagus to perform such an important function for very long. See Ostwald 517-9.

  Those laws...inspect: this sentence has regularly been taken to indicate permanent publication of the revised laws on a wall (consisting of a connected series of stelae) in the Stoa of the Basileus. Robertson, *art. cit.* 46-52 argues forcefully, however, that the present participle κυρουμένους indicates further temporary publication of the new laws for inspection by the public; and **where they were previously inscribed** refers to the same location as the earlier publication on boards, which he thinks was the courtyard of the Prytaneum. While accepting the main argument, Rhodes, *art. cit.* 90-1, 99 contends that the more natural place for the new laws was nevertheless the Stoa of the Basileus, the location of the laws of Draco and Solon (and we do not know where the statues of the tribal heroes were situated). This is where Andocides seems to place them in **82** and **85**, and he also implies their permanent publication, as the basis of his argument in **86**.

85.   **The laws...in the stoa:** again, it was the additional laws with which the decree was in fact concerned, and Andocides goes on to list a number of procedural laws which were inscribed in 403/2.

  Magistrates...unwritten law: referring not to firmly established divine laws or social customs, but to those laws which had not been or were no longer inscribed.

86.   **When...decree:** this apparently watertight argument is holed by MacDowell 202-3: decrees were not always inscribed on stone (see **71-91**n.).

  suffering misfortunes: a euphemism for 'had committed crimes'. See further **2.7**n.

  to make false accusations: in the traditional view *sykophantai* were professional accusers, who made money either from bringing cases in which the successful prosecutor received a reward (as in *phasis*; see **88**n.), or from blackmailing their victim to pay them to drop the case. It has recently been argued, however, that the term συκοφάντης was used more broadly to denote a 'vexatious litigant' (i.e. an excessively enthusiastic amateur). See R. G. Osborne in *Nomos* 83-102 (*contra* F. D. Harvey in *Nomos* 103-121); Todd (1993) 92-4. Andocides later plays on their notorious reputation by accusing his prosecutors Cephisius and Epichares of being sycophants (**93, 99**).

87.   **No decree...is to override a law:** the first statement of the principle that laws (*nomoi*), which are of general application and permanent, are to be of greater validity than decrees (*psephismata*) of the council and assembly, which are of particular application and temporary.

  It is not to be permitted...six thousand: this law reappears in Demosthenes (23.86, 24.59, 46.12), but Rhodes argues that it soon became a dead letter (*art. cit.* 97-8; *contra* Hansen [1991] 173). On the quorum of six thousand see Rhodes (1981) 491.

  All judgments...Eucleides: cf. Dem. 24.56, where the second half of the law is omitted, but another law added concerning decisions made in both private and public cases under the Thirty (which was presumably omitted by Andocides as not being relevant to his case). In **88** Andocides interprets the first part of the law as referring to private cases (and indeed public arbitrators were not instituted until 399; see MacDowell [1978] 203-11); then **but the laws...Eucleides** is taken to refer to public offences (such as Andocides'), which can only be prosecuted if committed in or after 403/2. But Andocides, of course, had good reason to make this distinction, which may not have been intended by the lawgivers.

88. **indictments:** the procedure *phasis*, which was mainly used in cases involving trading offences and orphans, was particularly attractive to sycophants since, if successful, half the fine went to the prosecutor. See Todd (1993) 119.

90. **you all swore:** as they had all sworn in 410 (**97**). For the feasibility of oath taking on this scale see Rhodes (1981) 135.

except the Thirty and the Eleven: cf. Xen. *Hell.* 2.4.38; *Ath. Pol.* 39.6 (with Rhodes). Andocides (still in exile at the time) and Xenophon omit the Ten (the successors of the Thirty in 403), and Andocides also omits the Peiraeus Ten (appointed by the Thirty in 404). The Eleven, the annual officials who controlled Athens' police and prison, were included because they had carried out the orders of the Thirty (Xen. *Hell.* 2.3.54; *Ath. Pol.* 35.1).

and not even...he conducted: at a *euthyna* (see **73**n.).

91. **the oath of the council:** see Rhodes (1972) 194-9, (1981) 263-4.

those who fled: perhaps referring to those in **78**, or possibly an addition to account for those who did not return even after the amnesty was extended to the oligarchs at Eleusis in 401/0 (as MacDowell, followed by Ostwald 500 n. 8).

your oath...judgment: on the heliastic oath see **2**n.

92-100: attack on Andocides' accusers

Vilifying the character of an opponent (διαβολή) was naturally a common element in oratory, especially in prosecution speeches (e.g. Lys. 14.23-40 with Carey). Andocides contends that if it were not for the amnesty, his accusers would themselves be facing trial.

For the possibility that the prosecution of Andocides was brought by members of his old *hetaireia* in revenge for his betrayal of them see Missiou 50.

92. **Cephisius here...fled:** the charge is tacitly admitted in *Ag. And.* 42, where the point is made that this is irrelevant to the present case. On the **privilege** see **73**n.

93. **the law was this:** i.e. before 403. It was presumably superseded by the milder one at *Ath. Pol.* 48.1

from you: since the jury represented the whole Athenian *demos*, including the farmers.

a false accuser: see **86**n. The effect of the accusation is heightened by the use of συκοφάντης in the contrast instead of ἐπίτιμος ('a man with the franchise').

94. **Meletus here arrested Leon...Thirty:** recent opinion identifies Andocides' prosecutor as the accuser of Socrates. See Ostwald 495 with n. 141; Bauman 108-9 with n. 23; *pace* MacDowell App. M. Meletus was one of the five men ordered by the Thirty to arrest Leon of Salamis. He obeyed; another, Socrates, refused (Pl. *Ap.* 32c-d). Leon may have been the general of 412/1 (see Develin 1792) and, more speculatively, the father of the speaker of Lysias 10, *Against Theomnestus* (cf. 4, 27).

the person planning a deed...carrying it out: on the planning (*bouleusis*) of homicide see MacDowell (1963) chap. VI.

Meletus cannot be prosecuted...arrest: only those who had committed homicide with their own hands did not come under the amnesty (*Ath. Pol.* 39.5).

95. **Epichares:** see Develin 1012. (He was not the member of the Ten at Lys. 12.55; see P. Krentz, *The Thirty at Athens* [Ithaca, 1982] 92.)

a man...making: *pace* MacDowell, the way in which Epichares recalled his own misdeeds will have been by boasting about what he did under the Thirty (or so Andocides alleged, without giving any examples). That is why Andocides goes on to quote the law of Demophantus.

according to Solon's law: an excellent example of how even recent laws were classed among 'the laws of Solon'. See **81n.**

96. **the law:** datable by comparison with ML 84 (= Fornara 154) to the first prytany of 410/09, and indicating that the democracy was restored in summer 410 after the rule of the Five Thousand. This was one of a number of laws against attempts to overthrow the democracy. See Rhodes (1981) 220-2.

Cleigenes: perhaps the Cleigenes of Ar. *Frogs* 709.

the council...appointed by lot: the use of the lot characterises this council as a democratic one (cf. Thuc. 8.66.1, 69.4; *Ath. Pol.* 32.1).

the first secretary: the secretary changed in each prytany.

97. **All Athenians:** see **90n.**

tyrant: see **78n.**

98. **Harmodius and Aristogeiton:** Athenian heroes for killing Hipparchus, brother of the tyrant Hippias, in 514.

in the camp: by oligarchs in the Athenian navy at Samos in 412/1 (Thuc. 8.48).

before the Dionysia: this was not until Elaphebolion (March), and therefore about nine months from the passing of the law.

99. **you false accuser:** again the charge of sycophancy (see **86n.**). The sycophants' activities were temporarily halted by the Thirty (cf. Xen. *Hell.* 2.3.12).

practised rogue: lit. 'damned fox', a phrase used of Odysseus at Soph. *Aj.* 103. Hickie noted that there may be a play on κίναιδος ('catamite'), given the accusation made in **100**.

it has become invalid: *pace* MacDowell, the law may have lapsed in 403. See Rhodes (1981) 221.

100. **And you mention association to me...alone:** Andocides cleverly turns the tables on Epichares, who accused him of conspiracy (ἑταιρεία; see **49n.**), by using the verbal form of the word (ἡταίρησας) in its sense of homosexual 'association'. Such allegations were commonplace in oratory (e.g. Lys. 14.41; Aesch. 1.126) and, of course, comedy (e.g. Ar. *Wasps* 686-8).

according to your laws...himself: male prostitution, though not illegal, entailed the loss of citizen-rights (*atimia*). Prostitutes who attempted to exercise such rights (as Epichares was doing in prosecuting Andocides) were liable to prosecution and the death penalty. See MacDowell (1978) 126.

101-109: the importance of Andocides' acquittal for political unity
101-2 might be taken with the previous section, but they mark the transition to Andocides' next topic, the political significance of his trial, by bringing in a reference to trials under the divisive rule of the Thirty.

In **106-9** Andocides adduces historical parallels to emphasise the value of political unity: such use of example (*paradeigma*) was a commonplace form of argumentation (cf. Arist. *Rhet.* 2.20). On Andocides' reputation as an historian see **3.3-12n.**

101. **had I not offered him money:** speakers rarely admit in court to giving bribes (as opposed to paying hush-money to a sycophant), but cf. Lys. 12.8-10, 14-5 (also in the context of the Thirty). See F. D. Harvey in *Crux* 78. Ours is, of course, a hypothetical case.

Who but Charicles...before the trial: as the presiding magistrate at the preliminary hearing (*anakrisis*). On Charicles see **36n.**

Decelea: the Spartan base in north Attica during the Peloponnesian War, where the leading oligarchs fled after the overthrow of the Four Hundred in 411 (Thuc. 8.98.1).

You did not fight at sea: in the battles culminating at Aegospotami. Charicles may have in mind Athenian exiles fighting on the Spartan side, but Diodorus' account of Aegospotami mentions deserters (13.106.2), while Xenophon says the general Adeimantus, the only Athenian captive to be spared, was accused of having betrayed the fleet (*Hell.* 2.1.32; see **16n.**).

help to demolish its walls...to the city: cf. **80.**

103. **they made the denunciation...about others:** repeating the argument of **71.**

So if you vote...many other citizens: i.e. this is a test case. A similar type of argument is used at Lys. 1.36.

swore oaths: cf. **90-1.**

removed stelae: i.e. those inscribed with laws.

105. **the trial is concerned...as a whole:** impressing on the jurors both the gravity of the situation and the collective advantage which their correct decision will bring.

106. **when the tyrants were ruling the city...exile:** referring to the Peisistratid tyranny of the sixth century. It was perhaps natural, or at least necessary in the context of his trial soon after the fall of the Thirty, for Andocides to picture post-Solonian Athens as a democracy, and to assume that the tyranny meant the exile of the democrats; but in reality the opponents of the tyrants were the aristocrats. There is also an element of anti-Peisistratid propaganda here, as in **2.26** (see n. there).

near the temple at Pallenium: Andocides' version of events here will stem from his family's oral tradition, and is an example of the 'partial preservation and partial transposition of a genuine memory'. See Thomas 139-43. He clearly is thinking of the expulsion of Hippias in 511/0, but he puts the battle at Pallenium, almost certainly a confusion with the battle of Pallene in 546/5 in which Peisistratus was victorious (Hdt. 1.62.3; *Ath. Pol.* 15.3, 17.4). His ancestors will have been involved in both episodes, but in the family tradition the memory of the earlier battle has been telescoped and transposed to a later period. There is therefore no need to posit an otherwise unknown battle (as MacDowell App. O, rejected by Davies 27-8).

Pallene, with its temple of Athena, lay between Mts Hymettus and Pentelicon on the route between Athens and Marathon.

under the generalship of Leogoras...and Charias: Andocides exaggerates the role of his ancestors, since Hippias was expelled by the Spartan king Cleomenes, and Leogoras and Charias were probably rebel leaders rather than official *strategoi*. On Leogoras see **General Introd. I**; and on the theme of family service see **17n.**

107. **when the King...invaded Greece:** in 490, the expedition being led by Datis and Artaphernes.

they decided to recall exiles: otherwise unattested, but this does not necessarily indicate confusion with the amnesty of 481/0, as is often thought. See **77n.**

108. **receiving the city back devastated...city:** Andocides has moved on to the second Persian invasion, during which Athens was sacked by Xerxes (480). This telescoping of events, whereby Andocides emphasises the hoplite victory at Marathon at the expense of the sailors' victory at Salamis, reflects Andocides' oligarchic background (see Missiou 51-2). But it also, with the juxtaposition of Athens' greatest hour and lowest ebb, adds poignancy to Andocides' plea for unity, and the effect is heightened by the

repetition of thought in **it was for this very reason** (i.e. not recalling grievances)...**through this living together in unity**. Note too the emotive vocabulary (especially ἀνάστατοι); the tricolon with παραλαβόντες (**the city...its temples...its walls and houses**); the repeated prefix κατα- ('down'), changing in sense from bad (**burnt down...fallen down**) to good (**handed down**); and the climax in τοιαύτην καὶ τοσαύτην.

109. **later:** i.e. in 405-3, after Aegospotami.

110-16: the olive-branch

Andocides now deals with the secondary charge against him, that a short time before the trial he had placed an olive-branch on the altar of the Eleusinium. This was an act of supplication, and was taken to indicate that Andocides had a guilty conscience and was begging for pardon. Moreover, it was a religious offence to lay a branch at the time of the Mysteries (**110**, cf. **115-6**). Further on supplication see J. P. A. Gould, 'Hiketeia', *JHS* 93 (1973) 74-103.

110. **the Eleusinium:** the temple of Demeter and Core, south-east of the agora.
an ancestral law: such laws (cf. *Ag. And.* 10) will not have been included in the collection made recently by the *anagrapheis*. See Rhodes, *JHS* 111 (1991) 92.

111. **When we returned from Eleusis:** the last day of the Mysteries was Boedromion 23. See Mylonas 280.
the denunciation had been lodged: by Cephisius during the celebration of the Mysteries (cf. **121**), on the grounds that the decree of Isotimides debarred Andocides from attendance. The *endeixis* was made to **the basileus**, the archon responsible for trials involving religious offences (cf. *Ag. And.* 4; *contra* Hansen [1976] 28-9), and the case was firstly referred to **the council** (*pace* MacDowell, there is nothing surprising about this; see Rhodes [1972] 159-61).
Solon's law: another law that was probably post-Solonian (see **81**n.).

112. **Callias:** see Introd. 1.ii.
wearing his official dress: as dadouchos ('torch-bearer').
we were standing close by...us: as Rhodes (1972) 160 (the sentence is usually translated as 'Cephisius could see me'). Andocides and Cephisius were standing outside the Eleusinium, since Eucles **went off inside again after making the enquiry**.
Eucles: appointed herald of the council and people for his actions in helping to restore the democracy (*IG* ii^2 145, on which see Develin App. VI.xxvii).

113. **They said...114...even if I had not laid the olive-branch:** for the idea of the gods directly manipulating human thoughts see Dover (1974) 136-7. The sophistic nature of Andocides' argument here makes it unlikely that he was responding to the evidence of his witness (suggested as possible by S. C. Todd in *Nomos* 23 n. 6).
in ignorance of the law: on ignorance as an excuse in Athenian law see briefly Saunders 109.

115. **Cephalus:** one of Andocides' supporters (*synegoroi*; cf. **150**). A potter (for which he is naturally lampooned in comedy), Cephalus became a leading democratic politician and accomplished speaker (e.g. Dem. 18.219; Din. 1.38-9, 76). See Develin 1581.

116. **when it is not permitted...interpretations:** the interpreters of the ancestral laws connected with the Mysteries were the Eumolpidae. See Mylonas 235; Bauman 110-11.
you talk of an ancestral law...Eleusinium: this particular *patrios nomos* had presumably been superseded during the legal revision by state law. See Ostwald 161-9; but n.b. Bauman 109-10.
when the stele by which you are standing: suggesting that, despite the legal revision, reference to written records was rather haphazard. See Thomas 67-8.

a fine of a thousand drachmas: this would have meant a trial in a regular court, since the council was not competent to impose a fine of this magnitude (cf. *Ath. Pol.* 45.1 with Rhodes).

It was clear...himself: but Andocides does not go on to say (or produce witnesses) that Callias was fined.

117-31: attack on Callias

117. **Epilycus:** see 3.29n.

He died in Sicily: possibly on the Sicilian expedition. Makkink and MacDowell take this to mean on a recent visit in 401 or 400, because Epilycus' will remained unsettled for some thirteen years if he died in 415-13. But the girls may have been babies at the time of their father's death; and if their mother was in fact the second wife of Callias (as Davies 264-5) more time is needed between Epilycus' death and her re-marriage, and Andocides' trial. See Davies 297-8.

without male children...daughters: in this situation (i.e. when a man died with no male descendants in his own or his brother's line, but only female children, and leaving no will) the nearest male relatives of the deceased were entitled to claim the heiresses (*epikleroi*), who had an equal share of the estate (which passed to their sons when they came of age). When the heiress belonged to the lowest property-class (as may be the case here, given Epilycus' debts as stated in **118**), her nearest relative would be compelled either to marry her or to provide a dowry. See MacDowell (1978) 95-8.

On a lighter note, the situation of the heiress was used by comic dramatists as the basis of plots; cf. Menander, *Aspis*; Terence, *Phormio*.

Leagrus: son of Glaucon and Callias' brother-in-law. His claim to one of the daughters implies that he was, like Andocides, the son of a sister of Epilycus.

118. **visible property:** i.e. land and buildings, furniture, slaves and animals. Money was variously regarded as visible and invisible. See Harrison 1.230-1.

119. **because of our virtue:** MacDowell questions the extent to which Andocides' offer was really virtuous: he and Leagrus may have been obliged to marry the heiresses or provide dowries, and Callias was willing to go to great lengths to claim one of them for his son (**120-3**). On the other hand, since Andocides and Leagrus were their closest relatives and so had first claim on them, Callias' seemingly vindictive behaviour may imply that there was more to his quarrel with Andocides than we are told. Either way, Andocides takes the opportunity to make great capital out of his offer.

enter a claim: by the procedure *epidikasia*. A dead man's estate passed automatically to his sons or (if they were dead) to his subsequent descendants in the male line, but in other circumstances (as here) a claim had to be made to the archon. It was read out at the next regular meeting of the assembly (*Ath. Pol.* 43.4), where it could be challenged. Disputed claims were heard by a jury in the process *diadikasia* (see **28n.**). See MacDowell (1978) 102-8.

120. **a fee:** Andocides says he paid a *parastasis*, which in public arbitration was one drachma; but in inheritance cases claimants regularly deposited a sum equal to one-tenth of the value of the property (*parakatabole*). See MacDowell (1978) 239-40.

and firstly obtained leave...saying: the MS. simply reads προτέρῳ μὲν Λεάγρῳ ὅτι, to which MacDowell objects on the grounds that (i) the ὅτι-clause has no connection with the rest of the sentence; (ii) ἔλαχον Λεάγρῳ cannot mean 'I obtained leave to make a claim on behalf of Leagrus', since he had already made one on his own behalf (**120**); (iii) ἔλαχον Λεάγρῳ cannot mean 'I obtained leave to make a claim against Leagrus', since Andocides immediately afterwards says his intention was not to make a claim against Leagrus, but against Callias if Leagrus waived his claim. MacDowell therefore emends the text to read πρότερον μὲν <λέγων> Λεάγρῳ ὅτι ('I obtained leave to bring a case, firstly saying to Leagrus'). While agreeing with (i) and (ii), I take Andocides to mean that, on hearing of Callias' attempt to bribe Leagrus, he initiated a precautionary counter-claim against Leagrus, in case Leagrus agreed to drop his claim (which he had already made) in favour of Callias. Andocides in turn would drop his claim if Leagrus rejected Callias' offer, but he was not sure Leagrus would do so when he deposited the fee. So I have followed MacDowell in adding λέγων ('saying'), but assume that it fell out of the text after rather than before Λεάγρῳ; and I see no need to emend προτέρῳ.

121. **Callias obtained leave...son:** having firstly claimed the heiress for himself (or so Andocides alleges, **120**), Callias now claims her for his son by Chrysilla. This raises two questions:

(i) What legal right had Callias' son by Chrysilla to the heiress? He was her uncle, on her mother's side (see App. B), but a legitimate claim could only be made by a blood-relation of her father. There are two ways in which the son could have been so related to her: (a) if the son's mother Chrysilla was the daughter of Glaucon, the son was a great-nephew of Epilycus (but Chrysilla probably was not Glaucon's daughter; see **127n.**); (b) Makkink suggested that Callias was related to Epilycus' father Teisandrus, since the names Epilycus and Teisandrus are connected with the Philaid family (see Davies 296-7), and the Philaid Miltiades (the general at Marathon) was Callias' great-grandfather (Callias' grandfather of the same name married Miltiades' daughter Elpinice; see **Introd. 1.ii**).

(ii) Why did Callias not proceed with his own claim to the heiress, or seek to secure her for his other son Hipponicus (who certainly was a great-nephew of Epilycus, through his mother)? The obvious answer to this is that Callias and Hipponicus did not want to divorce their wives, whereas the other son was both available and entitled to claim her.

MacDowell notes that, viewed in this way, Callias' personal motives were not as lurid as Andocides makes them out to be (**121-3, 128**). Nevertheless, Callias may well have been using the heiress as a pawn in his feud with Andocides.

In order to prevent me from obtaining her: MacDowell emends the text (reading ἵνα <δὲ> μὴ ἐπιδικάσωμαι ἐγώ, ταῖς [δ'] εἰκάσι) to take this clause with what follows, on the grounds that (i) Callias could not prevent Andocides obtaining the heiress by claiming her for his son, since Andocides was more closely related to Epilycus; (ii) it would be Andocides' condemnation or exile that prevented him from pursuing his claim. But even if Callias knew full well that his claim could not succeed, by submitting it he would buy himself time to effect his (alleged) further plans; and if he bought off Leagrus but made no claim himself, Andocides might win the heiress by default before his trial.

122. **Lysistratus:** *pace* MacDowell, this is unlikely to be the Lysistratus of **52, 67**, whom Andocides had denounced.

123. **I think...in his turn:** 'life' in the sense of losing certain rights if he were to be condemned for sycophancy.

124. **Ischomachus:** probably to be identified with the wealthy Ischomachus of Lys. 19.46 and the hero of Xenophon's *Oeconomicus*. See Davies 265-8.

her mother: Chrysilla (**127**). She is probably the young wife of Ischomachus in Xen. *Oec.* 7.4ff. If so, those familiar with the innocent and inexperienced girl in Xenophon will be all the more shocked by the behaviour of the scarlet woman in Andocides. See F. D. Harvey, 'The wicked wife of Ischomachus', *Echos du Monde Classique* 28

(1984) 68-70; P. A. Cartledge, 'Xenophon's Women: A Touch of the Other', *Tria Lustra* (Liverpool Classical Papers 3, Liverpool, 1993) 9-10.

the Mother and Daughter: Demeter and Core.

126. **at the Apaturia:** the three-day festival of the phratries in Pyanepsion (October). The last day saw the registration as phratry members of newly-born children and newly-wed wives. See Parke 88-92.

they said, "Of Callias...your child": a particularly striking and effective use of dialogue.

he swore...family: usually the father swore that the child *was* his by a legally married wife (Is. 8.19).

127. **introduced...to the Ceryces:** i.e. he registered him with his clan (*genos*) rather than the phratry.

by now a grown lad: cf. similar implied disapproval of late registration at Lys. 30.2.

Callicles: following MacDowell's emendation of the MS. Callides.

Grasping the altar: repeated from **126** to emphasise that Callias is now swearing the opposite.

born of Chrysilla: the different wording from **126** implies that Chrysilla was not Glaucon's daughter.

129. **his name:** Makkink suggested that it was in fact Protarchus, who is called 'the son of Callias' at Pl. *Phlb.* 19b (and Callias had only two sons; cf. Pl. *Ap.* 20a). But there were many Athenians named Callias. This son was also called 'Callias' bastard' (Metagenes F13, I 708 K).

brother of another: i.e. the half-brother of the daughter of Ischomachus and Chrysilla.

uncle of the third: i.e. of Epilycus' daughter.

Oedipus or Aegisthus: such tendentious use of mythical names is very rare in oratory (cf. **4.22**; Ant. 1.17; implicit in Dem. 21.149). The parallel is, of course, more effective than precise: Oedipus married his mother Jocasta, Aegisthus was the son of Thyestes and his own daughter Pelopeia.

130. **the tiniest young children and weak women:** the diminutives in the Greek are contemptuous (cf. Dem. 19.305, 25.57).

was upsetting his balance: in the Greek there is a pun on τράπεζα, which means both 'table' (upset by the evil spirit) and 'bank' (upset by Callias' spending). The family fortune had allegedly diminished from 200 talents in the time of Callias' grandfather to less than 2 talents in his own day (Lys. 19.48).

132-6: attack on Agyrrhius

132. **even though I initiated:** it was the Eumolpidae and the Ceryces who performed initiation ceremonies into the Mysteries. But despite *Life of And.* 834C, it is most unlikely that Andocides was himself a member of the Ceryces, and he may mean that he introduced his friends for initiation by a priest.

A...from Delphi: following Bekker's emendation. The MS. reads ἀδελφόν, but Andocides tells us in **148** that he has no brothers.

these men...public services: because these *leitourgiai*, which Athens required of its richer citizens and metics, were very expensive. But in trying to cause him financial problems by proposing him for duties connected with religious festivals, Andocides' enemies were tacitly admitting that they did not consider him guilty of impiety.

gymnasiarch: to supervise the preparation of a team competing in the torch-race at one of several festivals. See Rhodes (1981) 638-9. Andocides was probably gymnasiarch in 402 or 401.

the festival of Hephaestus: in Pyanepsion. Torch-races were particularly appropriate for the celebrations in honour of Hephaestus and Prometheus, deities closely associated with fire, but were also run at the festival of Pan. See Parke 171-2.

architheorus: the official in charge of the Athenian deputation at one of the Panhellenic festivals. After Andocides' return in 403, the first Olympics were held in summer 400; the biennial Isthmians were held in 402 and 400. If Andocides was gymnasiarch in 402 or 401, he may have been architheorus at both games in 400 (but ἔπειτα, **then,** may have no temporal significance, and the Isthmians of 402 may be meant).

as treasurer: probably in 401/0. See MacDowell App. J; Davies 31. On the treasurers see 77n. MacDowell emends the text to read 'I was treasurer' (εἶτα δὲ ταμίας <ἦν>) in a new clause independent of **kept proposing me for public services,** on the grounds that (i) treasurers were chosen by lot; (ii) their office was not a *leitourgia*. But his opponents may still have put Andocides' name forward, and he may be using the verb λητουργεῖν loosely and with zeugma in a general sense of 'perform public duties' (LSJ, s.v. II).

133. **Agyrrhius:** see Davies 278-9; Develin 44. A leading democrat (cf. Dem. 24.134-5), Agyrrhius was most famous for creating or modifying the theoric fund (*contra* Rhodes [1981] 492), and for introducing pay for attendance at the assembly (*Ath. Pol.* 41.3; see Hansen [1991] 150). Andocides treats Agyrrhius, **our gentleman friend,** with bitter irony, a clue that, despite the support of the democrats Anytus and Cephalus (**150**), Andocides did not hold democratic beliefs after his return to Athens. See Missiou 50-1.

chief contractor: see 73n.

the two per cent tax: on imports and exports.

two years ago: in 402. See MacDowell App. J.

under the poplar tree: Andocides evidently expected the jurors to know this meeting-point, the location of which is unknown to us.

I think they met there...price: and thereby maximise their profits.

134. **I went myself...city:** see 73n.

135. **before the Athenian people:** i.e. into court. For this use of πλῆθος cf. Ant. 5.8 (with Edwards); in **136, 150** (cf. Ant. 6.9) it refers to the people as a whole. Compare also the use of ὑμεῖς (see 7n.).

137-9: the argument concerning Andocides' sea-voyages (*Ag. And.* 19)

For the commonplace, and by now well-worn presumptive argument of innocence from the fact that the gods exact punishment from sinners during sea-voyages cf. Ant. 5.81-4 (with Edwards); and for the gods as bringers of punishment cf. also Dem. 24.121; Lyc. 1.91.

139. **when he is not:** referring back to **92-3.** Cephisius is protected by the amnesty, as Andocides claims to be, and if the amnesty were invalid for Cephisius, it would be invalid for Andocides too. But how many of the jurors would have worked out the logical flaw in this remark?

140-50: epilogue

The aims of the ἐπίλογος, or concluding remarks, were fourfold according to Aristotle (*Rhet.* 3.19): (i) to inspire in the listeners a favourable opinion of yourself and unfavourable opinion of your opponent; (ii) to amplify or depreciate the importance of the subject or the heinousness of the crime; (iii) to arouse in the listeners emotions such as pity, indignation, anger, hatred or jealousy; (iv) to recall the facts of the case to the minds of the listeners. Some of these topics have already been treated at length or are inappropriate here, and Andocides concentrates on (i) and (iii). He interweaves the two major themes of utility, i.e. what Athens will gain from his acquittal (**140, 144-5, 149-50**), and due appreciation for the services to Athens of his family (**141-3, 146-8**), and makes an appeal for pity in **148-9**.

140. do not be willing...reputation: Andocides amplifies the importance of his case by the suggestion that an incorrect verdict will have an adverse effect on Athens' reputation throughout Greece (cf. Lys. 14.13 with Carey).

by chance rather than by design: for this antithesis cf. Ant. 5.92 (with Edwards).

141. my ancestors: see General Introd. i; 17n.

so that it may be possible...to imitate them: a desire to emulate the noble deeds of one's ancestors was regarded as healthy (see Carey on Lys. 14.25), and Andocides is · trying to create a favourable impression of himself. His task would, of course, have been made easier if he had been able to point to some military exploits of his own.

142. when...the fleet was destroyed: see 73n.

decided to spare the city: see 3.21n.

because of the valiant exploits...Greece: at Marathon.

144. through the misfortunes of the city: in the war, unless this is an oblique reference to the events of 415 and a subsequent confiscation of Andocides' property.

145. to suffer for one's mistakes: an admission unique in this speech (but cf. **2.7**) that Andocides had done anything wrong.

After meeting with many people...more: during his exile. See General Introd. ii. MacDowell (after Reiske) notes that the sudden change in the case of the participles from accusative to nominative probably indicates a short lacuna in the text.

146. If you cause me to perish...destroyed: Andocides now appeals to the social values of the jurors on the basis of his family pedigree, the potency of the appeal being enhanced by the use of the tragic word πρόρριζον. See S. C. Todd, 'Lady Chatterley's Lover and the Attic Orators', *JHS* 110 (1990) 146-73 (esp. 164); **17n**. An important element of these values was religious: it was the duty of the living members of the family to maintain the graves of its dead members, and the family's extinction would affect the dead of previous generations (cf. Is. 2.46; Dem. 43.83-4). This belief in family solidarity lies behind Andocides' entreaty to the jurors to show gratitude for the deeds of his ancestors by acquitting him (**147-9**; cf. Lys. 3.47 with Carey).

Cleophon the lyre-maker: the leading radical democrat after the fall of the Four Hundred. A strong opponent of peace with Sparta, it was only after his execution in 404 that Theramenes was able to conclude the negotiations. See Develin 1672. Andocides plays on Cleophon's regular sobriquet (on this and his alleged low origins see Rhodes [1981] 354-5; Ostwald 214-5), but in speaking to a jury which will have included a number of the poor, he is careful to add that his house was **always very open to anyone in need** (**147**). See M. M. Markle in *Crux* 286; Missiou 52 on the anti-democratic implications of the remark.

147. No wrong...need: MacDowell notes the chiastic arrangement of ideas: we have never harmed you, you have never harmed us; you have always been good to us (because the family has survived until now without troubles and so **is the oldest of all**), we have always been good to you.

any favour: the idea that good services to the city should be returned by the people is another indication of Andocides' aristocratic stance. See Missiou 52.

148. whom can I bring...children: apart from his supporting speakers, an accused might bring his children into court to arouse the jurors' sympathy (cf. Lys. 20.34-5; Pl. *Ap.* 34c-d). This custom, which is parodied at Ar. *Wasps* 568-74, 975-84, was still observed in the time of Demosthenes and later (cf. Dem. 21.99 with MacDowell, 186-8; Hyp. 2.9, 4.41). Andocides' lack of support is brought out by the proffering and rejecting of successive suggestions (hypophora, with repeated ἀλλά). See Denniston 10-11. That he can still look to having children is consistent with his being born around 440. See **General Introd. i.**

149. You, then...children: possibly an allusion to Andromache's statement to Hector at Homer, *Iliad* 6.429-30.

to enfranchise Thessalians and Andrians...manpower: war casualties, especially after the Sicilian disaster, and the disfranchisement of oligarchic sympathisers led to the shortage. Various measures were proposed to remedy the situation, including limiting the application of Pericles' citizenship law of 451/0 (which restricted citizenship to those whose parents were both of citizen-status) to those born after 403/2 (schol. Aesch. 1.39); the decree of Patrocleides **(77-9)**; and rewards for distinguished service **(2.23**; Diod. 13.97.1; ML 94, = Fornara 166; Tod 100). See Rhodes (1981) 474-7. Andocides' reference is obscure.

150. Anytus: see Davies 40-1; Develin 265; Ostwald 472-3. According to *Ath. Pol.* 27.5 Anytus was the first Athenian to secure acquittal by bribery, at his trial in 409 for failing to relieve Pylos. A supporter of Thrasybulus at Phyle, he became one of the leading democrats after 403, but is perhaps best known to us as the prosecutor of Socrates. He died in exile at Heraclea Pontica.

Cephalus: see 115n.

you fellow-tribesmen...advocates: for the use of fellow-tribesmen as *synegoroi* cf. Dem. 23.206; Hyp. 4.12; Harrison 2.158.

SPEECH 2: *ON HIS RETURN*

1-9: proem
The extended proem contains several of the regular topics which are designed to render his listeners well-disposed towards the speaker: indignation at the behaviour of his opponents (1-5); an appeal for pity (6-7); recalling of his past actions on the state's behalf and a demand for gratitude for them (8-9); and his persistent ill-fortune (8-9).

1. **or anyone else more lowly than I:** this arrogant remark spoils an otherwise carefully constructed opening (for εἰ μέν...ὅπου cf. 1.57).
    If the city is common...rights: the democratic principle of *isonomia*.
2. **the greatest astonishment...from me:** Andocides' astonishment is highlighted in the Greek by the metaphorical use of the rare verb περικαίω and the rare use in prose of ἐπαυρέσθαι, with the positioning at the end of successive clauses of the sounds παρ-/περι-/ἐπαυρ-. The effect is maintained in the next sentence by the superlatives.
    If indeed...3...hostile towards the city: a variation on the commonplace sentiment that the individual was subordinate to the state; cf. Thuc. 2.60.2-4 (with Hornblower); R. Garner, *Law and Society in Classical Athens* (London and Sydney, 1987) 18-19.
5. **To me...6...bad luck:** according to Dover (1968) 74-6, this kind of psychological generalisation about the human condition (cf. **24 if men's persons...opinions**) is common in Antiphon and Thucydides, but is notably absent from Andocides' later speeches and those of Lysias (except speech 3). But cf. **3.13, I think that all men would agree...wronged.**
6. **most sensible...the quickest:** cf. Lys. 19.53; Dover (1974) 122.
    If you were...with fellow-feeling: see 1.57n.
7. **through my youthful folly...madness:** an apologetic reference to Andocides' involvement in the Hermae affair (cf. **1.58-9**, where he faces the same dilemma as here). The use of συμφορά ('mishap'; cf. **1.86**) is regular in passages where the speaker is trying to evoke sympathy for an act committed under the influence of external forces which were too powerful for him to resist. See Dover (1974) 153-4.
    it became necessary for me to choose...evils: a type of argument known as *dilemmaton* ('double-trap').
9. **It is therefore reasonable...gratitude:** Andocides swiftly forgets his humility of 7-8 in making this rather complacent claim to gratitude, but his audience will not so easily have forgotten his admitted responsibility for events in 415.

10-16: narrative
Andocides' narrative is designed to arouse the sympathy of his audience by showing how the earlier actions which he had taken on behalf of the democracy had cost him his freedom, and almost his life, because they happened to coincide with the hated regime of the Four Hundred. Missiou 26-7 doubts that Andocides' story was found convincing by the assembly, but it is certainly related in a dramatic way. Andocides begins in melancholy mood (10), but having decided to be positive, he builds up his hopes in 11-12. On discovering the situation in Athens, however, his optimism is immediately shattered (13), and the melancholy returns in 15-16, though he ends on a note of renewed determination. This is a vivid narrative, then, and the swings in Andocides' mood are reflected by the vocabulary. For example, note the emotive vocabulary when he is feeling down, especially κακῶν (10)...κακά (15)...κακοῦσθαι...κακά...κακόν (16). Note also the use of ἄγω and its cognates: the triple εἰσήγαγον and also ἐξάγεσθαι in the upbeat section 11 (Andocides *supplies* and is allowed to *export*) stand in stark contrast to ἤγαγον in 13 (the Four Hundred *arrest* him) and the use of

εἰσαγαγόντα against Andocides by Peisander in **14** (he *supplied* the enemy). Finally, Andocides' actions lead in **12** to victory (ἐνίκησαν) and safety (ἔσωσαν, cf. σῶσαι...σωθῆναι), but by **15** they have caused his own safety to depend on the gods (οἱ διασώσαντες) and he himself is in prison (δεσμά).

10. **for this exile:** Andocides is speaking vividly, as if he were in Cyprus, where the longing to return entered him.
it was better for me...to die: cf. Dem. 57.70.
to do this city...you: Andocides lists two services, supplying the navy at Samos with oar-spars, corn and bronze (**11**) and the city with corn (**19-21**). He claims credit for them (**12, 22-3**), as if he were performing a liturgy (public service), and strengthens the claim by referring to his family connections (**11**). Missiou 28-32 argues, however, that such an appeal based on the wealthy liturgical system and family ties reflected Andocides' oligarchic background and will not necessarily have commended him to a democratic audience; and it was further weakened not only because Andocides was technically acting outside the liturgical system, but also by his explicit statement of self-interested motives (in itself not uncommon; cf. Lys. 21.11, 25.11, 13).

11. **I never spared...possessions:** acting like a good citizen (cf. Lys. 19.58, 25.4, 31.15; ps.-Dem. 42.25).
oar-spars: for the crucial importance of northern Greek and especially Macedonian timber for building and in particular ship-building, cf. Dem. 19.265, 49.26, 36; Thuc. 4.108.1; Xen. *Hell.* 6.1.11; Theophrastus, *Char.* 23.4.
when the Four Hundred...here: in 411.
Archelaus: king of Macedon 413-399. Andocides' father led an embassy to king Perdiccas in 426 (see **General Introd. i**), and he again refers to his ties of friendship with foreign kings in **1**.145 (cf. *Ag. And.* 48).
I also supplied corn and bronze: there is little reason to doubt this, or the supply of corn in **20-1**, but Andocides' opponents in 400 denied that he made any such benefactions (*Ag. And.* 49).

12. **those men...at sea:** possibly at Cyzicus. See **Introd. 2.i**.
I might justly claim...themselves: again the arrogant, aristocratic tone.

13. **the situation here...expectation:** Andocides claims that he was performing a service on behalf of Athens in order to secure his recall; and his surprise on his return to the city was not that the government had changed (which he already knew, cf. **11**), but that he was arrested, instead of being commended, for helping the army at Samos, to which the Four Hundred were by now hostile (**14**).
before the council: of Four Hundred (cf. Thuc. 8.70.1). **13-15** show that they acted as a court of law. See Rhodes (1981) 387-8.

14. **Peisander:** see **1**.27n.
I denounce: taken by Hansen (1976) 31, 125 as evidence for the use of *endeixis* to the council before 403/2 - a dangerous inference in view of the circumstances (as Hansen is aware).

15. **the altar:** cf. **1**.44 with n.
despite my disgrace...gods: an admission that he had committed impiety.
My subsequent imprisonment: cf. *Ag. And.* 27. The Four Hundred refused to recall exiles (Thuc. 8.70.1), and this will have further justified Andocides' imprisonment. See Ostwald 386 n. 174.
the number and nature...I endured: cf. *Ag. And.* 27, but not implying that Andocides was tortured (for the decree forbidding the torture of Athenian citizens see **1**.43n.). There is some amount of rhetorical exaggeration here.

16.   **who on the one hand...because of this:** i.e. Andocides' confession had ended the panic that followed the discovery of the mutilation of the Hermae but had caused his exile, while the services he performed in Samos led not to his recall but to his imprisonment by the Four Hundred.

17-23: proofs

Andocides' contentions in this section, as in the narrative, are centred around his public services, which in his view deserve a reciprocal favour. This is a common type of argument in the orators, but Andocides' boasting over them is quite unusual, and for Missiou 40-6 he again reveals his oligarchic stance in three sets of comparisons. In **17-18** there is an element of competition between the city's officials and the private donor, with the outcome that civic excellence could only be achieved by individuals of Andocides' status, who alone could make the financial contributions that were of supreme importance. He goes on in **19-20** to attribute sounder decision-making to the council than the assembly, as if they were completely separate entities (when in reality the two bodies worked closely together), and thereby reveals his distrust of the latter. Finally, in **22-3** he compares his actions with those of foreigners and slaves, reflecting contemporary debate over the citizenship - whereas in general democrats favoured extension, oligarchs favoured restriction.

17.   **furnish you with money:** there was in this period an office of *poristes*, or 'provider' of funds. See Rhodes (1981) 356.
18.   **they are crowned by you...heroes:** cf. 1.45.
        But you must understand...citizens: see Introd. 2 (n. 72).
19.   **five hundred of you:** i.e. the council (cf. 3).
        in secret: the secret proposal was probably connected with ensuring the future corn-supply from Cyprus, which had equally mysteriously been threatened (**20**).
        far less likely: one of only two examples in Andocides of argument from probability (*eikos*). See **1.51-3n.**
        it is possible for them...citizens: at their *euthyna*. See **1.73n.**
        you have no others...wish: on the supremacy of the assembly and its majority decisions see Dover (1974) 290-2.
20.   **Cyprus:** on Andocides' connections with Cyprus see General Introd. ii, **1.4n.**
21.   **I would have given all the money in the world:** Albini compares similar expressions, which may derive from the commercial world, at Isoc. 13.11; Dem. 1.1, Pr. 3.1, 33.1; Hdt. 1.86.4; Thuc. 1.33.2; Xen. *Mem.* 2.5.3.
        so that you might know: προῄδετε is an example of the use of the historic tenses of the indicative in final clauses, to denote that the purpose is dependent on an unaccomplished action or unfulfilled wish (and so is not or was not attained). See Goodwin 333.
22.   **I am asking of you...not:** Missiou 40-1 rightly follows Dover (1974) 283 in connecting this sentence with the following section, so producing the argument that if the Athenians granted citizenship to slaves and foreigners, they should *a fortiori* bestow it on men like Andocides who were of Athenian birth.
23.   **I often see you giving citizenship...service:** see **1.149n.** Andocides may be referring in general terms to service in recent battles like Cyzicus, and perhaps more specifically to the assassination of Phrynichus in the autumn of 411, which precipitated the fall of the Four Hundred (cf. ML 85, = Fornara 155). The latter was long ago suggested by H. Röhl, 'Zu Andocides II 23', *Hermes* 11 (1876) 378-81.

24-8: epilogue

Andocides begins his peroration by attempting to allay his listeners' doubts about the sincerity of his contrition (24-5), supporting this with the standard reference to his ancestors' services to the state (26). But his final claim (27-8) not to feel resentment that the assembly has been misled in his case as in that of the Four Hundred is both arrogant and unconvincing - nor was the assembly persuaded that Andocides' true concern was other than his own personal interest. See Missiou 46-9.

24. **For if men's persons...before:** sophistical but sound, as Dover (1974) 123. See further Saunders 112 on the rarity of claims that repentance is a ground for diminution of penalty. Note the parechesis in the Greek (γνώμη...σῶμα; cf. Ant. 5.5, γλώσσης...γνώμης).

26. **These are far more befitting me...family:** Andocides' audience is to infer from his ancestor Leogoras' opposition to the tyrants his own support for the democracy. On the concept of inherited virtue see Dover (1974) 93.

     my father's great-grandfather Leogoras: Andocides is probably referring to the same Leogoras who appears at 1.106 as his own great-grandfather. This has led some editors to emend the reading here to πάππος ('my father's grandfather'), but in view of the confused nature of Andocides' family tradition (see 1.106n.), he may himself have been unsure of his relationship to this Leogoras. See Thomas 141-2. The text was also defended by V. G. Ramírez, 'De nuevo sobre And. II, 26 y I, 106', *Nova Tellus* 5 (1987) 115-25.

     to be banished with the democrats: Missiou 47-8 argues that, since our other sources report the exile of aristocrats, this passage should be viewed in the context of anti-Peisistratid propaganda. See further 1.106n.

SPEECH 3: *ON THE PEACE WITH THE SPARTANS*

1-12: proof 1
Andocides dispenses with a proem and begins with his first proof, a refutation of the claim
that peace with Sparta will endanger the democracy. See **Introd. 3.iv.**

1.　　**the public speakers:** *rhetores,* the term used in the fourth century of politicians who
　　　spoke in the assembly and council. There is an element of scorn in the use of the word
　　　here, as Andocides immediately distances himself from his popular opponents.
　　　the name of peace...actions: a variation of a regular rhetorical antithesis (e.g. Lys.
　　　13.15; Dem. 9.8).
　　　there is a very great danger...overthrown: in democratic ideology after the Thirty,
　　　public safety was identified with democracy and Sparta was seen as a threat to both.
　　　Charges of oligarchic tendencies and attempting to overthrow the democracy reflect the
　　　vocabulary of political abuse. See MacDowell on Ar. *Wasps* 345; Missiou 56-8.
2.　　**how is it not reasonable...then?:** the first of thirty-five rhetorical questions in the
　　　speech.
　　　For it is necessary...future: a commonplace concept; cf. Lys. 25.23; Isoc. 2.35; Thuc.
　　　1.22.4; Nouhaud 88. For Aristotle (*Rhet.* 3.17.10) deliberative oratory was more
　　　difficult than forensic because it concerned the future.

3-12: first set of historical examples
Sections **3-9** of the speech in particular have won Andocides the most notorious reputation
among the orators for historical inaccuracy. See, for example, S. Perlman, 'The historical
example. Its use and importance as political propaganda in the Attic orators', *Scripta
Hierosolymitana* 7 (1961) 150-66, esp. 163; G. E. M. de Ste Croix, *The Origins of the
Peloponnesian War* (London, 1972) 245; *contra* W. E. Thompson, 'Andocides and
Hellanicus', *TAPA* 98 (1967) 483-90. It is clear, however, that the Athenians were far less
concerned with such inaccuracies than modern scholars. See Pearson 214; Perlman, *art. cit.*
156.

　　　The errors themselves are probably due largely to faulty recollection in Andocides' oral
family tradition. Andocides divides the Pentecontaetia into two periods of war, in Euboea and
over Aegina (followed by the war over Megara, i.e. the Peloponnesian War), and in so doing
he inverts the temporal order. **The war in Euboea** refers to the Euboean revolt of 446, which
Pericles was sent to suppress. While he was on the island, Megara revolted (so Athens was no
longer **holding Megara**), and Athens was in addition threatened by a Peloponnesian invasion,
which necessitated his immediate recall (Thuc. 1.114). This was followed by the Thirty
Years' Peace, in which Athens gave up control of Nisaea, Pegae, Troezen and Achaea. The
'fifty years' peace' negotiated by Cimon must be the five years' truce of 451 (Thuc. 1.112.1),
on the expiry of which Euboea revolted. **The war because of the Aeginetans** (Thuc. 1.105.2;
Diod. 11.78.3) was fought some ten years previously and was over by 457/6. The significant
guarantee in the Thirty Years' Peace of Aegina's autonomy within the Delian League may be
the reason behind the idea that Aegina caused this second war. See Thomas 119-23.

3.　　**recalled Miltiades, son of Cimon:** Andocides is the earliest source for the tradition
　　　that Cimon, son of Miltiades, was recalled to Athens from exile early by a special
　　　decree in 452, in order to negotiate the five years' truce with Sparta. See Meiggs 111,
　　　124-5, 422-3. Cimon **had been ostracised** in 461 after the Mt Ithome fiasco. He
　　　persuaded the assembly to respond to Sparta's plea for help in suppressing a helot
　　　revolt and a large force was sent under his command, but it was dismissed soon after

arriving at Mt Ithome, where the helots were firmly entrenched. On the confusion of Cimon and Miltiades in the tradition see Thomas 203-5.

was in the Chersonese: perhaps staying on family property there (*contra* Davies 311).

an official representative of the Spartans: *proxenos*, a person who assisted citizens from another city in his own city. Andocides' rival Callias was also a Spartan *proxenos*. See **Introd. 1.ii**; Meiggs 215-19.

4.   **for thirteen years:** assuming the Thirty Years' Peace as a starting point, this takes us down to 433, when Athens became involved in the conflict between Corinth and Corcyra.

5.   **we fortified Peiraeus...period:** the fortification was in fact completed by Themistocles in 477 (Thuc. 1.93.3-8).

built the northern Long Wall: to Peiraeus. It was in fact built between 458 and 456, along with the southern wall from Athens to Phalerum (Thuc. 1.107.1, 108.3).

in place of the old...one hundred triremes: Cimon altered the design of the old triremes, making them stronger and broader so that they could carry more hoplites, for his Eurymedon campaign in the 460s (Plut. *Cimon* 12.2). These will not have replaced the old fleet, which numbered between 200 and 300 vessels. Aeschines, who gives a version of this passage (see **Introd. 3.iii**) simply has 'we added one hundred new triremes to our fleet' (2.173).

we firstly then established...archers: Andocides probably refers again to actions of Cimon, from the 470s, though Athens had cavalry long before then. See Rhodes (1981) 303 (Aeschines says 'we also equipped three hundred cavalrymen'). The archers kept order in the assembly and courts.

6.   **Andocides, my grandfather:** see **General Introd. i**.

was there a time...show this: strong emphasis is added here by the rhetorical questions, of which there are three in the Greek (**I ask you** translates τί δέ;).

7.   **this peace raised...so high:** an expression with a tragic flavour; cf. Eur. *Heraclid.* 322, *Suppl.* 555; also Soph. *OT* 914. Note too the use of the abstract **peace** (εἰρήνη) as the subject of the transitive verb.

one thousand talents...besides...reserve: this in fact happened *after* the outbreak of the Peloponnesian War (Thuc. 2.24, cf. 8.15.1), the money being drawn from the reserve of 6000 talents (id. 2.13.3). Thucydides says the Athenians voted to put aside 100 ships every year.

we built shipsheds: an initiative of Themistocles, completed between 451 and 448.

the southern Long Wall: i.e. the Middle Wall connecting Athens to Peiraeus, which was built at the time of the Thirty Years' Peace. See **1.45n**.

twelve hundred cavalry and as many archers: Thucydides (2.13.8) gives 1200 cavalry, including mounted bowmen (of whom there were 200), and 1600 unmounted bowmen in 431. These archers were citizens, to be distinguished from the Scythians of **5**.

From the peace...democracy: Andocides ends the second example with the same words as the first in **5**.

8.   **we went to war...Megarians:** reflecting the view in comedy (and cf. Thuc. 1.139) that the Megarian Decree was the cause of the Peloponnesian War. See Nouhaud 122-3, 254-5.

abandoned our territory...waste: a derogatory reference to Pericles' defence strategy.

Nicias, son of Niceratus: see **1.11n**. His fifty years' peace in 421 was short-lived; further on Andocides' account of it see Nouhaud 267-70.

I think you all know this: a commonplace type of expression in the orators, which enables them to avoid giving the impression that they are lecturing their audience. See Pearson 212-19.

seven thousand talents: this recalls the figure of 6000 talents at the outbreak of the war, and the reserve cannot have been anywhere near this sum in 421-419 (when hostilities resumed). It could, however, be the amount due to the gods from borrowing during the Archidamian War, which the Athenians determined to repay after the Peace of Nicias. See *ATL* 3.346-7, 356.

9. **more than three hundred ships:** the MSS have 400, but Markland emended comparing Aesch. 2.175; Thuc. 2.13.8. Andocides once more appears to be transposing to 421 the figure of 431; *contra* D. M. MacDowell, 'An expansion of the Athenian navy', *CR* 15 (1965) 260 (but see Nouhaud 268 n. 72).

   tribute...twelve hundred talents: this figure is regarded as far too high by most scholars (e.g. Nouhaud 268), though Meiggs 343 argues that a sum of 1000 talents of tribute plus 200 talents of other revenue might be correct. See further *ATL* 3.347-53.

   we were holding...Euboea: yet again this seems to reflect an earlier situation, at the time of the Thirty Years' Peace, since the balance of evidence suggests that no colony or cleruchy of Athenian citizens was sent to Euboea after the crushing of the revolt in 446. See *HCT* 1.345; Meiggs 565-70. Cleruchies were sent to the Chersonese in 457 and to Naxos in 450.

   persuaded then, as now, by the Argives: Andocides repeatedly attempts to sway the minds of his listeners against the Argives and in favour of the Spartans by insisting on the Argives' role as instigators of war (cf. **27, 31, 41**). See **Introd. 3.vi.** For the Athens-Argos alliance of 420 cf. Thuc. 5.40-8. When the Argives invaded Epidaurus the following year, Athens was induced by Alcibiades to support them.

10. **the Thirty were established...exile:** see, for example, the descriptions of atrocities committed by the Thirty in Lysias 12, *Against Eratosthenes* and 13, *Against Agoratus*. Andocides attempts to gloss over these with his argument in **11**.

11. **a peace and a truce are very different things:** the speciousness of the argument is emphasised by Nouhaud 303-4.

   enjoined us...exiles: and also to withdraw from all occupied cities; to have the same friends and enemies as the Spartans and follow them wherever they might lead by land and sea; and (perhaps) to be governed under the ancestral constitution; cf. **1.80**; Xen. *Hell.* 2.2.20; Arist. *Ath. Pol.* 34.3; Diod. 13.107.4. The last of these, which is missing from Xenophon's list, is not accepted by many scholars (e.g. Rhodes [1981] 427), but see Ostwald 458 n. 165.

12. **Consider too the actual recorded provisions...stele:** the details given by Andocides suggest that he may have consulted the actual stele. See Thomas 67. If so, as Thomas notes, it is interesting that the stone still survived in 392/1. Andocides naturally selects the three relevant conditions of the imposed settlement with which the present terms compare favourably, and omits the one concerning withdrawal from occupied cities - the currently proposed guarantee of autonomy for the other Greek communities (except in Asia and Boeotia) will have been highly unpopular in Athens.

   we demolish the walls...build them: cf. **14, 23, 36, 37, 39** (similarly for the ships).

   twelve ships: this figure is also given by Xenophon and Diodorus.

   those holding Lemnos...ours: cf. **14** and n., **23, 39**. On the importance of these islands to Athens see A. J. Graham, *Colony and Mother City in Ancient Greece* (Manchester, 1971) 174-89; Rhodes (1981) 686-7, 695.

and today there is no compulsion...overthrown: Andocides may here be attempting to shift the blame for the establishment of the Thirty from the Spartans to the Athenian oligarchs in exile. See Missiou 65-6.

peace means safety...but war means...the democracy: a neat correlation. The 'benefits' of **5** and **7** have now become 'safety', enabling the contrast to be made between the results of peace and war.

13-16 proof 2
Refutation of the claim that continuing the war was a necessity imposed by justice.

13. **Some say...should make war:** both sides employ the regular deliberative topic of necessity.

For I think...those wronged: for the generalisation see **2.5n**.

we were...being wronged: i.e. this was a just war of self-defence (cf. ps.-Anaximenes, *Rhet.* 2 p. 25 Spengel-Hammer), but in **22** the Athenians are made the aggressors. Note that Andocides carefully avoids naming the wrongdoers.

if the Boeotians...autonomy: the Spartans have conceded to the Thebans the continued existence of the Boeotian Confederacy (minus Orchomenus) and thereby won them over.

for what reason...war?: commencing an effective succession of rhetorical questions and answers in hypophora (cf. **1.148**). The questions reflect the aims of Andocides' pro-war opponents.

14. **That we may recover the islands:** the regular meaning of the middle κομίζομαι is 'recover', which suggests that Athens was not yet in full possession of these islands, despite Xen. *Hell.* 4.8.15 and the inferences to the contrary made from that passage by modern scholars.

15. **that we may regain...abroad:** reflecting the demands of the lower classes in particular. See Missiou 82-3.

our debts: on the practice of lending money outside Athens see Millett 298 n. 11. This was only done under exceptional circumstances: if the parties were bound by ties of reciprocity; if the lender was a merchant or involved in trade; or if Athens' power could be brought to bear, to ensure the recovery of monies owed or foreclose on securities.

But neither the King...for that: the regular deliberative topic of practicability.

Then if we are successful...this?: see **Introd. 3.vi**. This remark may imply that Andocides believes the Persians are still Sparta's allies, and if so, the news of Artaxerxes' rejection of Tiribazus' proposals is not yet known. See **Introd. 3.iii** (n. 87).

16. **any reason for us...nor anyone against whom...nor anything with which:** note the effective polyptoton in the Greek (i.e. repetition of words from the same root in different cases), ὅ τι...ὅτοισι...ὅτου.

17-23: proof 3
Confirmation of the advantages that peace will bring, employing the topic of expediency.

17. **a common peace:** *koine eirene* (cf. **34**). This is the earliest occurrence in literature of what was to become a prominent theme in fourth-century political philosophy.

18. **three battles:** in July 394 at Nemea (here **at Corinth**) followed sixteen days later by a **victory** at Coronea; and the attack on the long walls connecting Corinth and **Lechaeum** in 393. Andocides' account displays a heavily pro-Spartan bias, amplifying the Spartan victories (accomplished **by themselves**) and omitting mention of the other forces which fought on the Spartan side (cf. Xen. *Hell.* 4.3.15). The war was, in fact, inconclusive, and the Spartans themselves suffered heavy casualties (including the death of Lysander) and the comprehensive naval defeat off Cnidus.

19.   **Yet what kind of peace...battle?:** Andocides develops the theme of Spartan generosity and Athenian ingratitude in 21-3.

20.   **for they could have allowed...peace:** Andocides' derision of Athens' Boeotian allies again contrasts with his attitude towards the Spartans.

21.   **If any of you...facts:** Andocides' apology reflects how unpopular the idea would be that Athens owed Sparta a debt of gratitude (*charis*). The following string of rhetorical questions once more helps to emphasise the ethical conduct of the Spartans, in contrast to the behaviour of Athens' **present allies** (especially the Corinthians and Thebans) after the defeat in 404. See further Missiou 87-9.
        when we lost our ships in the Hellespont: at Aegospotami (405).
        Was it not the Spartans, dissuading their allies: on this tradition (cf. **1.142**; Xen. *Hell.* 2.2.19-20) and Andocides' use of it see Missiou 92-100, 106-7. It served to rehabilitate the Spartans' reputation as the patrons of the Thirty and promote a picture of a magnanimous Sparta.

22.   **But then we made an alliance...sea?:** Andocides makes the ungrateful Athens responsible for Sparta's recent misfortunes. Hence, whereas in **17** and **19** (where he is lauding Spartan invincibility and generosity) he says the Spartans were prepared to give up control of land and sea for the sake of peace, now they have **lost their sovereignty of the sea** (in the **sea-battle** of Cnidus, 394). Similarly, in **13** the Athenians are the ones wronged, here they are the aggressors. See further Missiou 90-1, 145-6.

24-32: proof 4
The disadvantages of alliance with Corinth and Argos.

26.   **Yes we can...allies:** i.e. Athens' alliance with Corinth and Argos was a major issue for Andocides' opponents. He attempts to counter this in **26-7** by portraying the Argives as warmongers (cf. **9, 31, 41**). See **Introd. 3.vi**.
        to make the Corinthians' territory the Argives': Andocides' fears were soon realised by the Union of Corinth and Argos, on which see Cartledge 255-6.

27.   **but they themselves...hostilities:** on this 'ancestral peace' see S. Payrau, 'Sur un passage d'Andocide (*Paix*, 27)', *REA* 63 (1961) 15-30.

28-32: second set of historical examples
Andocides adduces three more examples from the fifth century to illustrate his criticism of Athens' policy of siding with the weak instead of the strong and of choosing war instead of peace. For the policy itself cf. Thuc. 6.13.2; Pl. *Menex.* 244e; **Introd. 3.vi**.

29.   **We firstly made a truce with the Great King:** the existence of a Peace of Epilycus is supported by an inscription (ML 70, = Fornara 138), which honours Heraclides for helping an Athenian embassy on which (it seems) Epilycus served in 424/3. See Meiggs 134-5; *contra* Rhodes (1981) 492-3.
        Epilycus: cf. **1.117**; Davies 297; Develin 1049. Andocides' family tradition recorded Epilycus' action with pride. See Thomas 119, 143.
        but after this we were persuaded by Amorges: the dating of Athens' involvement in the revolt of Pissuthnes (see next n.) is controversial, and it has been argued that Andocides distorts the chronology of events here. See H. D. Westlake, 'Athens and Amorges', *Phoenix* 31 (1977) 319-29; but see E. Badian, 'The Peace of Callias', *JHS* 107 (1987) 35.

the runaway slave of the King: Amorges was in fact the bastard son of Pissuthnes, satrap of Sardis, who revolted from Persia at an unknown date. The Persian king, Darius, sent Tissaphernes, Spithradates and Parmises to suppress Pissuthnes, who was supported by some Greek troops led by the Athenian Lycon. The Greeks were bribed to desert Pissuthnes, who was captured and executed. Amorges fled to Caria, where he was sheltered by Iasus, until the town was stormed, on Tissaphernes' instigation, by the Spartans in 412. Amorges was handed over to the Persians. Cf. Thuc. 8.5.5 (with *HCT*), 19.2, 28.2-5, 54.3; Ctesias 52; Meiggs 349-50.

five thousand talents: cf. Isoc. 8.97. This probably inflated figure was the Persian subsidy to the Spartans between 412 and 405. See Cartledge 88-9.

30. when the Syracusans came: it is generally accepted that Andocides has invented this embassy. He was perhaps resentful at the death of his uncle Epilycus on the Sicilian expedition (see 1.117n.), hence the best before the rest.

31. we were persuaded...Laconia: in the summer of 414 (Thuc. 6.105).

33-41: proof 5
Justification of the referral of the decision to the assembly.

35. you are accustomed...brought you: cf. similar criticism at Ar. *Eccl.* 193-203. See further Dover (1974) 24-5.

36. if it is walls and ships...them: see Introd. 3.vi.

37-9: third historical example

37. partly by persuading...against them: Andocides' praise of Athens' fifth-century empire, tainted by his reference to stealth and bribery, is less than fulsome and conceals Themistocles' role in the rebuilding of the walls. On this technique of denying credit see Missiou 78-82. A similar passage is found at Isoc. 3.22.

38. Hellenotamiae: the ten Athenian officials who administered the funds of the Delian League.

by acting unobserved...walls: a reference to the famous trick perpetrated on the Spartans by Themistocles, when the Athenians were rebuilding their walls after the Persian Wars (Thuc. 1.90-2).

by bribing the Spartans: this was an alternative version to the story of trickery, in which Themistocles bribed the Spartan ephors not to oppose his rebuilding project. The tradition is also preserved by Theopompus (cf. Plut. *Them.* 19.1), in a passage close in tenor to this one. See further Missiou 81-2.

eighty-five years: the figure fits if taken from Marathon (490) to Aegospotami (405). The length of Athens' hegemony was frequently and variously cited, e.g. Lys. 2.55; Isoc. 4.106, 12.56; Dem. 3.24, 9.23; Lyc. 1.72.

41. Therefore...regret: the speech ends with the briefest of epilogues.

SPEECH 4: *AGAINST ALCIBIADES*

1-10: proem

The extensive introductory remarks include sections on the dangers of public service (**1-2**), criticism of ostracism (**3-6**), an appeal for a fair hearing (**7**), and the contrast between the speaker's probity and Alcibiades' improbity (**8-10**). The antithetical structure of **1-2** immediately raised Jebb's suspicions concerning the work's authenticity (p. 133).

1. **I consider it the duty of a good citizen:** the speaker opens his attack in the manner of a prosecutor in a trial, taking care not to appear like a sycophant or to be displaying meddlesomeness (πολυπραγμοσύνη), but stressing his public service and patriotism (cf. Aesch. 1.1-2; Lyc. 1.3-6).
2. **this prize:** n.b. the use of the plural in the Greek (ἄθλων), which is presumably influenced by δέκα ἔτη.
    Alcibiades: for his career see **1.11**n.; and the biographies of Hatzfeld and Ellis.
    Nicias: see **1.11**n.
3. **the author of the law:** Cleisthenes. For a convenient summary of the ostracism law and the problems over its attribution to Cleisthenes see Rhodes (1981) 267-71.
    you swear...trial: on this fundamental principle see Saunders 97.
    with no accusation made nor defence allowed: and so, it would seem, excluding the possibility of there being a real occasion on which to deliver a speech such as the present one.
    nor with the voting in secret: most editors follow Schleiermacher in deleting the third οὔτε (i.e. 'and with the voting in secret'), and it is true that the whole process of ostracism acquires its name from the inscribing of the votes on sherds of pottery (*ostraka*). But the author is not talking about the situation in the assembly, where there was a show of hands; rather, he is emphasising that ostracism violates the principle that no man should be exiled, imprisoned or executed without due legal process (ἄκριτον), which involved accusation, defence and secret vote. Stylistically, the emendation ruins the tricolon, which is set in direct antithesis (with μέν...δέ) to the preceding tricolon with μήτε. The MSS reading was similarly defended by Raubitschek, *TAPA* 79 (1948) 193-4.
4. **those who have political friends...others:** on political clubs see **1.49**n. Manipulation of the voting at ostracisms was proved by the discovery of 191 votes against Themistocles written in only fourteen hands. See ML 21 (p. 43).
    for it is not men appointed by lot...courts: for the details of the appointment of jurors by lot see MacDowell (1978) 35-40.
    a light and valueless penalty for public wrongs: a strained antithesis, since living in exile was thought terrible. See **1.5**n.
    when it is possible to punish...death: on these penalties see MacDowell (1978) 254-8. Imprisonment was in fact used sparingly in the ancient world in comparison with modern times.
6. **we alone of the Greeks use it:** an inversion of the regular *topos* (e.g. Lys. 1.2; Is. 2.24; Isoc. 19.50; Dem. 21.50). Ostracism was in fact used by other states, including Argos, Megara and Miletus (Arist. *Pol.* 5.3, 1302b18; schol. Ar. *Knights* 855).
7. **But I do ask you to be fair and impartial:** as if the speaker were addressing a jury. Such appeals were regular elements of forensic proems (cf. Ant. 5.4 with Edwards).
    presidents over our speeches...them: ostracisms were directed by the archons and the council, which was presided over by an *epistates* (cf. schol. Ar. *Knights* 855). The

speaker is urging his listeners to regard themselves as being in the same position of responsibility as the archons and *epistates*.

each of the circumstances: reading ἔκαστον with Maidment for the MSS ἑκάστου.

8. **my membership of a faction:** στασιωτεία is a virtual hapax legomenon (cf. Pl. *Laws* 8.832c).

9. **the laws forbid...charge:** cf. **36**; Dem. 20.147, 38.16 (but n.b. Hyp. frgs 28-9).

you have sworn to employ the laws: a reference to the jurors' oath, on which see **1.2n.**

10. **If I had to speak in detail...behaviour:** cf. similar descriptions of Alcibiades' lifestyle at Ant. frg. 67; Thuc. 6.15.4; and n.b. Lys. 14.41-2. There are various commonplace elements in the argument here: Alcibiades is characterised by his illegal and excessive behaviour (cf. **19, 21, 22, 23, 30, 34, 39, 40**), which puts the speaker in a state of loss (*aporia*) and in a dilemma.

11-40: these sections of the speech are effectively a series of anecdotes, typical of the many told about Alcibiades (cf. Plutarch's *Life of Alcibiades*).

11-12: Alcibiades' public conduct

11. **he persuaded you to assess anew the tribute:** apparently a reference to the re-assessment of 425/4 (ML 69, = Fornara 136; CW 200). Alcibiades was only about twenty-five at the time, whereas thirty was the regular lower limit for public appointments, but the story is accepted by, among others, Ostwald 292-3. The speaker's opposition to the raising of the allies' taxes is an indication of oligarchic sympathies, since this was a traditional feature of oligarchic politics (Antiphon, for instance, wrote speeches *On the Tribute of the Samothracians* and *On the Tribute of the Lindians*). For further indications in **8** and **32** see **Introd. 4** (n. 116).

which was set by Aristeides with extreme fairness: after the formation of the Delian League in 478. On these events and Aristeides' reputation for fairness see Meiggs chapters 3-4.

12. **to settle at Thurii:** the panhellenic colony in south Italy, founded in 443.

The enmity of the allies...Spartans: as it did in the Ionian War after the disaster in Sicily. This looks suspiciously like *vaticinatio post eventum* (prophecy after the event), but see **Introd. 4.**

13-33: Alcibiades' private conduct

13-15: his marriage

13. **I am amazed...democracy:** the speaker attempts to impugn Alcibiades' credibility by accusing him of harbouring tyrannical designs (cf. **24, 27**), as do his enemies at Thuc. 6.15.4, 28.2. See further Furley, *Hermes* 117 (1989) 146-8.

greed and arrogance: the speaker seems resentful of Alcibiades' wealth (cf. **16, 30-2**) and the fact that his excesses made him all the more popular (**18, 21, 24, 29, 30-1**). See Furley, *art. cit.* 153-4.

married the sister of Callias: Hipparete. The marriage will have taken place sometime in the late 420s (see Davies 19). For Callias see **Introd. 1.ii.**

a dowry of ten talents...another ten: cf. Plut. *Alc.* 8.2-4. Twenty talents was an enormous sum, but Davies (*ibid.*) thinks it credible given the reputed wealth of the family. Alcibiades' financial problems in c. 416 (see Davies 20-1) will explain why he insisted on the payment of the second instalment, and also why he refused to let Hipparete divorce him, in which case he would have had to repay the dowry.

after the death of Hipponicus...at Delium: Hipponicus' death is connected by Athenaeus (5.218b-c) with the production of Eupolis' *Kolakes* in spring 421. This does not rule out the possibility of his demise at Delium in 424, but this is usually thought to be a confusion with that of Hippocrates (cf. Thuc. 4.101.2), and Hipponicus' generalship in 424/3 is denied by Develin p. 133. Further on Hipponicus see **Introd. 1.ii.**

had a child: in the regular manner, Alcibiades' first son should have been named after the child's grandfather, Cleinias, but we only know of two legitimate children, a daughter (Lys. 14.28) and a son Alcibiades who was born about 417/16 (Isoc. 16.45-6). The first-born son, therefore, probably died in infancy (as Hatzfeld 137 n. 1). We are also told of four illegitimate children, including the son of **22** (cf. Plut. *Alc.* 16.4).

14. **bringing mistresses...to desert him:** Plutarch says they were both Athenian and foreign courtesans, and Hipparete went to live with her brother.
     go to the archon...law: in order to file for divorce. See MacDowell (1978) 88; Todd (1993) 214-15.

15. **as he accused him of doing:** note the awkward change of subject here from Alcibiades (ἐπεβούλευσε, κατάσχοι) to Callias (κατηγόρει).

16-19: Agatharchus

17. **he persuaded Agatharchus:** cf. Dem. 21.147 (with MacDowell); Plut. *Alc.* 16.4. In Plutarch's account Agatharchus adorns the house with paintings and is then dismissed with a handsome present. Demosthenes, however, preserves a different version of the story, that Alcibiades 'caught Agatharchus in some transgression', which the scholiast (506 Dilts) explains as intercourse with Alcibiades' concubine. This would then justify Alcibiades' conduct, since the adultery law permitted the confinement of a free man apprehended in these circumstances (cf. ps.-Dem. 59.41 with Carey).
     Agatharchus, son of Eudemus, came from Samos (Harpoc. s.v.) and worked on the Acropolis buildings (Plut. *Per.* 13.2).

18. **to carry even malefactors off to prison:** by *apagoge* (summary arrest), which was permitted against certain categories of criminal, including thieves, if they were caught in the act. Closely related procedures to *apagoge* were *endeixis* (by which Andocides was prosecuted in 400; see **1.2n.**) and *ephegesis* (in which the arrest was made by a public official). As with most public suits, if the prosecutor in an *apagoge* failed to **gain one-fifth of the votes,** he suffered **a fine of a thousand drachmas** and partial loss of rights (*atimia*; see **1.7n.**). This penalty was designed to prevent frivolous prosecutions, and **I am annoyed to think that it is not safe** to bring an *apagoge* is something of an exaggeration for the purposes of the antithesis here.
     shut up a man: εἱργνύω is used three times in this speech (cf. below, **27**) but is only elsewhere found (from the form εἵργνυμι) at Homer, *Od.* 10.238. It is therefore, like στασιωτεία in **8**, a virtual hapax.
     our treaties with other states: on these *symbola* see Meiggs 228-33.

20-1: Taureas

20. **Taureas:** cf. Dem. 21.147 (with MacDowell); Plut. *Alc.* 16.4. Taureas may be the cousin of Leogoras in **1.47** (see n. there).

choregus of boys: the choregus undertook the financing and general responsibility for training a chorus of boys for one of the major dramatic festivals (cf. Ant. 6.11-13). Here the Dionysia is the festival involved, since non-citizens were allowed to be choristers at the Lenaea but not the Dionysia (schol. Ar. *Wealth* 953). Alcibiades presumably undertook his *choregia* before 415, again at an exceptionally early age. See Davies 29.

The law: cf. Dem. 21.56-61 (with MacDowell). The description is very confused, but Alcibiades apparently ejected Taureas, who was objecting to an alien member of Alcibiades' chorus (the Greek might mean that Alcibiades was objecting to a member of Taureas' chorus). Alcibiades thereby fell foul of the clause in the law which forbade interference. But Demosthenes says (21.147) that the law had not yet been enacted in Alcibiades' day, and this was simply a matter of one chorus-producer striking another. If Demosthenes is right, this suggests that the author of our passage is guilty of an anachronism (which adds to the anomalies discussed in **Introd. 4**), but the existence of a similar procedure in the fifth century is defended by Ostwald 120-1.

Two grammatical features are noteworthy here:
(i) the use of ὥστε with the participle by assimilation to a preceding participle. Goodwin 607(b) notes only one other example of this construction (Dem. 45.83), when the ὥστε-clause does not depend on a participle in indirect speech;
(ii) the abrupt change of subject from Alcibiades (ἐξήλασεν) to Taureas (ἔπραξεν).

22-3: the Melian woman

22. **after declaring...slavery:** the Athenians reduced Melos in the winter of 416/15, killing the men and enslaving the women and children. Thucydides' view of the unique importance of this event is reflected by the unparalleled Melian Dialogue (5.84-116). For Alcibiades' role in the massacre, which is not mentioned by the historian, cf. Plut. *Alc.* 16.5; Hatzfeld 126-7; *HCT* 4.190-1; Ostwald 305-12. It is exaggerated in **23**, to the point where Alcibiades becomes personally responsible.
whose birth was more illegal than that of Aegisthus: see **1.129n.**

23. **whose city he had devastated:** note the change of tense from the aorist (κατέστησε...ἀπέκτεινε) to the perfect (πεποίηκεν). Furley, *art. cit.* 143 n. 17 takes this as an indication that the work was written before Melos' status was restored by Sparta at the end of the Peloponnesian War, but a later forger who knew of the restoration could also have written in this way.
when you watch such things in tragedies: cf. Isoc. 4.168 (with Usher).

24: Alcibiades' behaviour in his youth does not bode well for his future conduct

I think that the city...wrongs: on this apparent prescience see **Introd. 4.**

25-33: Alcibiades' behaviour at the Olympics

25. **his victory at Olympia:** in 416; cf. Thuc. 6.16.2 (with *HCT*); Plut. *Alc.* 11-12. In his speech in Thucydides, Alcibiades says he alone entered seven teams at the Olympics and came first, second and fourth (Plutarch quotes a victory ode written by Euripides, in which he comes first, second and third). For his victories at Nemea, Delphi and the Great Panathenaea see Davies 20-1. Through his horse-breeding and victories at the games Alcibiades became a panhellenic personality, adding to the reputation he gained at Athens by means of his lavish public expenditure.

26.   **Diomedes:** cf. Isoc. 16.1-2; Diod. 13.74.3-4; Plut. *Alc.* 12.2-3. In the other sources the story runs that one of Alcibiades' friends persuaded him to buy an outstanding team belonging to Argos (where he was influential), but Alcibiades then entered it in his own name. It was alleged that he used the friend's money, and this led to the suit in which Isoc. 16 was delivered. While three of the accounts name the friend as Diomedes, Isocrates calls him Teisias, which suggests that either there were two partners, one of whom died before the suit, or (preferably) the name Diomedes has erroneously entered the tradition (perhaps because the Argive horses were thought to be descendants of the mares that Heracles took from Diomedes). Teisias, the brother-in-law of Charicles (Isoc. 16.42; see **1.36n.**), is probably the general of 417/16 and 416/15 (see Develin 2859), who led the expedition to Melos. This would explain why he apparently did not protest against Alcibiades' conduct during the games themselves. See Davies 501-2; Ostwald 310-11; *contra* Ellis 51-2.

possessing moderate means: an understatement, especially if the man was really Teisias.

the first person he met: most editors add οὐ, i.e. 'no casual competitor' or 'a person of some distinction' (Maidment), but for this sense of the verb see LSJ, s.v. ἐπιτυγχάνω II.4. In this version (which omits the friendship of the two men) Alcibiades happened to meet a man who was an Athenian citizen and owned a team he coveted.

the presidents of the games: presumably referring to the *Hellanodikai*, who according to Pausanias (5.9.4) numbered two at this time.

27.   **shutting up others in prison:** see 18n.

28.   **He differs so much from the Spartans:** on this praise of the Spartans see 11n.

29.   **the leaders of the delegation:** on the *architheoroi* see **1.132n.**

30.   **The Ephesians...Lesbians:** cf. Plut. *Alc.* 12.1; Satyros ap. Athenaeus 12.534d. In Thucydides (6.16.1-2) Alcibiades later boasted that his victory celebrations brought glory to Athens at a time when her reputation was suffering. This may have been an element in the rivalry between Alcibiades and Nicias, who was renowned for his lavish public expenditure. See Ellis 51.

render an account of their term: at their *euthyna*. See **1.73n.**

31.   **public maintenance in the Prytaneum:** like Diocleides (cf. **1.45** with n.).

has doubled his wealth: but see 13n.

32.   **those who are thrifty:** see 11n.

you ostracised Callias, son of Didymius: in the 440s. See Rhodes (1981) 271.

33.   **they ostracised Cimon...sister:** the popular tradition, initiated by Eupolis; cf. schol. Aristeides 3.515 Dindorf; Plut. *Cim.* 15.3; Thomas 204 n. 28. For the real reason see **3.3n.** (and note that the relationship between Cimon and Miltiades is stated correctly here). The accusation of incest depends on Cimon and Elpinice having the same mother, but there was also a tradition that they were legally married, which was permitted between children of the same father but different mothers. See Davies 302-3.

Yet not only was he himself an Olympic victor...Miltiades: in fact, these victories were achieved by their sixth-century ancestors Cimon (the father of the Marathon general), who won the chariot-race three times, and his half-brother Miltiades (cf. Hdt. 6.103, 36.1).

34:   **comparison between the families of the speaker and Alcibiades**

his mother's father Megacles...ostracised: cf. Lys. 14.39. Megacles, father of Deinomache, was ostracised in 487/6 (*Ath. Pol.* 22.5), Alcibiades the grandfather perhaps in 460. See ML 21 (p. 43); Davies 15, 379. There is no reason to follow

Markland in adding δίς ('twice') to the text here on the basis of the Lysias passage, since Lysias' statement is itself most probably erroneous. See Carey's n. *ad loc.* (but n.b. Rhodes [1981] 275).

35-40: comparison between the speaker's and Alcibiades' experience of the law

35. **noticing that whenever...misdeeds:** it was a cardinal rule of the democratic legal system that a trial should be impartial, and that social status should not influence the verdict or the level of penalty. See A. P. Dorjahn, 'Intimidation in Athenian Courts', *CP* 32 (1937) 341-8; Saunders 98.

I have been tried four times: resuming the argument of **8-9** (ring-composition).

37. **who caused the deaths of two of those...me:** the reference is obscure.

those who are unwilling...life: cf. **30**.

38. **if somebody resolved...tolerated:** sim. Ant. 5.95, but see **1.7n.** For the construction ἀνασχέσθαι τῶν ἐπιχειρούντων see Goodwin 879.

40. **you should be concerned...decent:** for this *topos* cf. Lys. 14.12 (with Carey), 15.9; Dem. 21.37, 25.17.

41-2: past services of the speaker

The details given are consistent with what we know of the career of Phaeax, but this does not prove his authorship. See **Introd. 4.**

41. **I also wish to remind you of what I have done:** a commonplace element of speeches (e.g. **1.149**; Lys. 7.30-1).

42. **physical fitness:** the contest of *euandria*, a tribal competition in military prowess for which the prize was a shield (*Ath. Pol.* 60.3) or an ox worth 100 drachmas (*IG* ii^2 2311.75). See further Rhodes (1981) 676.

torch-race: see **1.132n.**

without hitting my rival choregi: cf. **20.**

Appendix A

The Family of Andocides

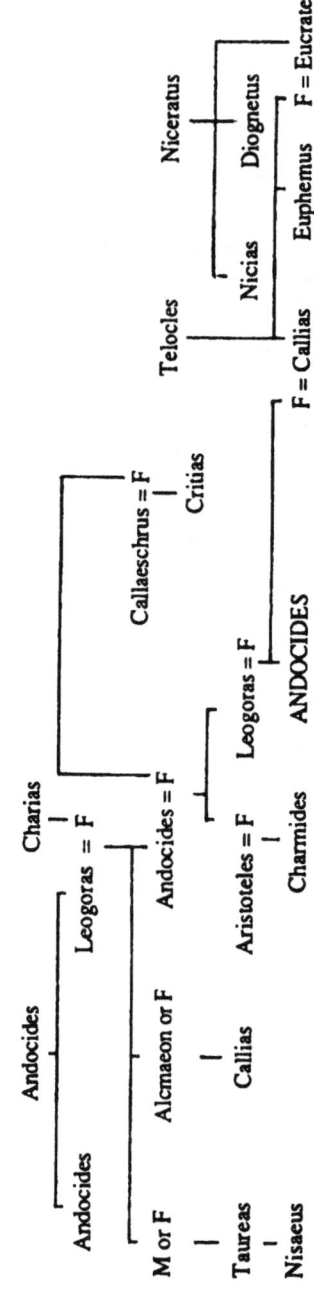

M = male; F = female. Phrynichus (1.47) may have been the cousin of either Andocides or Callias, son of Telocles.

Appendix B

The Family of Callias

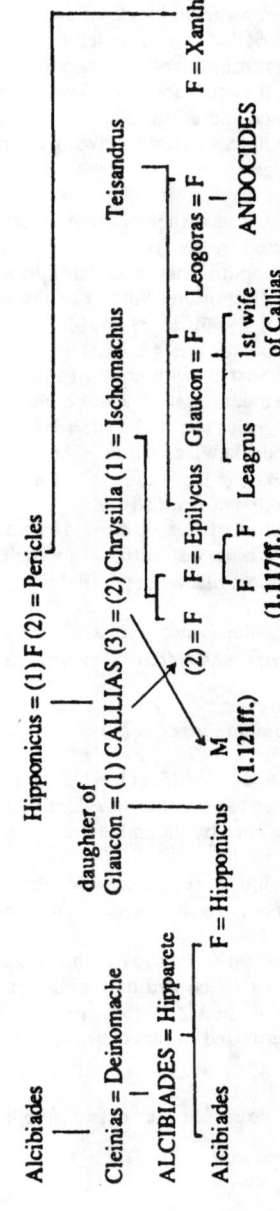

I follow MacDowell in allotting two daughters to Ischomachus; Davies 264-5 argues for only one.

Appendix C

The Language and Style of the *Against Alcibiades*

Simonetta Feraboli's analysis of the language and style of the *Against Alcibiades* (in *SIFC* 44 [1972] 5-37; cf. *Maia* 26 [1974] 245-6) led her to conclude that the work is spurious. For Feraboli, the *Against Alcibiades* differs from the other speeches above all in its formality: the variety of style, grammar and syntax that characterises Andocides' writing is replaced by a formal method based on correspondence and antithesis. The data collected by Feraboli is too extensive to be included in its entirety here, but the following are some of the main points she adduces, which fall under three headings.

I. Feraboli begins with a lexical survey. The author of the *Against Alcibiades* makes a careful choice of vocabulary, which is reflected in the frequent use of synonyms and synonymous expressions. These serve simply as repetitions or to strengthen expressions, to create a parallelism of structure or as a means of avoiding the use of the same word twice. Examples include: σφαλερόν - χαλεπόν (1); ἡγοῦμαι - νομίζω (1, 4, 8-9, 12, 24-5); χρή - ἀναγκαῖον (2); τιμωρία - ζημία - κολάζειν (4, cf. 18); χρήματα - οὐσία - πλοῦτον (15); but instances may be found in almost every section of the speech. Words in which there is only a slight shade of difference in meaning may also be classified here, among the many examples of which are: τυγχάνων - χρώμενος (2); ἐπιστάτας - ἄρχοντας (7); ἐπιδείξω - διηγήσομαι (25). Antonyms are used likewise: ἴδιος - δημοσίος/κοινός (1, 4, 18, 35; 1, 11, 35, 42); συνειδότας - ἀγνοήσαντες (5); φίλους - ἐχθρούς (5); πολλοῖς - ὀλίγοις (6, 41); λόγους - ἔργα (27); ζῶντας - τεθνηκότας (38).

In contrast to Andocides, the author of the *Against Alcibiades* constantly strives after symmetry. Sentences are arranged in a binary structure, in which the clauses assume a two-member form with subject, verb and object placed in parallel positions:

διὰ μὲν γὰρ τοὺς τῶν ἰδίων ἐπιμελουμένους οὐδὲν αἱ πόλεις μείζους καθίστανται,
διὰ δὲ τοὺς τῶν κοινῶν μεγάλαι καὶ ἐλεύθεραι γίγνονται (1);

τοὺς μὲν λάθρᾳ ἀδικοῦντας κολάζοντες,
τοὺς δὲ φανερῶς ἀσελγαίνοντας θαυμάζοντες (21).

Parallelism is often achieved by the use of οὐ (μόνον)...ἀλλὰ (καί): 1, 4, 5, 7, 15, 20, 22, 36, 39, 40; and the stylistic correspondences are the more evident in passages in which the binary structure is made more complex, sometimes by parenthetical remarks:

προθύμων μὲν καὶ ἀγαθῶν ἀνδρῶν ὑμῶν τυγχάνων, δι' ὅπερ σῴζομαι,
πλείστοις δὲ καὶ δεινοτάτοις ἐχθροῖς χρώμενος, ὑφ' ὧν διαβάλλομαι (2).

The author does, however, seek variation (*variatio*) within parallel or antithetical clauses. Verbs of declaration are followed by two co-ordinate clauses: νομίζω (1), οἶμαι (5), συνειδότας (5), δέομαι (7), δεινὸν νομίζω (9), νομίζω (24), ἡγοῦμαι (25), cf. ὁρῶντες (21). Attributive adjectives are used in two clauses, and in the second limb a pair of adjectives strengthens the expression:

μεγάλην τιμωρίαν νομίζω...μικρὰν καὶ οὐδενὸς ἀξίαν ἡγοῦμαι ζημίαν (4; cf. 1, 9, 11, 16, 18, 34, 40).

The use of the tricolon may be noted here:

τοὺς μὲν διαφόρους ὄντας διήλλαξα, τοὺς δ' ἐπιτηδείους ἐποίησα, τοὺς δ' ἀπὸ τῶν ἐχθρῶν ἀπέστησα (41; cf. 3 twice, 4, 14 twice, 23, 30, 37, 39, 42; four limbs are found at 10 twice, 27).

On the other hand, the strict formalism of the *Against Alcibiades* is reflected in the restricted use of correlative particles, in contrast with Andocides' extreme variety of correlation, for example: τοῦτο μέν...τοῦτο δέ (1.103, 2.16, 17, 3.40); πρῶτον μέν...εἶτα δέ/ἔπειτα δέ (1.46, 47, 50, 3.5; 1.116, 132, 144). In the *Against Alcibiades* τοῦτο μέν...τοῦτο δέ and ἔπειτα are absent, while εἶτα is used only to introduce a logical conclusion (4, 28). Further, Feraboli finds no example of πρῶτον μέν introducing an argument (wrongly taking 4.11 as temporal), in comparison with its numerous such uses in the other speeches (1.2, 10, 39, 46, 3.2, 4, 10, 13, 17, 24).

Other lexical differences between the *Against Alcibiades* and Andocides include the use in speech 4 of the particle combinations ἀλλὰ μήν (15, 34) and καὶ μήν (34), which are absent from Andocides (who uses ἀλλὰ γάρ, 1.22, 23, 72, 101, 103, 124, 128, 130, 132; cf. 4.32); while the particle δή, which is common in Andocides, is only found in the *Against Alcibiades* at 14. The author of speech 4 uses three transitional formulas in 42 sections: προσέτι (31), ἔτι δέ (5) and πρὸς δὲ τούτοις (4, 24); while Andocides prefers ἔτι δέ (1.7, 25, 50, 51, 52, 58 twice, 132, 138, 144, 150) with a few instances of πρὸς δὲ τούτοις (1.25, 31, 51, 135). Finally, to reinforce a comparative the author of speech 4 uses πολύ (19, 31, 42), τοσούτῳ (22), τοσοῦτον (28), μᾶλλον (5) and ἔτι (23), as opposed to πολύ (1.2, 5, 7, 30, 32, 109, 146, 2.18 with πλείστου, 26, 3.11, 34), πολλῷ (1.24, 64, 2.19) and ὅσῳ (2.17, 3.30).

II.   Feraboli turns next to modes of expression, where, despite Andocides' striving for variety, she finds a certain monotony in the repetition of some formulas. Three examples are:

(a) For good deeds and behaviour Andocides uses εὖ ποιέω (1.136, 149 twice, 3.33), εὖ πράττω (2.5), ἀγαθὸν ποιέω (2.1, 18, 23), ἀγαθὸν ἐργάζομαι (2.10, 16, 18), εὖ πάσχω (2.16, 23) and the poetic τι ἀγαθὸν ἐπαυρέσθαι (2.2). The only similar expression in the *Against Alcibiades* is ἡ πόλις οὐδὲν ἀγαθὸν ὑπὸ τούτου τοῦ ἀνδρὸς πείσεται (5). In the same way, Andocides has κακῶς πράττω (2.5, 6, 9), κακῶς ποιέω (1.1, 122), κακὸν ποιέω (1.102, 3.6) and also ἁμαρτάνω, ἐξαμαρτάνω, ἀδικέω and the expression πολλὰ κακὰ παθόντες πολλὰ δὲ ποιήσαντες in 3.6. The *Against Alcibiades* has greater variety: οὐδὲν κακὸν πέπονθεν (18), πάσχειν κακῶς (19), κακὰ τὴν πόλιν ὑπὸ τούτου πείσεσθαι (24), τοῖς πεποιθόσι κακῶς (36), as well as ἀδικήσαντα τὴν πόλιν (2), τὴν πόλιν διαφθερεῖ (5) and κακὰ κατασκευάσειεν (11), ἁμάρτημα (10, 22) and ἀδίκημα (4, 24, 36).

(b) For flight and exile Andocides uses φεύγοντες ᾤχοντο (1.13, 15, 34, 52, 66, 3.10; cf. 1.4, 19, 49); 4.12 has φυγάδες γίγνονται καὶ εἰς Θουρίους οἰκήσοντες ἀπέρχονται.

(c) To introduce his own thoughts Andocides usually employs οἶμαι (1.19, 22, 39, 89, 99, 123, 139, 3.8, 13), less frequently νομίζω (1.56, 132, 2.1) and ἡγοῦμαι (1.9, 139, 2.1). But in the *Against Alcibiades* there is a greater frequency of νομίζω (1, 4, 9, 12, 19, 24, 35) and ἡγοῦμαι (1, 4, 8, 25, 42), with only one occurrence of οἶμαι (5).

There are many words and expressions which are frequent in Andocides but are not found, or are rarely found, in the *Against Alcibiades*. These include: ἄλλο τι ἤ, τί ἄλλο ἤ, εἰκός (but for εἰκότως cf. **8, 21**), ὅπου (locative at **8**), τε...καί, οἷος, οἷον ἐστί, αὖ, εἴ τι, τι as the object of a verb (τι παθεῖν, τι ἠσέβηκα, ἐξαμαρτεῖν τι) or with a neuter adjective (βραχύ τι, ἀγαθόν τι, διάβολόν τι), εὖ, περ (only found in ὥσπερ, εἴπερ and ὅπερ), colloquial forms such as νυνί, ταυτί, οὑτοσί and δευρί, the neuter pronouns αὐτό, αὐτά, τόδε, τάδε, ἐκεῖνο and ἐκεῖνα (cf. τὰ αὐτά **41**, ἐκεῖνα **23, 36**), ἄξιος with πολλοῦ, πλείστου, τινός and οὐδενός (cf. οὐδενὸς ἄξιον **4, 27**), οὕτως ἔχει, the use of the participle as a substantive is rare (cf. τὰ ὑπάρχοντα **26**, τὰ διαφέροντα **19**, τὰ προστατόμενα **42**, τὰ πεπραγμένα **34, 41**), as is the use of the neuter of the relative (cf. ἃ εἴργασται **10**, ὧν ἐβιάσατο μετέμελε **17**).

On the other hand, some words and expressions are found more frequently in the *Against Alcibiades* than in Andocides, including: καταφρονέω (**14, 16, 39**, cf. **1.119**), ἐπιμελοῦμαι (**1 twice, 12, 40**, cf. **2.13**), φροντίζω (**23, 27, 39**), πλέον ποιέω (**7**), πράττω (**20**), φέρομαι (**4**, cf. **1.7, 149**), δηλόω (**12, 14, 27**, cf. **1.33**), ἀγνοέω (**5, 19**), ἀλλότριος (**10, 15, 27**), καίτοι (**6, 10, 15, 23, 26, 32, 33, 36, 41, 42**, cf. **1.20, 57, 146, 2.10, 3.19**), whereas τοίνυν (which is exceptionally common in Andocides) is found only at **15, 35, 40**, ἐπιτήδευμα (**16, 33, 39**), ἐπιτηδεύων (**31**), ἐπιτήδειος (**25, 36, 41, 42**, cf. **1.4, 63, 2.12**) and the use of the article with the names of peoples (**22, 26**).

Finally, some words are used with a different shade of meaning in the *Against Alcibiades*, such as συνειδότας in **5** ('know', as opposed to συνειδότα in **1.41, 47**, 'in the know'), the passive of καταλαμβάνω in **23** ('be compelled', cf. **1.40, 80, 2.11**) and καθίστημι with a predicative (**1, 7, 23, 40**, only so used by Andocides at **2.26, 3.7**).

III. In the third section of her article Feraboli examines figures of speech and the arrangement of sentences, to underline the contrast between Andocides' striving to avoid monotony and symmetry by variety of expression, and the more rigid and static parallelism of the author of the *Against Alcibiades*.

Among figures of speech, chiasmus occurs frequently in Andocides (cf. **1.7, 19, 24, 136, 2.12, 3.2, 5, 7 twice, 21, 28, 29**) and in the *Against Alcibiades* (cf. **14, 15, 25, 36**), but is more perfected in the latter:

τοῦτον μὲν ἀγαπᾶτε, τὸν...κατεργασάμενον, Καλλίαν δὲ... νικήσαντα... ἐξωστρακίσατε (**32**).

Andocides employs anacoluthon and etymological figure, both of which are lacking in the *Against Alcibiades*, while asyndeton, frequent in Andocides, is only found at **26** (where there are two instances).

Clauses in the *Against Alcibiades* are frequently opened by a verb in the first person singular (**5, 7, 13, 18, 19, 25 twice, 35, 39, 41**), more rarely with an address to the audience (**11, 20, 30, 33**). Andocides' practice is the opposite (**1.18, 32, 89, 92, 144, 2.8, 24, 29, 3.12, 17 twice, 25, 41** compared with **1.6, 8, 129, 141, 150, 2.23, 3.8, 13, 34**); he also uses the third person plural (**1.19, 105, 110, 113, 137, 3.1, 13, 27, 33, 41**) and very often emphasises his personal thought with ἐγώ (compare one example of ἐγὼ δὲ νομίζω at **4.12**).

Andocides has a tendency towards repetition of the same idea affirmatively and then negatively, as διδάσκειν πάντα...καὶ παραλείπειν μηδέν (**1.9**), and towards joining two verbs with καὶ οὐ/μή or οὐδέ/μηδέ (e.g. ὑπομεῖναι καὶ μὴ οἴχεσθαι **1.19**; εἰπεῖν...οὐδὲ βουλεῦσαι **1.75**). This is very rare in the *Against Alcibiades* (**1, 12, 37**), as is hendiadys with two verbs (cf. **7**).

The positioning of participles is more set in the *Against Alcibiades* than in Andocides. If we call *P* the participle and *p* the words it governs, *V* the main verb and *v* the words it governs, Andocides uses all possible schemes, but the *Against Alcibiades* regularly has only two schemes, *P p v V* (**1, 2, 7, 11 twice, 14 twice, 17, 22, 35**) and *p P v V* (**1, 10, 12, 30, 34, 35, 40 twice**), with one instance of *p P V v* (**4**). Similarly, the placing of the verb between the two objects it governs (e.g. στρατιὰν ἐκπέμπετε καὶ παρασκευὴν **1.11**) is very common in Andocides but absent from the *Against Alcibiades*. The same applies to the order object - subject - verb (only found at **4.24, 30**); the indirect object is usually placed in front of the verb in the *Against Alcibiades*, whereas it frequently follows it in Andocides (but cf. **4.15, 17, 42**); and the object of comparison joined by ἤ always follows the first element of the comparison in the *Against Alcibiades* (**5, 11, 21, 25 twice, 31, 42**), whereas other words may be inserted between the elements by Andocides.

As for syntax, the author of the *Against Alcibiades* has a predilection for consecutive clauses, which suits well the binary structure of his sentences (**14, 16, 17 twice, 20, 22 twice, 24, 28, 30, 34, 36**). In all these except **24** ὥστε is followed by the indicative, and all are preceded by a correlative except at **20** and **34**. Andocides makes less use of consecutive constructions, of which only five have ὥστε with the indicative (**1.36, 110, 122, 2.8, 3.7**) and several lack a correlative (**1.40, 113, 119, 2.5, 8 twice, 16, 27, 3.32**). In final clauses with ἵνα in historic sequence Andocides regularly uses the subjunctive but twice has the optative (**1.42, 137**), whereas the *Against Alcibiades* only has two optatives (**15, 29**). Genitive absolutes in the *Against Alcibiades* are largely unconnected to the surrounding expressions and without dependent clauses (**3 three times, 10, 11, 13, 20 four times**; but cf. **17, 20**).

Finally, Feraboli makes some observations on word-order in constructions. For example, in the *Against Alcibiades* accusative and infinitive constructions tend to follow the pattern *V...I* (where *V* is the governing verb and *I* the infinitive), as νομίζω...ἔχειν (**35**; cf. **2, 5, 8, 9, 12, 13, 15, 20, 24 twice, 25, 28, 32, 35, 38**; less frequent are the patterns *...V I...*, as **3, 16, 21, 37, 42**; and *...I V*, as **19, 24**); in Andocides the infinitive has no fixed position. Similarly with participial constructions, which are very common in the *Against Alcibiades*, the order tends to be verb...participle, as γνῶναι...ὄντα (**6**; cf. **14, 18, 21, 23, 24, 26, 27, 29 twice, 31, 34, 37**; but cf. μὴ μόνον Διομήδην...ὑβρίζων ἐπιδείξειε **29**); but the position in Andocides is again less regular.

As Feraboli is aware, such stylistic differences between the speeches do not prove conclusively that Andocides did not write the *Against Alcibiades* ('ripeto, non certezza, ma molti dubbi tutt'altro che infondati'). But when added to the historical anomalies discussed in the **Introduction** to the speech, their sum total places a heavy burden of proof on those who would defend its authenticity.

Index

www.ingramcontent.com/pod-product-compliance
Lightning Source LLC
Chambersburg PA
CBHW071105100726
47908CB00008B/2272